PERGAMON GENERAL PSYCHOLOGY SERIES

EDITORS

Arnold P. Goldstein, *Syracuse University*
Leonard Krasner, *Stanford University &*
SUNY at Stony Brook

THE TROUBLED ADOLESCENT
(PGPS-158)

Pergamon Titles of Related Interest

Apter/Goldstein YOUTH VIOLENCE: Programs and Prospects

Feindler/Ecton ADOLESCENT ANGER CONTROL: Cognitive-Behavioral Techniques

Goldstein/Glick/Irwin/Pask-McCartney/Rubama REDUCING DELINQUENCY: Intervention in the Community

Hollin COGNITIVE-BEHAVIORAL INTERVENTIONS WITH YOUNG OFFENDERS

Horne/Sayger TREATING CONDUCT AND OPPOSITIONAL DEFIANT DISORDERS IN CHILDREN

Matson TREATING DEPRESSION IN CHILDREN AND ADOLESCENTS

Oster/Caro/Eagen/Lillo ASSESSING ADOLESCENTS

Rhodes/Jason PREVENTING SUBSTANCE ABUSE AMONG CHILDREN AND ADOLESCENTS

Van Hasselt/Hersen HANDBOOK OF ADOLESCENT PSYCHOLOGY

Related Journals
(Free sample copies available upon request.)

CHILD ABUSE AND NEGLECT

CLINICAL PSYCHOLOGY REVIEW

JOURNAL OF ANXIETY DISORDERS

JOURNAL OF CHILD PSYCHOLOGY AND PSYCHIATRY AND ALLIED DISCIPLINES

THE
TROUBLED
ADOLESCENT

JOSEPH L. WHITE
University of California, Irvine

PERGAMON PRESS
New York • Oxford • Beijing • Frankfurt • São Paulo • Sydney • Tokyo • Toronto

Pergamon Press Offices:

U.S.A.   Pergamon Press, Inc., Maxwell House, Fairview Park, Elmsford, New York 10523, U.S.A.

U.K.   Pergamon Press plc, Headington Hill Hall, Oxford OX3 0BW, England

PEOPLE'S REPUBLIC OF CHINA   Pergamon Press, Qianmen Hotel, Beijing, People's Republic of China

FEDERAL REPUBLIC OF GERMANY   Pergamon Press GmbH, Hammerweg 6, D-6242 Kronberg, Federal Republic of Germany

BRAZIL   Pergamon Editora Ltda, Rua Eça de Queiros, 346, CEP 04011, São Paulo, Brazil

AUSTRALIA   Pergamon Press (Aust.) Pty., Ltd., P.O. Box 544, Potts Point, NSW 2011, Australia

JAPAN   Pergamon Press, 8th Floor, Matsuoka Central Building, 1-7-1 Nishishinjuku, Shinjuku-ku, Tokyo 160, Japan

CANADA   Pergamon Press Canada Ltd., Suite 271, 253 College Street, Toronto, Ontario M5T 1R5, Canada

---

Library of Congress Cataloging in Publication Data

White, Joseph L., 1932-
   The troubled adolescent / Joseph L. White.
     p.   cm.--(Pergamon general psychology series ; 158)
   Bibliography: p.
   Includes index.
   ISBN 0-08-036820-4 : ISBN 0-08-036819-0 (pbk.)
   1. Adolescent psychopathology. 2 Mental Disorders--in adolescence. I. Title. II. Series.
   [DNLM: 1. Adolescent Behavior.   WS 463 W585t]
RJ503.W48 1989
616.89'022--dc19
DNLM/DLC   88-38345
for Library of Congress   CIP

Printed in the United States of America

The paper used in this publication meets the minimum requirements of American National Standard for Information Sciences -- Permanence of Paper for Printed Library Materials, ANSI Z39.48-1984

Dedication

To the Memory of Dorothy Lee White, who as a single parent guided Bunkey, Mary Jane, and Joe through the storms and stresses of childhood and adolescence in the 1930s and 1940s.

I would like to thank the many people who made this book possible. I am especially indebted to three of my former undergraduate psychology students, Tracy Ann Whalen, Jacqueline Foster, and Kathy Harris, who spent long hours in the library doing background research. Ms. Whalen was the one who first encouraged me to begin this project and provided valuable assistance in preparing the first outline. I am also thankful to Lissa Forehan and her partner, Lee Richards, for reading and fine-tuning the manuscript at each critical stage of development. I could not have completed this project without the assistance of my executive secretary, Edna Mejia. She typed the original manuscript, made the necessary corrections as the manuscript progressed, and kept me on schedule. Finally, I am deeply grateful for the help, support, understanding, and patience my wife Lois provided me with throughout the many months it has taken to complete *The Troubled Adolescent*.

Contents

Chapter 4: Depression   *111*

Chapter 5: Suicide   *144*

Introduction

This book is about America's troubled and distressed teenagers. While adolescence is certainly a time of opportunity and growth, statistics indicate that it is also a time of severe distress and trouble for many teenagers. There are 2 million runaway and homeless youth in America, 10% to 20% of America's teenagers have serious problems with drugs and alcohol, 5% to 10% of adolescents suffer from severe depression; increasing numbers of female adolescents are experiencing fasting, binging, and purging eating disturbances; and one of the highest suicide rates is in the 15–24-year age category. *Newsweek* magazine (Gelman, 1986) states that adolescent mental health is the most rapidly growing area in the fields of psychiatry, psychotherapy, and counseling. The number of in-patient admissions to psychiatric services for troubled youth under the ages of 18 more than doubled between 1970 and 1980. Between 1980 and 1984, adolescent admissions to private psychiatric hospitals increased more than 350%.

This book consists of ten chapters. The first two set the stage for the clinical chapters by introducing the role of conflict, frustration, coping, prevention, and treatment in troubled and distressed adolescent behavior. The next seven chapters cover the clinical and behavioral syndromes of running away, depression, suicide, eating disturbances, schizophrenia, drug abuse, and juvenile delinquency. Each syndrome is discussed from a perspective that includes historical notes, descriptive symptoms, statistics, etiology, causation and dynamics, consequences and outcomes, treatment, prevention, discussion questions, and suggestions for parents, educators, counselors, and youth workers. Case histories are used to illustrate the behavioral and clinical symptoms. The author attempts to describe the phenomena in clear English. DSM-III-R (American Psychiatric Association,

1

1987) criteria are included and so designated where appropriate. The closing chapter addresses the implications of troubled and distressed adolescent behavior for American society as a whole and recommends solutions which involve strengthening prevention and treatment services available to teenagers and their families.

This book is written from a psychosocial perspective of adolescent development, conflict, coping, stress, and maladaptive behavior. The major focus in the psychosocial model is on prevention, empowerment, and competency. It stresses helping adolescents to generate new ways of experiencing themselves, of satisfying their needs, and of replacing maladaptive behaviors with adaptive, growth-enhancing strategies to cope with frustration and distress. Adolescents are viewed as people who have the power to initiate growth, recover from setbacks, and discover what they need to move toward fulfilling their goals and actualizing their potential. In the psychosocial model, the causes or triggers for maladaptive behavior are to be found in excessive current stresses, conflicts, frustrations and negative psychosocial learning, faulty interaction between the adolescent and the psychosocial environment, and vulnerabilities carried over from incomplete previous developmental stages. Disordered adolescent psychological moods, response styles, and behavior are viewed within an adaptive-maladaptive context. When adolescents run into conflicts and stresses that overtax their support systems and coping resources, maladaptive behaviors or psychological disorders are likely to occur. Disordered behavior, which is reflected in the clinical and behavioral symptoms, causes and consequences of running away, depression, suicide, eating disturbances, schizophrenia, drug abuse, and delinquency, is seen as an exaggeration of the normal adolescent developmental stresses, conflicts, and coping processes.

This book was written for a mixed audience. It is designed for people who come into daily contact with troubled and distressed adolescents in their roles as youth counselors, mental health technicians, social workers, teachers, school administrators, family and adolescent psychotherapists, parents, juvenile officials, and recreation directors. Other groups that could benefit from reading this book are undergraduate and graduate students in the behavioral sciences, human services, and mental health training programs, preparing for careers that will bring them into close contact with troubled and distressed adolescents.

1

Adolescent Conflict, Stress, Coping, and Approaches to Understanding and Helping Troubled Youths

PREVIEW

Adolescence is a transition time when the individual is leaving a familiar psychosocial space and entering another. As adolescents try to work their way through major developmental tasks; resolve identity issues; reach out to explore, adventure, and challenge; establish a sense of power, competency, and belongingness, some degree of conflict with self, others, and society is inevitable. Certain conflicts — e.g., future shock, mixed messages about values and standards for conduct, and the role of women and minority youth — are due to the complexity, organization, and structure of society. Conflict can be perceived as an essential condition of growth that often serves as a stimulus to start the movement toward higher levels of social maturity and personal integration in adolescents. If not properly handled, conflict can generate unproductive stress, frustration, and tension. The important question is how adolescents cope with conflict. Coping is a term that refers to active efforts to resolve stress and create workable solutions to the challenges and demands of each growth stage. Coping involves three primary components: understanding the meaning of a troublesome situation, engaging in competent action, and keeping powerful emotions, such as anger or fear, from being too overwhelming. Styles for coping are reviewed within an adaptive–maladaptive framework. Adaptive coping is growth facilitating

3

and allows adolescents to move forward to complete the essential development tasks. Maladaptive coping is defined as disordered behavior because it
blocks psychological growth and prevents adolescents from actualizing their
potential. Disordered behavior and maladaptive coping are reflected in the
syndromes of troubled and distressed adolescent behavior, which will be
reviewed in subsequent chapters.

Three approaches to helping troubled and distressed youth through counseling and psychotherapy are reviewed: psychodynamic, humanistic-existential, and cognitive-behavioral. During the past 10 years, psychoeducational
techniques have been widely utilized to assist adolescents in improving self-
concept, social skills, communication skills, conflict-resolution skills, negotiation skills, and decision-making skills. Psychoeducational strategies
involve such techniques as role playing, rehearsal, practice, relaxation training, discussions, values clarification, feedback, and a variety of other methods to help adolescents cope with the predictable problems and stresses of
growing up. Psychoeducational tools can be incorporated into counseling
and prevention formats.

ADOLESCENT CONFLICT, STRESS, AND COPING

Adolescence is a transition time during which the individual leaves a
familiar psychosocial space and enters another. Adolescents have to adapt to
changes in their biological, cognitive, and physical development at a time
when the changing demands of parents, peers, and school are likely to be
accelerated. To successfully complete these changes with a sense of mastery,
power, and meaningful relationships with others, teenagers need to develop
new behavior, cognitive, and social skills. New skills are necessary because
the expectations and demands are new. When the individual leaves the world
of childhood and enters the world of adolescence, new assumptions about
self, values, and identity must ultimately be confronted. During this time of
intense and often rapid change, the early learning, resourcefulness, and
adaptiveness of the individual are severely tested. Some degree of conflict,
stress, frustration, and confusion is inevitable. Adolescents or young adults
cannot be in complete harmony with themselves, their peers, parents, and
with society at all times.

For some adolescents, the changes, expectations, and new demands are
perceived as a challenge. For them, confusion and stress are part of a
process that leads to a higher level of integration. They quickly recover from
setbacks and minor disappointments. For others, the changes have a more
threatening quality, causing temporary or more prolonged periods of disruption, fear, mood changes, rebellion, and despondency. Adolescence can also
be a time for catching up. For an insecure adolescent, making the team or

being selected for an important class office often provides a boost in self-esteem that generalizes to other areas. Whether adolescence is experienced as a challenge, as an opportunity to catch up, or as an extremely painful period of life depends on a variety of factors. These factors include the nature of the conflicts and the types of stresses, the presence or absence of a supportive environment, and the degree of mastery achieved in previous developmental stages (Jensen, 1985; Conger and Petersen, 1984; Forisha-Kovach, 1983).

There are three major adolescent conflict areas: social and interpersonal, situational, and internal psychological. Conflict can be defined as a clash between opposing emotional, social, motivational, or interpersonal forces (Goldenson, 1984). Social conflict consists of discord between the adolescent and peers, parents, adult authority, or society. Situational conflicts are dilemmas triggered by a specific stressful situation that has a well-defined onset. Internal psychological conflicts refer to dilemmas that occur within the person.

Social and Interpersonal Conflicts

The sources of social and interpersonal conflicts are external. There are two types of social and interpersonal conflicts. Personal conflicts within the personal-individual space of the adolescent involve peers, parents, relatives, acquaintances, or adult authority figures such as teachers and employers. The second type of social conflict comes about as a result of the status of adolescents living in a complex, fast-moving society. In this type of conflict, the triggering sources are more at the macro level, because the forces of society are vague and impersonal.

Conflicts between adolescents and parents or other adult authority figures usually occur in areas involving independence–dependence issues. Within the independence–dependence dimension are two somewhat incompatible issues: increased power and control versus continued support and understanding. Adolescents want greater power and control over such things as curfew, choice of friends, sexual activity, school performance, social activities, and conditions under which they can use intoxicants. Where they once accepted parental standards without question, they now question the rationale for their parents' decisions. As a result of growth in their conceptual reasoning and abstract thinking skills, adolescents can produce sophisticated arguments to support their point of view. Parents and other adults in positions of power may be reluctant to give up their power, regardless of the teenager's proficiency in debating and arguing. However, while fighting for their independence, adolescents still need to be loved and understood by those with whom they are locked in a power struggle. The independence–

dependence struggle is confusing to parents. They are accused of not letting go on the one hand, and not being loving and supportive enough on the other.

Discord between adolescents and their peers generally centers around issues concerning values and standards, cooperation versus competition, intimacy, and conflicting expectations within the peer group. For example, in any large high school, there is a diversity of acceptable standards and values with respect to school performance, sexual activity, drugs, athletics, obeying parents and teachers, and social class norms. By joining a peer group that represents a certain set of values, an adolescent is expected to go along with the group despite personal misgivings. Joining one group may also put the adolescent at variance with other peer groups that share different values. In a high school where the athletes, socializers, and party goers are the most popular teenagers, an adolescent whose major focus is academics may feel left out if he or she doesn't give the appearance of joining in. Adolescents also face dilemmas between cooperation and competition. If two adolescent males are friends and both want to date the same girl or play the same position on the football team, the competition may interfere with their attempts to work together cooperatively in other areas. Another example of the discord between adolescents and their peers is the adolescent's need for peer intimacy and acceptance. When adolescents reach out to others, there is no guarantee they will be accepted. Sometimes they are accepted and build close, intimate relationships only to see those relationships fall apart when one party changes directions or wants to be with someone else. Lastly, different peers have divergent expectations. For example, several activities can be scheduled for a Friday night. Choosing one activity may mean the adolescent will have to reject invitations to other activities. Each of these questions and situations poses dilemmas adolescents have to figure out a way to resolve.

At the macro level, there are five conflicts that come about as a result of the complexity, organization, and structure of society. These can be labeled as conflicts due to: (1) mixed messages about values, (2) future shock, (3) the status of adolescents as marginal people, (4) minority and gender issues, and (5) laws and social customs.

Sexual restraint versus sexual expressiveness, obedience to authority versus doing your own thing, concern for others versus "looking out for number one," hard work and self-denial versus having fun and doing it now, and abstinence from drugs and alcohol versus recreational use of drugs and alcohol are several of the mixed messages society communicates to adolescents about values and standards. Teenagers are encouraged to abstain from sex or to carefully restrict their sexual behavior, yet all around them are movies, magazines, records, TV, and cosmetic advertisements that bombard adolescents with sexual content. Having sex appeal and being desirable are very valued commodities in American society. Without clear guidelines and standards for sexual behavior, many teenagers feel anxious, confused, guilty, and ashamed. Obedience to authority and following mainstream norms are stressed, yet people who are successful in doing their own thing are admired. For example, one of the most popular songs of the 1970s contains the lyrics "I did it my way" (Sinatra, 1969). Another way in which adolescents receive mixed messages about values is that while they are encouraged to show respect and concern for others, society seems to be moving on a course where "looking out for number one" is becoming more widespread (Lasch, 1977). On one hand, hard work, self-denial, and preparation for the future are stressed as part of the achievement ethic. On the other hand, we live in a now society where TV commercials tell us "You only go around once, go for the gusto." The use of drugs and alcohol by teenagers is discouraged, yet the use of tranquilizers, mood elevators, alcohol, and illegal drugs are multibillion dollar businesses in our society.

Toffler (1971) coined the term future shock to describe the rapidly changing, fast-paced society we live in. In a rapidly changing society, the traditional values and life-styles are no longer sacred. Old landmarks disappear, social customs change, and new occupational and economic trends emerge as old trends become obsolete. Future shock can impact on adolescents in terms of occupational choices, family structure, and adult guidance. In the midst of a changing economic marketplace and shifting trends in the work force, young people are expected to make occupational and career choices that will have a decisive effect on the rest of their lives. The east and midwest are filled with towns where high paying jobs in the steel and manufacturing industries no longer exist. The adolescents of a generation ago, who went to work in these industries with faith in hard work and traditional American values, are now unemployed, trying to hang on until retirement, or seeking retraining for jobs in lower sectors of the economy. Watching fathers, mothers, uncles, aunts, and neighbors go through the trauma of mid-life unemployment and economic decline through no fault of their own can be very stressful for adolescents trying to make decisions about their own occupational future.

The second area of future shock pertains to changes in the family. Children and teenagers no longer have a reasonable certainty that they will remain in a family with their natural parents and siblings until late adolescence. Between childhood and middle adolescence, at least 50% of America's teenagers experience major family changes. Today, it is not uncommon to talk to teenagers who have spent periods of time in a two-parent family, a single-parent family, and/or a reconstructed family consisting of stepparents or coparents, half-siblings, and/or stepsiblings. To further complicate matters, adults who live in a world where their own lives are undergoing major changes may be confused about how to advise adolescents with respect to questions about standards, values, and personal conduct. Adolescents are often forced to turn to their peers for advice and answers to troublesome questions.

The marginal status of adolescents is commonly described as a stage where adolescents are expected to act like responsible adults without having the social, legal, financial, or political franchise and power of adults (Jones, 1980). It is not acceptable for adolescents to show the spontaneity, forgetfulness, and playfulness of children, yet they are not allowed the assertiveness, independence, and inherent decision-making prerogatives of adults. This is especially the case when adolescents and adults are dealing with major differences of opinion. The term *anomie* has been used to describe the alienation adolescents experience when they find themselves caught between two worlds, while not belonging to either.

The combination of future shock and marginal status has produced a situation in contemporary American society in which teenagers and preadolescents have to make major decisions at younger and younger ages about drugs, sex, how to spend free time, the role of their parents as authority figures, and a variety of other value-laden issues. Elkind (1981, 1984) thinks the blurring of distinctions between childhood and adulthood in modern society has placed pressure on children and adolescents to grow up too rapidly and to make critical decisions before they have acquired a base of experience and coping strategies. In Elkind's view, the stresses and turmoil resulting from being pushed to grow up too fast are the underlying causes of the depression, suicidal behavior, delinquency, runaways, drug and alcohol abuse, sexual promiscuity, and other signs of troubled behavior seen in many of today's adolescents.

Low-income minority adolescents and female adolescents are presented with a contradictory set of messages and images from society. They are told that they are equal and that success is possible, if they work hard. Yet, they see evidence that this is not so. In low-income minority neighborhoods, unemployment and crime rates are high, the neighborhoods are falling apart, the schools are inadequate, and drugs are plentiful. When these kinds of conditions exist in one's environment every day, it is hard to believe that one can overcome them with hard work and persistence. Similarly, female teenagers are told that they can move to the top of the educational, political, economic, and occupational ladders in America. Despite major changes brought about by the women's movement, women still have a long way to go toward equality. A second complication female adolescents face is how to balance the roles of wage earner, mother, and spouse, and still have time left over for personal interests and personal development. While there has been much dialogue about women "having it all," it may not be possible to have it all simultaneously. Models need to be developed to help adolescent females begin to learn how to balance these roles and considerations over the period of their adult life.

The final conflict between youth and society involves laws and social customs. The laws and social customs of society require that teenagers control expressions of anger and sexuality, respect private property, contain their hedonism, and follow the juvenile laws of their particular state. Freud (1923, 1933) and G. Stanley Hall (1904) believed that society's expectations set up a conflict wherein the individual was forced to control his or her desires for the good of society. Children and adolescents were socialized to internalize society's standards through guilt, fear, and the power of adults to reward and punish. In this view, the storms and stresses of adolescence were due to intensified conflicts between instincts (e.g., sexual and aggressive drives) and society's needs for control.

In reconstructing the conflict between society and adolescents to fit the 1980s, it seems that the conflict between youth and society is not solely a conflict between adolescent desires versus society's controls. Perhaps the major reason for the conflict between youth and society results from the fact that society makes laws and sets up controls without consulting teenagers. Since teenagers are not part of the power structure that makes and enforces the laws and social customs, they may not feel committed to obey these laws and social customs.

Situational Conflict

Situational conflict, sometimes referred to as situational crisis, is a highly stressful dilemma that has either a rapid onset or a clearly identifiable onset. Situational conflicts cause an abrupt change in the life-space of the adolescent. Events that fall into this category are: the death of loved ones, life-threatening injuries and illnesses, breakups in boyfriend–girlfriend relationships, parental divorces, unplanned pregnancies, perceived failures, and the like. These events trigger feelings of grief, disappointment, shock, guilt, shame, and loss. In situational crises, adolescents are exposed to the unpleasant reality that things can no longer be the way they once were. Pain, loss, unrequited love, and sudden misfortune are part of the existential conditions of life from which adolescents cannot be completely shielded. With time, support, and understanding, most adolescents can recover from situational crises and continue to move forward in their growth.

Intrapersonal and Internal Conflicts

Internal psychological conflict or intrapersonal-intrapsychic conflict can be defined as strife within the adolescent caused by competing ideas, motives, values, and goals. Intrapersonal conflict occurs primarily within the internal psychological space of the adolescent. There are three important intrapersonal conflicts: (1) conflict caused by unresolved past events or developmental stages; (2) conflicts between the past and present; and (3) conflicts between the present and the future.

Conflicts caused by unresolved past events usually involve the failure to successfully complete the preadolescent psychosocial developmental stages. Faulty preadolescent psychological development can leave a residual of persistent feelings of shame, guilt, fear, self-doubt, and mistrust. Adolescents may not understand these feelings or know how to protect themselves from the turmoil they can generate. For Freud and Erikson, mastery of the childhood psychological challenges was the foundation for successful adolescent and adult development. Adolescents who are struggling with doubts and fears from unresolved childhood conflicts are at a disadvantage when it comes to coping with the new demands of adolescent living.

Conflicts between the past and the present occur when previously internalized standards conflict with present thoughts, actions, and explorations. In growing up, most children internalize the standards of their parents and bring these standards with them into adolescence. As adolescents, they are likely to question old beliefs and explore new behaviors in the areas of sex, morality, values, achievement, and drugs. When new ideas and behaviors conflict with internalized standards, the resulting effect can be guilt and shame. Feelings of guilt and shame can be very confusing to adolescents who feel they have rationally discarded old beliefs. What these young people fail to understand is that deeply internalized childhood beliefs have an unconscious residual component that can remain with them long after they have intellectually rejected childhood beliefs. Thus, conflict between past and present standards can have an unconscious component of which the adolescent is not fully aware. When this happens, young people feel a lingering sense of shame, guilt, or depression but cannot connect these feelings to conflicts between their present life-style and past internalized beliefs.

Conflicts between the present and future can be defined as a lack of congruence between the way things are now and the way the adolescent would like them to be. A good example of conflict between the present and the future is a discrepancy existing between the real self in the present and the idealized self in the future. Some adolescents experience themselves in the present as unattractive, powerless, and not very lovable. They project a future in which they will be powerful, lovable, and attractive. If they are not careful, the conflict between the ideal future self and the real present self can be a source of self-deprecation.

As noted in the discussion of conflicts between past and present standards, the source of intrapersonal or intrapsychic conflicts and conflicting ideas and motives may not always be fully conscious. When adolescents are trying to move forward toward their goals but constantly feel stuck, depressed, and guilty, yet don't know why, it may be that unconscious feelings and experiences are holding them back. Unconscious motives may be at work when adolescents have the grades and the apparent motivation to attend college, but avoid taking the admissions exams until it is too late, or when adolescents claim they want close, intimate relationships with others, yet always carefully structure their activities when they are with others so that there is very little time for intimacy and sharing.

Ambivalence

Although conflict has been described as existing between opposing forces, in many conflicts the same goal is sometimes desirable and sometimes undesirable. These types of situations are defined as ambivalence. A boy may want to date a girl but is apprehensive about calling her because she might say no. The closer he comes to making the call, the more anxious he becomes. The more he thinks about not calling her, the stronger the motive to call her becomes. This is called an approach-avoidance conflict. An approach-avoidance conflict occurs when an adolescent wants to do something but has to choose between two possible negative outcomes. For example, a teenager wants to please both his parents and his peers, although the latter may have different expectations and values about issues such as drugs, sex, and school performance. Making one set of choices will bring disapproval from either parents or peers (Atkinson et al., 1983).

Conflicts in Early, Middle, and Late Adolescence

Conflicts and dilemmas are likely to have different themes in early, middle, and late adolescence (Goldenberg, 1977). In early adolescence, conflicts are usually concerned with the impact of sexual drives, acceptance of changing body and physiology, and defining one's self as an individual in the junior high school or middle school peer network. Middle adolescence is a time of experimentation with sex, drugs, challenges to parental authority, and value conflicts. Late adolescence is a time for confronting identity dilemmas, such as the meaning of one's life; career decisions; and how to implement choices and values. Intimacy concerns also tend to surface during late adolescence (Sarason and Sarason, 1984; Newman and Newman, 1984).

Stress

Interpersonal and social conflicts, situational conflicts, and intrapersonal conflicts can cause stress and frustration. Stress is a condition of physical or psychological strain that imposes pressures for adjustment on the individual. The triggers of stress can be internal or external, brief, transient, or persistent. If stress is severe or prolonged, it may overtax the individual's resources and lead to disordered psychological functioning or maladaptive behavior. The types of events that are stress-producing include external and internal strife, frustrations, deprivations, conflicts, and pressures. The concept of stress was introduced by Hans Selye around 1940 (Goldenson, 1984; Selye, 1976). Frustration refers to thwarted or blocked motives, desires, and actions by internal or external forces. Internal forces are internalized standards and intrapsychological conflicts. Frustrating external forces are usually the rules of society, parents, and other authority figures, or the refusal of others to fulfill our needs. Stress has become a popular generic concept that has preempted such terms as anxiety, frustration, emotional upset and disturbance, psychological tension, trauma, and alienation. Stress is a term very much in vogue among mental health professionals and lay people. These days one hears adolescents using terms like "stressed out." A stressor is any experience or event that produces physical or emotional stress (Goldenson, 1984; Lazarus and Folkman, 1984).

Research evidence indicates that some of the major stresses during adolescence include the following: failing grades, serious illness or death of family members, breakups with boyfriends or girlfriends, changing schools, school suspensions, punishment and restriction, trouble with the police, loneliness and isolation, unplanned pregnancies, personal loss, and significant changes in the family such as divorce (Elkind, 1981, 1984; Tyerman and Humphrey, 1983; Fuhrman-Schneider, 1986; Sarason and Sarason, 1984).

A number of physiological and psychological characteristics are associated with stress. At the physiological level, mild-to-moderate levels of stress seem to focus attention and increase alertness and efficiency. In gearing up for an exam or an important athletic contest, mild-to-moderate stress helps adolescents focus and concentrate on carrying out their assignments. High levels of stress can generate crippling fear, panic, disorganization, restlessness, and irritability. It is difficult to perform tasks that require a high level of skill and organization, such as playing chess, when an individual is experiencing panic and disorganization.

There are corresponding physiological changes with stress. Blood pressure and heart rate increase, respiration becomes more rapid, the blood sugar level increases to provide more energy, and the pupils dilate. Positive stresses such as joy and excitement create the same physiological effects. Most of the physiological changes that take place during stress arousal result from the activation of the sympathetic division of the autonomic nervous system (White and Watt, 1981; Atkinson et al., 1983).

Some degree of stress arousal and emotional activation seems to be necessary for optimal human cognitive and psychological functioning. In laboratory experiments with perceptual isolation and sensory deprivation in which the arousal level generated by incoming stimuli was reduced to extremely low levels, cognitive and perceptual functioning deteriorated to a point where subjects showed the following: disorientation, confusion, hallucinations, significantly reduced intellectual performance, and a marked decrease in ability to concentrate (Atkinson et al., 1983). In real-life situations, when children and adolescents are bored they will seek out stimulating activities. Most adolescents enjoy the mild-to-moderate emotional arousal generated by the stress and excitement of adventure, minor risk taking, stimulating challenges, and curiosity seeking. Adolescence is a time when learning can be enhanced by the excitement and pressures involved in discovery, exploration, experimentation, struggle, challenge, and confronting the unknown.

Conflict, Stress, Struggle, and Growth

According to the theories of Erikson (1959, 1963, 1968), Kohlberg (1975, 1976), and Jourard (1967) stress, struggle, and conflict are essential features of psychological growth and development. In Erikson's view, psychosocial growth comes about as a result of conflict between opposing forces, ideas, and values. Each developmental stage from infancy through adulthood has a growth crisis which, if successfully resolved, allows the individual to move forward. The growth crisis in late adolescence revolves around identity issues and shaping the dream of what one wants to become (Levinson et al., 1978; Sarason and Sarason, 1984). An actualizing, growth-facilitating, integrated sense of who one is cannot be achieved without struggle, disappointment, conflict, experimentation, confronting the unknown, giving up old ideas, and making difficult choices about values, beliefs, and future goals. Mastery of the adolescent growth crisis involving identity and interpersonal relationships, builds self-confidence and belief in one's ability to handle troublesome circumstances.

In Kohlberg's theory of moral development, moral growth moves through a process of empathy, exposure to different ideas, role taking, conflict, dissonance, and disequilibrium, and is finally resolved by moving toward a higher level of psychological and moral integration. Through exposure, role taking, and empathy, youths encounter beliefs and values that differ from their internalized beliefs and values. The confrontation with different ideas produces conflict, dissonance, and disequilibrium. In order to successfully resolve the moral dissonance, adolescents move to levels where narcissistic concern with self, and concern with social approval and blind adherence to rules are replaced by universal, logically comprehensive moral principles such as honesty and justice. Universal ethical and logical moral principles represent a higher level of moral development than egocentric self-interests or blind rule-following.

Sidney Jourard feels that conflict, stress, and struggle should be welcomed rather than feared, and approached rather than avoided because conflict, stress, and struggle can provide a source of growth that deepens one's appreciation for life, broadens one's life-experience base, and enriches relationships. While all psychologists recognize the potentially harmful effects of severe conflict and stress, the critical question is how adolescents can find growth-enhancing outcomes and challenges in dealing with strife, discord, and conflict rather than growth-blocking outcomes, such as prolonged bitterness, despair, fear, anger, and depression.

The two themes stressed in this section involve the inevitability of conflict and stress as part of the adolescent experience and the premise that conflict and stress are essential for psychological growth. The important question at this juncture is how adolescents deal with conflict and stress and to what extent their responses can be classified as adaptive growth-facilitating or maladaptive growth-blocking.

COPING WITH CONFLICT AND STRESS

The degree of resourcefulness, resilience, persistence, and effectiveness displayed by adolescents when they encounter developmental dilemmas, conflicts, and stresses is largely dependent on what psychologists refer to as coping behavior. Informally, coping can be defined as how one deals with external and internal demands, pressures, and conflicts. Formally, coping can be defined as a process that consists of active efforts to resolve stress and create workable solutions to the developmental challenges and expectations of each psychological growth stage. Coping involves three primary components:

1. Understanding the meaning of a troublesome situation.
2. Engaging in competent action.
3. Keeping powerful emotions, such as anger or fear, from being too overwhelming (White and Watt, 1981; Newman and Newman, 1984; Brammer and Abrego, 1981).

We will begin our discussion of coping with the case of Jill.

Case Example 1-1: Jill

Jill is an attractive, likeable, 16-year-old high school junior who has been going steady with Harry since she entered high school as a ninth grader 2 years ago. As the relationship became closer, she and Harry spent more and more time together. They rode to school together every morning and saw each other between classes and after school. Because Jill was happy with Harry, she didn't see any need to participate in school activities or cultivate close relationships with peers. She was deeply in love with Harry, had her first and only sexual experiences with him, and was sure she would some day marry him. Although she was very bright and came to high school with excellent junior high school grades, she showed only a mediocre interest in her studies, and her grades were mostly C's with a few B's. Her parents were concerned about her lack of interest in anything outside of Harry. Each time they tried to discuss the subject of her relationship with Harry and her lack of interest in other friends and activities, Jill would get very irritable and defensive. She pointed out that she was passing all her courses, didn't use drugs, and wasn't "wild" like some of the other girls. At the start of her junior year, she gradually began to notice some unpleasant changes in her relationship with Harry. Harry seemed distant and spent less time with her. He said he needed more time to study, and his boss wanted him to work more hours on his part-time job. When Jill confronted Harry about what was really going on, Harry at first denied there was any change in his feelings. Later, during a very emotional discussion in which Jill and Harry both cried, Harry finally told Jill that he felt their relationship was too confining. He thought they both needed to see other people (this is what Harry's dad told him to say) and that they were missing out on the excitement of dating, parties, and "being young." He also told Jill that he changed his mind about going to a local college next year and wanted to go to college at his dad's alma mater, which was in another part of the country. Jill was devastated. Between intermittent outbursts of anger and tears, she begged and pleaded with Harry to keep their relationship as it was. Harry also cried, but was adamant that they break up their one-to-one relationship and date other people. He hoped that they would continue to see each other as friends. Jill refused the offer of continuing the relationship on a friendly dating basis.

After the breakup, Jill went through a period of heartbreak. She felt blue, cried frequently, had days when she didn't feel like getting out of bed or eating, and spent a considerable amount of time thinking and pining about the good old days with Harry. Gradually, she began to absorb the shock. She started spending time with her favorite aunt, who helped her sort out her feelings of hurt and disappointment. Slowly, with her aunt's encouragement, she started initiating new peer relationships, improving her grades, participating in school activities, and thinking about what she wanted to do with her life. She knew it would be a long while before she would be ready for another intimate, long-term male–female relationship. Although she was not completely over the hurt and pain, Jill gradually began to see her freedom from Harry as an opportunity to think about future goals and explore things she had been missing out on in school, such as social relationships, extracurricular activities, and academic courses that would prepare her for college.

As a junior high school student, Jill had been very good in music and English. She was an excellent singer, and was very fluent with words. With encouragement from her teachers and the school counselor (who knew about the breakup because of the school's grapevine), she started singing with the school choir and joined the debate team. Through these activities, she started building peer relationships. She also joined a young people's social activities and discussion group at her church. As Jill recovered and rebuilt her life, she thought more and more about the future in terms of what was important to her. She thought about what she wanted to do with her life and the roles future relationships, a career, and a family would play in her life. During the latter part of her junior year, her grades showed dramatic improvement, and by the beginning of her senior year she was being considered for a scholarship at a good university, where she is thinking about majoring in music or prelaw. She now feels good about her life, enjoys her freedom, and looks back on her relationship with Harry as both a happy and a painful experience. In retrospect, she thinks she was too young to get that deeply involved and wants to continue to sort out who she is before she gets in another "long-term" relationship.

Meaning, Appraisal, and Reframing

The case of Jill illustrates the major issues in understanding a stressful situation. These involve absorbing the first emotional shock waves, establishing initial meaning, appraising and reappraising the situation, reframing the problem, and establishing new meanings that allow the growth process to move forward (Brammer and Abrego, 1981). For adolescents, the initial meaning of highly stressful situations is likely to be determined by the intensity of the emotional impact. Initial judgments about the effects of stress on one's well-being are referred to as appraisal. In Jill's case, her first reaction to the breakup was one of disappointment, despondency, and hurt. Her responses to these emotions, with tears, anger, and pining, were attempts at damage control. Releasing her feelings in this manner enabled her to absorb the initial shock waves. Subsequently, through discussions with her aunt, teachers, and the school counselor, she slowly reappraised the situation and reframed her perceptions from hurt and disappointment to opportunity. She began to see her freedom less in the context of rejection and more in terms of the opportunity to get involved in productive activities she had ignored because of her involvement with Harry. Finally, she started to think about her future, her values, and what she wanted from life. In dealing with these identity-related issues, she is beginning to dream about what she wants to become; this is a critical developmental task of adolescence. She was able to take what started out as a teenage tragedy and turn it into an opportunity for personal growth.

While the initial appraisal of a stressful situation can be a threatening one, subsequent reassessment over time can change the meaning from a threatening one to one of opportunity and promise. Reframing the problem to one of challenge or promise releases energies that can be utilized to pursue the challenge. In order to reassess, reappraise, and reframe the problem, the individual has to be able to control the meaning of the situation and contain powerful disruptive emotions.

As adolescents mature intellectually and gain more experience, their capacity for conceptual and reflective thinking improves, and they can then see the same situation from multiple perspectives and envision new possibilities. The ability to see and experience from multiple perspectives is one of the critical skills that enable adolescents to reframe a problem, allowing for new growth possibilities.

Problem Solving and Competent Action

The second component of the coping process involves taking competent action. This step is often referred to as problem solving. The basic aspects of the problem-solving process can be demonstrated with the case of Tom.

Case Example 1-2: Tom

Tom is a 15-year-old, black high school sophomore. He lives in a single-parent, low-income household with his mother and two younger sisters, ages 11 and 13. His father is not in the picture. Tom has an 18-year-old, high school dropout brother who spends most of his time "in the streets." Tom and his family live in a rundown inner city neighborhood that has the usual problems of urban decay, high teenage and adult crime, drugs, teenage pregnancies, unemployment, and 50% high school dropout rate. For males, the dropout rate is probably closer to 75%. Tom would like to stay out of trouble, get a good job someday, marry, and be able to support a family. He also wants to be in a position to help his mother and two younger sisters. He has some vague ideas about wanting to enter the field of medicine. He doesn't know exactly what he wants to do in the field of medicine, and he's unsure about how or where he would get the training or the financing to do so. He is attracted to medicine because he would like to do something to help the people in his neighborhood. He also thinks that physicians "make good money." His interest in medicine was stimulated by a career-day film on occupations when he was in junior high school. Every time he goes to see the high school counselor to talk about jobs and careers, the counselor is too busy with emergencies (gang fights, drugs, unplanned pregnancies, truancy, and the like) to really help Tom get the information he needs to establish a sense of direction. Tom has plenty of ability, but isn't working too hard in school. He has a C+ average he thinks is pretty good, considering the dropout rate. He doesn't use drugs or have unprotected sex, avoids the gangs, and hasn't been in trouble with the law. He is close to his mother and sisters.

His uncle is a substitute father figure. The uncle, when he is able to, spends time with Tom and tries to guide him away from drifting into the "streets." The uncle works in the maintenance department of a large metropolitan hospital near Tom's home and runs a janitorial service on the side. Tom works with his uncle's janitorial service on some evenings and on weekends. He gives half of his pay to his mother, saves a fourth, and "finger pops" the other fourth. Tom says he has learned to stay out of trouble by not jumping into things until he has had a chance to "lay back and check it out." He thinks that if he jumps into things too quickly he might get strung out on drugs, "fall into" the gang life, become a teenage father, or get into some other situation that could get out of hand.

Tom's uncle got him connected to a job as a laboratory helper through a work-study program for low-income high school students at the hospital where he works. Tom works for an experimental psychologist who is doing studies with rats on learning, perception, and neurophysiology. Tom's job is to feed the rats and keep the cages clean. Because he is a hard worker, the psychologist gives him additional responsibilities. After 6 months, Tom is able to record time trials, enter low-level statistics into a computer, and set up the mazes for experiments. In the career-counseling part of the work-study program, Tom is exposed to how the hospital works, the range of medical services and departments, and the functions of professionals, paraprofessionals, and administrators. When an opening occurs for a higher paying clerical job in the admissions office, Tom's boss encourages him to apply.

As a junior in high school, Tom works in a hospital admissions office where he becomes acquainted with the financial and management side of health care. He gets to meet a number of the senior physicians, department heads, and administrators and gradually starts thinking about a career in hospital management or public health (Tom doesn't like blood). His boss, who likes Tom's positive attitude and hard work, encourages and helps him to find information about how to prepare for careers in public health and hospital administration. She is a recent graduate from a hospital management master's degree program. She arranges for Tom to talk to minority recruiters from different colleges, stays on him about pulling up his grades, and takes him to visit colleges around the state on weekends.

Tom decided to enter college as a business major with a psychology minor. He felt this background would give him the flexibility to move in several directions as he improves his people skills and business skills. He continued working at the hospital during summers and vacation periods. As a college student, he established a good relationship with a black psychology teacher who helped him think through his choices and what he wanted to do with his life. At the time of this writing, Tom is a second-year graduate student in public health administration and has decided to pursue a career in either hospital administration or as an administrator of a prepaid health plan located in the minority community.

Tom began his problem solving and movement toward his ultimate goal with a vague idea of the direction he wanted to go in. Over the next few years, he acquired the information he needed to clarify the career possibilities and the strategies for moving toward them. Tom showed remarkable persistence. When his counselor was not available, Tom either sought out or made the best use of other possible sources of information, such as programs and people in the hospital. When adolescents start out with a vague idea of what they want to do, the information, strategies, and choices may not be highly visible. This is especially true for low-income, minority youths who are trying to find out about educational preparation and experience tracks for entering occupational areas that are new in that family members and neighbors have not been traditionally employed in these areas. Tom learned to avoid impulsive choices, not only in establishing career choices, but in his overall style of responding to decision-making situations. Learning to "lay back and check it out" helped him to examine a range of possibilities before committing himself to a final course of action. Sometimes adolescents and adults who are in a hurry to look good or appear decisive make quick choices based on poor information, decisions they later regret. "Laying back" gives vague ideas the time to gel. Tom was able to utilize support systems and people networks in his environment. He regularly talked to his mother and his uncle. He managed to establish good relationships with his supervisors and teachers, and they, in turn, spent time guiding him toward his goals. In problem solving, there is a reciprocal interaction between the person and the environment. Tom's actions and style of relating to people generated positive feedback he used to shape and refine his goals and strategies for achieving them. Finally, Tom was able to invest his psychological energies into getting things done rather than being bottled up by fear, anger, or bitterness. His actions opened up new possibilities for growth.

In a brief synopsis, the major steps in problem solving involve taking competent action to resolve obstacles and move toward goals. The successful problem-solving adolescent learns to size up the situation, examine a range of alternative possibilities, generate accurate information, develop a workable course of action, make mid-course corrections using feedback to refine goals and strategies, utilize available environmental support systems, and develop new support systems as needed. Effective problem solving does not occur instantly. Time, persistence, and flexibility are usually required to move toward major goals and accomplish major growth steps. Problem solving has a strong cognitive component. Sequential thinking, organizing information, and capitalizing on opportunities are critical to effective problem solving. These skills should improve as adolescents evolve through the social-psychological maturity process during their early through late teens (Brammer and Abrego, 1981; Bolton, 1979; Johnson, 1981).

Protective Strategies and Defense Mechanisms

The third component of the coping process involves protective strategies. Protective strategies are actions designed to control powerful, disorganizing feelings such as fear, anger, and guilt. When adolescents are paralyzed by fear or wild with anger, it is difficult for them to work their way through stressful and frustrating experiences. The most effective protective strategies keep the adolescent from being too badly upset by stress. These strategies strengthen such supportive emotions as calmness, serenity, and enthusiasm and give the adolescent time to complete the appraisal and reappraisal process necessary to work through the problem and generate workable solutions (Brammer and Abrego, 1981; White and Watt, 1981). There are three aspects of protective responses: (1) damage repair, (2) defense mechanisms, and (3) complex protective reactions.

Damage control mechanisms enable the individual to reduce or minimize personal discomfort without actively working on the major conflict. Relaxing, ventilating feelings by grieving, crying, pining, or mild expressions of anger can be part of a sequential coping process which allows the teenager to ventilate crucial feelings before the problem-solving phase can begin (Coleman et al., 1984). Defense mechanisms are the most commonly used and widely known protective strategies. Defense mechanisms were described by Freud (1966, 1974) and elaborated upon by his daughter Anna Freud (1937). Defenses are conscious and unconscious protective strategies used by the individual to reduce such anxious feelings as guilt, shame, or fear without necessarily working on the problem. The goal of defense mechanisms is to help the individual maintain a sense of equilibrium in the face of threat. The mind is very clever and creative and can find all sorts of ways to reduce uncomfortable feelings (Goldenberg, 1977). Defense mechanisms have several important characteristics. Defenses involve the alteration of internal or external reality; they have an automatic, habitual quality; and they can be used in growth-enhancing or growth-restricting ways.

Case Example 1-3: John

John is a 17-year-old high school junior. He has been going with his girlfriend for about a year. In the past, he described her as "beautiful, devoted, honest, smart, and caring." Two months ago, she told John she wanted to break up their relationship because she had secretly started seeing someone else she had grown very fond of. His girlfriend said she was reluctant to tell John about her new male friend because she knew he would be hurt, but she was tired of lying and feeling guilty. She still cares about John, but no longer wants to be in a boyfriend-girlfriend relationship. John reacted with anger. He refused her offer of trying to continue the relationship as friends. He let loose a verbal tirade at his girlfriend, degraded her morality and integrity as a woman, and said he never wanted to see her again. He now says he has put her out of his mind "like she never existed." He devaluates her character, says she was no good for him, and that he is glad to be rid of her. He told one of his friends he was intending to break up with her anyway because he was tired of being tied down and had been thinking about checking out some of the other girls at school. Since he broke up with his girlfriend, John, who used to be very outgoing, spends a considerable amount of time alone in his room at home watching TV and sleeping. He has very little energy and avoids seeing his friends and going to parties. He says he thinks he has mononucleosis. John's doctor says he is in excellent health. His mother thinks he cries in his room when he is alone. When she asked him about feeling blue and sad over the breakup, John became very angry, denied any feelings of heartbreak, and said he needed time alone to think about his future.

John is using a mixture of defense mechanisms to handle his feelings about the breakup and bolster his deflated self-esteem. He appears to be trying to tune out feelings of hurt and loss by denial, suppression, and screening out thoughts and images of his girlfriend. He fortifies this denial, suppression, and possible repression of feelings about his girlfriend by rationalizing that she was not a very good person and that he was going to leave her anyway. He emotionally distances himself from embarrassment about the breakup by insulating himself from his friends. Repression, suppression, denial, rationalization, avoidance, and insulation are frequently used defensive mechanisms. Several commonly used defense mechanisms are described in Table 1-1.

All defenses involve alterations of unpleasant internal or external realities by distortion, distancing, or filtering. Repression, the unconscious screening out of painful feelings, and denial in varying degrees are integrated into most defensive strategies. Defenses that successfully reduce anxiety, threat, and other uncomfortable feelings are retained because they work. The tension-reducing quality acts as a reinforcer to sustain the defensive behavior. Defenses that are retained and reinforced because they work have a way of

Table 1-1. Commonly Used Defense Mechanisms

Repression—The automatic or unconscious screening out of unacceptable wishes, drives, images, and impulses. Repression begins in childhood and is one of the basic defense mechanisms.

Suppression—Consciously tuning out unpleasant feelings, ideas, or emotions by trying not to work it out. Suppression is conscious, whereas repression is unconscious.

Denial—Denial usually refers to the screening out of unpleasant external values or feelings generated by unpleasant external realities. Repression usually refers to intrapsychic feelings. All defenses involve some degree of repression or denial.

Displacement—A shift of feelings from one object to another. The second object becomes a more acceptable target of such feelings as anger or hostility.

Rationalization—The assessment of a socially acceptable explanation for our behavior so we appear to be acting rationally or logically.

Intellectualization—Dealing with anxiety and stress-provoking problems as if they were intellectually interesting, emotionally neutral events.

Projection—Attributing one's own anxiety, arousal, or unacceptable or acceptable motives to someone else.

Sublimation—Channeling unacceptable aggressive and sexual energies into socially approved behaviors such as athletics, school, or the performing arts.

Acting out—Poorly controlled release of sexual, aggressive, or angry impulses to reduce tension.

Regression—Retreating to earlier ways of behaving when one is under stress.

becoming habitual, automatic, and mostly unconscious mechanisms to reduce stress and may continue to be used after the original stressful situation has passed. Existing patterns of protective behavior are maintained because they are familiar and because they provide us with a source of security (Coleman et al., 1984). Once in place, defenses are resistant to change. The automatic and unconscious use of defenses prevents the person from learning to utilize new behaviors to face a situation that was once unpleasant. Adolescents who, because of an unpleasant experience on a blind date, avoid situations in which they will have to meet new people are protecting themselves from threat and embarrassment; at the same time, they are restricting their opportunities to develop social and interpersonal skills through interactions with new people. Protecting one's self by restricting growth opportunities does not allow the individual to reappraise an originally threatening situation to discover other ways of coping. In facing a situation that was threatening in the past, the individual could also find out the situation is no longer threatening (White and Watt, 1981).

Defenses can have growth-enhancing or growth-inhibiting qualities, according to Haan (1977) and Kroeber (1963) who have examined the healthy and unhealthy aspects of defense mechanisms. Intellectualization and rationalization can be seen as distorted forms of logical thinking. Excessive repression is an indiscriminate use of our powers to hold back uncomfortable feelings until we can consciously deal with them. Projection, or attributing one's unacceptable impulses to someone else, is a misuse of empathy, that is, the capacity to put one's self in another's place and accurately understand that person's feelings. Concentrating on other activities or working on hobbies allows one to temporarily set aside disturbing thoughts until a more opportune time, whereas denial represents a refusal to face painful thoughts and stressful situations. Defenses or protective strategies may be necessary before more effective problem-solving ideas can develop. When used properly, defenses can be ways of buying time to allow workable solutions to emerge. The ideal defense provides protection, is low on distortion of reality, allows for some expression of feelings and gratification of needs, and does not block the appraisal and reappraisal process that is essential in finding workable solutions. Unhealthy defenses prevent fulfillment of needs, involve excessive distortion of internal and external reality, and severely reduce the flexibility needed to work through stressful conflicts. A 14-year-old girl who excessively fasts to the point where her menses cease, yet sees herself as fat and develops elaborate denial and justifications for not eating sufficient calories for her body to develop normally, may be protecting herself from feeling guilt and fear as a result of sensuous impulses. She may use a complex process of denial, repression, rationalization, and intellectualization. The cost of such a defensive system could be catastrophic, if her defenses continue to prevent the kind of reappraisal of her conduct that can lead to a healthy diet.

Complex protective strategies involve the integration of damage-control and defense mechanisms with other behaviors. Relaxation exercises and jogging in the evening and the morning before an important exam are ways of reducing stress, which can be an essential part of a productive test-taking strategy. Seeking excitement and adventure can relieve distress caused by boredom and stimulate the process of discovery. A protective strategy that involves the persistent use of rebellious behavior or abuse of drugs to tune out unpleasant feelings and avoid coming to grips with challenging situations can be growth inhibiting because additional adverse stresses are likely to be created by these protective behaviors. Youths who have persistent feelings of shame, guilt, anger, fear, and lack of trust because of unresolved childhood developmental conflicts may have to invest a considerable amount of energy in constructing complex protective strategies. These strategies, in the end, don't solve the original issues and generate adverse reactions from the environment, which make things worse. Even when complex protective strategies are partially successful in protecting us from uncomfortable feelings, threatening images and vague anxiety-producing ideas, involving shame, guilt, and fear, can seep through.

Synopsis of General Coping Principles

Coping is a learned behavior that should become more sophisticated with age and psychosocial maturity (Vaillant, 1977). As teenagers progress through adolescence, they develop the potential and the experience to become more resourceful, reflective, and more able to contain disruptive emotions. More mature problem-solving approaches and protective strategies allow for closer access to internal feelings and involve less distortion of external reality. Greater self-knowledge, which comes about through honest reflection, creates a stronger awareness of one's needs, values, and goals. Knowledge of values, goals, and needs is essential in making accurate judgments about the meaning of events in one's life and what one wants to do.

Coping is not an end-state that always results in success, leads to happiness, and ties everything up in a neat bundle. No solution to conflict is likely to work all of the time; initial solutions must be refined through trial and error, successive approximations, and persistence. Disappointment, setbacks, and misfortunes occur, even when there has been careful planning, appraisal, and competent action. It took Jill awhile to work through her feelings about the breakup with Harry. She still occasionally misses him, despite the fact that she has successfully moved on to new things in her life. Tom tried a variety of approaches before he made his final decisions about career direction.

Coping can be either reactive or proactive, or a combination of both. Jill initially reacted to the loss of Harry with sadness and pining. Her behavior became proactive when she started thinking about going to college, what she would major in, and how she would finance it.

Different coping skills may be required during early and late adolescence. In early adolescence, teenagers need to develop social and interpersonal skills in order to make the transition into the peer group networks. In late adolescence, when young people are confronted with identity-related issues, reflective, integrative, and planning skills are essential. Establishing who one is, what one believes, and where one is going with his or her life often requires making new assumptions about self, beliefs, and values.

Successful copers use a variety of strategies (Brammer and Abrego, 1981). Adolescent life presents a variety of demands, pressures, and conflicts in relationships, personal goals, emotions, and society's expectations. No one set of protective mechanisms, problem-solving approaches, or decision-making strategies will work in all situations. There are times to lay back and check things out, times for direct action, and times when adolescents need to call time out and set their problems aside for a while. Coping responses can be refined and updated as adolescents receive feedback and assess results.

Coping is a reciprocal process involving interaction between the adolescent and the environment. By having a good attitude, showing persistence, and being a hard worker, Tom impressed significant adults. They, in turn, opened up opportunities for him. Had his attitude been one of hostility and sullenness, however justifiable, he probably would have met with resistance and avoidance. In the process of successfully coping with disappointing situations, adolescents discover new strengths, increase their self-confidence, and learn to manage transitions. After a period of disruption and disillusionment, Jill began to take charge of her life. She began to develop new academic and interpersonal skills and started looking forward to the challenges of the future.

Finally, coping should be viewed over time. John, who was into denial and rationalization about the breakup of his relationship with his girlfriend, may need more time before he can successfully absorb the shock and start moving forward in his growth.

Adaptive and Maladaptive Coping

Coping behaviors can be divided along an adaptive-maladaptive continuum with strategies that concentrate on helping adolescents maintain the status quo or their equilibrium in the middle (see Table 1-2). Adaptation is a concept that refers to the individual's ability to achieve and maintain a workable relationship between one's needs and goals and one's available options and society's expectations (White and Watt, 1981).

Adaptive coping prevents emotions from becoming too disorganizing and allows a competent course of action to develop. Adaptive coping facilitates the development of mastery and positive self-esteem and keeps the growth process moving forward. Maladaptive coping does not resolve the original stressful events, often generates negative feedback from the environment, tends to make the problem worse, and blocks the growth process. Maladaptive coping blocks the flexibility and resourcefulness needed to overcome troublesome dilemmas and challenges. Responses that concentrate on survival and on calming strong emotions help us to maintain the status quo, but do not change the situation. Screening out unpleasant feelings of shame or

Table 1-2. Adaptive-Maladaptive Coping Continuum

Excessive, rigid defenses; distortion; acting out; making things worse prevents growth	Adjustment-survival, keeps stress low, doesn't change situation, growth possible at later date	Facilitates growth, makes environment more conducive to mastery, allows actualizing drives to move forward
Maladaptive coping	Equilibrium status quo	Adaptive coping

guilt doesn't change the feelings, but helps us to remain calm and buy time to use on another occasion. Jill and Tom put together adaptive coping strategies over a period of time. The key element in each of their adaptive strategies was the growth-facilitating factor. Both Jill and Tom were able to develop coping styles that allowed them to move forward toward making career choices, defining values, developing a positive self-concept, and ultimately make significant progress toward resolving identity issues.

The growth-blocking effects and adverse consequences of maladaptive coping are highlighted in the case of George.

Case Example 1-4: George

George is a 16-year-old male, who was looking forward to getting his driver's license and buying his first car. George lives with his mother and younger sister. His parents are divorced and he sees his father about once a month. By saving money from his part-time job, he has accumulated enough to purchase a good used car a neighbor agreed to sell him. His mother put him on restriction for coming home drunk, violating curfew, poor grades, and school truancy. He considers the restriction fair because he violated a contract he had signed with his mother and his counselor, which included the following: pull up his grades, attend school regularly, maintain the agreed upon curfew hours, no drinking outside the home, and no drug use at all. George had used drugs intermittently in the past. George really wants to go to a party on Friday night but won't be able to because of being on restriction. He has heard that all the popular kids are going to be there, and the kids at school describe it as "the party of the year," complete with a teenage rock band and local singer. George angrily demands that his mother permit him to attend the party despite the restriction. She points out to him that not attending the party is one of the consequences of violating their contract. The discussion between George and his mother quickly escalates. George triggers the escalation in an angry, confrontational style, accusing his mother of not caring and of not being fair. He tells her that he hates living with her, accuses her of being responsible for the divorce, and says he doesn't like her boyfriend. He uses a considerable amount of profanity. In response to George's attack, his mother counterattacks. She accuses him of being irresponsible and ungrateful, claims his misbehavior has made her life more stressful, and tells him that if he cannot abide by her rules and respect her, he can find some place else to live. Because of his behavior, she is not going to give her permission for him to purchase the car or to get his driver's license. George finally leaves the room, slams the door, and spends most of the next several days brooding in his room. Notices are sent from school indicating that he has not been attending. He hangs out with old drug buddies in the daytime, when he should be in school, and starts drinking and using marijuana again. More confrontations and restrictions ensue. Between bouts of anger and rebellion, George is depressed, thinks more and more about suicide, and ruminates about past hurts and disappointments.

George's angry confrontational response to not being able to go to the party was maladaptive, because it made things worse and did not resolve the major problem between himself and his mother. Maladaptive coping often creates negative responses from others. George's angry, confrontational style generated counter-escalation from his mother and made her more adamant in refusing to permit him to attend the party, and she also withdrew her permission for him to purchase the car and get his driver's license. George's case illustrates the major paradox contained in maladaptive coping and protective strategies. Rather than solving the original problem, maladaptive coping actually makes things worse by creating additional stresses.

Maladaptive responses block growth because they restrict the flexibility and resourcefulness needed to reassess the situation, make mid-course corrections, and generate alternative workable responses. Some adolescents faced with similar situations have tried to negotiate by offering to do additional chores or serve additional time on restriction for the opportunity to attend the party. Others might decide to cool out for the weekend, watch TV, and use the time to catch up on their school work. George's subsequent responses of apathy, helplessness, powerlessness, and suicidal ideation following the blowup with his mother can also be classified as maladaptive coping. The presence of these feelings indicates that there has been a breakdown in the coping process. When suicidal ideation becomes pervasive, adolescents no longer feel that life has any meaning. They often stop thinking about problem solving and don't feel they have the protective resources to shield themselves from feelings of worthlessness, powerlessness, and self-deprecation.

Adaptive and maladaptive coping are learned behaviors and responses. As learned behaviors, coping responses are guided by the principles of reinforcement, modeling and imitation, identification, and internalization. Maladaptive behavior, no matter how dysfunctional and misguided it seems, represents misdirected attempts to meet the problems of living (White and Watt, 1981). George's angry confrontational style has some elements of an assertive response that got out of hand when he became overly aggressive.

Learned behaviors, whether adaptive or maladaptive, are resistant to change once they become habitual, familiar, and integrated into one's personality. Because maladaptive responses may have once worked well in serving a protective function, they are difficult to relinquish without evoking anxiety and stress.

When youngsters are rebelling, using drugs, running away, not eating, and talking about suicide, we as parents, teachers, and clinicians need to ask ourselves what purpose is this behavior serving, what's holding it in place, what's reinforcing it, who are the teenagers identifying with, why are they hanging on to these behaviors, and what are they protecting themselves from? They may well be holding on to maladaptive behaviors because they are too frightened and distressed to relinquish these behaviors, thereby preventing the opportunity for more constructive behaviors to emerge. In a later section of this chapter, disordered adolescent behavior is defined as maladaptive coping.

Coping Styles

Adolescents display a variety of coping styles and different approaches in managing the developmental tasks of adolescence. In a study carried out in the midwestern area in the 1970s, Moriarty and Toussieng (1976) classified adolescent coping styles in terms of sensers and censors. The sensers sought out diversity, showed a willingness to encounter new experiences, questioned traditional values and inconsistencies in society's standards, and explored ways of changing the rules. The sensers were accepting of their emotions, tended to trust their own experiences and perceptions, and wanted to work out new solutions for living in a rapidly changing world. The censors tended to follow the rules and adopt parental standards without a great deal of questioning. Their interest was more in clarifying traditional values and finding out which behaviors were acceptable. The censors tended to be more oriented toward carefully controlling their feelings and impulses. Answers to troublesome questions were sought externally rather than by relying on one's own experiences and judgments. The censors saw little need to explore new ideas and did not seek out people with diverse ideas and values. Both styles can be successful in our society and are needed for the growth and continuation of society. The censors maintained the existing pathways and values in sharing stability and continuity in traditions. Sensers are part of the cutting edge that creates new values and ideas.

Adolescent males and females may have slightly different coping styles, especially during early adolescence. Adolescent males tend to be more oriented toward overaction, whereas females tend to be more thoughtful and reflective. Properly balanced, action and reflection are essential components of an adaptive coping style. An extreme action or reflective style can be part of a maladaptive coping process. Excessive action can be impulsiveness; excessive reflection can magnify self-doubts, fears, and guilt (Kimmel and Weiner, 1985; Cramer and Carter, 1978).

PSYCHOSOCIAL FACTORS ASSOCIATED WITH COPING

Several personality, environmental, and background factors influence, shape, or constrain the coping process an adolescent is likely to use in a given situation. The major psychosocial factors are: (1) the nature of the conflict or stress, (2) the degree of environmental support, and (3) personal competence (Schlossberg, 1981; Brammer and Abrego, 1981; Lazarus and Folkman, 1984).

The Nature of Stress

The nature of the conflict and how it is perceived is influenced by the following: the number of stressful events or stressors occurring at the same time, the adolescent's values and goals, whether the stress is sudden or chronic, and the degree to which the stress is inevitable.

An adolescent who is encountering several stresses at once, such as divorce of parents, loss of peers or intimate relationships, movement to another community, failing grades, and constant criticism because of failure to live up to unrealistic parental standards, is likely to feel overwhelmed by the demands placed on her. This has been called the layering or hassle effect (Brammer and Abrego, 1981). When transitions are sudden and unpredictable, such as the loss of a parent through a fatal heart attack, teenagers are likely to experience a sense of discontinuity and disruption. It usually takes a while for them to mobilize the resources to work through the situation. Inevitability versus noninevitability is a decisive factor in how teenagers respond to loss. When teenagers think someone is responsible for their loss and disappointment in situations of divorce or unrequited love, they may tie up a lot of energy blaming themselves and others. Loss is also perceived differently at different time periods. Initially, it may be responded to with grief, anger, and disappointment. At a later point in time, teenagers may be able to perceive the loss situation as a challenge or opportunity to grow. Jill felt devastated when she first broke up with her boyfriend; later, she saw the breakup as an opportunity to grow. Acute versus chronic stress has different implications. Acute stresses demand an immediate response and cannot be ignored. Chronic stress from childhood carryovers of persistent feelings of shame, guilt, fear, or anger is likely to tie up energies in shielding, protecting, and defending for extensive periods that could otherwise be utilized to accomplish growth-oriented developmental tasks. When youths perceive loss and tragedy as inevitable circumstances of life which offer the opportunity to grow, they are in a position to discover that they have a variety of potential strengths that can be utilized to move forward. These beliefs help adolescents to gain control and maintain their self-esteem (Brammer and Abrego, 1981).

Environmental Support

The extent to which the adolescent perceives the environment as supportive and understanding is critical. All adolescents have needs for belonging, positive regard, and caring. If significant others in a network of parents, peers, relatives, and friends are perceived as understanding and supportive, the adolescent is likely to turn to them for comfort and counseling. This mitigates against feelings of loneliness and abandonment. Significant others can also provide realistic feedback and suggestions adolescents can use to shape the meaning of events and formulate constructive problem-solving responses.

Psychosocial Competence

Psychosocial competence is a term used to indicate the adequacy of self-concept, social skills, communication skills, problem-solving strategies, and conflict-resolution skills. A growing body of psychological literature suggests that the most stress-resistant individuals and the best copers are people who have achieved a high level of psychosocial competence. They think they have a reasonable control over their destiny and view change as part of life. They see stress as a challenge to change the situation to their advantage (Schlossberg, 1981; Brammer and Abrego, 1981). Teenagers who have completed preadolescent development tasks involving the building of trust and self in others, self-sufficiency and autonomy, initiative and curiosity, have developed the psychological foundation to cope with the stresses and conflicts of adolescence. Their coping reflects a spirit of self-confidence, personal pride, resourcefulness, resilience, and adequate interpersonal skills. When an adolescent feels capable, powerful, lovable, and secure, he or she does not have to invest an overabundance of energies in protective strategies to bolster self-esteem. They are free to devote their energies to problem solving, conflict resolution, creating workable alternatives, and refining goals and strategies.

Conversely, teenagers who fail to complete the preadolescent, psychosocial developmental tasks bring a strong residual of guilt, shame, fear, anger, and low self-esteem into adolescence with them. When there are unextinguished childhood anxieties, future development must be affected by this limitation (White and Watt, 1981). Excessive baggage from unresolved preadolescent developmental conflicts places teenagers at a disadvantage. They are confronted with the challenges and dilemmas of adolescence while still struggling to complete the unfinished business of childhood. The psychological struggle involved in trying to resolve issues from several developmental stages at the same time can overload the adolescent's coping mechanisms. Significant energies are tied up in self-protective strategies and defenses against feelings of shame, guilt, and fear. Complex protective systems can involve shielding one's self from further hurt by an armor of protective anger, excessive competence, or perfectionistic strivings to bolster low self-esteem and a host of other behaviors. The constant investment of energies in protecting and defending comes at a time when most adolescents need all their resources to cope with the daily pressures and demands of adolescent living.

Faulty preadolescent development and lack of environmental support often do not occur in isolation of each other. Lack of trusting, caring relationships from parents and significant others is the prime reason children are unable to complete the preadolescent psychosocial tasks. When children who have not been sufficiently loved, supported, and understood become teenagers, they are not likely to reach out for support in the same family or social environment in which they have not been supported in the past.

Sarason and Sarason (1984) use a formula of vulnerability plus stress to account for maladaptive and disordered behavior. Vulnerability refers to how likely we are to respond maladaptively because of predisposition based on prior learning and development. Faulty preadolescent development and lack of a supportive environment each create some degree of risk. Each risk factor increases the adolescent's emotional and psychosocial vulnerability. When vulnerable, at-risk adolescents encounter major new stresses, the likelihood of maladaptive coping increases proportionately. The mixture of vulnerability and current stress may not be obvious from the adolescent's overt behavior and present concerns. When an adolescent is able to establish sufficient trust in someone and is able to open up and share personal thoughts and feelings, information about preadolescent issues, support systems, and current demands becomes more visible.

For the purposes of this discussion, the components of the coping process and associated psychosocial factors were discussed separately. In real life, the individual acts as a holistic, integrated, synergistic unit with the primary coping factors and psychosocial conditions blending together to form either growth-enhancing, growth-restricting, or equilibrium-oriented responses.

MALADAPTIVE COPING AND THE SIGNS AND SYMPTOMS OF TROUBLED BEHAVIOR

No matter how resourceful adolescents are in coping with conflicts, pressures, and challenges, there will probably be times when they feel overwhelmed. When adolescents encounter demands, conflicts, and stresses that overtax their coping resources, the probability of maladaptive responses increases. Behaviors, persistent moods, and response styles are defined as maladaptive to the extent they block emotional, psychological, and cognitive growth or create adverse consequences that make the situation worse and, consequently, restrict growth. Disordered adolescent behavior can be defined as a breakdown or disruption in the adaptive coping process. Defining adolescent psychological disorders as maladaptive coping or as a disruption in the coping process avoids some of the complications inherent in the use of social norms, statistical frequencies, and terms such as illness, sick, abnormal, and pathological to describe troubled and distressed adolescents.

The signs and symptoms of disordered or maladaptive adolescent behavior, which will be discussed in subsequent chapters, are expressed in the syndromes of depression, suicide, anorexia and related eating disturbances, schizophrenia, drug and alcohol abuse, and persistent and delinquent criminal behavior. The appearance of these symptoms indicates that there has been a blocking, stuckness, or breakdown in the psychosocial growth tasks of adolescence. Each syndrome is the result of a core psychological conflict or dilemma the adolescent has not been able to resolve. Running away does not fit neatly into a classification of maladaptive or disordered behavior. Running away has adaptive and maladaptive connotations. The act of running away can be an assertive response to escape an oppressive home situation or a challenging search for adventure. The consequences of running away, however, can be maladaptive. When youths are out in the streets with no money or skills, they are vulnerable to delinquency and exploitation. The core conflict in running away seems to be a breakdown in the parent–adolescent relationship. Primary conflicts for the remaining syndromes are listed below.

1. *Depression*. Conflicts which are preventing the emergence of self-worth, hope, confidence, and feelings of being capable, powerful, and lovable.
2. *Suicide*. Suicide in adolescents represents the ultimate loss of hope. Core conflicts involve deficits in connectedness to others, unconditional love, and a sense of belonging.
3. *Anorexia and eating disorders*. Conflicts around body image and nurturance.
4. *Schizophrenia*. Core conflict involves difficulties in perceptual, cognitive, and emotional organization which may be caused by a combination of biochemical and psychological vulnerabilities and predispositions. Schizophrenia can also be a defense against further hurt by withdrawing from reality.
5. *Excessive use of drugs and alcohol*. Core conflict involves the inability or unwillingness to cope with the demands of adolescent life and feel good about one's self without using substances.
6. *Delinquency and conduct disturbances*. Conflicts between the adolescent and the rules of society. If delinquent behavior persists, society has the power to create adverse consequences by restricting personal freedom and punishment.

APPROACHES TO HELPING
AND UNDERSTANDING TROUBLED YOUTHS

Counseling and psychotherapy and psychoeducational experiences are two methods mental health professionals have developed to assist troubled and distressed adolescents and young people in coping with the normal problems of growing up. These approaches represent a combination of corrective and preventive philosophies. They can be used individually, with families, or in groups and are employed in educational, mental health, and youth agencies. The terms counseling and psychotherapy are sometimes used interchangeably. Differences between psychotherapy and counseling, to the extent that such differences exist, involve length of time, degree of psychological depth, role of past experiences, and the use of preventively oriented techniques. For the purposes of this discussion, the terms counseling and psychotherapy will be used interchangeably. All approaches to therapy and counseling have embedded within them a theoretical model for understanding how human growth and maladaptive behavior develop.

Three approaches to counseling and psychotherapy and their underlying principles of human growth and maladaptive development will be presented in this section: (1) psychodynamic, (2) cognitive-behavioral, (3) humanistic-existential. These three approaches do not exhaust the universe of adolescent counseling and psychotherapy, but after careful consideration appear to be sufficiently representative to give the reader an understanding of how the process of counseling and psychotherapy facilitates growth in adolescents. While the three counseling and psychotherapy approaches differ from each other, there is a considerable amount of overlap between them in two areas. First, each approach is designed to facilitate growth. Second, each model depicts the first step as building a relationship with the adolescent; the second step as uncovering and sorting out the issues; the third step as exploring new ideas, behaviors, or problem-solving techniques; and the final step as integrating the therapeutic learning and terminating the relationship.

Our discussion of helping approaches and underlying theoretical models of growth and maladaptive behavior begins with the case of Freddy.

Case Example 1-5: Freddy

Freddy is a 14-year-old, male adolescent who was brought to an adolescent mental health center for psychological evaluation and treatment by his parents and stepmother. Freddy's parents were concerned about his fighting with peers, school truancy, failing grades, thefts, angry outbursts against his mother, periods of withdrawal and sullenness, and recent experimentation with drugs and alcohol. His mother is thinking about returning Freddy to live with his father and stepmother because she "can't get along with him and he won't follow the rules." She says Freddy is frequently angry, irritable, and impatient, has trouble sitting still, and doesn't follow through on promises to attend school, obey curfew and household regulations, and do his chores. Freddy has started hanging around with 16- and 17-year-old boys who seldom attend school, use drugs and party a lot, have been arrested on various delinquent charges such as theft, public drunkenness, joy riding, and who have been counseled about running away and school truancy. The precipitating incident motivating Freddy's parents to bring him to the mental health center involved a $200 check Freddy had written on his mother's checking account without her permission and unauthorized charges on her accounts at local stores. While his mother was away on a business trip, Freddy cashed a check and treated his older friends to food, drugs, and alcohol. When asked why his parents brought him to the adolescent mental health center, Freddy said, "Family problems, my family is all broke up and messed up, it's no good, no good." Freddy's parents were divorced 3 years ago after a marriage of 25 years. Both parents agreed that the first 15 years of their marriage were good, but that during the last 3 or 4 years of their marriage things seemed to "fall apart." There was a lot of fighting, arguing, and threatening between the parents. Freddy has three older brothers, ages 24, 22, and 21. The 21-year-old brother is in the service. The two older brothers are married and do not live with either parent. When the parents were first divorced, Freddy and the brother, who is now 21, decided to live with their mother. Freddy is not sure why he chose to live with his mother, but he thinks it was because she was "easier to get along with." Approximately a year after the divorce, the brother that was living with Freddy and his mother joined the army, leaving Freddy alone with his mother. As the mother now looks back, she feels some of Freddy's problems started when his brother joined the army. The presence of the brother seemed to be a stabilizing force in Freddy's life, and she could count on the brother to look after Freddy while she was traveling frequently on her job as a buyer for a large business firm. When Freddy started cutting school, engaging in petty theft (his mother thinks he was also stealing from her), and violating curfew, she first tried to enforce rules with such punishment as restriction and taking away other privileges. When this didn't work, she sent Freddy to live with his father who resided in another part of the state. She said it was too much to handle Freddy, travel on her job as a buyer, and have time for her personal life. His mother was starting to date, and Freddy always managed to find something wrong with her boyfriends. At first, Freddy liked being with his father and his father's girlfriend. His father was an amateur race-car driver on weekends and Freddy liked going along. Shortly after Freddy started living with his father, his father and girlfriend were married. Freddy says his stepmother is "okay, but strict." She laid down the rules, which included regular school attendance, at least C grades, no drugs or alcohol, no curfew violations, and chores must be done. Freddy did alright for a while; then he started cutting school, getting into fights with other kids, and becoming more argumentative toward his stepmother. He accused her of being "overprotective" and not wanting him to "have any fun." His father tried to stay out of the arguments between the stepmother and Freddy. When Freddy's behavior continued to deteriorate, Freddy's stepmother told the father that either she or Freddy would have to leave. At a conference between the mother, stepmother, and father (Freddy was not included), it was decided that Freddy would be sent to live with his older brother and his wife and son.

The Psychodynamic Approach

Psychodynamic theory evolved from the psychoanalytic views of Freud (1966, 1974) and was modified by several of his followers: Sullivan (1953), Fromm (1941, 1955), Horney (1937, 1945), and Erikson (1959, 1963, 1968). There are six primary concepts in psychodynamic theory that are used to explain adolescent psychological disorders and psychotherapy: (1) levels of consciousness, (2) unresolved childhood developmental tasks as the major source of psychological distress, (3) defensive mechanisms and protective strategies, (4) catharsis, abreaction, and working through, (5) expansion of conscious awareness and bringing instincts under conscious control, (6) transference and countertransference.

In the process of moving through preadolescent and childhood psychosocial and psychosexual development, three levels of consciousness develop, the conscious level, subconscious level, and unconscious level. The conscious level contains two dimensions, information which is known to self and known to others and information that is known to self and not known to others. The two dimensions of the conscious level have also been described as the public dimension and the private dimension (Luft, 1970).

In Figure 1-1, the unconscious and preconscious levels make up the largest part of the triangle. This configuration depicts a person who is unaware of many significant feelings and needs. In Figure 1-2, the Johari Window, levels of consciousness are divided into four quadrants. Quadrant 1 refers to behaviors and feelings known to self and to others. Quadrant 2 is the blind area in which others can see things unknown to the person. Quadrant 3 is the private area. These are issues and feelings known to self but not to others. Quadrant 4 contains unconscious material not known to the person or to others. As adolescents become more aware and open to self through psychodynamically oriented therapy or other successful consciousness-

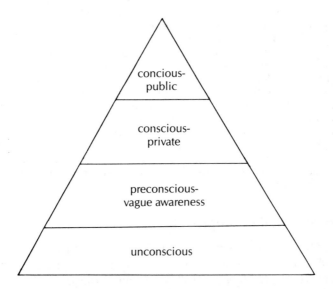

FIGURE 1-1. Levels of consciousness. (Adapted from Luft, J. (1970). *Group processes, an introduction to group dynamics* (2nd ed.). Palo Alto, CA: Mayfield Publishing Co.)

	Known to self	Unknown to self
Known to others	1. Free to self and others	2. Blind to self, known to others
Unknown to others	3. Hidden area, self hidden from others	4. Unknown to self

Figure 1-2. Johari Window. Identification of areas of self-awareness and consciousness. (Adapted from Luft, J. (1970). *Group processes, an introduction to group dynamics* (2nd ed.). Palo Alto, CA: Mayfield Publishing Co.)

expanding growth experiences, the blind, hidden, and private unknown areas should become smaller.

In the case of Freddy, his fighting, cutting school, anger, and some of his thefts were known to him and to his family; this would be the public level. The sadness, tears, and depression, which later became evident in therapy, would be the private conscious domain because these experiences were known to Freddy but not to others. The preconscious level contains material the individual is only vaguely aware of, but does not fully surface. In Freddy's case, this material turned out to be feelings of powerlessness, fear, and helplessness about events he couldn't control. He had no control over his parent's divorce, which started numerous changes in his family, and he felt abandoned when the one remaining brother who lived at home joined the army. At the unconscious level, Freddy, as it turned out, had a profound fear of loneliness and abandonment. He felt insignificant and that no one cared. He worried about whether he had been responsible for his parent's breakup, despite the fact that his behavior problems did not start until later. He began to remember arguments between his parents and his worries about them breaking up when he was 6 or 7 years old. He had forgotten about these unpleasant experiences and worries he had, and also about dreams he used to have during that time, about his family being destroyed by fire.

In psychodynamic theory, protective behaviors at one level of consciousness can be used to screen out upsetting feelings at another level of consciousness. Freddy seemed to be using rebellious and angry behavior to shield himself from feelings of sadness, depression, fear, and powerlessness. The use of defenses and protective measures can complicate diagnostic issues. Freddy's surface behavior might suggest a predelinquent, aggressive conduct or behavior disturbance, or hyperactivity. At a deeper level, it became more obvious that Freddy was frightened, depressed, and hurt.

The deeper sources of adolescent conflict are related to unresolved childhood developmental tasks. These tasks involve bonding, trust building, channeling sexual and aggressive feelings, and building a sense of pride, self-confidence, hope, and optimism for the future. Because of turmoil within their marriage and subsequent adult transitions, Freddy's parents may not have been able to create a sufficient degree of love, security building, and firm but fair discipline for Freddy during the last years of his childhood and early preadolescence. This left the residual fear, hurt, and aloneness Freddy had to shield and protect himself against, because such feelings are very uncomfortable. Through a combination of repression, denial, suppression, and acting out, Freddy built a complex pattern of defenses and protective strategies to shield himself. Acting-out is a defensive mechanism in which the adolescent avoids facing the original stresses and conflicting emotions, yet manages to discharge some of the anger by rebellious behavior, fighting, and rulebreaking. Early adolescents who have not yet developed the reflective capacity to clearly understand, conceptualize, or express their feelings verbally are more prone to acting them out than late adolescents. The goal of psychodynamic therapy is to expand conscious awareness, work through unresolved emotional conflicts, using a process of abreaction and catharsis, and bring behavior under conscious control and understanding. In his therapy, Freddy felt safe enough to ventilate feelings of sadness, fear, and hurt, and to reexperience earlier stressful feelings, look at his needs for love and companionship, and discharge some of his anger and disappointment. Once he started to face these feelings with the help and support of the therapist, he could reappraise his feelings, loosen his protective shield, and start thinking about more socially acceptable ways of meeting his needs. While getting in trouble brought him the attention of his parents, it created other stresses for him.

Freddy's parents, stepmother, and occasionally one of his brothers periodically met with Freddy and the therapist for family sessions. As the parents and other family members understood the dynamics of what was happening to them and to Freddy, they were able to make constructive changes in their relationships with each other and with Freddy. Finally, Freddy was able to make some conscious decisions about goals for school attendance and performance, social conduct, and school grades, which he started following through on. The therapy lasted for 18 months with weekly individual meetings supplanted with family meetings. In the later stages of therapy, Freddy attended group meetings with other adolescents. This expansion of conscious awareness in psychodynamic therapy is illustrated in Figure 1-3, which shows corresponding changes in the Johari Window. Transference and countertransference are vehicles the therapist uses to facilitate building a working relationship. Transference occurs when the client transfers strong feelings about people in his or her life-space onto the therapist. Freddy went through periods in which he was angry and sullen with his therapist and periods in which he was very loving and caring. The therapist tried to understand these feelings, what triggered them, and how he handled them in therapy and in relationships outside of therapy. Countertransference refers

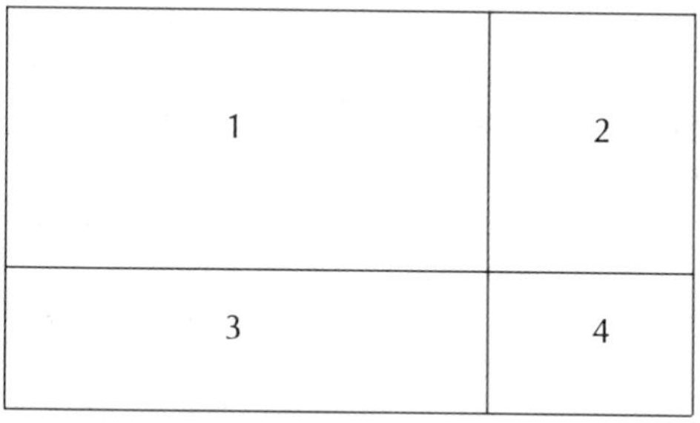

1	2
3	4

Area 1 consciousness or awareness open to self and others expands. Closed and blind areas decrease.

FIGURE 1-3. Johari Window. Changes in consciousness and levels of awareness as a result of successful psychotherapy. (Adapted from Luft, J. (1970). *Group processes, an introduction to group dynamics,* (2nd ed.). Palo Alto, CA: Mayfield Publishing Co.)

to feelings originating in relationships outside therapy that therapists have toward their patients or clients. In their training and personal therapy, therapists are expected to learn how to handle their feelings of countertransference toward patients in ways that facilitate rather than block the patient's therapeutic growth.

The Cognitive-Behavioral Approach

Cognitive-behavioral therapists use the principles of antecedent events, reinforcement, modeling, identification, and internalization to explain maladaptive behavior and to set up the conditions for changing maladaptive behavior (Skinner, 1953; Bandura, 1977; Rosenthal and Zimmerman, 1978). Cognitive-behavioral therapists would be concerned with Freddy's previous exposure to aggressive, rebellious, and argumentative behavior and what maintained and reinforced these behaviors. Freddy's acting-out behavior makes people pay attention to him and seems to reduce his internal stress. This draining off of anger and fear may be a way of identifying with and modeling after older boys he admires. In terms of antecedent conditions, Freddy was exposed to arguing and turmoil between his parents during the last few years of their marriage and, as a way to survive, may have started to model aggressive and argumentative behaviors at that time. Once behaviors are set in place, they are resistant to change because they become familiar, habitual, and automatic. Existing behavior patterns provide a source of security and take less effort to continue than to adopt new ones. Letting go of familiar behaviors, even maladaptive ones, makes us feel tense and uneasy (Coleman et al., 1984). In trying to help Freddy to change his behavior in the direction of socially approved actions and to increase his repertoire of adaptive coping responses, a behavioral therapist would be interested in changing the reinforcement contingencies and role-identification models. The therapist would encourage Freddy's parents and teachers to award and approve such positive behaviors as school attendance, efforts to improve grades, friendly relationships with peers, and the like. Since new behaviors do not occur all at once, the therapist would help Freddy and his parents break the desired behaviors into smaller steps so that successive approximations could be encouraged and rewarded. Changing the reinforcement and reward schedules would allow new behaviors to become consolidated and strengthened.

The cognitive aspects of Freddy's maladaptive behavior pertain to the faulty beliefs Freddy arrived at through overgeneralization and arbitrary inferences. Because of a few unfortunate experiences in family and peer relationships, Freddy seems to have concluded that his family doesn't care for him, other kids don't like him, and that he must be prepared to defend himself by fighting. He also feels he is not a very good person and is powerless to change the things he doesn't like. These faulty beliefs can be labeled as erroneous beliefs about himself, his experiences, and about the future. These beliefs or attributions influence Freddy's behavior and how he interprets his experiences. A cognitive-behavioral therapist would gently, but firmly, challenge Freddy's beliefs, expose him to alternative ways of interpreting his experiences, and guide him toward forming new beliefs.

New beliefs and reappraisals would acknowledge that Freddy has experienced disappointment and pain in family and peer relationships, but these experiences do not mean he is absolutely unlovable, powerless, or a bad person. As an adolescent, Freddy's logical reasoning skills are expanding to the point where he can look at alternative ways of interpreting and conceptualizing his experiences. Freddy can change his beliefs, change the kinds of statements he makes to himself about his work, and has the power to do something positive about his situation. In looking at the consequences of his present behavior and thinking about his beliefs, Freddy might decide that his life would be much happier if he attended school, pulled up his grades, acted friendlier to peers, parents, and others, and treated himself a little better. Since adaptation involves reciprocal interaction between the person and the environment, positive changes in Freddy's behavior will probably generate positive feedback from the environment to inforce new behaviors and beliefs. Changing faulty beliefs and patterns of reinforcement, modeling, identification, and internalization are the major themes of cognitive-behavioral therapy (Beck, 1976; Ellis, 1970).

The Humanistic-Existential Approach

The humanistic-existential psychologists use three primary assumptions to explain human growth and psychological development, conflict, and maladaptive coping. The first premise is that human beings have strong needs to grow, develop, and actualize to the fullness of their potential

(Rogers, 1959, 1980). Growth involves moving forward toward the constructive fulfillment of human potential through a hierarchy of human needs, beginning with physiological needs and progressing upward through safety and security needs, belongingness and love needs, self-esteem needs, and finally, self-actualizing needs (see Fig. 1-4; Maslow, 1968).

Second, the basic conditions of human growth involve positive regard, empathy, and genuineness. If children and adolescents are related to in caring ways, understood from their perspective, and feel that parents and significant other people are genuine, then belongingness and self-esteem needs will be fulfilled. If children and adolescents are not provided with a psychosocial environment that meets the conditions of positive regard, empathy, and genuineness, it will interfere with the actualization of their potential. This blockage in actualization is usually reflected in a significant incongruence between the real self and the ideal self. Children and adolescents learn to value themselves because others value them. If they are not treated with warmth, genuineness, and understanding, a negative self-concept de-

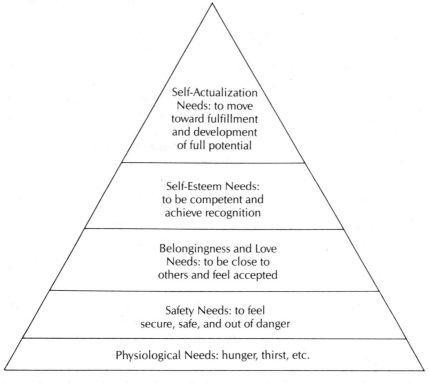

Self-Actualization
Needs: to move
toward fulfillment
and development
of full potential

Self-Esteem Needs:
to be competent and
achieve recognition

Belongingness and Love
Needs: to be close to
others and feel accepted

Safety Needs: to feel
secure, safe, and out of danger

Physiological Needs: hunger, thirst, etc.

In Maslow's hierarchy of needs, needs that are on the hierarchy must be partially satisfied before needs in the higher levels can be fulfilled.

FIGURE 1-4. Maslow's hierarchy of needs. (Adapted from Maslow, A. H. (1968). *Toward a psychology of being* (2nd ed.). Princeton, NJ: Van Nostrand.)

void of hope, faith, and optimism can develop. A narrow and rigid self-concept can prevent children and adolescents from reaching out positively to new experiences, because opening up to new experiences is likely to be threatening. Children or adolescents who are afraid to reach out because of past hurt and devaluation are forced to invest vital psychological energy in protecting and defending their fragile self-image against additional hurt. The restricted level of awareness caused by the defensiveness prevents the individual from utilizing new information and opportunity because they can't let go and open up in a spontaneous manner to allow the learning-by-discovery process to work.

The third premise of the existential-humanistic perspective is that some degree of pain and struggle cannot be avoided in this life. Since human beings are neither perfect, omnipotent nor omniscient, we cannot always control what happens to us nor make things come out exactly the way we want them to be. If we can free our energies from bitterness, anger, hurt, and fear, which many times accompany disappointment and misfortune, we can discover that we have the strength to overcome adversity and to move on to higher levels of personal growth and fulfillment.

Looking at the case of Freddy, existential-humanistic psychologists would say that because of the breakup in his family, turmoil between his parents created pressures of new adult transitions they were forced to cope with after the divorce, preventing them from being able to fulfill Freddy's needs for safety and security, belongingness, love, and positive self-regard. Consequently, Freddy's growth was blocked, as evidenced by his anger, fear, rebellious behavior, sadness and depression, and self-doubt. In order to help Freddy's growth move forward, a humanistic-existential therapist would develop a therapeutic relationship with Freddy based on the growth-facilitating conditions of positive regard, empathy, and genuineness. Relating to Freddy in a nurturing, caring, trust-building, understanding, and genuine manner over a sufficient length of time should help Freddy rebuild his sense of trust, faith, hope, and self-confidence and set the stage for the actualization process to move forward. In caring about Freddy and respecting him, the therapist doesn't have to approve of Freddy's conduct. Freddy's family would also be encouraged to rediscover loving, caring ways of relating to each other, to Freddy, and to themselves. Finally, the therapist would accept Freddy's disappointments, losses, and family misfortunes as a reality, with faith in the belief that Freddy has within him the power to overcome these misfortunes if he can free his energies from defending himself against fear, anger, bitterness, and self-doubt.

Psychoeducational Approaches

Psychoeducational approaches involve a group of techniques, strategies, and tools, developed by psychologists, educators, and other mental health workers, to teach adolescents adaptive coping skills (Adams and Gullotta, 1983; Jensen, 1985; Meichenbaum, 1985). The use of the word "teach" in this context means that psychoeducational approaches have a systematic, didactic flavor. The approaches are sequentially planned and follow an organized script. These strategies were devised to help adolescents learn, through a process of modeling, discovery, and practice, how to cope more effectively with the unpredictable conflicts, stresses, and pressures of adolescence. Psychoeducational strategies are geared toward improving the base of social competency, a term used to denote the adequacy of self-concept, social skills, communication and negotiation skills, problem-solving and decision-making skills, and conflict-resolution skills. Through role playing, discussions, rehearsal, feedback, desensitization, values clarification, relaxation training, and a variety of other techniques, the psychologist tries to help adolescents improve their effectiveness in understanding the meanings and alternative meanings of challenging and stressful events in their lives. Through these techniques, adolescents learn to anticipate and employ possible courses of competent action to reduce stress, generate positive feelings and statements about themselves, and how to sort out discordant values, ideas, feelings, and motives. Psychoeducational approaches can be used in conjunction with psychotherapy and counseling, or they can be used in a preventive context. Psychoeducational strategies are now being used in working with adolescents in mental health clinics, hospitals, college counseling centers, youth centers, churches, and schools to help young people meaningfully confront such issues as teenage sex, birth control, drugs, suicide, running away, anger, and resolving adolescent-parent conflicts and the like. In high schools and colleges, psychoeducational techniques are frequently part of psychology courses in personal adjustment and the applied principles of mental health. For example, in psychology classes, areas like social skills and conflict resolution are broken down into understandable units that can be learned through practice and rehearsal in the classroom and applied in real-life situations. A psychoeducational skills unit on communication and conflict resolution would contain skill-building in active listening, expressing feelings, negotiation and constructive confrontation, defining and reframing conflicts, and include relaxation strategies to reduce stress and tension when negotiating with parents and others about critical issues (Johnson, 1981; Bolton, 1979).

The use of psychoeducational strategies in a preventive, therapeutic, or counseling context rests on two underlying assumptions. First, that social competency and coping skills are learned behaviors that can be taught and improved through use, understanding, and discovery. Second, that interpersonal and social conflicts, situational conflicts, and intrapersonal conflicts are inevitable. We know that adolescents have a vast potential for growth, and we know that they are going to run into stressful situations. This being the case, it seems to make sense that psychologists devise strategies to equip adolescents to cope in a growth-enhancing fashion with the predictable hormonal changes, values-questioning, sexual awakening, family changes, peer changes, self-doubts, and school changes they most probably will experience. Because of their preventive emphasis, psychoeducational strategies have been referred to as stress-inoculation techniques (Meichenbaum, 1985).

SUMMARY AND CONCLUSIONS

During the adolescent passage, some degree of conflict with self, others, and society is inevitable in today's fast-paced society wherein young people encounter contradictory messages with respect to sex, drugs, values, and standards for conduct. How young people cope with conflict is the key element in determining whether conflict is growth enhancing or growth restricting. Coping refers to the degree of resourcefulness, resilience, persistence, and effectiveness adolescents display when they encounter conflict, stress, and dilemmas in psychological development. Coping can be adaptive or maladaptive. Adaptive coping prevents powerful emotions from becoming too disorganizing and allows a competent course of action to develop. Adaptive coping facilitates the development of positive self-esteem and keeps adolescent psychological growth moving forward. Maladaptive coping makes things worse, does not resolve the original conflict, and prevents growth. Successful copers use a variety of strategies. Adolescent life presents a variety of demands, pressures, and conflicts in relationships, personal goals, emotions, and society's expectations. No one set of protective mechanisms, problem-solving strategies, or decision-making approaches will work in all situations. Different coping skills may be required during early and late adolescence. In early adolescence, teenagers need to develop social and interpersonal skills in order to make the transition to peer group networks. In late adolescence, when young people are confronted with identity-related issues, reflective, integrative, and planning skills are essential.

Counseling and psychotherapy and psychoeducational strategies are methods developed by mental health professionals to assist troubled and distressed youths in coping with the normal problems of growing up. These methods represent a combination of corrective and preventive approaches that can be used with individuals, with families, or with groups and are employed in educational, mental health, and youth agencies. Psychodynamic therapies focus on working through unresolved conflicts from childhood and preadolescence as the major sources of distress as well as on expanding conscious awareness and conscious control of behavior. Humanistic-existential therapies view positive regard, empathy, and genuineness as the basic conditions of growth in therapeutic relationships. Cognitive-behavioral therapists use the principles of antecedent events, reinforcement, modeling, identification, and internalization to set up the conditions for changing maladaptive behavior. Psychoeducational strategies are geared toward improving psychosocial competency through an active process of modeling, discovery, role-playing, feedback, practice, and rehearsal. The use of psychoeducational tools in a preventive or counseling framework rests on the assumption that social competency and coping skills are learned beʰ ᵥᵥ-iors that can be taught in an organized, systematic fashion.

SUGGESTIONS FOR PARENTS, TEACHERS, COUNSELORS, AND YOUTH WORKERS

1. Positive self-esteem and emotional support are two primary components of effective coping. As parents, make sure your teenagers know you are available whenever they need you for companionship or to talk out issues. Periodically, parents should let teenagers know they care. Caring from significant others is an important element of positive self-esteem.
2. Conflicts are an inevitable part of growing up and can be useful in building self-esteem, identity, problem-solving skills, and adaptive-coping behaviors. Do not wait until conflicts reach crisis proportions to start working on important issues. Anticipate conflicts about sex, peers, social conduct, drugs, and curfew and start discussing these issues ahead of time.
3. It is essential that adolescents have opportunities to learn psychosocial competency skills. Psychoeducational programs are available designed to teach positive self-concept building, coping and conflict-resolution skills, social skills, interpersonal relationship skills, problem-solving strategies, clarification of values, negotiational skills, how to utilize and develop support systems, stress reduction skills, achieving nonchemical highs, and goal-setting. Find out if such programs exist in local school districts or youth organizations. If they do not, form a group of counselors, educators, and parents and request psychosocial competency programs be developed in local school districts and youth organizations.
4. Teenagers do not want to be sullen, angry, unhappy, miserable, or depressed. Maladaptive coping usually contains a disguised message. When teenagers act out with explosive anger or withdraw into sullen, despondent moods, they are usually trying to tell adults that something is going wrong, and they do not know how to handle the problem constructively. Be patient. Try to listen for subtle indications of what they are trying to communicate. Let them know you are willing to listen, and hear them out.
5. As children become teenagers, they will want more freedom and a loosening of parental controls. Parents should be prepared to move from an autocratic decision-making model to an interpersonal decision-making model based on two-way communication, shared power, collaborative

decision making, empathy, and participatory problem solving. Continued autocratic decision making by parents is likely to create resentment and fails to prepare young people for independent, responsible behavior.

6. Young people who are experiencing loss, setbacks, and major disappointments need time and emotional support to absorb the psychological shock and begin the recovery process. Try to be there for them. Remember, as time passes they are likely to reappraise the meaning of the troublesome situation in ways that will allow them to continue their growth.

7. If you decide to seek out professional counseling for continuing adolescent–parent conflicts or troublesome experiences adolescents cannot resolve, two considerations are important. First, you and your adolescent should feel comfortable with the person you have decided to work with. Personal chemistry and confidence are very important ingredients of successful counseling. Second, the counselor or mental health professional should lay out a treatment plan early in the process so you and your teenager know what the goals are, how they will be achieved, and in what sequential order.

DISCUSSION QUESTIONS

1. Discuss the major types of psychological conflicts adolescents are likely to encounter. Why have macroconflicts increased in the past 25 years and what kinds of decision-making skills must adolescents acquire to deal with the contradictory messages they receive from contemporary society?

2. Why are coping skills so important for today's teenagers? Define the major components of coping behavior and discuss examples of how each component of the coping process can change over time.

3. What are the primary differences between adaptive and maladaptive coping? In what ways is maladaptive coping likely to block growth? How does adaptive coping enhance growth?

4. What is personal competency or psychosocial competency and why is it such an important ingredient in the coping process?

5. Discuss the primary differences between healthy and unhealthy protective or defense mechanisms. Why are healthy defense mechanisms essential for adaptive coping and, on the other hand, why are unhealthy defenses detrimental to the coping process?

6. Compare and contrast the psychodynamic, cognitive-behavioral, and humanistic-existential approaches to psychotherapy with teenagers. Think of a case in which all three approaches could be integrated.

7. Discuss the major components of psychoeducational approaches in working with adolescent stresses and conflicts, and what are some of the underlying assumptions of the psychoeducational approach? Why does the psychoeducational approach blend easily into prevention efforts?

8. Discuss differences in the stresses and conflicts of early and late adolescence. Why are the stresses and conflicts of early and late adolescence different, and what kinds of coping mechanisms are likely to be needed during each period?
9. Discuss some of the positive aspects of adolescent psychological conflict and how conflict can be an essential condition for building positive self-esteem, self-confidence, and a well-integrated identity and value system.

2
Adolescent Mental Health Practitioners, Psychiatric Diagnostic Systems, and Conceptual Models

PREVIEW

This chapter begins with a discussion of the training backgrounds, goals, and approaches of adolescent mental health practitioners and social scientists. Three major medical-psychiatric models are examined: the traditional medical model, the holistic health model, and the psychodynamic model. The major components of the current psychiatric diagnostic and classification system, as outlined in DSM-III (1980) and DSM-III-R (1987), are presented. The traditional medical model is built on the concept that disease has a typical beginning, etiology, characteristic course, outcome, and treatment. The power to heal or arrest the disease belongs to the physician. The traditional medical model has been criticized because of its overemphasis on disease and thinking in terms of pathology, the unproductive side effects of labeling, and attributing the power to heal to the mental health practitioner or physician. In the holistic health model, the emphasis is on wellness and prevention rather than on pathology. The mental health practitioner in the holistic health model works as a copartner with the troubled and distressed adolescent to unlock enabling and growth forces. The psychodynamic model conceives of troubled and distressed adolescent behavior as an outgrowth of a failure to resolve childhood psychosexual stages and aggressive drives. Integration of the three medical-psychiatric models provides a comprehensive foundation for modern psychiatric education. This chapter closes with a discussion of the psychosocial model and the rationale for using the psychosocial model as the conceptual orientation of this book.

ADOLESCENT COUNSELORS, MENTAL HEALTH PRACTITIONERS, AND SOCIAL SCIENTISTS

Human services and mental health professionals, paraprofessionals, and lay people, interested in understanding troubled adolescents and young adults, come from a variety of training backgrounds and disciplines. While all share a common interest in guiding the development of youths, they tend to differ in their methods, goals, and approaches. Some are more interested in prevention and wellness, some work with social systems and institutions that impact on adolescents rather than with individual clients, and some are more interested in the normal course of growth and development. There may be times when short-term goals and approaches conflict. In many communities greater coordination is needed across different professional and lay groups to insure that the psychosocial needs of the youth population are adequately served. In this section, we will try to acquaint the reader with some of the major goals, approaches, and objectives of the juvenile justice system, educational psychologists and school counselors, family counselors and social workers, churches and religious organizations, sociologists, and developmental, clinical, and counseling psychologists. Psychiatrists, psychiatric nurses, medical social workers, and other medically oriented personnel are reviewed in the next section on psychiatric and medical-psychiatric models.

The Juvenile Justice System

Human services personnel in the juvenile justice system include judges, probation officers, parole officers, and youth counselors. The juvenile justice system is interested in reducing juvenile lawbreaking, decreasing the number of repeat offenders, and preventing predelinquent youths and first-time offenders from becoming more seriously involved in lawbreaking activities. Changing and guiding the behavior of youths who come to the attention of the juvenile justice system is likely to take place through diversion programs, behavior modification, and counseling, with emphasis on the reality consequences of lawbreaking and changing antisocial behavior by helping youths learn to set constructive goals. Counselors and mental health workers in the juvenile justice system are also interested in restructuring juvenile laws so that youths who violate status laws, such as curfew or school truancy, will be treated through external counseling programs rather than within the juvenile justice system.

Educational and School Psychologists

Educational and school psychologists are interested in learning and achievement, social conduct and behavior, values, emotional adjustment, career goals, classroom performance, ability assessment, and teacher effectiveness and how these factors impact on adolescents in educational settings. Since they view the school as a social institution, educational psychologists are also concerned about how the school as a socialization system impacts on adolescents with respect to such issues as school governance, how decisions are made in the educational system, and how youth can become a part of the decision-making process.

Family Counselors and Social Workers

Family counselors and social workers are concerned with the family as an organization. In working with troubled and distressed families, they help the family look at the roles of each family member, how decisions are made, how blame is assigned, the nature of family alliances, who is scapegoated or praised, how conflicts are resolved, and the role of the adolescent within the family. Family counselors and family social workers are interested in helping families develop clear lines of communication and establish loving, actualizing ways of relating to each other. Social workers and family counselors often serve as a link between the family as a social system and other social systems in the community when the family needs additional social services because of violence and abuse issues, economic problems, placement for youths outside the family, unplanned teen pregnancies, treatment for alcohol- and drug-abuse problems, and the like.

Churches and Religious Organizations

Many churches and religious organizations have programs designed to work with the social, emotional, and spiritual growth needs of youths and their families. While churches may sponsor a variety of counseling and prevention activities, they are likely to have a primary interest in helping youths struggle with questions of morality and values. Churches and religious organizations, like many other organizations that work with adolescents, may experience conflicts between wanting to indoctrinate adolescents in a particular value system versus allowing them to learn by discovery, experimentation, and exploration.

Sociologists

Sociologists are concerned with institutions and the impact of institutional change on adolescents. An adolescent-sociologist examines issues such as future shock and how changes in the family, youth culture, and values impact on adolescents as a social group. From studies on changing trends in society due to technology, population shifts, values, and male–female roles, sociologists can use their findings to assist in updating institutions, such as the school, the family, and the juvenile justice system.

Psychologists

Psychologists are concerned with identifying the primary psychosocial variables involved in normal adolescent development and in maladaptive development such as perception, learning, motivation, intelligence, social relationships, conflict, and stress. Developmental psychologists examine the normal pattern of psychosocial development across the life cycle and try to identify the vital growth issues and challenges at each stage. Counseling psychologists, affiliated with high schools and colleges, tend to be involved in the short-term counseling and therapy of troubled and distressed youths. Counseling psychologists have a major interest in wellness and prevention and in adolescent and young adult transition issues such as identity, intimacy, and the changing perceptions of youths toward self, others, and family as they progress through adolescence. Clinical psychologists tend to focus on troubled and distressed adolescents who are experiencing serious maladaptive behavior and who are likely to require extensive therapy and possible hospitalization. Clinical psychologists are also trained to do comprehensive, psychological, and psychodiagnostic assessment with personality, neuropsychological, and projective tests. The line of demarcation between clinical and counseling psychologists is often very blurred and the roles are somewhat interchangeable. Community psychologists see the community, rather than the individual adolescent, as the patient. Community psychologists are interested in making social systems more responsive to the needs of youth, especially in the context of prevention. In working with such problems as runaways, teen pregnancies, drugs, or delinquency, a community psychologist would bring together parents, teachers, adolescents, juvenile justice counselors, and other interested community agents and civic groups to initiate a dialogue as a first step in moving toward the development of responsive programs. Shelters and youth homes for runaway adolescents, delinquency diversion programs, and confidential access to birth control are programs that have been developed with the participation of community psychologists.

In most states, providers of mental health services to adolescents and their families, in private practice on a fee for service basis, are required to have at least a master's degree in counseling, social work, human services, or marriage, family, and child counseling. A variety of mental health workers with a B.A. and a 2-year community college A.A. degree work with adolescents, under the supervision of a licensed professional, as counseling assistants and associates, psychiatric technicians, and behavioral specialists in hospitals, mental health clinics, youth shelters, youth homes, substance abuse centers, counseling centers, and other youth facilities.

In psychology, the preferred degree for licensure as an independent practitioner is the Ph.D. or Psy. D. (Doctor of Psychology). Persons with a master's degree in psychology can work as psychological associates and assistants under the supervision of a licensed psychologist.

For your state licensing, certification, and training requirements for counseling, social work, human services, psychology, or marriage, child, and family counseling, write the Department of Mental Health in your state or contact the national associations listed below.

1. National Association of Social Workers
   7981 Eastern Avenue
   Silver Spring, MD 20915
2. American Association of Counseling and Human Development — For counseling psychology and youth guidance and human services.
   5999 Stephenson Ave.
   Alexandria, VA 22304
3. American Psychological Association
   1200 17th Street, N.W.
   Washington, DC 20036
4. American Association of Marriage and Family Counselors
   1717 K St., N.W. #407
   Washington, DC 20006

Medical-Psychiatric Personnel

Psychiatrists are medical doctors who have completed an internship plus a 3-year residence period of specialty training, following medical school, in mental illness, psychology and human behavior, and psychotherapy. Because psychiatrists are medical doctors, they are the only members of the mental health profession who are licensed to prescribe medications and psychoactive drugs.

Within the family of medicine, there are pediatricians and family physicians who have a primary interest in adolescent health care. In order for family physicians and pediatricians to be effective in working with an adolescent's mental and medical health concerns, they should be sensitive to adolescent growth conflicts and psychosocial needs, as well as aware of how the mind and body interact and cognizant of the role of stress, conflict, and pressures on adolescent growth and functioning. Family physicians and pediatricians in many cases are the first health care professionals to become aware of maladaptive adolescent behavior and distress with respect to issues such as depression, suicidal ideas, eating disturbances, unprotected sex, and drugs.

Psychiatric Nurses

Psychiatric nurses are nurses who have had specialty training in emotional and behavioral disturbances, human growth and behavior, and counseling. They usually work in hospitals or other inpatient settings as part of a professional mental health team that includes psychologists, psychiatrists, social workers, and counselors.

Medical-clinical social workers are social workers who have been trained at the master's degree level in psychotherapy, counseling, case management, psychiatry, and community services to work in medical-psychiatric and outpatient settings with an emphasis on mental health needs of adolescents.

MEDICAL-PSYCHIATRIC MODELS AND PSYCHIATRIC DIAGNOSTIC CLASSIFICATION SYSTEMS

Historically, medicine has been concerned with illness, pathology, abnormality, and sickness. When physicians moved into the area of mental processes, emotions, behavior, psychological conflict, and stress, they brought with them from traditional physical medicine, concepts of sickness, abnormality, pathology, and illness. Deviance from expected psychosocial norms in adolescents, children, and adults was considered a pathological emotional disturbance, mental illness, or evidence of an underlying psychological disease. Thus, the concept of illness and pathology as a way of accounting for the behavior of troubled and distressed adolescents is deeply ingrained in adolescent psychiatry.

Within adolescent psychiatry, three models, saturated in varying degrees with illness and pathology metaphors and analogies, have emerged to describe, explain, diagnose, and treat disordered adolescent behavior. These models are called: (1) the medical model, (2) the holistic health model, and (3) the psychodynamic model.

The Traditional Medical Model

The traditional medical model is built on the concept of disease. The medical model of physical illness starts with the premise that diseases or pathological states can be traced to concrete causes, such as tissue and chemical dysfunctions, injury, genetic predispositions, biochemical defects, viruses, infections, or defects in hormones, organ systems, body tissues, and neurological functions. Each disease has a typical beginning and etiology, characteristic course, and outcome and treatment. The power to heal, arrest, or alter the disease belongs to the physician. The disease model follows the following steps: The physician diagnoses the causes or etiology of the pathology on the basis of an examination of the signs and symptoms. This step generally produces a diagnosis or label for the disease. Based on the label or diagnosis, recommendations for treatment or therapy are made.[1] Treatment is directed toward cure, arrest, or reversal of the disease. Based on previous experience with similar cases, a prognosis is made predicting the final course of the disease toward recovery, arrest, or continued deterioration (Schumer, 1983; Levy, 1982; White and Watt, 1981). When the disease model or analogies to the disease model are used to explain, describe, or treat adolescents displaying disordered behavior or maladaptive coping styles, a similar process is followed. Attempts are made to identify the overt and underlying causes of the pathology, a label for the disease or emotional abnormality is designated, predictions about the course of the disturbance are made, and a program of treatment is initiated. In the medical model, it is assumed that maladaptive adolescent behavior reflects an underlying disease process. The biogenic hypothesis, which is the outgrowth of the medical model, looks for the correlates and causes of maladaptive and disordered adolescent behavior in the nervous system and its biochemical environments, genetic predispositions, and tissue and biophysical malfunctions. In the treatment phase, medical practitioners have a variety of psychoactive and psychotropic drugs they can administer to adolescent psychiatric patients. These drugs are used to stabilize moods, control depression, reduce agitation and anger, and reduce confusion in thought processes. Psychoactive and psychotropic drugs are used in conjunction with counseling and psychotherapy.

Critique of the Medical Model

A great deal of controversy and criticism surrounds the medical or disease model. These criticisms and controversies center around the following topics and issues:

1. Overemphasis on disease-thinking and pathology analogies.
2. Confusion of correlation and causality in biochemical and biogenetic research.
3. The unproductive side effects of labeling.

---

[1]The Diagnostic Classification System of the American Psychiatric Association as outlined in DSM-III-R (1987) and DSM-III (1981) is presented on pp. 56–66.

4. Attributing the power to heal to the psychiatrist or mental health professional.
5. Contradictions in the use of psychoactive and psychotropic drugs with adolescents.
6. Lack of valid mental illness concepts.

Overemphasis on disease and pathology analogies leads mental health workers to look for the causes and etiology in the adolescent rather than in the interaction between the adolescent and the social environment. The strict medical model tends to minimize adverse conditions in the psychosocial environment which could be triggering maladaptive responses. Overemphasis on disease results in a focus on emotional limitations, biochemical deficits, and pathological themes rather than the competencies of adolescents and the strength of forward-moving growth drives. Excessive concern with disease seems to generate a focus on arriving at the proper diagnosis at the expense of focusing on how to change the interaction between the adolescent and the social environment which may be inhibiting growth. Finally, disease analogies between the body and the mind, or the body and social and emotional behaviors tend to get confused with the reality that the mind and the body are very different entities. Since the mind is not a physical organ of the body, it cannot be diseased in the same sense the body is diseased (Schumer, 1983).

Biogenic research, which looks for the causes of maladaptive behavior in genetic deficits, biochemical malfunctions, and the biochemical environment of the brain, is vulnerable to a confusing correlation with causality. For example, in asking the question, "Are some kids born to be bad?" Jensen (1985) points out that there appears to be a correlation between hyperactivity, minimal brain disorder, and attention deficit disorder. Some adolescents who become delinquent are found to show a pattern of hyperactivity, minimum brain disorder, and attention deficit. When this type of correlation is found, it cannot be automatically assumed that the hyperactivity, minimum brain disorder, and attention deficit caused the delinquency. Three events have to be explained before we can justify the cause-effect link. First, we have to show why adolescents with the same neurophysiological or neuropsychological pattern did not become delinquents. Second, we have to show that the neurophysiological effects preceded the delinquency rather than came about as a consequence of the delinquency. Third, the statistical correlation between two events in neurophysiological research (or any other research for that matter) has to be almost perfect before enough of the variance is accounted for to raise the cause-effect predictions above the chance level (Guilford, 1954).

Labeling can have unproductive side effects. From educational psychology, we have learned that labeling youngsters as culturally deprived or as having social learning and behavioral problems seems to create a self-fulfilling prophecy (White, 1984; Rosenthal and Jacobson, 1968). Labeling tends to freeze people into categories that stigmatize them. Expectations of behaviors implied by these labels causes teachers and counselors to treat students as if they were educationally and emotionally disabled. Teachers respond to the label rather than to the person. The same effect seems to occur in psychiatry. Labeling an adolescent sick or emotionally ill has social meanings that not only can contribute to how others see the adolescent but to how adolescents see themselves. Thinking of one's self as a depressive, anorexic, or delinquent can lead to unidimensional thinking because the individual now defines himself or herself as sick, abnormal, or different. The individual and others in the social environment begin to attribute all of the person's behavior to the label, even when the emotional disturbance or conduct disorder has disappeared. For example, if a depressed person has a good day, he or she could be accused of denying depressive feelings or manipulating the therapist away from focusing on painful material. Extreme proponents of the labeling theory assert that labels may cause the adolescent to react in a delinquent or pathological manner once the label is attached, or else severely exacerbate existing maladaptive behaviors (Goldstein et al., 1980).

In the medical model, the power to heal is controlled by the physician or mental health professional. Cure depends on professional intervention (Korchin, 1976). Adolescence is a time in which young people, however misguided, are trying to take over control of their lives and develop the resources to shape and pursue their dream. Putting them in a treatment relationship where the professional person has the power, can generate conflicts around issues of power, control, and independence. If the professional person who is using the medical model is not perceptive or insightful, he or she could attribute power conflicts between his- or her-selves and the adolescent to resistances and psychopathologies in the adolescent rather than to the legitimate independence strivings that are conflicting with the control-oriented style of the professional.

A number of contradictions are involved in the use of psychoactive and psychotropic drugs to control and stabilize the moods of troubled and distressed adolescents. At the time of this writing, the President and the Congress, as well as other powerful and respected agencies of American society, have declared "war" on teenage drug use. What kind of metamessages or covert messages do we send to teenagers when we condemn drugs as a way of controlling moods and feelings, yet we give them drugs when they are upset or behaving in ways upsetting to adults? The contradiction between the overt message and the metamessage can inadvertently contribute to teenage drug use. Psychotropic and psychoactive drugs can certainly have positive effects when properly used, but we should not be afraid of facing the difficult questions and dilemmas surrounding the therapeutic use of drugs for adolescent mental health patients.

Questions of validity have been raised about concepts used within the medical model. There is no consensus on the real meaning of terms like schizophrenia or psychosis. Individuals can display some of the behaviors characterized by a given illness, but their behaviors may not be due to the particular mental disease. Rosenhan (1973), in a widely quoted study, attempted to demonstrate that experienced mental health practitioners cannot separate insane or psychotic people from noninsane or nonpsychotic people. Eight nonpsychiatric patients or normal research volunteers gained admission to several mental hospitals by displaying phony symptoms such as hearing voices. After these research volunteers were admitted to psychiatric units of hospitals, they dropped the phony symptoms and acted normal. They were diagnosed as schizophrenic, never detected during their stay in the hospital, and some of them were discharged with poor prognoses for recovery. While no one study is conclusive, Rosenhan's work demonstrates that there are weaknesses in psychiatric labels.

The most devastating criticism of the emotional disease or mental illness model comes from within the profession of psychiatric medicine. Dr. Thomas Szasz (1961, 1963, 1973), a psychiatrist, thinks that what has been called mental or psychological illness is basically a myth. Psychosocial and emotional conflicts are not identical or analogous to physical diseases. To pursue this myth according to Szasz prevents us from understanding fundamental issues which are questions of human conduct, values, and conflicts. In Szasz's view, the fundamental human struggle involves moral, ethical, legal, and value dilemmas about questions regarding how we should live and what choices we should make. Those who have the power to set conduct and value standards and enforce the rules, as do the courts, schools, and the healing profession, can use labels such as mental illness to devaluate those who are different and force them into abiding by recommendations for treatment and institutionalization. Parents with troublesome adolescents diagnosed as emotionally disturbed or mentally ill can be forced to have their children treated in order for them to remain in school. Labels indicating behavioral problems and emotional disturbances are all too often placed on young people who are responding in an understandable and, at times, even in an appropriate manner to an environment that does not support their legitimate developmental needs. Under the rubric of the concept of mental illness, individuals whose life-styles, conduct, and values differ from the mainstream can be labeled as crazy and deprived of their right to pursue life as they see fit. The disease model provides a shield that can be used to advance some social interests and retard others.

Since Szasz's first book, *The Myth of Mental Illness* was published in

1961, most states have passed laws designed to protect the legal and human rights of adult mental patients with respect to the rights to treatment, to refuse treatment, and not to be detained for prolonged periods against their will unless they are a danger to themselves or to others. As minors whose legal rights are controlled by adults, adolescent psychiatric patients are more vulnerable to being forced to participate in treatment when they express deviant values and conduct.

Psychiatric Diagnostic and Classification Systems, DSM-III-R and DSM-III

DSM-III-R (1987), the revised *Diagnostic and Statistical Manual of Mental Disorders* prepared by the American Psychiatric Association (APA), is a classification system of emotional disturbances, mental illnesses, and maladaptive behaviors. DSM-III-R (1987) is an update of DSM-III which was originally published in 1980. DSM-III-R makes no attempt to define the term mental illness in either adults or adolescents. It offers a description of signs and symptoms commonly associated with maladaptive behaviors and emotional disturbances such as depression, eating disorders, alcohol and drug abuse, schizophrenia, and conduct disturbances. Signs are moods, attitudes, or behaviors that the mental health professionals observe. A symptom is something expressed by the patient. A syndrome is a cluster of signs and symptoms. A disorder is a group of signs and symptoms that regularly occur together to form the basis for the diagnosis (Levy, 1982).

The term diagnosis has two meanings (Mezzich, 1979). In medicine, diagnosis means sorting out categories of illness, on the basis of available information provided by the signs and symptoms, to precisely identify the patient's illness. The second meaning of diagnosis refers to the process, or how a clinician goes about obtaining a comprehensive picture of the adolescent's condition, which usually involves interviews, observations, history-taking, and psychological and neuropsychological assessment. A meaningful diagnosis helps us to develop a working picture of what the adolescent is like.

DSM-III-R and DSM-III represent vast improvements over DSM-I (1952) and DSM-II (1968), which were regarded as vague and unreliable. Because specific characteristics of diagnostic classifications and objective criteria were lacking in DSM-I and DSM-II, mental health clinicians often had to fall back on interpretations and hunches in defining categories such as neurosis, psychopath, transient situational adjustment, latent schizophrenia, or inadequate personality. DSM-III-R and DSM-III were developed by mental health professionals and behavioral scientists from a variety of disciplines over a period of several years. DSM-III was evaluated on a trial basis in over 100 facilities before being finalized. A glossary of terms is provided in the DSM-III-R manual, and all major diagnostic categories contain the following information:

1. Primary clinical features
2. Frequently but inconsistently associated secondary symptoms
3. Age and onset
4. Course of the disorder
5. Complications
6. Predisposing factors
7. Familial patterns
8. Prevalence
9. Sex ratio
10. Differential diagnoses
11. Operational criteria for making the decision

DSM-III-R acknowledges the importance of previous and current levels of adaptive functioning and the role of psychosocial stressors in triggering maladaptive behavior by requiring ratings on these dimensions.

While there are still problems with reliability and validity, DSM-III-R provides a system of classification with descriptive guidelines that mental health clinicians can use to categorize adolescent psychosocial problems, assess etiology and possible outcomes, and discuss their findings with each other using a common language system. Because the system is widely used in mental health settings, it provides a good basis for research data and common record-keeping. For patients who have health insurance, the DSM-III-R classifications are used as documentation for payment for diagnostic, assessment, and treatment services rendered by mental health professionals.

DSM-III-R and the Multiaxial Diagnostic Approach

DSM-III-R uses a multiaxial classification system. The patient is rated on five categories, each called Axis. Axis I contains the formal diagnosis of clinical syndromes exhibited in the signs and symptoms revealed during assessment, examination, observation, interviews, psych testing, and case history. The five Axes are described below.

AXIS I

Contains the principal diagnostic categories such as eating disorders, schizophrenia, substance abuse, depression, and conduct disturbances. Diagnostic categories for adolescents can be used from the list of Disorders First Evident in Infancy, Childhood or Adolescence (see Table 2-1) or from the general list of Axis I categories (see Table 2-2). The list for basic childhood and adolescent disorders can be divided along five dimensions: intellectual, behavioral, emotional, physical, and developmental. The predominant factor in mental health retardation is intellectual; behavioral themes are crucial in conduct disturbances and attention deficit disorders, whereas emotional themes are central in anxiety disorders. Themes that relate to body functions are pervasive in eating disorders. The areas of learning and development are covered in specific and pervasive developmental disorders. Multiple diagnoses can be used on Axis I. If an adolescent is abusing alcohol regularly, shows signs of depression, and has periods of binge eating, purging, and fasting, then alcoholism, depression, and eating disorder can be labeled a primary diagnosis on Axis I.

Axis II—Developmental Disorders and Personality Disorders. With adolescents, Axis II is usually used to designate specific developmental and learning disorders—i.e., difficulties in reading, language, speech, math, and coordination. Axis II should not be used for slow learners. For a diagnosis on Axis II, there should be a significant discrepancy between the actual and expected levels of development. The adolescent should have the intellectual and physical potential to accomplish the behaviors. A blind child who cannot read would not be designated as being a specific developmental disorder on Axis II. Axis II specific developmental disorders are listed in Table 2-3. If no Axis II diagnosis is present, Axis II can be left blank. With adults, Axis II is used to designate personality disorders and enduring personality traits likely to hamper growth and adjustment. The personality disorders or traits are characterized as enduring, inflexible, and maladaptive styles of relating to, perceiving, and experiencing the psychosocial environment. These personality traits usually start to develop in childhood, but do not become fully consolidated until adulthood. The basic personality traits and disorders are listed in Table 2-3. Sarason and Sarason (1984) divide these personality disorders and traits into three clusters. The first cluster includes individuals whose behavior is likely to seem strange, odd, or bizarre, such as paranoid or schizoid personalities. The second cluster includes people who often appear highly emotional, dramatic, or erratic in their behavior. This cluster would include the hysterical, narcissistic, antisocial, and borderline personalities. The third cluster consists of the avoidant, dependent, compulsive, and passive-aggressive personality disorders. If adolescents show a pronounced personality disorder or a pronounced pattern of personality traits, it can be listed on Axis II along with any specific developmental disorder.

Axis III—Physical Disorders and Conditions. Axis III refers to any physical or medical condition relevant to the adolescent's case, such as epilepsy, a history of heart problems, or life-threatening diseases. Adolescents in inpatient settings are always given a physical examination, and it is a good policy for clinicians working with adolescents in outpatient settings to have a working knowledge of their medical history.

Table 2-1. DSM-II, DSM-III-R and Axis I Classifications for Disorders Usually Arising in Childhood or Adolescence

DSM-II (1968)[a] (Taken from all categories where there is mention of childhood)	DSM-III-R (1987)[b]

Mental Retardation
  Borderline
  Mild
  Moderate
  Severe
  Profound
  Unspecified
	Mental Retardation
	  Mild
	  Moderate
	  Severe
	  Profound
	  Unspecified

Special Symptoms
  Speech disturbance
  Specific learning disturbance
  Tic
  Other psychomotor disorders
  Disorders of sleep
  Feeding disturbance
  Enuresis
  Encopresis
  Other special symptoms
	Pervasive Developmental Disorders
	  Infantile autism
	  Early childhood psychosis
	  Pervasive developmental disorder of childhood, residual state
	  Unspecified

Transient Situational Disturbances
  Adjustment reaction of infancy
  Adjustment reaction of childhood
  Adjustment reaction of adolescence
	Stereotyped Movement Disorders
	  Motor tic disorder
	  Gilles de la Tourette
	  Unspecified tic disorder
	  Other

Behavior Disorders of Childhood and Adolescence
  Hyperkinetic reaction
  Withdrawing reaction
  Overanxious reaction
  Runaway reaction
  Unsocialized aggressive reaction
  Group delinquent reaction
  Other reaction
  Schizophrenia
  Childhood
	Speech Disorders Not Elsewhere Classified
	  Stuttering
	
	Disruptive Behavior Disorders
	  Attention-deficit hyperactive disorder
	  Conduct disorder
	    Group type
	    Solitary aggressive type

	Eating Disorders
	  Anorexia nervosa
	  Bulimia nervosa
	  Pica
	  Rumination
	  Other or unspecified

	Anxiety Disorders
	  Separation anxiety disorder
	  Shyness disorder
	  Overanxious disorder

	Disorders of Late Adolescence
	  Emancipation disorder of adolescence or early adult life
	  Specific academic or work inhibition

(continued)

Table 2-1.
Continued

DSM-II (1968)[a] (Taken from all categories where there is mention of childhood)	DSM-III-R (1987)[b]
	Other Disorders of Childhood or Adolescence Introverted disorder of childhood Oppositional defiant disorder Academic underachievement disorder Elective mutism
	Other Disorders Commonly Diagnosed in Childhood, But Not So Designated in DSM-III-R
	Sleep Disorders Somnambulism Night terrors
	Psychosexual Disorders Gender identity or role disorder of childhood or adolescence
	Adjustment Disorders

Adapted from: [a]American Psychiatric Association. (1968). *Diagnostic and statistical manual of mental disorders* (2nd ed.). Washington, D.C. and [b]American Psychiatric Association. (1987). *Diagnostic and statistical manual of mental disorders* (3rd ed., rev.). Washington, D.C.

Axis IV—Severity of Psychosocial Stressors. Axis IV provides a code graded along a 7-point scale to assess the severity of enduring and current psychosocial stressors which have contributed to the adolescent's clinical problems and could influence the course of treatment. Stressors for adolescents include such events as changing schools, chronic parental fights, and loss caused by divorce or breakup with girlfriend or boyfriend. Examples of stressors and severity ratings for stressors are shown in Table 2-4.

Axis V—The Highest Level of Adaptive Functioning. Axis V permits the mental health clinician to make an overall estimate, based on the available evidence, of the adolescent's psychological, social, educational, and occupational functioning for two time periods: (1) the current level of functioning at the time of the evaluation, and (2) the highest level of functioning for a few months during the past year. For adolescents, the estimate of the highest level of functioning should include at least one month during the school year. A high level of functioning is indicated by minimal everyday

Table 2-2. DSM-III-R[a] General Axis I and II Categories
(Can be used for adolescents or adults)

AXIS I

Organic Mental Disorders
(Symptoms include delusions, dementia,
delirium, and/or depression.)

Senile and presenile dementias

Substance-induced
Alcohol
Barbiturate or similar-acting sedative or
hypnotic
Opioid
Cocaine
Amphetamine or similar-acting stimulant
Hallucinogen
Cannabis
Inhalant
Tobacco
Caffeine
Other or unspecified substance
Cause unknown

Substance-Use Disorders
Alcohol abuse
Alcohol dependence (alcoholism)
Barbiturate or similar-acting sedative or
hypnotic abuse
Barbiturate or similar-acting sedative or
hypnotic dependence
Opioid abuse
Opioid dependence
Cocaine abuse
Cocaine dependence
Amphetamine or similar-acting stimulant
abuse
Amphetamine or similar-acting stimulant
dependence
Hallucinogen abuse
Cannabis abuse
Cannabis dependence
Tobacco-use disorder
Other or unspecified substance-abuse
Other specified substance-dependence
Unspecified substance-dependence

Factitious (Psychophysiological) Disorders
Factitious illness with psychological
symptoms
Chronic factitious illness with physical
symptoms

Schizophrenic Disorders
Disorganized (hebephrenic)
Catatonic
Paranoid
Undifferentiated
Residual

Delusional Disorders
Grandiose
Erotomanic
Jealous
Persecutions
Somatic
Unspecified

Schizoaffective Disorders

Affective Disorders
Episodic affective disorders
Manic disorder
Major depressive disorder
Bipolar affective disorder
manic
depressed
mixed

Chronic affective disorders

Atypical affective disorders

Psychoses Not Elsewhere Classified
Schizophreniform disorder
Brief reactive psychosis
Atypical psychosis

Anxiety Disorders
Phobic disorders
Panic disorder
Obsessive compulsive disorder
Generalized anxiety disorder
Atypical anxiety disorder
Post-traumatic stress disorder

Disorders Usually Arising in Childhood or
Adolescence
(This section lists conditions that usually
first manifest themselves in childhood or
adolescence. Any appropriate adult
diagnosis can be used for diagnosing a
child.)

(continued)

Table 2-2.
Continued

Somatoform Disorders
  Somatization disorder
  Conversion disorder
  Psychalgia
  Atypical somatoform disorder

Dissociative Disorders
  Psychogenic amnesia
  Psychogenic fugue
  Multiple personality
  Depersonalization disorder
  Other

AXIS II

Personality Disorders
(Notice: These are coded on Axis II.)

  Paranoid
  Introverted
  Schizotypal
  Histrionic
  Narcissistic
  Antisocial
  Borderline
  Avoidant
  Dependent
  Compulsive
  Passive-aggressive
  Other or mixed

Psychosexual Disorders

  Gender identity disorders

  Paraphilias

  Psychosexual dysfunctions

  Other psychosexual disorders

Disorders of Impulse Control Not Elsewhere
    Classified
  Pathological gambling
  Kleptomania
  Pyromania
  Intermittent explosive disorder
  Isolated explosive disorder
  Other impulse-control disorder

Mental retardation

Pervasive developmental disorders
  Infantile autism
  Atypical childhood psychosis

Specific developmental disorders (Notice:
    These are coded on Axis II.)
  Specific reading disorder
  Specific arithmetical disorder
  Developmental language disorder
  Developmental articulation disorder
  Enuresis
  Encopresis
  Mixed
  Other

Attention deficit disorders

Conduct disorders

Anxiety disorders of childhood or
  adolescence

Other disorders of childhood or
  adolescence

Disorders characteristic of late adolescence

Eating disorders

Speech disorders (stuttering)

Stereotyped movement disorders

Reactive Disorders Not Elsewhere Classified
  Post-traumatic stress disorder

Adjustment disorders

(continued)

Table 2-2.
Continued

Sleep Disorders

  Nonorganic

  Organic

Other Disorders
  Unspecified mental disorder (nonpsychotic)

  Psychological factors affecting physical
    disorder

  No mental disorder

Conditions Not Attributable to a Mental
    Disorder
  Malingering
  Adult antisocial behavior
  Childhood or adolescent antisocial
    behavior
  Marital problem
  Parent-child problem
  Child abuse
  Other interpersonal problem
  Occupational problem
  Uncomplicated bereavement
  Noncompliance with medical treatment
  Other life-circumstance problem

Administrative Categories
  Diagnosis deferred
  Research subject
  Boarder
  Referral without need for evaluation

aAdapted from: American Psychiatric Association. (1987). *Diagnostic and statistical manual of mental disorders* (3rd ed., rev.). Washington, D.C.

problems or concerns, psychosocial effectiveness, and good overall judgment in major areas of school, family, and peer relationships. A poor level of adaptive functioning is indicated by serious difficulties in family, peer, and school relationships, suicidal ideation, poor judgment, impulsive behavior, and persistent danger of hurting self or others.

The practical use of DSM-III-R will be illustrated with the following case example.

Table 2-3. Axis II Diagnostic Categories[a]

Specific Developmental Disorders
  Primarily in Children and Adolescents
Academic Skills Disorders

  Developmental arithmetic disorder
  Developmental reading disorder
  Developmental language disorder
  Developmental articulation disorder
  Developmental coordination disorder
  Mixed developmental disorder
  Atypical developmental disorder

Personality Disorders and Traits
  Primarily in Adults

Paranoid	Exaggerated suspiciousness, mistrust, and hyperactivity
Schizoid	Extreme reserve, social withdrawal, loner, seclusive
Schizotypical	Oddities in thinking, speech, perceptions, communicating, not as extreme as found in schizophrenia
Histrionic	Emotional overreaction to minor events, self dramatic, exaggerated expression of emotions, extreme drawing of attention to self, out bursts, and tantrums
Narcissistic	Inflated sense of self, absorbed in self, requires constant attention, and admiration
Center Social	In adolescents, truancy and suspensions from school, running away, lying, delinquency. In adults, doesn't respect rights of others, failure to accept social norms, poor attachments to others, inability to maintain work
Borderline	Impulsivity and unpredictability, unstable and intense personal relationships, chronic feelings of emptiness or boredom, and identity confusion
Avoidant	Social withdrawal and isolation to avoid being hurt
Dependent	Passive, self-belittling attitudes, always looks to others for direction
Compulsive	Exaggerated preoccupation with small details, rules, loses sight of big picture
Passive-aggressive	Aggressive, indirect resistance expressed by procrastination, seeming compliance, intentional forgetting

aAdapted from: American Psychiatric Association. (1987). *Diagnostic and statistical manual of mental disorders* (3rd ed., rev.). Washington, D.C.

Table 2-4. Rating Scale for Severity of Stress on DSM-III-R, Axis IVa

Rating	Level of stress	Acute/Current events	Enduring events
1	None	No acute events relevant to disorder	No enduring events related to disorder
2	Mild	Change of school, breakup with boyfriend or girlfriend	Family arguments, overcrowded household
3	Moderate	Expelled from school, birth of sibling	Chronic parental fighting, serious parental illness
4	Severe	Divorce of parents, arrest, unplanned pregnancy	Several foster home placements, chronic life-threatening parental illness, rejecting parents
5	Extreme	Death of parent, sexual or physical abuse	Recurring sexual or physical abuse
6	Catastrophic	Death of both parents	Chronic life-threatening illness
0	Unspecific	No information available	No information available

aAdapted from: American Psychiatric Association. (1987). *Diagnostic and statistical manual of mental disorders* (3rd ed., rev.). Washington, D.C.

Case Example 2-1: Susie

Susie is a 16-year-old female who was brought into an inpatient adolescent psychiatric facility for an evaluation. The evaluation was initiated by the school after Susie was arrested by an undercover narcotics officer for using and possessing drugs at school. Her parents report increasing concerns with regular alcohol and drug abuse, school truancy and deteriorating school performance, failure to obey household rules, curfew violations, past arrests, running away, and defiant and rebellious attitudes toward parents (especially when questioned about her behavior), and periodic episodes of depression. Susie seemed tearful and depressed on admission. She admitted to using drugs and alcohol on a regular basis for the past 2 years. She smokes two to three marijuana joints daily, drinks to get drunk on weekends, and has experimented with cocaine and speed. She says she has tried to stop using drugs and alcohol, but can't seem to do so for more than a week. She says she started using drugs to have fun, but now uses them because she feels "bummed out" and depressed when she isn't high. She reports that depressive feelings are more pronounced when she is alone and not high. She likes to be with her friends who are into partying, having a good time, using drugs and alcohol, and defying adult authority. Susie cuts school frequently, and during the past few weeks has only been attending school about one day a week. Prior to her present arrest for possessing and using narcotics at school, she has been arrested once for shoplifting and once for being drunk in public. She has been suspended from school once for truancy. Her grades are poor despite above average intelligence. Recently, she was transferred to a special high school for problem students. Susie is two grades below her grade level in reading and math. The only courses she likes in school are music and photography. She sings with a teenage rock band and has won prizes in amateur photography. She is in good health and has never experienced any drug-related seizures, blackouts, amnesias, or hallucinations. Recent stresses include a breakup with her boyfriend. Her parents are having trouble with their marriage and fight a lot. Susie claims the reason she often stays away from home is because there is too much confusion and "hassling" at home. She says "Someone is always fighting. I'm not the only one in the family who needs help, my parents should come in here for help too." Susie has agreed to be admitted for further evaluation, and is thinking about working on her depression, drug, and alcohol problems.

In assessing Susie's overall situation, current adjustment, and primary conflict areas, her initial DSM-III-R diagnoses and ratings would look something like this:

Axis I   Multiple diagnosis
           1. Substance abuse
           2. Depression
           3. Conduct disturbance
           4. Family conflict
Axis II   Specific learning disorders in math and reading
Axis III   None
Axis IV   Moderate to severe recent stress: breakup with boyfriend, parental fighting
Axis V   Poor level of adaptive functioning in recent year and during past 2 months

Linda Webb et al. (1981) and her associates have edited a training guide for students and mental health workers who are interested in gaining more experience in using the current diagnostic system. The training guide provides case histories, and video cassettes can be ordered separately. Working with the training manual is a very good way for beginners to learn to use the system.

Critique and Evaluation of Psychiatric Diagnostic Systems

DSM-III-R is not the last word in the diagnosis of maladaptive and disordered behavior. There will surely be a DSM-IV and DSM-V, but questions of validity and reliability still remain. Validity pertains to the accuracy, truth, predictive effectiveness of the system, and how well it measures what it says it measures. Reliability refers to how well clinicians agree on the diagnosis of a particular patient. Some questions that concern reliability are: is there a consensus on how the symptoms are viewed and are identical or highly similar signs and symptoms always diagnosed the same way? Evidence reviewed by Schumer (1983) suggests that the percentage of agreement on diagnosis varies between 40% and 85% depending on the training, level of experience, and views of pathology on the part of clinicians doing the ratings. Many psychologists also have questions about what the diagnoses mean and whether categories such as depression or adjustment reaction really tell anything about adolescents other than that they are troubled and distressed and may be causing others trouble and distress.

There is a tendency in some mental health settings to overuse the adjustment disorder category in working with adolescents. Adjustment disorders are a group of maladaptive reactions to adolescent stresses such as divorce, family discord, situational crisis, relationship breakups, and the general stresses involved in moving through the transition from one developmental stage to another. The symptoms of adjustment disorders are beyond the usual range of reactions to adolescent stresses and transitions, and interfere with psychosocial functioning in relationships, family, school, and the social environment. These symptoms can be combined with other moods, behaviors, and subcategories, such as adjustment disorder with depressed mood or adjustment disorder with disturbance of conduct or withdrawal. The major adjustment disorder combinations are shown in Table 2-5.

DSM-III-R does not discuss the relationship between the psychosocial developmental tasks of adolescence and the pressures, challenges, and threats adolescents encounter in trying to grow up in today's world. Although DSM-III-R recommends that clinicians be sensitive to ethnic and cultural differences in arriving at diagnoses, no specific directions are provided for understanding social class and sociocultural differences in how adolescents respond to the world around them.

In trying to refine the system and come up with sufficient descriptive categories, the system has become too cumbersome and detailed. There are now approximately 230 diagnostic categories compared to 145 in DSM-II (Schumer, 1983).

Despite DSM-III-Rs attempt to be high in descriptive clarity and avoid vague definitions of mental illness, the aura of disease surrounding psychiatric diagnoses still remains, as does the presumption that before young people can start resolving the conflicts blocking their growth, we must arrive at a proper diagnosis. A second presumption is that once we have the diagnosis, we will automatically understand the adolescent and know what to do.

Other diagnostic systems being explored for working with adolescents are prototype models and broad-band disorder models. These models attempt to describe maladaptive behavior along major dimensions such as aggressive-impulsive, depressive-withdrawn, borderline-disorganized, or externalization–internalization (Schumer, 1983).

Table 2-5. Types of Adjustment Disorders[a]

---

1. Adjustment disorder with anxious mood
2. Adjustment disorder with depressed mood
3. Adjustment disorder with conduct disturbance
4. Adjustment disorder with mixed disturbances of mood and conduct
5. Adjustment disorder with mixed emotional features
6. Adjustment disorder with physical complaints
7. Adjustment disorder with withdrawal
8. Adjustment disorder with work or academic inhibition
9. Adjustment disorder: unspecified

---

[a]Adapted from: American Psychiatric Association. (1987). *Diagnostic and statistical manual of mental disorders* (3rd ed., rev.). Washington, D.C.

The Holistic Health Model

The second psychiatric model which has evolved in medicine is the holistic health model. The holistic health model focuses on the total person and his or her relationship to the psychosocial environment rather than on emotional, behavior, and intrapsychological symptoms. The emphasis is on wellness and prevention rather than pathology. The physician or mental health professional is considered as a copartner, coequal with the patient. As part of a cooperative team, the mental health professional and the patient try to discover and unlock the natural growth and enabling forces inside the patient. According to the holistic health model, each patient carries the power to grow and actualize within. In short, patients have the power to heal themselves, and the mental health professional acts as a guide. Emotional difficulties come about when the body, mind, and spirit are in disharmony. This is due to unresolved stress and the failure of the person to listen to the internal growth and wellness signals of his/her mind and body (Siegel, 1986; Miller, 1981).

Three levels of mental health prevention have been outlined by mental health practitioners: primary prevention, secondary prevention, and tertiary prevention (Caplan, 1964, 1974). Primary prevention is directed at reducing the incidence of new cases of maladaptive or disordered behavior. Secondary prevention seeks to reduce the length of time an adolescent persists in using disordered behavior. Tertiary prevention attempts to insure that an adolescent who has participated in a rehabilitation program will maintain his/her gains and not be adversely affected by long-term consequences. Prevention involves coordinated efforts of civic agencies, educational institutions, mental health professionals, volunteer groups, parents, and teenagers to facilitate the development of actualizing life-styles.

In primary, secondary, and tertiary prevention, the emphasis is on combatting harmful psychosocial growth effects in adolescents by making existing social systems more responsive to their needs, and by creating new social systems as the need arises. A comprehensive drug program can be used as an example of a coordinated primary, secondary, and tertiary prevention effort. Primary prevention involves education, community organization, competency promotion, and natural care-giving (Adams and Gullotta, 1983). At the primary level, workshops, community forums, psychoeducational groups, and joint parent–adolescent groups could be set up to equip adolescents with the social-competency skills and problem-solving tools essential for drug-free living. This would enable adolescents to find nondrug oriented ways of constructive problem solving, relating to others, seeking out adventure, reducing stress, completing goals, and feeling good about themselves. In doing so, they will become less vulnerable to needing to feel good or avoiding uncomfortable feelings by using drugs. Natural care-giving involves people in the community coming together to solve psychosocial problems of mutual interest. The organizations people form and the activities they engage in when they come together serve as a mutual support system and let the adolescents in the community know that someone cares. Education, organization, competency promotion, and natural care-giving can also be used as part of secondary and tertiary prevention.

Secondary prevention in this comprehensive drug program would consist of outpatient clinics and inpatient settings working with teenagers whose drug use had progressed to the point where it was interfering with their social, family, personal, and school adjustments. Emphasis on drug education and competency building would continue in this phase of the treatment program. This is because adolescents need to continue to improve their coping skills and understanding of the effects of drugs in order to remain drug free once they have completed the counseling or rehabilitation phase of the drug program. Tertiary prevention in drug circles is known as aftercare. The emphasis on follow-up and aftercare is to help adolescents maintain their treatment gains when they reenter the social environment in which they started to use drugs.

The Psychodynamic Model

The third medical-psychiatric model, the psychodynamic model, historically evolved out of the work of Charcot, Janet, and Freud (White and Watt, 1981). The psychodynamic model considers psychopathology, mental illness, and disordered behavior as outgrowths of the failure to resolve childhood psychosexual and aggressive strivings. Because of unresolved, childhood instinctual conflicts, the process of mental and emotional development cannot move forward effectively. As a result of faulty interaction between parents, the child has internalized images, values, and fears that produce severe intrapsychic (unconscious conflicts) tensions and anxieties. These anxieties and tensions, which teenagers bring with them into adolescence, must be defended against by the excessive use of rigid, habitual, and mostly unconscious defense mechanisms and protective systems. The intrapsychic struggle prevents fulfillment of instinctual sexual and aggressive drives while the emphasis on protection against anxiety prevents the individual from reaching out to experience the satisfactions of living in a creative, productive manner.

Freud's original deterministic, instinctual model of unconscious, childhood sexual and aggressive strivings as the basic human energy system was subsequently modified by Sullivan (1953), Horney (1937, 1945), Fromm (1941, 1955), and Erikson (1959, 1963, 1968). Modifications by these writers stressed reciprocal interaction between the individual and the environment. These neo-Freudians, as they are called, picture the individual as an active, rather than passive, agent of learning and development, and emphasize the importance of interpersonal relationships, identity and self-concept, and the psychosocial environment.

The Comprehensive Medical-Psychiatric Spectrum

The three medical-psychiatric models that have been presented — the medical model, the holistic model, and the psychodynamic model — make up the foundation for modern adolescent psychiatry. Taken together, these three models form a comprehensive view of the biological, biochemical, neuropsychological, and psychosocial dynamics and causes of adaptive and maladaptive adolescent behavior. This comprehensive view of adolescent psychiatry is based on an integration of the major medical-psychiatric models. It balances out many of the criticisms inherent in the traditional medical model and constitutes a broad spectrum for the education of adolescent psychiatrists and psychiatrically oriented mental health workers.

The Psychosocial Model

The primary conceptual orientation of this book will be grounded in a psychosocial view of adolescent development, conflict, and maladaptive behavior. The psychosocial model, which evolved from psychodynamic psychiatry, clinical psychology, academic psychology, and holistic psychology, emphasizes learning, mastery, and competence. Adolescents are viewed as people who have the power to initiate growth, recover from setbacks, and discover what they need in order to move toward fulfilling their goals and actualizing their potential. Growth comes about through maturation, development of cognitive and biophysical processes, social learning, and feedback between the individual and the environment. In the psychosocial model, the causes or triggers for maladaptive coping are to be found in faulty interaction between the adolescent and the psychosocial environment.

Excessive stresses, conflicts, frustrations, negative psychosocial learning, and vulnerabilities carried over from incomplete previous developmental stages can all be triggers for maladaptive coping. The emphasis in the psychosocial model is on prevention, empowering, and helping adolescents set the stage so they can generate new ways of experiencing themselves, satisfying their needs, and learning and conceptualizing about the world around them.

The psychosocial model, with its emphasis on growth being a function of reciprocal interaction between events within the individual and events outside the individual, is broad enough to include psychobiological, neurophysiological, and biochemical events as part of the internal properties of the organism. Where a critical mass of evidence exists to support a biogenetic or biochemical predisposition or etiology of adolescent disordered behavior, this evidence will be reviewed. In reviewing the evidence for the biogenetic or biochemical causes of adolescent disordered behavior, we should be mindful of the fact that correlation and causation are not synonymous. Correlations do not automatically mean causation; there is a wide range of psychological differences in the reactions to the challenges, stresses, and pressures of adolescence in teenagers with a similar biochemical or biogenetic makeup.

SUMMARY AND CONCLUSIONS

Adolescent mental health-care practitioners and lay people interested in understanding the troubled and distressed youth come from a variety of professional-training backgrounds and disciplines. While all share a common interest in resolving major adolescent behavioral, emotional, and psychological conflicts, they differ in their methods, goals, and approaches. Some adolescent mental health experts work with social systems that impact on adolescents and their families. Some are more interested in wellness and prevention, and some are more interested in the normal course of growth and development. Three major medical-psychiatric approaches were reviewed: the traditional medical model, the holistic health model, and the psychodynamic model. The traditional medical model has been criticized because of its overemphasis on pathology, illness, and classification. The holistic health model is more concerned with prevention than with psychopathology.

Three levels of prevention—primary, secondary, and tertiary—were discussed. Successful prevention involves the coordinated efforts of civic agencies, educational institutions, volunteer groups, parents, mental health practitioners, and teenagers to facilitate the development of actualizing adolescent life-styles. The psychosocial model of adolescent development, which is the conceptual view of this book, perceives adolescents as young people who have the power to initiate growth, recover from setbacks, and discover what they need to fulfill their goals and actualize their potential. Maladaptive behavior is due to faulty interaction between the adolescent and the social environment. Faulty interactions result in excessive stresses, conflict, frustrations, negative learning, and vulnerabilities often carried over from incomplete previous developmental stages. Adolescents are likely to be more receptive to prevention and treatment efforts if they are recognized as potentially capable individuals who can significantly contribute to their own growth.

SUGGESTIONS FOR PARENTS, TEACHERS, COUNSELORS, AND YOUTH WORKERS

1. Since high school counselors and school psychologists are often called on for referrals, they should keep an up-to-date list of local, adolescent, mental health professionals and community mental health agencies that offer services to youths. The list should contain fee schedules and whether or not referral sources accept insurance payments. Special treatment areas should be noted, such as drugs, eating disturbances, suicide, depression, etc.
2. There are many qualified mental health professionals in most communities. Parents seeking help should talk with counselors, other parents, and visit one or two practitioners or clinics before making a final decision on who might be the best person to work with their concerns. Personal chemistry and confidence in the practitioner are very important elements of individual and family psychotherapy.
3. High school counselors, educators, parents, and youth workers should set up periodic conferences and workshops on important topics adolescents and their families are likely to encounter — e.g., drugs, sex, suicide, teen pregnancies, pressure for grades, and peer relationships. Invite teenagers to participate in the planning of workshops and conferences. Teenagers often have good ideas, intentionally or unintentionally ignored by adults.
4. Many teenagers are interested in careers in the mental-health field. High school counselors and administrators should invite mental health practitioners from several disciplines to participate in career days and workshops. Brochures on careers in mental health can be obtained by writing to the professional organizations listed in Chapter 1.
5. Adolescents are likely to resist counseling when they feel they have been designated as the "bad" person in the family, and the counselor's job is to correct their attitudes or behavior. Parents should let adolescents know they are willing to reexamine their attitudes, expectations, and decision-making strategies as part of the counseling process.
6. Be careful of diagnostic labels. Labels are a convenient shorthand, necessary for insurance purposes and for allowing professionals to communi-

cate with each other. More important than the diagnostic label is getting a clear picture of why young people are expressing troubled and distressed moods or behaviors. What are the underlying family, personal, and social conflicts contributing to the depression, suicidal behavior, mood swings, or angry outbursts, and what kind of treatment plan can be formulated to resolve these issues?

7. During initial interviews with therapists and counselors, much of the focus is on what is going wrong in the adolescent's life and how it is affecting family interaction and school performance. Remember, every adolescent has a number of strengths and likeable qualities that may not be visible because of personal and family turmoil. Counselors and parents should discuss the adolescent's strengths and potential strengths as well as weaknesses to maintain a balanced view.

8. Under carefully controlled, supervised conditions, psychotropic medications and psychoactive drugs can reduce disruptive symptoms and elevate despondent moods. When drugs are part of the treatment, parents should become knowledgeable about dosages, pharmaceutical properties of the drugs, side effects, and how long the drugs will be administered. Periodically, it is important to reevaluate the situation to make sure medication is having its intended effect, and to carefully observe the adolescent to make sure that the drugs are not being abused.

DISCUSSION QUESTIONS

1. Discuss the major differences between clinical and community psychology. Why does the philosophy of community psychology blend in with the rationale for prevention?

2. Compare and contrast the traditional medical model and the holistic health model. Which model is likely to work better with today's troubled and distressed teenagers and why?

3. Several major criticisms have been directed toward the traditional medical model. Discuss some of these major criticisms and how they can be corrected. What is the myth of mental illness and how can this myth have detrimental effects on teenagers?

4. Why are psychiatrists the only mental health care professionals allowed to administer psychoactive and psychotropic drugs? What are some of the advantages and disadvantages of using psychoactive drugs in working with troubled and distressed adolescents?

5. What are the major differences between primary, secondary, and tertiary prevention? Outline a prevention approach to a major adolescent mental health problem such as suicide, running away, eating disturbances, or depression, which would combine all three approaches.

6. Explain the role of etiology, diagnosis, prognosis, and prescriptive treat-

ment in the traditional medical model. How did the traditional medical model develop and what are the two major purposes of diagnosis?

7. Discuss the axis system in DSM-III-R (1987). What are the advantages of the axis system over a simple diagnostic classification system with only one axis? What major changes do you think will occur in DSM-IV?

8. How is the psychosocial model different from the traditional medical model, especially with respect to philosophies of growth, power to initiate change, illness, maladaptive behavior, and social learning?

3
Running Away

PREVIEW

The term runaway refers to youths between the ages of 10 and 17, who leave home overnight without permission. The number of runaway adolescents has increased dramatically in the past 25 years; estimates vary between 1 and 4 million annually. The number of female runaways is slightly higher than male runaways. Running away has been depicted as adventure seeking, escaping from oppressive conditions, delinquent-pathological behavior, and/or as an assertive first step in dealing with family conflict.

In contemporary America, reasons for running away primarily involve breakdowns in family relationships characterized by conflicts related to independence and individuality or conflicts involving rejection and lack of support. Runaways who stay on the streets for an extended period of time are vulnerable to exploitation by adults, often become involved in delinquent behaviors, and exist on the fringes of society as street people. Prior to 1974, treatment approaches were concentrated in the juvenile justice system and psychiatric detention centers. With the passage of the Runaway, Homeless and Youth Act of 1974, running away was decriminalized and to some extent depathologized. Funding was given to runaway-youth shelters, which offer a combination of temporary shelter to runaway youths and individual, family, and group counseling. Examples of youth shelters and family counseling models are discussed. Runaway prevention is divided into two parts: the first is helping young people and their parents resolve problems prior to running away and the second is helping young people survive once they have decided to run away. Concluding statements are directed toward the implications of teenage runaways for American society with respect to changes in legal rights and emancipation for young people. Included in this is the reorganization of mental health services for adolescents and their parents, increasing our awareness of adolescent abuse, and the need for long-term noninstitutionalized group homes for adolescents who cannot or will not live with their families.

Case Example 3-1: Dave

Dave, a 16-year-old high school junior, his mother, and his 14-year-old sister were referred to an adolescent mental health center for family counseling by a family social worker at a runaway-youth shelter. A month prior to the referral, Dave ran away from home after an argument with his mother about issues related to curfew and choice of friends. During the argument, Dave claims his mother said, "If you don't like the rules here, you can leave. I'm sick and tired of trying to provide a home for you, which you don't appreciate." The first few days Dave was away from home, he stayed with different friends each night. Next, he spent a few days on the streets sleeping in abandoned cars and houses. He had $75 when he left home, which he let a friend hold. He would meet his friend every other day to get enough money for food and for doing his laundry. Dave recalled the name of a runaway-youth shelter in his community from a high school class on social issues, but was reluctant to call the shelter because he wasn't sure whether he would be forced to return home or be sent to juvenile hall.

Dave has no prior juvenile arrest record. He is an A minus student in a college preparatory high school program. He plans to attend a local state university to study engineering and computer science when he graduates. He works 16 to 20 hours a week in a fast-food restaurant. His boss considers him a very good worker. While he was away from home, Dave called his boss and asked for a 2-week leave because of family problems.

During the second week away from home, Dave decided to call the runaway-youth shelter. A friend told him that he would not be forced to return home and would not be sent to juvenile hall. At the runaway shelter, Dave agreed to let the intake worker call his mother who gave permission for Dave to stay there temporarily. During the 3 weeks he was at the runaway shelter, Dave received individual, group, and family counseling. He attended school and resumed his part-time job. From Dave's perspective, he perceived his mother as overprotective, trying to control his life, and overly critical of his choice of friends and the way he dressed. Dave felt that his mother seldom complimented him on his positive accomplishments, such as his grades or his good work record. He was angry with his mother and said he often felt depressed when he thought about his home life. Mother told the family counselor that she had to keep a firm grip on Dave's life because he could be led astray by some of his older college friends from work, who drank and engaged in premarital sex. She would frequently call the restaurant to make sure Dave was at work, maintained a rigid curfew, and would not allow Dave to entertain his friends at home.

Before he ran away, Dave and his mother would try to discuss their differences but the conversations would quickly deteriorate into heated, verbal arguments about lack of love and appreciation, overprotectiveness, and who was responsible for the parent's divorce. Dave's younger sister says the reason Dave and his mother can't talk is that neither of them listens to the other. During the family counseling sessions at the runaway center, the counselor helped Dave and his mother learn to listen without constantly attacking, interrupting, and criticizing. They were encouraged to express their differences without accusing one another of lacking love and respect for choosing to disagree. Once the intensity of anger, hurt, and disappointment between Dave and his mother was reduced, they were able to rediscover mutual caring feelings and start working toward ways of solving their differences, which involved constructive communication and collaborative decision making. Dave agreed to return home on the condition that he, his mother, and his sister continue family counseling. Dave's father also agreed to participate in the family counseling.

DEFINITION AND RUNAWAY STATISTICS

The term runaway refers to youths age 10 to 17, who leave home overnight without parental or guardian permission (Nye and Edelbrock, 1980; Opinion Research Corporation, 1976). As part of independence and psychosocial maturity development, youths are expected to demonstrate their ability to function and survive in society, on their own, by leaving home. Leaving home usually occurs during late adolescence or early adulthood, with the implicit or explicit approval of parents. What distinguishes runaways is that they leave early, without the explicit approval of their parents.

There has been a dramatic increase in the number of runaway youths in the past 25 years (Moses, 1978). Estimates of the annual number of runaway teenagers range from 1 million to 4 million. The most stable figure is 1.3 to 1.4 million (Bucy, 1985). Studies using probabilistic sampling techniques predict that one out of every eight adolescents between the ages of 12 and 18, will run away from home at least once (Young et al., 1983). Estimates of the total number of runaways vary because investigators use different sampling techniques, definitions, and reporting procedures. Many parents don't report their children as runaways when they leave home without permission, because they know where they are or think they will return in a few days.

Fifteen- and sixteen-year-olds make up the largest percentage of runaways (Adams and Gullotta, 1983). Between 56% and 60% of runaway teenagers are girls (Mann, 1983; Langway, 1982). Eighty to ninety percent of runaways return within 48 hours (Langway, 1982; Mann, 1983) and only 18% travel more than 50 miles from home (Adams and Gullotta, 1983). Sixty percent of runaways had never been in trouble with the law before running away (Langway, 1982). While runaway youths represent an ethnic and economic cross-section of the population, the majority of runaway youths are white (Rice, 1984; Nye, 1980).

Most runs away from home are poorly planned. Few youths run away with companions and only a minority run away more than three times (Adams and Gullotta, 1983). Many of those who do not return home in a few days head for big cities like New York, Chicago, and Los Angeles. New

York City police estimate that there are 20,000 runaways in New York City (Ritter, 1979). Many of these long-term runaways are self-emancipated adolescents who have become a permanent part of the street society. Approximately 5,000 runaways are never heard from again. Runaway juveniles make up a large percentage of the missing persons listed by the National Crime Information Center (Bucy, 1985; Mann, 1983).

There are two subgroups within the category of youths commonly referred to as runaways. The first group consists of youths who depart from home voluntarily with no sense of being pressured by their parents to leave. The second group of runaways consists of push-outs, castaways, and throwaways. These are youths who leave home because they feel rejected or have been physically or sexually abused. In some cases, they have been abandoned by their parents or actually asked to leave. Research evidence suggests that 40% to 50% of youths generally classified as runaways are actually push-outs, castaways, or throwaways (Langway, 1982; Adams and Gullotta, 1983). Gullotta (1978) defines castaways as youths who did not willingly choose to leave home, but were pushed out of the home by their parents and then reported by either the parents or the police as runaways.

June Bucy (1985), Executive Director of the National Network and Youth Services located in Washington, D.C., suggests that we should use five definitional categories to describe the runaway youth.

1. *Runaways*.   Teenagers who are away from home at least overnight without parental or caretaker permission. Thornberg (1982) refers to this group as true runaways.
2. *Homeless*.   Youths who have no parental, foster, institutional, or alternative home. Often these youths have been urged to leave with the knowledge of their parents or legal guardians.
3. *System Kids*.   These are youths who have been taken into custody by the state because of child abuse, neglect, or other serious family problems. Often these youths have had few opportunities to establish long-term ties with any adult, or are school dropouts and have few independent living skills.
4. *Street Kids*.   These are long-term runaway youths who have become skilled at surviving on the streets, usually by illegal activities.
5. *Missing Youths*.   This category refers to teenagers whose whereabouts are unknown. This term is often used to refer to youths who have been the victims of exploitation, foul play, or who have been abducted.

The Meaning of Running Away in American Life and History

How running away is interpreted, explained, and categorized depends on the historical period and on the moral or theoretical views of the observer.

Four views of running away that have evolved in American life, literature, and professional discourse are presented in this section. First, running away has been viewed within a romantic adventurous context. Second, running away has been considered as a way of youth to escape oppressive conditions. Third, running away has been interpreted as pathological-delinquent behavior. Fourth, running away has been viewed as an assertive step toward defining independence and individuality.

A theme of ambivalence surrounds the meaning of running away in American society. On one hand, running away has been romanticized and glorified in American fact and fiction (Marshall, 1981; Adams and Gullotta, 1983). Fictive characters, such as Dorothy in the Wizard of Oz and Mark Twain's Tom Sawyer and Huckleberry Finn, have been enshrined and admired as youthful heroes who ran away in the spirit of adventure, challenge, and exploration. Real-life American heroes, such as Davy Crockett and Ben Franklin, regarded their youthful running away as challenging, adventure-filled, character-building experiences. In the 19th century, Horace Greeley (1850), a successful journalist and political leader, advised America's youth to leave their current surroundings and seek their fortunes by following the expansion of the American frontier westward (Liebertoff, 1980). On the other hand, adults have attempted to control and contain runaway behavior on the part of children and teenagers by classifying running away as a crime, moral transgression, or deviant psychological behavior (Walker, 1975; Gordon, 1981).

A second theme embedded in runaway behavior in America is the theme of running to and running from (Homer, 1973). While youthful runaways are seeking excitement, adventure, challenge, and fulfillment of the American dream, they are also running from controlling parents, boring existences, unfulfilled lives, and limited economic opportunities. Huckleberry Finn fled from a punitive, drunken father when no other avenue was open to him. The early immigrant youth of America fled from harsh conditions in Europe.

The themes of escape and adventure come together in Irene Hunt's novel, *No Promises in the Wind* (1970). The story is set in the economic depression of the 1930s. Josh, the novel's 15-year-old protagonist, leaves his home in Chicago, along with his brother and a friend, not only to escape an impoverished home situation and the harshness of his father, but also to find adventure and success. Through the process of struggle, tragedy, and disappointment he encounters during the runaway, Josh gradually shapes his identity and comes to understand his parents' frailties as well as his own. Because of this deeper understanding and acceptance of self and others, Josh is finally able to return home and start the process of building a new relationship with his parents. In this context, running away is a first step toward individuality, independence, and self-determination.

In the early years of colonial America, thousands of immigrant children and teenagers ran away from abject poverty, social oppression, and harsh masters to seek a better life in America. These young immigrants indentured themselves to American families as farm hands, apprentices, and servants for periods of 7 to 10 years. Following the completion of the period of indenture, they were free to seek their fortunes as bona fide citizens.

As America settled into a farm economy, colonial society took a harsh attitude toward running away by its own children. In the early puritan colonies, young people who left home without permission were regarded as a loss to the family's agricultural economy, since they performed essential work as laborers, apprentices, and domestic servants. Runaways were also regarded as violators of the community's religious morality (Gordon, 1981). Their elders found justification for their beliefs against running away in the Bible: "God settleth the solidarity in families" (Psalms 68:6). Laws against running away, in the 17th and 18th century Commonwealth colonies and early American states, were severe (Liebertoff, 1980).

In the mid-to-late 19th century, as America slowly changed from a predominantly agricultural economy with the building of the railroads, expansion of the west, and development of the early factories in urban areas, children and teenagers were no longer essential for the economy of the rural towns and villages. Young people ran away from the farms and sought jobs in the city's factories, or heeded Horace Greeley's (1850) advice and headed west to seek their fortunes. Land was available in the west; anyone (except Blacks and women) who was willing to stake claim to it and work it could eventually own the land. In America's mid-19th century factories, a large percent of the labor force was made up of youths under the ages of 16, who were used as cheap labor (Hopkins, 1983). During this early period of westward expansion and growth of factories, a tolerant attitude toward running away prevailed because youths were still productive contributors to the economy.

As America approached the last quarter of the 19th century, attitudes toward runaway youths changed in the direction of greater control and confinement. Between 1875 and 1925, unionization of the labor force with its demands for higher wages and the development of more complex industrial machinery reduced the need for the employment of children and teenagers under 16 in the labor force (Bakan, 1971). With the closing of the frontier, opportunities to go west were no longer readily available. Runaway teenagers and unemployed youths congregating, loitering, and drinking on the streets of the cities, were regarded by their elders as a menace to the morals and stability of the community.

Humanitarian reformers, educators, parents, and child-guidance workers, concerned about the welfare and morality of teenagers, joined forces with labor unions, law enforcement, and employers to redefine the status of young people who were no longer needed as productive members of the labor force. Out of their combined efforts came child labor laws, compulsory education, and the juvenile justice system. Minors between the ages of 12 and 18 (in some states, 12–16) were covered by a special body of juvenile laws, forced to attend school, and their access to employment was severely restricted (Bakan, 1971). Adolescence, as a specially designated period of life for juveniles between the ages of 12 and 18, became a sociological and legal reality. The psychological foundation for adolescence as a stage of psychosocial development was provided by the writings of G. Stanley Hall (1904).

THE DELINQUENCY-PATHOLOGY MODEL OF RUNAWAY BEHAVIOR

By 1925 running away was classified by the juvenile justice system as delinquent behavior. In most states running away was regarded as a status offense, like truancy, curfew, or unmanageability, which was a crime only if it occurred in adolescents or minors under the age of 18. The roles of the juvenile justice system and child-guidance clinics, which started in the early 1900s, were to guide and counsel youth, such as runaways, whose behavior was not congruent with community standards. The early child-guidance clinic counselors, social workers, psychologists, and psychiatrists were influenced by the work of G. Stanley Hall (commonly known as the Father of Adolescence), and later by the psychodynamic theory of Sigmund Freud. Adolescence was conceptualized as a critical period of human development when young people needed the active supervision of adults in family, social, educational, and recreational settings to prevent the development and continuation of impulsive, deviant, or runaway behavior. Psychologically speaking, running away was perceived as a failure to internalize the values of parents who represented the standards of the society. Failure to internalize parental values, or a defective internal conscience, was viewed as a developmental emotional disorder that could be part of a larger syndrome involving deviant behavior, low self-concept, poor impulse controls, deviant actions, and depression. This syndrome has been labeled as the delinquency-pathology syndrome, or the bad-sick model of runaway behavior (Brennan, 1980).

Once the delinquency-pathology or bad-sick model of runaway behavior was set in place, it persisted until the early 1970s with one exception. During the economic depression of the 1930s, many young people lived in communities where their parents lacked jobs and the necessary resources to feed, clothe, and house them. Thousands of male and female teenagers and pre-teenagers, with the tacit approval of their parents, were on the road looking for shelter, food, clothing, and work. Transient service bureaus were set up in several communities, during the 1930s, to provide support for these young people in the form of employment assistance, counseling, health care, recreation, and job training (Liebertoff, 1980).

Many books, articles, and studies published in professional journals prior to 1975 supported the delinquency-pathology or bad-sick model of runaway behavior. In an extensive review of the runaway literature, Walker (1975) concluded that a large majority of the studies utilized the individual psychopathology model to explain runaway behavior. Another review of the runaway literature, conducted by the Scientific Analysis Corporation (1974), reached essentially the same conclusion. The Scientific Analysis Corporation study labeled two of the major runaway categories used in the literature as the "sick" and the "bad." A third category, called "free runaways," was used to designate youths whose motives for running away involve the search for independence, pleasure, adventure, exploration-seeking, wanderlust, and the excitement of new experiences. Several research studies emphasizing the delinquency-pathology or bad-sick model are summarized below.

Armstrong (1932, 1937) studied 660 runaway boys and 122 runaway girls arraigned before the domestic courts as delinquents and seen in the children's division of the New York Courts Clinic. She described running away as a psychoneurotic reaction in unstable and emotional young people who were experiencing fear, distress, and insecurity. The intelligence range of these youth was below average. In a 30-year follow-up study of former child-guidance clinic patients who had been diagnosed as schizophrenic, O'Neal and Lee (1959) found that runaways, compared to nonrunaways, exhibited more evidence of antisocial behavior. These behaviors included incorrigibility, delinquency, lying, and violence. In Hildebrand's (1968) studies of runaway youth referred by the courts, runaways were described as second generation delinquents with the potential for becoming future felons.

In a series of articles, Jenkins and his associates (1968, 1969, 1971) described delinquent runaway boys confined to a state training school as insecure, timid, immature, furtive, seclusive, rejected, and inclined toward stealing. Delinquent acts other than running away were considered more common in runaways than in nonrunaways. The personality makeup of runaway delinquents was not as well organized as the personality makeup of the nonrunaway group. Stierlin (1973) found that runaways have more contacts with the police and a higher incidence of drug abuse than was seen in nonrunaways.

Greene and Esselstyn (1972), in their study of runaway, delinquent, incorrigible girls, outlined three distinct types: the rootless, the anxious, and the terrified. The rootless runaway is primarily interested in pleasure-seeking, requires immediate gratification, cannot handle limits, and rebels against authority. The anxious runaway is frequently from a multiproblem family, may have experienced sexual abuse from her father, and worries about the family's welfare. The terrified runaway is fleeing from her father or stepfather's advances toward her.

The American Psychiatric Association concurred with the delinquency-pathology model of runaway behavior described in the literature. The 1968 Diagnostic and Statistical Manual of the American Psychiatric Association (DSM-II) included runaway reaction as a separate diagnostic category of mental disorder (APA, 1968). The work of Jenkins and his colleagues (1968, 1969, 1971), cited earlier, was used to support the inclusion of the runaway reaction as a psychiatric diagnostic category. Youths exhibiting the runaway reaction were described in DSM-II as immature, timid, rejected, inadequate, and friendless individuals who characteristically escaped from threatening home situations by running away from home without permission, and who steal secretively.

There are three major criticisms of the delinquency-pathology model of runaway behavior. First, from the design of the studies it was not always clear whether delinquency and emotional maladjustment were a cause or an outcome of runaway behavior (Rice, 1984; Adams and Gullotta, 1983). Over half the youth in detention in America, prior to 1974, were confined because of runaway behavior (Moses, 1978). It has been repeatedly observed that once runaways or other juvenile offenders are detained and adjudicated within the supposed corrective influence of the juvenile criminal justice system, the probability of future lawbreaking increases (Justice and Duncan, 1976). This may be related to being labeled a juvenile delinquent or to the association with veteran juvenile offenders in detention centers and other juvenile facilities. It is also a reasonably well-documented fact that the longer runaway youths are on the streets without money, job skills, or a place to stay, the more vulnerable they are to violating the law in order to survive (Ritter, 1979; Loveless, 1981a,b).

Second, the delinquency-pathology model assumes that the causes or triggers for the emotional disturbance are inside the adolescent. It does not consider the possibility that depression, poor self-image, poor impulse controls, and angry outbursts may be a result of environmental influences. Some of these influences may include poor communication, legitimate differences in values, and interpersonal conflicts within adult-adolescent relationships.

Third, the bad-sick hypothesis does not take into account socialization differences in males and females. Female adolescents are usually expected to follow stricter controls with respect to sexual behavior, obedience, curfew, drugs and alcohol, and acting out. Historically, punishment for violations of juvenile codes has been much harsher for adolescent females than for adolescent males (Schlossman and Wallach, 1978). Even with the changes in attitudes and in female childrearing practices that have occurred since the beginning of the women's movement, adolescent girls are still expected to be more constrained in their behavior and are given mixed messages about assertive behavior, equality, and their role outside the home.

CONTEMPORARY RUNAWAY EXPLANATIONS, DYNAMICS, AND TYPOLOGIES

In the 1970s and early 1980s, two important changes occurred in explanatory models and classification systems psychologists, mental health workers, and social scientists utilized to account for runaway behavior. First, the reasons for running away were no longer confined to personal characteristics or motives operating inside the psychological makeup of runaway youth. Runaway behavior occurs in a psychosocial context involving interaction between the adolescent and the social systems in which the family is a major force. There is a significant body of evidence suggesting that the emotional quality of family relationships, the degree of parent–adolescent conflict, the level of support and understanding, and the openness of communication affect the runaway process (Roberts, 1982; Orten and Soll, 1980; Brennan, 1980). The counter literature, as Rice (1984) refers to it, rejects the delinquency-psychopathology explanation and projects an image of many runaways as capable, goal-directed young people who are experiencing family-related stresses. While school dilemmas, peer relationships, and adventure-seeking can trigger runaway behaviors, the primary reasons for running away appear to be family connected. The second change, which occurred in runaway classification systems and explanatory models, involves the development of new typologies. The new typologies use a range of different motives, reasons, and dynamics to account for runaway behavior rather than relying on one or two major explanations, such as the delinquency-pathology model or the escape versus romantic-adventure models. An expanded discussion of family dynamics and new runaway typology systems will be presented in this section.

Family Dynamics and Runaway Behavior

Studies by Gullotta (1978) and Brennan (1980) indicate that parent-adolescent interaction in runaway homes is characterized by lack of nurturance, parental dissatisfaction and rejection of the adolescent, lack of companionship, physical abuse, negative labeling and devaluation, and conflicts around power and control issues such as choice of friends, dating, school issues, dress and grooming, and curfew. Wolk and Brandon (1977) examined the relationship between runaway behavior, self-concept, and treatment by parents, using a matched sample of 47 runaways and 47 nonrunaways. Their study reports four significant outcomes:

1. Runaways reported more punishment and less support from their parents than did nonrunaways.
2. Runaway females experienced more issues regarding parental control than did runaway males.

3. Runaways showed a lower self-concept than did nonrunaways.
4. Runaways acknowledged a greater need for personal counseling than did nonrunaways.

In his review of the literature on runaways and their parents, Rice (1984) concluded that alienation, rejection, lack of warmth, and lack of support were the primary family conflicts. Parents and stepparents of runaways were described as absorbed in their own problems and marital turmoil. Female offspring were overly controlled in runaway families, whereas male offspring had minimal controls.

The family is a vital influence in adolescent psychosocial development. Families have impact on young people's values, self-esteem, personal worth, physical well-being, and degree of freedom in choices and decision making. It is difficult for adolescents to maintain feelings of worth and self-esteem when they do not feel a sense of affirmation and appreciation from their parents. Youths who are rejected and abused by parents are vulnerable to feelings of depression and self–doubt. Parent–adolescent conflicts associated with running away can be divided into two groups: (1) conflict around issues of individuality, independence, and control, and (2) conflicts involving lack of support and understanding or involving verbal, physical, and sexual abuse (Thornberg, 1982). Adolescence is a time when teenagers begin to push for greater independence, increased differentiation of themselves as individuals separate from their parents, and more control over decisions that impinge on their lives. The parents who heretofore have been in control of the power to define, validate, and set limits have to determine how and when to relinquish their authority in order for adolescents to gradually take control over the direction of their lives. In the best of households there will be disagreements about curfew, dating issues, choice of friends, school performance, and free-time activities. If the lines of communication shut down, and parents refuse to understand the need for changing family power dynamics from autocratic to collaborative, minor adolescent–parent conflicts can escalate into heated arguments, accusations, threats, and negations of self-worth, with the possible outcome being an adolescent runs away.

A more covert kind of control-oriented conflict can be seen in an adolescent's needs for challenge, excitement, and adventure. Adolescents need to test themselves against risk, encounter danger in less than catastrophic amounts, and experience the thrill of discovery and adventure. If the families or immediate environments are too confining and restrictive, adolescents may need to break out temporarily to experience the unknown and test themselves against its challenges. This may explain why seemingly well-adjusted young people, experiencing very little visible conflict with their family, occasionally run away. Boredom can be stressful and unfulfilling. Clinically speaking, boredom can also be a symptom of mild depression.

Issues of support, understanding, and belongingness are many times missed by parents when they find themselves locked into battles with their teenagers over issues involving power, control, and independence. While less obvious than full-blown power conflicts, issues of support, understanding, and belongingness are a critical element of adolescent self-concept and self-esteem. Despite close relationships with their peers and challenges to parental authority, adolescents are still deeply bonded to their parents and need to be supported, appreciated, and affirmed by them. Adolescents may not know how to ask for parental support when they need it, and in some cases parents withdraw their support because of disagreements with their teenagers.

Verbal abuse and threats, hostile rejecting attitudes, threatening to throw teenagers out, asking them to leave, and actual physical or sexual abuse represent blatant examples of parental lack of support and affirmation. Estimates of physical and sexual abuse by parents, stepparents, and adult family members of runaway youths vary from 20% to 50% (Lourie et al., 1979). Until the 1970s, child abuse was thought to occur primarily in children below the age of 12. Now, more and more runaway teenagers are reporting physical and sexual abuse. The sexual abuse of female teenagers is receiving independent confirmation from studies on father–daughter incest (Herman, 1981). Angel (1983) estimates that one of every six teenagers is sexually assaulted by family members before the age of 18 and that there are 100,000 to 200,000 incest cases each year.

A second type of lack of parental support and understanding occurs when parents become so overwhelmed by the demands in their own lives, they are no longer psychologically or emotionally available to their children. This category includes parents who have serious problems with alcohol, drug abuse, or emotional disturbances; parents going through major personal changes and adult transitions such as divorce, economic reversals, or existential redefinitions; and parents who for one reason or another have dropped out of the responsibilities of adult life. The abuse, family disturbances, and lack of support runaway adolescents report is part of a larger pattern of family disruption that has come about as a consequence of rapid social, economic, occupational, and geographic changes in the past generation. Divorces, occupational changes, redefinition of gender roles, adult transitions, and family relocations generated by job transfers and economic necessity have created severe stress and confusion in families. The effects of these stresses are seen in adult drug and alcohol abuse, family turmoil, mental illness, child abuse, and parental role confusion. Many adults are not confident in their role as parents, they are not sure of their own values or how to guide their adolescent offspring with a balance of firmness, flexibility, and support through the pressures and demands of growing up. In cases in which family conflict and disruption are severe, families may need special help in the form of parenting advice, homemaker assistance, network building, and employment; this would be a first step in developing a growth-facilitating family environment (Thornberg, 1982).

In contrast to the delinquency-pathology explanations of runaway behavior prevalent a generation ago, recent studies suggest that many runaways, despite family conflict, are reasonably well-adjusted adolescents struggling with the normal developmental tasks involved in growing up. Thornberg (1982) estimates that one-third of runaway teenagers are well-adjusted, successful in school experiences and peer relationships, and have good self-concepts, self-control, and the capacity to regulate their behavior. In a study of 201 randomly selected females and 91 males who used runaway facilities between 1977 and 1979, Jorgensen et al. (1980) report that 91% had future goals. Nye (1980) and Orten and Soll (1980) described groups of psychologically healthy runaways who handled themselves well on the streets, learned from their travels, developed a better adjustment to family life when they returned home, and viewed themselves and their runaway experiences in a positive light.

Runaway Typologies and Classification Systems

Runaway typologies generally employ three categories based on the degree of alienation and conflict teenagers are experiencing in the family and in their immediate social environment. The first category describes young people running away primarily to seek adventure and excitement. They are reasonably well-adjusted and show few signs of overt family conflict. Covert family conflicts may exist in terms of overprotectiveness or in a highly structured environment that prevents adolescents from experiencing a sense of risk, challenge, and adventure. The runaways in this category don't stay away too long; they reunite in positive ways with their families; and they look back on running away as a positive experience. In the second category, there are obvious signs of conflict and alienation within the runaway's family, which are usually around issues of power and control with respect to dating, style of dress, choice of friends, school performance, and the like. Runaways in the second group stay away from home a little longer, but are usually reunited with their family. Category three contains the push-outs, castaways, and throwaways. These young people are seriously alienated from their families, feel that they were driven away because of threats, abandonment, or actual abuse, remain on the streets for an extended period of time, are likely to be involved in delinquency and drug use, and show other signs of maladaptive behavior.

From a review of the runaway research and runaway program literature, Nye (1980) developed a runaway typology involving three categories. Category I involves young people who are running to increase their rewards.

Category II consists of young people who are running to reduce costs, and Category III involves push-outs.

Category I runaways make up about 20% of the runaway population. Youths in Category I value adventure, freedom, and opportunity. They are generally upbeat and feel optimistic about life. They are not so much running from unhappy situations as they are running to meet new people and encounter new experiences. They have good relationships with their families, peers, and teachers; but they feel a more rewarding life awaits them on the road. They have, to some extent, idealized the world away from home and its potential for enjoyment in contrast to the unexciting routine of home and family life.

Category II runaways make up about 75% of the runaway population. This is the largest group of runaways. Adolescents in this group have been disappointed in one major area of family, school, or peer relationships. Areas of serious conflict and alienation most frequently involve turmoil with parents, feelings of rejection by teachers, and poor performance in school. Some operate on the fringes of delinquent groups and have been in trouble with the police. They are running from an unhappy situation with hopes that they will find an accepting, happy place somewhere else.

Category III runaways make up approximately 5% to 10% of the runaway population. This group is usually referred to as push-outs, castaways, and throwaways. Youths in this group feel chronically rejected, and parents do not strongly oppose their leaving. Many runaways in this group have been forced to leave home because of physical abuse, sexual abuse, or continuous degradational experiences. In some instances, parents may not have actually asked them to leave, but it has been made clear to them that they are not wanted. In other cases, parents have actually abandoned teenagers, ejected them from the house, or are unable to care for them because of problems such as alcohol, drugs, mental illness, and physical illness. Some parents have gotten into new marriages or adult relationships where they feel the adolescent would be a burden.

In a comparable system based on the degree of alienation from family and home environment, Orten and Soll (1980) classified runaways as first-degree, second-degree, and third-degree.

First-degree runaways are fairly stable youths who generally have good family relationships. They typically run away from home only once, don't stay long, and handle themselves carefully on the streets. Their reasons for running away usually have an existential theme, such as searching for identity or looking for new discoveries. Youths in this group return home with a renewed appreciation for family, and their parents tend to be willing to try to be more understanding of their needs when they return. There is a second subgroup, labeled fugitives, within the first-degree runaway group. These adolescents usually feel rejected, powerless, vulnerable, and frightened, and have few problem-solving skills. They are psychologically dependent on home, and they generally return after a few days.

Second-degree runners have run away several times, have major problems with parents, and are ambivalent about returning home. They have learned how to survive on the streets, and feel a sense of power and mastery because of their ability to survive away from home. Second-degree runners experience alienation from family and home.

Third-degree runners are usually 16 or older, and have been on the streets for a year or more. The degree of alienation from their homes is severe. They have little or no contact with their homes, and no desire to return. In learning to survive on the streets, they have become skilled at theft, manipulation, con games, and exploiting others. They may have juvenile records for offenses such as prostitution, drugs, theft, and/or burglary.

Brennan and his associates (1978, 1980) developed a statistically derived, runaway classification system based on cluster analysis. The data analyzed came from interviews and questionnaires that considered such variables as family relationships, peer relationships, school aspirations, school performance, beliefs and attitudes, delinquent behavior, and personal characteristics. They also include a behavioral description of the adolescent's most recent run in terms of spontaneous versus premature departure, length of time gone, mode of travel, companionship during the run, victimization during the run, mode of return, and parental responses. Brennan's system contains two classes of runaways encompassing seven types. Class I contains runaways who exhibit positive self-esteems, have nondelinquent friends, and do not seem to feel powerless, estranged, or alienated from their family. Class II runaways are more estranged from their families and are likely to be delinquent. Approximately 45% of the runaways are in Class I and 55% are in Class II. The seven runaway types are described in Table 3-1.

Roberts (1982) arranged runaways along a parent-youth conflict continuum (see Fig. 3-1). The 0 to 1 category, *the nonrunaways*, was made up of teenagers whose conflicts with parents were worked out or tolerated without the youth running away. If the youngsters wanted to travel or wanted more independence in choosing friends, a compromise was worked out. In level 1+, *the runaway explorers and social pleasure seekers*, runaways wanted to travel or to assert their independence against the wishes of their parents. The level 1+ pleasure seekers were usually girls who had conflicts with their parents over issues related to dating, curfew, and their choices of friends. Level 1+ runaways usually stayed away only for a short time, and they left notes for their parents telling them where they were. Level 2+ runaways, *the runaway manipulators*, had frequent conflicts with their parents and experienced verbal criticisms and arguments regarding their attitudes, their handling of responsibilities, and their choices of friends. They perceived running away as a way of manipulating their parents into worrying about them

Table 3-1. Runaway Classes and Types[a]

Class I

Type 1:   *Young, overcontrolled escapists.* Parents deny autonomy, are not nurturing, and use
          negative labels for the adolescent. Harsh discipline is exercised by means of physical
          punishment, social isolation, and rejection. Adolescents are bonded to their parents,
          and are successful in school and peer relationships. This group consists mostly of
          early teenage boys.

Type 2:   *Middle-class loners.* Teenagers tend to be around 16. They have good relationships
          with their parents, they do well in school and are not involved in delinquent behav-
          ior; they are successful and involved in school. Their parents support their educa-
          tional aspirations. They are isolated from their peers, and they spend much time
          alone. They are given high scores on autonomy from their parents.

Type 3:   *Unrestrained, peer-oriented runaways.* The approximate age is about 16. There are
          low companionship and nurturance levels within the family; they have minimal
          achievement demands and a high level of freedom and autonomy from the family.
          They are not doing well in school, they dislike school, and have low aspirational lev-
          els. They spend much of their time with a few friends.

Class II

Type 4:   *Rejected and constrained peer-oriented runaways.* These teenagers have been re-
          jected from both family and school. They spend most of their time with peers,
          who have been involved in delinquent behavior. They have poor relationships
          with their parents. Their parents are involved in negative labeling, harsh disci-
          pline, rejecting attitudes, and physical punishment. They have high commitments
          to their friends, who are usually delinquent.

Type 5:   *Rebellious and constrained middle-class dropouts.* This group is composed mainly
          of girls. There is rejection and stress in both family life and at school. These girls are
          angry and rebellious. Their parents deny their autonomy, and are overprotective and
          indulgent. These teenagers perceive their parents as giving preferential treatment to
          their siblings, and denying them their freedom. They have high commitments to their
          personal friends who are delinquent.

Type 6:   *Homeless, rejected, and unrestrained youth.* This group contains mostly boys. Their
          family relationships are characterized by severe rejection, negative labeling, high
          alienation, and low nurturance. They are uninvolved in school, spend a lot of time
          alone, and their friends are likely to be delinquent. Their parents are disinterested.

Type 7:   *Push-outs; socially-rejected youth.* This group experiences extreme parental rejec-
          tion. Their parents are very dissatisfied, unconcerned, not nurturing, and distant.
          These adolescents sense emotional rejection and feel their parents do not care about
          them. They feel totally alienated from school; they feel rejected by teachers, and
          have no expectations of their occupational achievement. Their self-esteem is low and
          they feel powerless. They lack norms and values, and spend time with delinquent
          friends.

---

[a]Adapted from: Brennan, T. (1980). Mapping the Diversity Among Runaways. *Journal of Family Issues*, 1 (2),
189–209.

while they were gone. Their parents would then cool off and hopefully allow
them to return on their own terms. Level 3+ runaways, *the retreatists*, were
impulsive youths who experienced repeatedly heated arguments and conflicts with their parents that included yelling and some occasional hitting
and throwing of things. These youths had problems in school, used drugs,
and many of their parents were divorced. Level 4+ runaways, *the endan-*

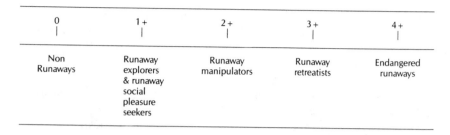

0	1 +	2 +	3 +	4 +
Non Runaways	Runaway explorers & runaway social pleasure seekers	Runaway manipulators	Runaway retreatists	Endangered runaways

FIGURE 3-1. Formulation of the degree of parent-youth conflict continuum. (Adapted from Roberts, A. R. (1982). Adolescent runaways in suburbia: A new typology. *Adolescence, 17* (66), 387–396.)

gered youths, were from homes in which they were the victims of repeated physical and verbal abuse as well as occasional sexual abuse from parents or stepparents, sometimes while the parent or stepparent was in a drunken state. When they left home, it was usually because of a beating or the threat of another beating. Many of these youths had problems in school and used drugs or alcohol on a regular basis. Roberts' continuum is shown in Figure 3-1.

Miller and her colleagues (1980) devised a system involving six runaway categories: (1) immigrants, (2) rebels, (3) victims, (4) exiles, (5) refugees, and (6) fugitives. The immigrants and rebels were running to seek adventure or independence. The victims and the exiles were forced out of their homes, thrown out, or abused. The refugees and fugitives were fleeing from institutions, boarding schools, foster homes, or the police.

As noted earlier, runaway behavior and the intrafamilial conflict usually preceding it is ultimately interpreted based on the values, training, and psychological views of the observer. A generation ago, running away was interpreted as impulsive, disordered behavior indicative of emotional maladjustment, delinquency, impulsiveness, lack of controls, failure to internalize mainstream values, and excessive pleasure seeking. Parents tended to agree with the delinquency-pathology interpretation, probably because placing the blame for runaway behavior on the adolescent absolved parents of the responsibility for looking at themselves and what they may have contributed to the adolescent's distress. When family conflict was apparent, it could also be blamed on the adolescent who was supposedly emotionally and behaviorally disruptive, impulsive, and lacked respect for authority.

Today, running away is likely to be interpreted by counselors and mental health professionals as an assertive, coping response to family conflict perceived by the adolescent as controlling, restricting, or rejecting. Running away, no matter how ill-conceived or poorly thought out, can be thought of in this context as a first step in the direction of self-determination, or as defining one's individuality and independence. The runaway adolescent temporarily steps outside the family environment to cast off negative self-statements, experience self in a positive fashion, seek growth-facilitating challenges, or to symbolically signal a need for reducing and resolving family conflict.

As we saw in Chapter 1, coping is a way of dealing with stressful, frustrating situations. The extent to which running away, as a coping strategy, has adaptive or maladaptive consequences depends on the response of the social environment, and on the flexibility and resourcefulness of the runaway. Parents tend to resist interpretations of runaway behavior as a potentially adaptive coping response to parent–adolescent conflict. It is easier for parents to agree with interpretations of runaway behavior which assign the blame to adolescents than it is to engage in critical self-examination.

OUT ON THE STREETS:
THE CONSEQUENCES OF RUNNING AWAY

First-time runaways who leave home with romantic visions of adventure or feelings of relief because they are escaping from stressful, and often abusive, home situations are in for a rude shock when they end up on the streets of America for extended periods of time. Runaways who impulsively leave home with no job skills or work permits, no money, no place to stay, and no organized plan of action run the risk of being exploited, sexually or physically abused, and often have to turn to crime in order to survive. In many cases, the art of survival runaway youths learn in the streets consists of sleeping in garages, parked cars, and abandoned houses, of huddling with other runaways over heating grates to keep warm, of begging and stealing for food, of dope peddling, and of prostitution. The grimness of runaway life on the streets, the lessons of survival, and the tragedies and hopes of day-to-day existence were vividly portrayed in *Streetwise*, a movie documentary about teenage runaways in Seattle, Washington (Bell et al, 1985). The longer a runaway youth is on the street, the greater the likelihood he or she will become a victim of exploitation or become involved in delinquency (Mann, 1983; Orten and Soll, 1980). Loveless (1981a,b) cites a study conducted by the Behavioral Research and Evaluation Corporation of Colorado which revealed that 33% of their runaway sample committed petty thefts while on the streets; 15% of these runaways were involved in thefts of $50 or more; burglary, car thefts, and shoplifting were frequently reported, and 20% of the sample sold drugs. Not only does criminal activity increase with the length of time runaways are on the streets, but runaways become harder to reach in terms of counseling and attempts to help them reunite with their families or reenter the mainstream. Father Ritter (1979), who directs Covenant House in New York City — one of the largest runaway shelters, outreach, and 24-hour counseling programs in America — claims that time is the great divider in working with runaways. According to Father Ritter, after 48 hours one-tenth of New York City's runaway population is into prostitution and, after 6 months on the streets, it is nearly impossible to rescue runaway youths and interest them in continuing their education, looking for employment, reestablishing relationships with their family, giving up drugs, or learning to survive economically without relying on stealing, drug-dealing, and prostitution (Langway, 1982).

Thousands of runaway youths congregate in cities like Chicago, Los Angeles-Hollywood, and New York's Time Square which supports approximately 10,000 runaways (Scott, 1980). The pimps, procurers, and "chicken hawks" (male homosexuals interested in sex for hire with young teenage boys) know the youth hangouts and points of entry for new runaways. They wait at these places — e.g., railroad and train stations — with offers of money, emotional support, and a place to stay. For tired, frightened, lonely, hungry runaway adolescents, the chance to earn some money by going out on a "date" with older males can sound like a workable offer. On Hollywood's Santa Monica Boulevard, or in Chicago, boy hookers too young to be legally employed can support themselves by charging from $300 to $450 for a weekend date. One section of New York was renamed the "Minnesota Strip" in street parlance because it attracted so many blonde teenage boy and girl prostitutes.

According to Satchell (1986), half of the runaways on the streets for longer than a month are involved in forms of prostitution that range from occasional tricks to daily hustling. Satchell cites data collected by two physicians for a study of teenage prostitution. Information provided by 595 police departments in 50 states helped them to estimate that there are between 100,000 and 200,000 adolescent prostitutes in the United States, with an average age of 15. In 1977, adolescent pornography in Texas was a $15 million business; most of the actresses were runaway females with an average age of 15 (Thornberg, 1982).

Runaway youths who become involved in prostitution, pornography, and hustling are vulnerable to violent actions by customers and pimps, and can be victimized by robbery and thefts. Pimps have been known to physically harm young people for not earning enough money, or for refusing to work the streets anymore as hustlers. In Houston, in 1973, and in Chicago, in 1978, there were mass sexually related murders of runaway males and of unsuspecting teenagers who allowed themselves to be picked up by sadistically oriented men (Mann, 1983; Sullivan and Maiken, 1984). With the increased fear of AIDS on the part of adults, younger teenage prostitutes of both sexes are becoming more in demand, which means increased risk for youths. It is ironic that many youths who leave home to escape from physical and sexual abuse often end up being sexually and physically abused again once they are forced to survive out on the streets.

Throwaways, castaways, push-outs, abandoned youths, and other parental rejects are likely to stay on the streets for extended lengths of time because they feel they have no home to return to. Many of these neglected, abandoned, and homeless youths need health care, job placements, counseling, and safe living quarters. They are reluctant to seek out the services of runaway youth shelters because of understandable distrust. Unsatisfactory past contacts with adults in authority, combined with a history of abusive family interaction have left them wary and suspicious. The decriminalization of juvenile-status offense laws prevents authorities from insisting on or coercing them to receive essential services in institutional settings, so these youths fall through the cracks. States such as Missouri have passed laws to designate Youth In Need of Service (YINS) in order to require that homeless street youths receive essential protective services (Lourie et al., 1979).

In recent years, a new phenomenon of runaway youths referred to as the "rat pack," has appeared in suburban areas, such as the San Fernando Valley of Los Angeles (Hawkins, 1985). These are groups of youths from middle-class homes, who refuse to go to school, who stay away from home for extended periods of time, and who spend their days and nights in discos, shopping malls, arcades, and in the homes of friends. They call their parents periodically to let them know where they are. They don't want to return home on a permanent basis because of parent rules regarding school attendance, curfew, drugs, and sexual activities. As long as they stay within the confines of juvenile-status offense laws, such as truancy, curfew, running away, and disobeying, they are immune from long-term detention by the police because many states have decriminalized juvenile-status offenses. Rat-pack youths survive economically by borrowing money from friends, staying for brief periods at the homes of different friends, and by occasionally doing odd jobs. One teenage girl told reporters that she made $50 by asking the middle-class teen customers for loose change at a teen night club.

While the grim side of life on the streets has been presented during this discussion, there is another side of the picture. Youths who master the art of survival on the streets develop a certain toughness, resilience, resourcefulness, and ability to cope adaptively with a variety of stressful situations. The toughness, adaptiveness, and resilience of young people faced with difficult circumstances was evident in the movie, *Streetwise* (Bell et al., 1985), and has been projected as a primary theme in the works of such writers as psychiatrists Robert Coles (1972) and Claude Brown (1966, 1973), a former New York City runaway teenager. The survivors learn to band together; they establish quasi-extended families with other street youths, and share information about where to find food, shelter, health services, and adults they can trust. They learn to operate in the gray areas between juvenile-status and nonstatus offenses to stay out of jail and confinement. They seem able to retain their humanness and capacity to love, to maintain an upbeat, hopeful attitude about the future, and to avoid serious drug abuse; some even manage to continue their education on a part-time basis.

Runaway street-life survivors who eventually return home are likely to have a stronger sense of themselves as self-reliant, capable young people. Because they now feel a greater degree of security within themselves, they may be more appreciative of their families and more willing to work toward collaborative solutions to family problems. For those street survivors who do not return home, the qualities of adaptiveness, resourcefulness, resilience, and self-confidence they have developed can become part of a sound foundation for adult living.

TREATMENT APPROACHES FOR RUNAWAY YOUTHS

From the beginning of the 20th century, when adolescence became a sociological reality in America supported by the creation of the juvenile justice system, compulsory school attendance, and labor laws restricting the access of juveniles to employment, treatment approaches for runaway youths were based on definitions of running away as an emotional disturbance or delinquent behavior. The delinquency and emotional-disturbance treatment approaches often went hand-in-hand. Runaway youths were apprehended and detained by juvenile authorities for violating the law and, as a condition of their probation, were referred to child guidance clinics for psychotherapy. When teenagers persisted in running away, they were confined for longer periods at detention centers and psychiatric hospitals. Parents generally went along with the decisions of the courts and juvenile officials. If adolescent runaways did not show cooperative attitudes toward this enforced guidance and counseling, they were considered to be resistant and in need of closer supervision or further confinement until such time as they showed proper respect for the authority of their parents and counselors. The point of view of the runaway adolescent was seldom taken into consideration in making treatment and diagnostic decisions, and the blame for failures in their treatment was assigned to the runaway.

In the 1970s, there was a definite shift away from the delinquency-pathology definition of runaway behavior and away from treatment models based on control, coercion, and denial of the legitimacy of the runaway's point of view. Runaway youths were increasingly being looked upon as potentially responsible, capable young people who needed growth-facilitating experiences to develop the coping tools, problem-solving skills, competencies, and support systems that would enable them to resolve stressful intrapersonal and intrafamily conflicts. Runaway youths, as a group, are not emotionally sick or bad but are sometimes confused, sad, angry, and disappointed because they cannot change the troublesome psychosocial conditions and family turmoils blocking their growth. Because they cannot change these dilemmas, they sometimes internalize the turmoil, which results in self-blame and depression; they act out their emotions with angry outbursts, defiant behavior, and reckless adventure-seeking, or reduce their stress level by turning to drugs and alcohol. Since self-blame, depression, acting out, and drug use are considered signs of psychopathology or delinquency, runaways and prospective runaways exhibiting these behaviors run the risk of being diagnosed as delinquent or emotionally disturbed.

The transition from the delinquency-pathology treatment models to approaches based on wellness, enabling, and empowering gives runaway adolescents the potential to become responsible, capable young people who are struggling with family problems and the developmental tasks of adolescents. This transition came about as a synergistic effect from several intersecting cross-currents: the youth movements and counterculture of the 1960s; changes in juvenile laws regarding the detention of status offenders; the emergence of social systems theory, family therapy, and collaborative decision making; and an increased tendency on the part of mental health workers, youth counselors, and developmental psychologists to conceptualize development as an interactive process between the individual person and the psychosocial environment (Gordon and Beyer, 1981).

The runaway-youth shelter was the guiding force in organizing a comprehensive system of treatment for runaways. This system brought an understanding of social consciousness, psychological theory, volunteer efforts, and community activism to runaways, their families, and professional mental health workers. Runaway shelters are temporary youth homes staffed by concerned adults and mental health workers, where runaways can live on a voluntary basis while they sort out their lives. Runaway-youth shelters developed in the wake of the civil rights, antiwar, and hippie movements of the 1960s in communities such as San Francisco's Haight-Ashbury district and in college towns such as Berkeley, California, and Boston-Cambridge, Massachusetts. On the fringes of these youthful protest movements were a number of teenage runaways, sometimes called flower-children and teeny-boppers, who were attracted by the excitement, by the antiestablishment and antiparent rhetoric, and by experimentation with alternative life-styles exhibited in dress, drugs, sexual values, communal living, and humanistic concern for the rights of the oppressed. It soon became obvious that these runaway teens needed food, shelter, health care, emotional support, and someone to help guide them through the obstacles they encountered on the streets. Young activists, street veterans, former runaways, community organizers, citizen volunteers, and mental health workers stepped into this vacuum to create the runaway-youth shelters.

Two of the earliest runaway shelters were founded in 1967: Huckleberry House, in the Haight-Ashbury district of San Francisco (Beggs, 1969), and Project Place, in Summerville-Boston, Massachusetts (Washton, 1974). Project Place started in a one-bedroom apartment in Summerville, Massachusetts. In its first 2 years, the small staff was overwhelmed with runaways, and drew a considerable amount of hostility from the community. It was against the law at that time to harbor a runaway youth. The organization was brought to court on 14 charges of contributing to the delinquency of minors and harboring runaways. Parents of the youths who ran away felt that if there were no runaway shelters, the teenagers would not have run away. The staff was given the choice of leaving the community or going to jail. They chose to leave, and then reopened in a four-story townhouse at the south end of Boston. After moving to Boston, Place developed into a residential shelter, with the capacity to house 12 youths for up to 14 days, and provided individual, family, group, health care, drug, and alcohol counseling. A staff of 13 employees and volunteers performed outreach talks in the community, conducted a 24-hour hot line and referral services, and provided drop-in counseling (National Youth Workers Alliance, 1979). Project Place, a one-time funky antiestablishment agency for kids, is now an established agency offering a comprehensive range of services for runaway youths and their families.

Larry Beggs (1969), one of the founders and directors of San Francisco's Huckleberry House, states that most of the 664 runaways who used Huckleberry House services in its first year left home because of pain and discomfort in the family. Their average age was 15.3 years. Most heard about the shelter on the streets, and eventually over one-half returned home. Beggs concluded that running away is a desperate S.O.S. signal to the family that the runaway young person wants to have his or her feelings honored, would like an increased measure of self-determination, wants to change the family situation, and does not intend to leave the family permanently. Runaways are not just escaping stress, but are taking the initiative to get something done (Walker, 1975).

As the social protest movements of the 1960s wound down, large numbers of runaway youths continued to be on the streets of urban and suburban America. While the runaways of the 1970s and 1980s were not interested in building countercultures, raising consciousness, or revolutionary changes in society, their protests and conflicts seemed to be directed toward their parents, families, and social institutions in their immediate environment. Since many of the runaway shelter's young-adult counselors, volunteers, and mental health workers had participated or been fellow travelers of social protest against dominant-submissive relationships based on age, gender, race, and political and familial power, it was not difficult for them to understand and legitimatize the perspective of runaway youth who felt they were being controlled, suppressed, and abused by their families and other adult-controlled institutions.

In the runaway-home atmosphere in which they were treated with warmth, empathy, positive regard, and respect by counselors who tried to be genuine human beings in relating to them, runaways classified as unmanageable, delinquent, and emotionally disturbed found that they could function within the democratically set limits of the youth shelter. As runaways opened up in group meetings with other runaways, and in individual sessions with counselors, they learned to reassess their views of themselves and their reasons for running away, and to examine alternative ways of coping with family and developmental stresses. Many youths had internalized views of themselves as bad or emotionally unstable, which mirrored the views of their parents. In exchanging experiences with other runaways, they could see that their views and experiences were not unique. Part of the adolescent experience involves confrontations with family and personal value conflicts concerning power, control, sexuality, school performance, choice of friends, dress styles, and morality. During the period of reassessment and self-examination, running away was redefined as a self-initiated, assertive action to cope with a stressful family and social environment. Running away was a first step in coping actively and in defining oneself as a person who would no longer tolerate restrictive, controlling, or abusive family conditions (Gordon, 1981). As the process of reappraisal and self-definition continued, runaway youths could explore new ways of coping and defining themselves.

Without the parents present, it was easy for the counselors and runaway groups to slip into a style of blaming and condemning the family as the sole cause of the runaway's trouble and distress. The early runaway counselors saw themselves as protectors of youth against the oppressive nature of parents, families, social structures, and adolescent institutions. Gradually, however, both runaway youths and their counselors saw a need to meet with the parents to try to work things out. As Gordon (1981) points out, 15- and 16-year-old runaways are dependent on their families legally and economically. At a deeper level, the emotional bonding between parents and their children is one of the strongest human ties. No matter how angry and disappointed adolescents are with their parents, they still want their love and respect.

Runaway counselors and mental health professionals turned to the work of family therapists and family systems theorists to guide them in their counseling sessions with runaways and their families (Satir, 1983). Family systems theorists and family therapists see the family as a social organization with parents and children as interdependent members. In order to function smoothly and to facilitate the psychosocial growth of its members, decisions need to be arrived at through a mutual and collaborative approach based on two-way communication, caring, empathy, shared power, and participatory problem solving. In many runaway families, counselors saw just the opposite. Decisions were arrived at autocratically, communication had a hostile, devaluative, and defensive flavor, and attempts at mutual problem-solving discussions tended to escalate into accusations and counter-accusations usually centering on the adolescent's deficiencies.

Runaway counselors learned to assist families in searching for a common constructive language members could use to articulate their concerns by taking on a collective responsibility for collaborative decision making. In this type of family atmosphere, differences of opinion or behaviors, such as running away, can be perceived as a catalyst or challenge for creative change and movement toward consensus, rather than as evidence of pathology of one or more family members. Family members can learn to disagree without becoming bitter enemies.

The runaway family mediation-counseling model, outlined by Palmer and Patterson (1981), contains five interrelated components: (1) decreasing emotional intensity, (2) improving communication, (3) reestablishing loving feelings, (4) increasing youth independence and responsibility and lessening overprotectiveness, and (5) constructive problem solving.

1. *Decreasing emotional intensity*. At the point in time when running away occurs, negative emotions within the family, such as anger, hostility, hurt, rejection, and disappointment, are generally at their peak. Before parents and youths can communicate or relate to each other in a more positive fashion, it is necessary to decrease the intensity of negative emotions. Time is a critical variable. By the time the adolescent arrives at the runaway shelter and the parents are called, emotions have had a chance to cool off a bit. Further reduction of emotional intensity can be accomplished by having runaways and parents talk to counselors individually in order to ventilate their feelings before beginning family sessions.

2. *Improving communication*. This step can be accomplished by demonstrating, to family members, active listening skills such as summarizing, paraphrasing, clarifying, empathy, and accurately reflecting feelings. A simple technique many counselors use in family sessions is to encourage family members to rephrase what has been communicated by the previous speaker, to the satisfaction of the previous speaker, before giving their response. Other constructive listening techniques include avoiding quick, pat solutions, advice giving, put-downs, and criticism. Providing clear feedback to let family members know you are listening, owning one's feelings rather than blaming others, and not engaging in threats to withdraw love when there are disagreements, are also ways to improve communication. By listening empathically and nonjudgmentally, the counselor serves as a positive communication role model for family members to emulate in moving away from a communication style based on threats, counterthreats, accusations, defensiveness, and criticism.

3. *Reestablishing loving feelings*. Beneath the angry, hostile feelings

that preceded the running away, most families have, at some time, experienced positive and caring feelings toward each other. These positive feelings often get lost in the power struggles that surround family turmoil. In order to reactivate caring feelings, the counselor should encourage positive emotional sharing. Many families of runaways are briefly stunned when counselors ask, "When was the last time you've hugged each other or said I care?"

4. *Increasing youth independence and responsibility and lessening overprotectiveness.* This is one of the most difficult steps for many families caught up in a struggle for power and dominance over their teenager's behavior. If young people are going to eventually take charge of their lives and define their own identity and individuality, they must have the opportunity to gradually start making their own decisions. Running away is a signal that the balance of power has shifted (Gordon, 1981). The adolescent is no longer willing to acquiesce passively to parental control. The act of running away can be used as a catalyst for constructive confrontation and change, and can influence the way power and control are exercised within the family. As communication and positive sharing improve and emotional intensity decreases, it is easier for families to calmly discuss and define areas where youths should have the major say in what happens—e.g., dress, hair styles, and choice of friends. The goal in increasing youth responsibility and lessening overprotectiveness is to move away from a parent-centered decision-making style toward one based on mutual and participatory interaction. At the other extreme are extremely permissive parents. In these cases, parents need to understand that youths need help and support in learning to establish values and make their own decisions.

5. *Constructive problem solving.* When families have succeeded in improving communication, in sharing loving feelings, in decreasing the intensity of negative emotions, and in lessening overprotectiveness, they can begin to examine ways of problem solving that involve mutual decision making, negotiations, and identifying common goals. Many family problem-solving attempts break down because the members are unable to communicate common goals. For example, a 16-year-old runaway and her father got into a series of heated arguments when he refused to let her work in a fast-food establishment located in a high-crime area near their neighborhood. When the counselor helped the family sort out the issues, the parents agreed that wanting a job was a positive step in their daughter's development. Once the positive features of wanting a job were clarified, the family could focus its energies on discussing what sorts of jobs were available and where they were located.

To briefly summarize, as runaway-youth shelters gained more experience in working with troubled and distressed runaway youths, the treatment approach that developed represented a combination of individual, group, and family therapy. The goal is to help runaway youths reassess their reasons for running away, redefine themselves in a more positive manner, and develop a wider range of coping and social competency skills to handle the problems of family living and the developmental demands of adolescence. Running away is defined as an assertive act that can trigger a process of self-affirmation, adaptive coping, and personal and familial growth. Since family conflict appears to be the major reason associated with running away, and since most runaways ultimately return to live with their families, family counseling-mediation is a central feature of runaway treatment. After a period of 14 to 30 days in a runaway shelter treatment program with family, individual, and group therapy, and some follow-up or aftercare, most runaways, when reunited with their families, can look back on running away as a positive growth experience that resulted in higher self-esteem, reduced family conflict, and improved coping skills (Gordon, 1981).

CONGRESSIONAL ACTS: FUNDING OF RUNAWAY-YOUTH SHELTERS AND DECRIMINALIZATION OF RUNNING AWAY

In 1974 Congress passed the Runaway Youth Act (later amended to the Runaway and Homeless Youth Act) authorizing funding for runaway shelters and recommended that state and local jurisdictions no longer arrest, detain, and process runaway teenagers through the juvenile justice system. Congress was spurred into action by the serial mass murders of 27 runaway teenage males in Houston, in 1973, and by advocacy on the part of the early runaway-youth shelters. Elmer Wayne Henley was convicted of the Houston slayings. He and a 33-year-old accomplice, Dean Allan Corll, who was killed by Henley in an argument, befriended runaway youths, exploited them for sexual purposes, and subsequently killed many of them. He buried their bodies in groves around the Houston area (Mann, 1983). A few years later, in 1979, another mass murderer, John Wayne Gacy, a Chicago contractor, precinct level politician, and part-time clown, was convicted of killing 30 young males in a series of homosexual torture episodes. Many of Gacy's victims were runaways whose bodies were found buried under the crawl space beneath his home (Sullivan and Maiken, 1984).

The $10 million appropriated by Congress in the Runaway Youth Act was used to fund approximately 166 youth shelters. Hot lines and crisis services were also supported. The financial support was badly needed; the few runaway shelters in existence were struggling along on small grants, local charities, and volunteer contributions of staff time and money. The 166 shelters, with an average capacity of 8–10 beds, could house approximately 2,000 runaways for short-term stays of 14–30 days. Within 24-72 hours after runaways arrive in the runaway shelter, their parents are contacted, and within 30 days, young people have to make a decision whether to go home or to seek out a long-term alternative solution, such as a youth home, foster home, or residential school. Entry and departure in runaway shelters are voluntary.

Tough Love, a parent organization that believes in firm, fair, clearly stated limits on teenagers, operates its own network of runaway shelters. After warning teenagers of the consequences, Tough Love encourages parents to lock the door behind repeat or difficult runaways until they promise to change. Runaway youths are given a list of other Tough Love parents who will provide shelter. Substitute Tough Love parents expect runaway youths to conform to the rules of their household (Mann, 1983; York et al., 1983).

In 1982 Congress increased the funding from $10 million annually to $21 million. Most of the money goes into shelters, 24-hour drop-in counseling, crisis services, hot lines, and referral systems (Langway, 1982). The national hot line numbers are listed in Table 3-2. There are now over 500 runaway-youth shelters and facilities funded by public and private sources with a nationwide capacity of 6,000 runaways (Hopkins, 1983).

In 1983–84 runaway shelters provided at least one night of shelter to approximately 50,000 youths — 27,000 females and 23,000 males. The shelters provided additional services to 101,000 nonsheltered youths and responded to 171,900 hot line calls and contacts. The average rate of positive resolution, defined as reuniting youth with their families, placing them in a foster care or group home, or helping them to attain independent living arrangements, was 57% (Bucy, 1985). Half of the youths served were between 15 and 16 and the majority were females (Services to Runaways, 1984). While the number of runaway youths served by the shelter seems impressive, it must be remembered that there are 2,500 to 3,000 new runaways each day (Thornberg, 1982). One runaway center in Tucson, Arizona, turned away 16,000 runaway youth in 1984 (Hawkins, 1985).

Over the years, runaway shelters have adapted to fit the needs of the local populations and changing demographics. A large percentage of minority youths find their way into runaway houses in urban areas. Since female runaways make up 56% to 60% of the runaway population, many runaway shelters offer special programs designed to meet the concerns and conflicts of adolescent females growing up in a society where the role of women is

Table 3-2. National Runaway Hot Line Numbers

1. 1-800-621-4000—24-hour, toll-free, National Runaway Switchboard in Chicago, Illinois.
2. 1-800-231-6946—24-hour, toll-free hot line sponsored by Operation Peace of Mind in Houston, Texas.

undergoing major changes. Specialized counseling programs exist to assist rape and incest victims (Gordon, 1981).

In recommending the decriminalization of running away, Congress noted that over 50% of the juveniles being detained in many states and local jurisdictions were guilty of nothing more than the offense of running away. In some cases, the detained runaway youths were actually throwaways, pushouts, and castaways who had been asked to leave or who were being physically and sexually abused by their parents. Congress was also aware of the repeated observation that placing runaway youths experiencing family conflicts, as well as other status offenders, into the juvenile justice system increases the probability that they will be arrested again in the future.

The other half of the delinquency-pathology model was also about to undergo a change. In the 1987 edition of the *Diagnostic and Statistical Manual of Mental Disorders*, published by the American Psychiatric Association (DSM-III-R, 1987), running away was no longer classified as a separate distinct category of mental disorder. Running away is now one of the criteria for conduct disorders. The pattern of running away must involve two runaways where the teenager stays away from home overnight or once without returning.

The events leading up to the passage of the Runaway Youth Act, the mass murders, and cooperation between runaway shelter advocates and Congress, illustrate how a behavior that was considered to be deviant can be brought into the normal range of adolescent behavior for treatment within a non-pathological framework. The shelters, which started as an underground, quasi-legitimate alternative to juvenile and psychiatric detention facilities, were given a stamp of approval by Congress, reflecting the growing belief that runaways are neither delinquent nor sick and should not be treated as such (Moses, 1978).

LONG-TERM RUNAWAY-YOUTH HOMES

After a 14- to 30-day stay in a shelter, some runaways and their families jointly or individually decide that the runaway is not going to return home. In a few cases, even after a 30-day period of intensive counseling, the degree of alienation is too severe, old conflicts about issues of control and independence cannot be sufficiently resolved, or the residual feelings from abuse and rejection are too strong for the healing process to begin. In other cases, the parents may not have worked out alcohol, drug, divorce, economic, or adult transition issues to the point where they feel comfortable having the runaway adolescent in their residence. To fill this void, runaway-youth counselors and mental health workers developed alternative living residences in the form of youth homes, group foster homes, and supervised apartment living. A youth home or group foster home is a specially designated residence for former runaways who have decided not to return home or who cannot return home because of continuing parental alienation. Residents of youth homes are usually not wards of the courts as dependent children or under the supervision of the courts for delinquency. One of the paradoxes of the Runaway Youth Act reforms is that the decriminalization of status offenses created a gap in residential placement services for youths who cannot, or will not, live at home. Youth homes and group foster homes were created as alternatives to traditional youth institutions such as juvenile justice system facilities, psychiatric hospitals, and foster homes where the house parents had neither the training nor the desire to work with assertive youth who were not under the supervision of the courts (Gordon, 1981).

A youth home or group foster home usually consists of four to six former runaways who are supervised on a 24-your basis by specially trained house parents and counselors. The focus in these alternative living systems is on developing the transitional skills needed to function successfully in the adult world. The goals for youth homes were developed to coincide with adolescent psychosocial-developmental tasks such as: (1) moving from dependence to independence, (2) getting along comfortably with peers, (3) preparing for a vocation, developing marketable skills, or continuing one's education, and (4) adjusting to sexual maturity (Berlin, 1981).

Youth are encouraged to learn the day-to-day survival skills involved in applying for and interviewing for jobs, budgeting money and financial management, developing a social support network of nondelinquent peers, good work habits, goal setting, and personal, mental, and physical health care. Households are run according to participatory democracy, and residents are expected to abide by household rules, obey the laws and customs of the community, and respect the rights of others. The use of drugs and sexual interaction on the premises is generally taboo.

Counselors and house parents are expected to be able to understand the pressures on young people who are growing up without the day-to-day support of their natural parents; they are also expected to have a profound belief that with supportive guidance, troubled and distressed adolescents can, despite occasional setbacks, figure out their destiny. Adolescents are encouraged to stay in touch with their parents and keep working on moving toward adult-to-adult relationships with their parents. Huckleberry House in San Francisco, the Bridge Program in Boston, and Covenant House in New York have developed long-term group homes or group foster homes for runaway youth.

In circumstances where youth and their parents cannot be reconciliated, even after 6 months to a year has passed, a dozen or more states allow teenagers to become emancipated from their parents (Langway, 1981). Emancipation is a process where youths between the ages of 16–18 can be legally separated or divorced from their parents and guaranteed the right to live independently, engage in contracts, and work for a living. Usually the parents must consent, or at least acquiesce. In making decisions on emancipation issues, juvenile judges take into consideration the adolescent's level of psychosocial maturity and survival skills as demonstrated by job skills, work history, money management, completion of high school or passing the high school's equivalency exam, future educational and vocational plans, absence of arrests during the past year, and no current history of alcohol abuse. Since emotional and psychological feelings for parents do not end when youths are legally emancipated, the process of building an adult-to-adult relationship between parents and emancipated adolescents should not be discouraged.

Many youth do not go through the refinements of the legal process to become emancipated. In America's cities and suburban areas, there are thousands of teenagers who are self-emancipated or quasi-emancipated from their parents. They no longer live at home, they support themselves economically, and they have their own support networks. Not all these long-term runaways and homeless youth are living in the streets and stealing, selling drugs, or doing prostitution for a living. Some are very enterprising, resourceful, and resilient when it comes to making it on their own.

RUNAWAY PREVENTION

There are two types of runaway prevention. The first is reducing the number of runaways. The second is reducing the abuse and exploitation of runaways once they are out on the streets. While these two types of runway prevention are interrelated, we will separate them for discussion purposes.

Prevention I: Reducing the Number of Runaways

Since the reasons for running away usually involve family dynamics in terms of conflict, alienation or stress, programs aimed at reducing the number of runaways should concentrate on strengthening relationships and improving understanding between parents and adolescents. Psychoeducational, wellness, and preventive mental health services, augmented by community forums, workshops, magazine and newspaper articles, and TV and radio programs addressed to parent–adolescent issues are powerful tools that can be used to facilitate a better understanding of runaway centers for adolescents. It offers rap sessions and in-depth individual counseling to assist parents with personal problems and adolescent issues. Child care is provided for children under 10 when parents are using the facility (Thornberg, 1982).

In order to cope with family stresses and conflicts that generate runaway behavior, adolescents need assistance in improving their self-image, and in expanding their base of social-competency skills. Through high school classes in the applied principles of mental health and workshops conducted by youth organizations, adolescents can be provided with opportunities to examine how they resolve conflicts with their parents, how they sort out their values, how they establish their goals and priorities, and how they build support systems. Adolescents who know how to develop a range of options with respect to appraisal and reappraisal of family conflicts, problem-solving skills, stress reduction, and support building are less likely to rely solely on running away as a problem-solving or stress-reducing mechanism. A large percentage of potential runaways who have received preventive counseling from runaway shelters and youth counseling services decide not to run away (Loveless, 1981a,b).

Adolescents and parents need practice working together in active listening, positive sharing and affirmation, collaborative decision making, mutual problem solving, communicating clearly without resorting to accusations and counter-accusations, and understanding each other's differentness. Parent-teen workshops using psychodrama, role-playing, vignettes, and films can dramatically cause conflictual issues — e.g., dating, dress styles, sexual issues, curfew, discipline, runaway threats, and values — to surface.

Providing preventive psychoeducational and mental health services to families and adolescents will require an expansion of advocacy and coordination efforts in many communities. Traditionally, mental health and social services have been organized around the needs of adults and children under 12. Services to adolescents were primarily downward extensions of adult services or upward extensions of children services. There was a deficit in terms of a well-organized network of counseling, employment, medical and preventive mental health services designed specifically for adolescents and their families. Runaway-youth shelters funded by the Runaway and Homeless Youth Act have attempted to remedy this deficiency in adolescent services by moving beyond their original mandate to provide temporary shelter and crisis counseling. In many communities, the original runaway shelters have expanded their role to provide a well-organized network of preventive counseling, referral, and advocacy services. A well-coordinated network of adolescent services also helps identify families at risk. Families at risk are families in which parent problems, such as excessive alcohol and drug use, mental illness, physical disabilities, chronic unemployment, or a past history of child abuse, suggest a need for special assistance in order to prevent destructive parent–adolescent interaction. In some states, these families are designated as Families With Service Needs and special assistance is provided (Adams and Gullotta, 1983).

Prevention II: Reducing the Risk of Exploitation and Abuse to Runaways on the Streets

In spite of the best prevention efforts, young people will continue to run away in large numbers. Running away is a historical and contemporary fact of life. When teenagers perceive no other feasible options and have made the decision to run away, Loveless (1981a,b) and other runaway experts suggest they take several steps to protect themselves. First, they should consider staying temporarily at the home of friends or relatives. Sometimes, after a brief cooling-off period, intrafamilial conflicts that seemed unmanageable are more amenable to problem solving, constructive communication, negotiations, and collaborative decision making. Second, runaways should have a plan. Most runaways leave home impulsively without money, a clearly thought out destination, or any knowledge of runaway resources. Teenagers who are thinking about running away should accumulate a reasonable amount of money, leave some of it with friends to reduce the risk of robbery or loss, and know the location and phone numbers of runaway shelters and hot lines (including the national hot lines) in areas where they may be headed. These numbers should be listed in teen discos, hangouts, bus stations, high schools, youth hostels, and other places where they are easily accessible. Runaways who know about shelters tend to use them (Loveless, 1981a,b). Third, once on the streets, runaways should be wary of strangers, especially older males offering promises of food, shelter, and support. There are people out on the streets waiting to exploit inexperienced teenagers economically, physically, and sexually. Fourth, if at all possible, teenagers should try not to burn their bridges behind them. Since most runaways eventually return home, making a bad situation worse before leaving will not help the reconciliation process. Fifth, runaway teenagers should let a trusted friend know where they are, or call friends from time to time for news about their families. Life-threatening family emergencies can occur. Not being in touch with one's family during catastrophic events such as a heart attack or the sudden death of a family member can leave lasting scars of guilt and shame. Finally, when runaway teenagers decide to return home, they should contact agencies such as the Traveler's Aid Society, which has representatives located in airline, bus, and train stations. Trailways Bus Service offers runaway youths free rides back home. The Trailways program requires a runaway youth receive their parents' permission to return home and verification of their status as runaways by the police (Banks, 1984).

SUMMARY AND CONCLUSIONS

Runaways were defined in this chapter as youths between the ages of 10 and 17 who leave home overnight without parent permission. Approximately 1.4 million teenagers run away annually. It has been estimated that 1 in 8 youths between the ages of 12 and 18 will run away. Runaways represent an ethnic and economic cross-section of America's teenagers. The average age of runaways is between 15 and 16. Some youths classified as runaways are actually push-outs, throwaways, or castaways. These are youths who have been rejected, abandoned, thrown out, asked to leave by their parents, or driven out because of physical and sexual abuse. Of youths generally classified as runaways, 40% to 50% are actually push-outs and throwaways. Running away has been characterized as adventure seeking, as a way of escaping from oppressive conditions, as delinquent-pathological behavior, and as an assertive first step in dealing with family conflict. Prior to 1974, runaway treatment programs were guided by the delinquency-pathology approach. Runaway youths were apprehended by juvenile authorities, confined in juvenile detention centers, and forced to undergo psychological counseling and treatment as a condition of probation. In the 1970s and 1980s, running away was decriminalized, and, to some extent, "depathologized." Contemporary mental health workers redefined running away as an assertive first step in coping with family and developmental conflicts. The Runaway and Homeless Youth Act recommended that runaway youths no longer be confined within the juvenile justice system and funded voluntary runaway shelters as an alternative to involuntary confinement. After a 14- to 30-day period of group, individual, and family counseling, youths and their families must decide if the runaway is to return home, seek placement in a long-term foster or youth home, or enter a residential school. Some states allow youths to become officially emancipated from parents so they can legally live on their own, but most runaway youths eventually return home.

The primary reasons for running away involve family conflict around issues such as individuality, independence, and lack of support and understanding. Current treatment approaches rely on a combination of individual, group, and family counseling. Family counseling was described in terms of a family mediation model.

Two types of runaway prevention were discussed. The first type of runaway prevention aims at reducing the number of runaways by strengthening adolescent-family mental health services, and by providing psychoeducational and wellness services, such as workshops, conferences, community forums, newspaper and magazine articles, and TV programs to increase the awareness of issues confronting adolescents and their families. The second type of runaway prevention is designed to reduce the exploitation and abuse of runaway youths once they are out on the streets. These programs are directed toward ensuring that runaway youths know about the available resources, such as hot lines and shelters, and have some plan of action before they leave home, which will help them survive while they are away.

In conclusion, the problems encountered in working with adolescent runaways have forced the American society to reconsider several major issues involving the juvenile justice system, adolescent legal and human rights, adolescent psychological development and coping styles, adolescent mental health and treatment approaches, and the emancipation of adolescents. As we conclude this chapter, five issues are briefly addressed. First, to what extent should adolescent status offenders, such as runaways, be incarcerated in juvenile detention facilities; to what extent should they be forced to undergo counseling to make them conform to adult expectations with respect to school attendance and performance, dress styles, curfew, sexual behavior, alcohol, and the like. The direction of the courts has been to decriminalize and to deinstitutionalize juvenile status offenses. In place of confinement and involuntary mental health services, adolescent status offenders, such as runaways, are now being offered growth opportunities in the form of voluntary counseling, job training, health services, and alternative home placements.

Second, the counseling, psychotherapy, and psychoeducational approaches utilized in working with adolescent runaways, which emphasized self-esteem building, adaptive coping, social competence, and collaborative family decision making, can be applied to a wide range of adolescent growth issues because they are congruent with the basic principles of adolescent psychosocial development. These growth-enhancing approaches can be adapted to assist adolescents in coping with the expected interpersonal, intrapersonal, social, and situational conflicts they will encounter in the process of moving from childhood to adulthood.

Third, the runaway problem brought to the surface the absence of adolescent-focused counseling and preventive mental health facilities in many communities. Runaway-youth counselors were instrumental as advocates in developing a more comprehensive, well-coordinated package of mental health services designed specifically to cope with the psychosocial needs of adolescents and their families. Fourth, the problems of sexual, physical, and emotional abuse experienced by many castaways, push-outs, and throwaways helps society become aware of the fact that child abuse is not confined to children below the age of 12.

Finally, the presence of thousands of self-emancipated runaways and abandoned and homeless youths on the streets of America has made us think about long-term alternative home placement and how to help these young people develop the economic and social skills as well as the legal support they need to function independently. The notion that nearly all youths can or will live with their parents or guardians until they become legally self-sufficient young adults is a myth that needs to be addressed economically, legally, and sociologically.

SUGGESTIONS FOR PARENTS, TEACHERS, COUNSELORS, AND YOUTH WORKERS

1. Since running away generally involves conflict surrounding independence and individuality on the one hand, and support and affirmation on the other hand, parents should strive to achieve a balance between providing adolescents with additional areas of freedom, emotional support, and understanding.
2. Notice early warning signs of runaway behavior and family turmoil such as cutting school, staying out late, breaking household rules, and frequent arguments with threats and counter-threats.
3. Assertive challenges to parental authority and struggling with conflicting choices are part of normal, adolescent identity development. Parents should try to use these occurrences as a signal for changing from an autocratic to a collaborative parent–adolescent decision-making style.
4. The peer group is very important to mid-teenagers as a source of support, recognition and understanding, and as a sounding board; parents should provide enough space and time so teenagers can interact with their friends.
5. Get into discussion groups with other parents of teenagers. Discussion groups can provide support, help parents ventilate frustrating feelings, and generate problem-solving ideas.
6. Parents need to look at the mid-life and early mid-life adult transition issues confronting themselves, their mates, and their significant others, and ask how these issues might be contributing to parent-adolescent turmoil.

DISCUSSION QUESTIONS

1. What are the two primary areas of family conflict or adolescent-parent conflict involved in running away, and what can parents and adolescents do to resolve these conflicts?
2. What changes in society during the past generation need to be considered in explaining the large number of female runaways?
3. Why does runaway behavior seem to peak between the ages of 15 and 16?
4. What is likely to happen to runaways once they are out on the streets for an extended period of time without skills, money, or place to stay?
5. How have the mental health and law enforcement models used in working with runaways changed over the past 20 years?
6. Discuss three major events, specific and general, that were responsible for changes in runaway-treatment models, and how have these events contributed to these changes.
7. Describe the major goals and components of the family mediation model used to work with runaway youths and their families.
8. Describe two types of preventive models used in working with runaway youths and their families.

4
Depression

PREVIEW

Depression is characterized by gloom, low self-esteem, dejection, downcast feelings, foreboding, helplessness, lack of energy, and loss of interest in usual activities. Historical references to depression extend back as far as biblical times. Depression has been described in poetry, literature, and in the biographies of many famous people. Mild-to-moderate depression is a common occurrence in adolescents. The primary symptoms of depression are classified as mood, cognitive, motivational-behavioral, and physical-vegetative clusters. DSM-III-R (1987) criteria for depression are presented. Depression is a generic term that can be analyzed along a continuum ranging from sadness and the blues through chronic, severe depression. Scales for assessing depression are reported. In the section on etiology, the causes and dynamics as well as psychodynamic, cognitive, learned helplessness, and behavioral models of depression are examined. Females tend to report depression more often than males. Differences in male-female rates of depression are explained in terms of divergent socialization practices concerning power and control, management of feelings, and relationship orientations. Late adolescents are more likely to show discernible symptoms of depression than are early adolescents because of differences in introspective, reflective, and self-analytical abilities.

Three approaches to psychotherapy with depressed adolescents are presented: cognitive, client-centered relationship, and psychodynamic. While approaches to psychotherapy can be differentiated for purposes of discussion, there is often considerable overlap among approaches in real-life treatment situations. Antidepressant drugs, such as the tricyclics, can be helpful

111

in working with depressed adolescents, although the use of antidepressants with adolescents is a controversial topic. The chapter concludes with a discussion of the adaptive possibilities in depression.

Case Example 4-1: Ellen, Part I

Ellen is a 16-year-old high school junior who was referred to a psychologist by her family physician with problems of depression and low self-esteem. For the past 6 months, Ellen has become increasingly despondent. She cries frequently, feels sad and dejected, is highly self-critical, ruminates about what she perceives as past mistakes, doesn't think she has what it takes to accomplish future goals in school, and is withdrawing from family, friends, and social activities. In the initial interviews with Ellen and her mother, the following picture of Ellen's situation emerged. Despite being an honor-roll student, holding a part-time job, and sharing responsibility for the care of her 13-year-old brother, Ellen described herself as lazy, not working hard enough, and not "a very good person." She was losing interest in school, dreaded going to her part-time job as a clerk-receptionist in a law office, and was avoiding her boyfriend and peers. She had to push herself to get out of bed in the morning, slept a lot, but felt tired most of the time. Her family physician reports that she is in good physical health. She spends a lot of time alone. When she is alone, she cries frequently, ruminates about past events, and worries about the future. She is not sure she has the ability to go to college, despite her excellent grades. Sometimes she thinks that life is too much of a struggle. Ellen denies any active suicidal plans, but admits that she occasionally thinks about dying as a way to get away from all the "hassles and unhappiness."

Ellen could not remember any specific events such as major disappointments, failures, or losses that might have triggered her feelings of despondency and downheartedness. Ellen said her relationship with her mother, which was never very good, was getting worse. Ellen felt her mother was too busy with work and her adult friends to spend time with Ellen and her brother. Her 13-year-old brother was becoming rebellious and would no longer obey her. Ellen perceived her brother's rebelliousness as her fault for not being a positive role model.

Ellen's parents were divorced when she was approximately 9 years old. The divorce was preceded by a period of angry arguments and turmoil between her parents. Ellen said that her world "fell apart" when her parents were divorced. She described herself as "daddy's girl." For a long time following the divorce, Ellen hoped that her parents would get back together. She now realizes that a reconciliation will never happen; however, she still "wishes" it would, "so we can all be a family again." She worries about her father working too hard, not exercising or eating properly, dating too much, and sometimes drinking excessively. Ellen claims, "he needs me to take care of him."

Ellen is losing interest in her boyfriend and in her peers. She says her girlfriends only talk about dating, sex, and abortions. She thinks there must be "more to life" than the concerns of her girlfriends. She thinks her boyfriend is getting tired of her being down in the dumps all the time, and she wouldn't be surprised if he left her. They have been "dating steady" for a year. Her boyfriend has been pressuring her for sex. Ellen says she isn't against teen sex, but thinks that sex should be part of a committed relationship. She isn't sure she is willing to make that kind of commitment at this time.

Psychological assessment revealed that Ellen's intellectual abilities were in the superior range. She has an excellent command of words. Her skills in quantitative and conceptual reasoning are highly developed. Her preoccupation with personal concerns (which Ellen said were family, school, boyfriend, and "other things I don't want to talk about now") occasionally interfered with sustained concentration.

A review of Ellen's psychotherapy will be presented later in this chapter.

GENERAL DESCRIPTION, STATISTICS, AND HISTORICAL REFERENCES

Depression is characterized by profound sadness, gloom, dejection, despondency, futility, sullenness, brooding, self-deprecation, low self-worth, pessimism, foreboding, loss of interest in usual activities, and a lack of energy. The zest goes out of living. Depressed teenagers feel dispirited, "bummed out," discouraged, and unhappy. They have trouble finding any sense of joy, optimism, hope, or excitement in their lives. Existence takes on a quality of darkness, gloom, and doom.

Mild-to-moderate depression is a fairly common experience during adolescence. Depressive themes, such as heartache, sadness, loneliness, pining, gloom, and dejection, are very prominent in the lyrics of the music on radio stations with large adolescent audiences. Forty to fifty percent of adolescents report experiencing moderate-to-severe symptoms of depression (Achenbach and Edelbrock, 1981; Albert and Beck, 1975). One-third to one-half of adolescents who visit mental health clinics display symptoms of depression such as crying spells, self-deprecation, despondency, and suicidal thoughts (Kimmel and Weiner, 1985).

Twenty-five to thirty percent of college students experience psychological distress associated with depression, such as feeling blue, sad, discouraged, downhearted, unhappy, and hopeless (Rosehan and Seligman, 1984). Depression seems to increase with age and is more prevalent in late adolescence than it is in early adolescence or childhood. Only one in nine 10-year-olds reports feelings of despondency, moodiness, and self-deprecation (Rutter et al., 1986). Depression occurs more often in females; two to three times as many females as males report episodes of depression (Weiner, 1980; Fuhrmann, 1986).

The symptoms of depression or melancholia appear throughout history, across cultures, and in all walks of life. References to depression are noted in the bible and in the early writings of Chinese, Egyptian, Hebrew, and Greek scholars. Depressive themes, such as futility, gloom, dejection, self-deprecation, and suicide, are prominent in the Book of Job. The term melancholia was derived by Hippocrates, around 400 B.C., from the Greek word *melan* to signify the blackness and bleakness of depressive moods. Robert Burton in his book, *The Anatomy of Melancholy*, written in 1621 under the name of Democritis Junior, presented a vivid literary portrait of the symptoms of depression. Descriptions of the sadness, despair, futility, and self-doubt of depression appear in the works of Shakespeare, Dostoevski, Poe, Hemingway, Kierkegaard, and Goethe. Famous historical figures such as Moses, Rousseau, Queen Victoria, Lincoln, Robert E. Lee, Churchill, and Freud suffered from episodes of depression. Profound sadness, gloom, sorrow, and melancholia are projected in the paintings of Vincent Van Gogh. The gloom, dejection, and foreboding of depression are reflected in poetry by metaphors of winters of sorrow, nights of discontent, and the heartbreak of unrequited love. Conversely, upbeat feelings, such as joy, optimism, and hope, are projected by images of the spring of joy, the dawn of hope, and the heart fluttering with love (Coleman et al., 1984; Wetzel, 1984).

Depression has been treated by burning, blood letting, whipping, hypnosis, spirit soothing, music, exortation, hot baths, and electroshock therapy (Rosenfeld, 1985). Depression has been attributed to curses, witchcraft, devil possession, and evil thoughts. Depression or melancholia was a key element in the development of modern psychiatry and clinical psychology. The diagnosis and treatment of depression are major topics in the works of Benjamin Rush, Emil Kraeplin, and Adolph Meyer. John Charot, Pierre Janet, Joseph Breuer, and Sigmund Freud, in their early writings, associated depression with hysteria in women. Hysteria and depression were thought to be caused by sexual repression and psychophysiological disturbances in the womb. Modern psychologists and mental health workers attribute the causes of depression to loss, erroneous beliefs, and faulty social learning (White and Watt, 1981; Wetzel, 1984).

Until two decades ago, depression was thought to be primarily an adult phenomenon. Reservations about diagnosing depression in children and adolescents were based on clinical and theoretical grounds (Carlson and Garber, 1986). Children were thought to lack the internalized conscience necessary for experiencing the shame, guilt, self-doubt, hopelessness, and negative self-evaluation that are part of depression. It was generally held that depression-like symptoms were part of the normal storms and stresses of adolescence; therefore depression could not be diagnosed separately in adolescents. Still others held that depression in adolescents was expressed through behavioral equivalents such as angry outbursts, defiance of authority, restlessness, school difficulties, promiscuity, and general behavioral problems.

Now, there is a growing consensus that adolescents and older children can show the major mood, cognitive, motivational, and physical signs of depression. DSM-III-R (1987), *The Diagnostic and Statistical Manual of Mental Disorders* of the American Psychiatric Association allows the depression diagnosis to be used for adults, adolescents, and children. Minor variations do occur, but the basic symptoms defining depression are approximately the same from late childhood to adulthood (Puig-Antich, 1986). In some cases, early adolescents and children defend themselves against crying, sadness, self-deprecation, and hopelessness, which are symptoms of depression, by utilizing restlessness, aggressive behavior, boredom, temper tantrums, or excessive involvement in activities and people. The symptoms of depression are actually present, but are hidden or masked by the adolescent's reluctance to share personal experience (Weiner, 1974).

PRIMARY DEPRESSION

The major symptoms of depression are divided into four symptom clusters: (1) mood, (2) cognition, (3) behavioral-motivational, and (4) physical-vegetative (Beck, 1972, 1978; Kaslow and Rehm, 1983).

I. Mood-emotional-affective
   1. Profound sadness, despondency, gloom, blue, low, heavy-hearted, downcast, somber, woe, sullen, dejected
   2. Zest and joy go out of living
II. Cognitive patterns, thoughts, and beliefs
   1. Poor self-concept, self-devaluation, self-criticism, self-deprecation, excessive guilt, and shame
   2. Belief that others don't care or that one is not worth caring about
   3. Sense of foreboding, doom, hopelessness, and futility about the future
   4. Overgeneralization of negative events
   5. Belief that one is not attractive or desirable
III. Motivational-behavioral
   1. Low energy, can't get started, person feels stuck, can't fight back
   2. Difficulty concentrating or engaging in activities that require sustained concentration, indecisiveness
   3. Withdrawal from social activities
   4. Loss of interest in fun activities, dating, partying, work, hobbies
   5. Loss of interest in daily activities
IV. Physical-vegetative
   1. Irregular eating, sleep disturbances, little interest in romance or love-making
   2. Excessive fatigue, person tires easily, slowing down of psychomotor activity

Mood and cognitive symptoms are the key features of depression. Depressed adolescents feel a pervasive sense of despondency and express negative beliefs about themselves, their experiences, and the future. The

DSM-III-R (1987) criteria for depression, listed in Table 4-1, correspond to the mood, cognitive, motivational-behavioral, and physical-vegetative symptoms described above. DSM-III-R (1987) criteria can be used for adolescents, adults, and children.

Depression has a self-sustaining, self-defeating quality, and has been described as a vicious cycle that seems unending. Once an adolescent is depressed, new experiences tend to filter through the gloom and doom of negative beliefs and despondent feelings. No matter how bright the day, how many compliments one receives, or what goals are accomplished, the depressed person finds some flaw or reason for self-criticism. The more one looks for gloom and doom, the easier it is to find. The more one believes that things will turn out bad and refuses to try, the greater the likelihood that things will turn out bad. Time seems to have an unending quality when one is depressed. A week of depression seems like a month. Even when one rationally knows that sadness and hopelessness will pass, time seems forever.

The Depression Spectrum

Depression is a generic term that can be ordered along a continuum into four distinguishable reactions; the blues, grief, reactive depression, and endogenous depression (Goldstein et al., 1980). The blues are mild, transient, emotional lows, moodiness, sadness, or downheartedness caused by specific experiences such as memories of good times with a former boyfriend or

Table 4-1. DSM-III-R (1987)[a] Criteria for Major Depressive Episode

The major DSM-III-R symptom of depression is dysphoric mood. Dysphoric mood is characterized by sadness, gloom, hopelessness, despondency, downheartedness, as well as a loss of interest in pleasurable activities, almost all usual activities, and past times. The dysphoric mood or mood disturbance must be prominent and relatively persistent. In addition to depressed mood or loss of interest in pleasure, four of the following eight symptoms need to be present daily, for a period of at least 2 weeks, and represent a change from previous level of functioning:

1. Appetite disturbance characterized by decrease or increase in appetite nearly everyday or significant weight loss or gain when not dieting.
2. Sleep disturbance: Not falling asleep initially, not returning to sleep after awakening in the middle of the night, early morning awakenings, or in some depressed patients, a desire to sleep a great deal of the time.
3. Shift in activity level, becoming either lethargic or agitated.
4. Loss of interest and pleasure in usual activities.
5. Loss of energy, excessive fatigue.
6. Negative self-concept, self-reproach and self-blame, feelings of worthlessness and guilt.
7. Complaints or evidence of difficulty in concentrating such as slow thinking and indecisiveness.
8. Recurring thoughts of suicide or death.
9. Psychomotor retardation or agitation. Others observe restlessness or a slowing down of movements and motor activities.

[a]Adapted from: American Psychiatric Association. (1987). Diagnostic and statistical manual of mental disorders (3rd ed., rev.). Washington, D.C.

girlfriend, having a bad day, getting a poor grade on a test, or by the general ups-and-downs of adolescent living. The blues usually last only a few days. Nearly all adolescents and adults have or will experience the blues. Grief is the profound feeling of loss, sadness, melancholy, or emptiness which comes about as a result of death or separation from a loved one. In grief, mood symptoms of depression are present, but not excessive self-criticism and self-devaluation. Reactive depression is characterized by moderate-to-severe despondency, negative beliefs about self and future, lack of motivation, and physical-vegetative symptoms. Reactive depression is precipitated by loss, failure, or major disappointments. Both grief and reactive depression are precipitated by real loss or personal setbacks. The difference between grief and reactive depression is that in normal grief there is not pervasive self-deprecation. Endogenous depression is a more chronic, severe form of depression in which the precipitating causes are not generally visible or specific, as in grief or reactive depression. The major depression symptom clusters are present in endogenous depression. The depression spectrum is presented in Table 4-2.

Depression Inventories

Several inventories or questionnaires have been developed to measure the extent and severity of depression (Beckham and Leber, 1985). One of the most widely known inventories is Aaron Beck's *Depression Inventory* (Beck, 1972, 1978). The *Beck Depression Inventory* consists of 21 items the subject ranks on a severity scale of 0 to 3 in terms of how well the items describe their feelings, thoughts, or behaviors during the past week. A sample of the items used in the Beck scale is listed in Table 4-3. Total scores can be ranked from moderate to severe. The items are straightforward and can be understood by older adolescents. The Beck scale has been adapted for use with children and early adolescents (Kovacs and Beck, 1977; Chiles et al., 1980). Other depression inventories that can be used with adolescents are outlined in Table 4-4.

Table 4-2. The Depression Spectrum Ranging from Mild Transient to Severe Chronic

The blues	Grief	Reactive depression	Endogenous depression
Mild mood symptoms, emotional lows, downheartedness, transient	Reaction to loss, profound sadness, emptiness, longing	Mood, cognitive behavioral, physical symptoms triggered by loss or major disappointment	Mood, cognitive behavioral, physical symptoms, no great signs of loss or disappointment
Mild-transient			Severe-chronic

Table 4-3. Sample of Items from the Beck Depression Inventory[a]

Subjects are instructed to circle the number preceding each item best describing how they have been feeling, behaving, and thinking during the past week.

What item measures	Item
Mood	0 I do not feel sad. 1 I feel sad. 2 I am sad all the time and I can't snap out of it. 3 I am so sad or unhappy that I can't stand it.
Thinking	0 I do not feel like a failure. 1 I feel I have failed more than the average person. 2 As I look back on my life, all I can see is a lot of failures. 3 I feel I am a complete failure as a person.
Motivation	0 I can work about as well as before. 1 It takes an extra effort to get started at doing something. 2 I have to push myself very hard to do anything. 3 I can't do any work at all.
Physical/vegetative	0 My appetite is no worse than usual. 1 My appetite is not as good as it used to be. 2 My appetite is much worse now. 3 I have no appetite at all anymore.

aAdapted from: Beck, A. T. (1972). *Depression: Causes and treatment*. Philadelphia, PA: University of Pennsylvania Press and Beck, A. T. (1978). *Beck depression inventory*. Copyright, 1978; Aaron Beck, Center for Cognitive Therapy, Room 602, 133 South 36th Street, Philadelphia, PA 19104.

Table 4-4. Inventories for Assessing Depression[a] in Adolescents

I. (CAS) Child Assessment Schedule (Hodges et al., 1982a & b). The child assessment schedule is a semistructured clinical interview for use with children and adolescents in the age range 6–18. The CAS consists of a series of standardized question-and-response items. Part I contains 75 items and records the adolescent's verbal responses to inquiries about school, peers, activities and interests, fears, family, self-concept, body concerns, anger, and thought processes. Part II records the clinical examiner's observations and consists of approximately 53 items that explore insight, grooming, motor coordination, activity level, cognitive abilities, and quality of verbalization, emotional expression, and emotional interaction. For each item, the adolescent's responses are recorded yes, no, ambiguous, no response, or not applicable. Copies of the CAS can be obtained from the Administrative Assistant, Dept. of Psychiatry, University of Missouri, Room 107, MMMHC, 3 Hospital Drive, Columbus, MO 65201.

II. (SRS) Self-Rating Scale (Birleson, 1981). The self-rating scale consists of 18 items such as "I feel very lonely" or "I feel bored." Adolescents are asked to rate whether the item applied most times, sometimes, or never during the past 2 weeks. The SRS can be used from age 7 to 17 years. Copies can be obtained by writing Peter Birleson, M.D., Royal Edinburgh Hospital, The Young Peoples Unit, Tipperlin House, Tipperlin Road, Edinborough, EH, 105 HF, United Kingdom.

aAdapted from: Beckham, E. E., & Leber, W. R. (Eds.). (1985). Handbook of depression: Treatment, assessment, and research. Homewood, IL: Dorsey Press.

MODELS OF DEPRESSION: DYNAMICS, CAUSES, AND ETIOLOGY

There are four major psychological theories or models of depression: (1) psychodynamic, (2) cognitive, (3) learned helplessness, and (4) behavioral. While the forces producing depression are conceptualized in several different ways, all theories acknowledge the presence of low self-esteem or self-deprecation in depression. Psychodynamic theorists are primarily concerned with the importance of real loss and symbolic loss in depression. Cognitive theorists examine the role of negative beliefs about self, experience, and the future. The learned-helplessness model of depression, which evolved out of social learning theory, looks at how adolescents develop the feeling or belief that they are powerless to control events in their lives. The behavior model perceives the key element in depression as the inability of adolescents to behave in ways that lead to consistent positive reinforcements.

The Psychodynamic Model

Loss and self-blame are the critical defining characteristics in the psychodynamic model of depression. In his classic paper, "Mourning and Melancholia," written in 1917, Freud outlined his theory of depression. Mourning or grief is caused by a real loss such as death. The person in mourning feels a profound sense of emptiness, longing, despondency, and sadness. The mood, behavioral, and physical symptoms of grief or mourning are similar to depression. In grief, however, there is one noticeable difference. The bereaved person does not engage in excessive self-blame or self-reviling for having caused the death or loss of the loved one. In depression or melancholia, the mood, behavioral, and physical symptoms of grief are present. The depressed adolescent feels despondent, has trouble getting started, loses interest in pleasurable activities, and may show wide fluctuations in sleeping and eating habits. In addition, the depressed adolescent engages in pervasive self-blame, self-criticism, and hopelessness about the future. Through a series of complex intrapsychological maneuvers, the depressed person turns the disappointment of loss inward, into self-deprecation, guilt, and self-blame. Personal standards prevent the person from expressing anger toward loved ones (White and Watt, 1981). Grief is always activated by real objective loss, whereas depression or melancholia can be activated by real loss or symbolic loss. Real loss is a known event usually visible to the person experiencing the loss and to outside observers.

When adolescents show the major signs of depression, including despondency and self-blame, after losses such as death, separation, or the divorce of their parents, this is called reactive depression rather than grief because of the presence of self-blame. For example, Charles, a 16-year-old adolescent, was repeatedly asked by his father to mow the lawn and clean up the yard on a hot summer day. Charles delayed getting started until it was almost early evening. Finally, the father, after growing increasingly angry and irritated with Charles, decided to mow the lawn and clean up the yard himself. While pushing the lawn mower, the father had a heart attack and died before he could be revived by Charles or his mother. Charles was devastated. His grief was compounded by severe self-blame, guilt, and self-deprecation. In this case, Charles's response to his father's death would be classified as reactive depression because he blames himself. Reactive depression, like grief, usually heals in time with new experiences, growth, and replacement of the lost object.

In symbolic or fantasized loss, the events and meanings surrounding the loss are not highly visible to the person experiencing the depression, or to the outside observer. In endogenous depression, the major mood, cognitive, behavioral, and physical symptoms are present, but no highly visible loss can be connected as an activating agent. When there are persistent signs of depression without known loss, psychodynamic theorists believe the source of the depression involves symbolic loss. Symbolic loss can be illustrated by the case of a 17-year-old high school senior who on the surface has everything going for her. She is attractive, has good grades, close friends, loving parents, social skills, and has been accepted to her first college choice. During the last semester of her senior year, she becomes increasingly depressed. The symbolic loss in this case is the loss of the security of childhood and the support systems of a familiar environment. Adolescence is a transition time when young people must sort out their values, cast aside old beliefs, resolve existential contradictions, and confront the dangers of the unknown as they struggle to define themselves in the context of a much broader world. These demands pose challenges to self-esteem and evoke questions concerning self-worth and adequacy in many adolescents. The push toward autonomy, separation, and individuation in adolescents can activate unresolved feelings of shame, doubt, fear, and guilt from unfinished preadolescent developmental tasks, which then need to be resolved before a more vibrant, confident, integrated identity can be developed.

The concept of loss in psychoanalytic theory has been extended to include anything the individual holds dear or feels is necessary for their well-being, such as persons, objects, beliefs, ideas, goals, or values (Weiner, 1974). Loss creates a psychological void, emptiness, or feeling that something vital is lacking. In this context, loss can involve the breakup of romantic relationships, failure to achieve goals, loss of goals through achievement, rejection by peers, or the loss of innocence and self-esteem, which comes about when adolescents feel guilty about violating internalized standards and values. Symbolic loss occurs when subtle, unrealistic beliefs about achievement, beauty, perfection, or needs for love are challenged. Because of these hidden, unrealistic beliefs, many adolescents experience feelings of unattractiveness, inadequacy, and not being loved. These feelings have no basis in fact. Real-life stresses, such as arguments with parents, conflicts with peers, tension in love relationships, changes in body size, injuries, or disfigurement, can intensify depressive episodes caused by real or symbolic loss.

In psychoanalytic theory, the symptoms of depression can have indirect meanings. The guilt, helplessness, and self-criticism depressed adolescents express may represent a disguised plea for help, a plea for forgiveness, or an attempt to expiate guilt and win back lost self-esteem by self-condemnation (White and Watt, 1981).

The Cognitive Model

The cognitive theory of depression considers negative beliefs about self, future, and one's experiences as the salient aspects of depression. Aaron Beck (1974, 1976), one of the leading cognitive theorists, acknowledges that real loss can and does cause depression. In Beck's view, however, symbolic loss is the key element in depression. Symbolic loss consists of negative beliefs that convince a person his or her life is lacking in some attribute essential to personal well-being and positive self-esteem, such as attractiveness, intelligence, likability, or successful future experiences. Beck refers to negative or faulty beliefs about self, experience, and the future as the negative cognitive triad. These beliefs determine how a person feels and acts. Because of gross errors in logical thinking, depressed adolescents erroneously conclude that they are worthless, unlovable, or doomed to a life of unhappiness because of perceived personal defects. Experiences are distorted to agree with negative conclusions. Depressed adolescents make statements about themselves, their future, and their world, reflecting their unrealistic negative beliefs such as "I'm terrible," "I'm no good," "I'm dumb," "No one will ever date me," "I'll never get into any college," or "If I do get in, I'll flunk out." They usually interpret what's happening as bad, unpleasant experiences, attributing these feelings to personal unworthiness. Small obstacles represent impossible barriers, and the future is depicted in the worst possible light (Rosenhan and Seligman, 1984). Some young people constantly see dire predictions for the future, a practice cognitive theorists refer to as "awfulizing."

Gross errors in logical thinking that generate and maintain depressive beliefs are due to faulty reasoning, misinterpretations, or misrepresentations of one's experience. Specific errors in logical thinking are labeled as arbitrary inferences, selective abstraction, overgeneralization, magnification or minimization, and personalization. Depressed adolescents tend to overemphasize minor disappointments and shortcomings while underemphasizing genuine successes and personal assets. A student who gets an A− on a test concludes that she is a failure. A boy at a teen dance asks five girls to dance during the course of an evening, four accept. They have pleasant conversations and exchange phone numbers. On the way home, the boy concludes that no one likes him because the one girl didn't accept his offer to dance. A girl applies for three part-time jobs, she gets two offers. She concludes that she is not a good prospect for employment because of the one refusal. A boy who has trouble fixing a flat tire concludes that he is inadequate. When events are filtered through negative beliefs about self, experiences, and the future, adolescents cannot avoid the pessimistic conclusions, despondent feelings, and self-devaluation associated with depression. Adolescents are more vulnerable to errors in logical thinking than adults because they lack experience and because mental structures for logical thinking are still in the process of developing.

To explain the causes of depression, cognitive psychologists examine the relationship between current stresses and a learned predisposition to negative beliefs. This has been called a stress-diathesis model of depression. In the stress-diathesis model, adolescents prone to depression have acquired a predisposition to depression-generating beliefs through early experiences that shaped the development of thinking styles. The depression-generating beliefs or faulty beliefs remain latent until activated by precipitating factors, conflicts, or stresses to which the adolescent is sensitized. Due to the loss of a parent during childhood, through divorce or death, some adolescents may develop a predisposition to depression caused by breakups in close relationships. This same adolescent might not be bothered by low grades or lack of athletic achievement. Failure to make the basketball team might precipitate depression in an adolescent who is expected to live up to excessively high athletic standards. According to Sacco and Beck (1985), the concept of specific areas of vulnerability explains why the relationship between depression and current stresses or conflicts is not perfectly correlated. Adolescents will not be seriously affected with depression when they encounter stressful events in areas to which they have not been sensitized by prior experiences. Negative belief systems remain dormant until activated by specific stressful events.

Underlying the negative beliefs about self, the future, and experiences, there is often a disguised form of perfectionistic thinking implying that if everything doesn't turn out perfectly, "I'm bad, no good or others won't like me." The hidden assumption is that one has to be flawless or perfect; anything less than perfect is not acceptable. If one is not flawless or perfect, he or she will be rejected by others. Beck refers to this rigid, perfectionistic orientation as a type of negative thinking based on depressogenic assumptions. Some of Beck's depressogenic assumptions are listed in Table 4-5.

Table 4-5. Aaron Beck's Depressogenic Assumptions[a]

1. In order to be happy, I have to be successful in whatever I undertake.
2. To be happy, I must be accepted by all people at all times.
3. If I make a mistake, it means I am inept.
4. My value as a person depends on what others think of me.

[a]Adapted from: Beck, A. T., Rush, A. J., Shaw, B. F., & Emery, G. (1979). *Cognitive therapy of depression*. New York: Guilford Press.

Depressed adolescents who engage in perfectionistic thinking are unable to distinguish between excellence and perfection. Since they cannot be all powerful or all knowing, they assume that they are incompetent and worthless.

Perfectionistic teenagers set standards for success so high, they are impossible to reach. Setting unreachable standards for attractiveness, performance, or love can have crippling or self-defeating effects, since impossible goals cannot be achieved. Even when the adolescent is successful, some flaw is found which negates the achievement. Since perfectionistically oriented teenagers equate minor flaws or shortcomings with failure and lack of self-worth, failure and disappointment are inevitable. Failure triggers loss of self-esteem, defeat, and despair. Furthermore, repeated exposure to self-judged failure inhibits the motivation to try new experiences. New experiences are an essential feature of adolescent psychosocial development. Adolescence is a time when new learning must be confronted. The competition for grades, athletic awards, artistic prizes, and social inclusion becomes more intense. It gets harder and harder to be the best in every situation. Avoiding challenges because of fears of failure can heighten one's sense of helplessness and inadequacy. Young people who cannot tolerate setbacks or less than perfect performances will find their self-esteem and sense of well-being continuously deflated. Perfectionistic teenagers are also vulnerable to thinking that others will judge them as harshly as they judge themselves. Therefore, they anticipate devaluation and rejection from others.

How is this perfectionistic thinking learned? How do adolescents come to believe that they must be flawless in order to be acceptable? How does this dichotomous, all or none, saint or sinner thinking get started? According to Burns (1982), one must go back to the childhood or preadolescent years to find the origins of perfectionistic thinking.

As children, perfectionistic adolescents were rewarded and loved for outstanding performances. Parents reacted to not-so-perfect performances with irritation, irritability, anxiety, or even punishment. When children are repeatedly censured and devalued for minor errors, they are likely to see themselves as bad, or they feel rejected. They associate personal worth with achievement and performance. Since imperfections are more likely to occur than perfections, children whose parents are perfectionistically oriented receive more censure than praise. The child begins to anticipate censure, doesn't learn the distinction between perfection and excellence, and starts to fear and avoid situations in which she is sure she will be judged as less than perfect. Once children are sensitized to an "I have to be flawless to be acceptable" mentality, it sets up a self-perpetuating, defeatist approach that carries over into adolescence. Cultural institutions, such as schools, religion, athletics, and commercial advertising, tend to reinforce the philosophy that only the best can be acceptable.

The Learned-Helplessness Model

The learned-helplessness model of depression, which evolved from social learning theory, is concerned with how depressed adolescents learn to believe that they have little power or control over what happens in their lives. In the learned helplessness view of depression, the depressed adolescent passively submits to events because he or she is convinced that his or her actions will have little effect on the outcome. They expect bad events to happen and believe there is little or nothing they can do to prevent their occurrence (Wetzel, 1984; Rosenhan and Seligman, 1984).

Supportive evidence for the learned-helplessness model of depression comes from laboratory studies in helplessness and fear with animals (Seligman, 1975). To produce the learned helplessness, Seligman first subjected dogs to inescapable electric shock. There was nothing the dogs could do to terminate this shock. Later, the dogs were given the opportunity to learn to escape the shock. They were placed in a two-sided compartment box where they had the opportunity to escape the shock by jumping from one side of the box to the other. Instead of escaping the shocks when they were given the opportunity to, the dogs remained passive and did not try to elude the shock. Other dogs that had not been subjected to prior inescapable shock quickly learned to avoid the shock by jumping to the other side of the compartment. Seligman concluded that when an animal or person is exposed to trauma they cannot control or escape, the motivation to take action to avoid future traumas diminishes, and the ability to perceive the possibility of success is undermined. Learned helplessness is defined as the interference with adaptive responses produced by trauma (Wetzel, 1984).

A parallel process caused by earlier life experiences the person is unable to do anything about is thought to occur in human beings. When the individual has experienced trauma he or she cannot control, the motivation to avoid trauma is reduced, and the ability to develop or imagine successful responses to stressful situations is diminished. Children who learn helplessness as a way of viewing the world attribute disappointment, failure, or loss to factors beyond their control, such as chance, the behavior of others, or their own lack of ability. Adolescents with this attitude respond to conflicts, demands, or frustrations by feeling helpless and unable to cope. It is not so much a traumatic experience that produces helplessness, but the belief that there is nothing one can do about it. Within this model of depression, the type of loss that makes an adolescent susceptible to depression is the loss of power or control over her or his destiny. For adolescents to be motivated to strive for mastery, power, and control over their lives, it is important for them to believe that their actions or decisions can affect the outcome. The strength of the learned-helplessness model is that it captures the defeatist and hopeless attitude of the depressed adolescent (Jensen, 1985). Defeatist statements such as "What's the use of trying?" or "I can't do anything about it anyway" prevent adolescents from trying responses that might work through successive approximations or trial and error.

Experiences that place adolescents at risk to develop learned helplessness can involve death of a loved one, where it is of course impossible to bring the person back to life, situations where the adolescent tries very hard to accomplish an academic, social, or athletic goal with no visible signs of success, physical disease or disfigurement, and being reared in an overprotective environment where the adolescent has very little opportunity for mastery experiences and self-determination. Also at risk are female adolescents who are repeatedly discouraged from learning to be assertive or self-directed (Goldenberg, 1977; Wetzel, 1984).

The Behavioral Model of Depression

In the behavioral model, depression is due to the inability of the adolescent to behave in ways that will be positively reinforced (Lewinsohn, 1974). The depressed adolescent lacks an adequate repertoire of rewarding responses, or he behaves in ways that will perpetuate the gloom, doom, and self-deprecation of depression. Several reasons are advanced to explain the depressed adolescent's inability to behave in ways that will result in positive reinforcement. First, the psychosocial environment can be a problem. Few opportunities for positive reinforcement exist, or the environment may be overweighted with punishment and adverse experiences. Second, the adolescent's skills in coping with stress or seeking out positive experiences may be limited. Third, the adolescent may be lacking in personality characteristics that have a high social reinforcement value, such as social attractiveness, friendliness, or communication skills. Fourth, reinforcements seem less positive when people are depressed and punishment seems more negative (Lewinsohn and Talkington, 1979). The decrease in the value of positive activities and the increase in value of negative activities happens in depression because experiences are filtered through a mood of doom and a belief system that anticipates unpleasant events. Sudden changes in the environment can affect any of these factors. A shy, retiring adolescent who moves to another community because of a divorce may not have the social skills to start over in an unfamiliar environment to replace close friendships and rewarding social activities.

According to the behavioral model, depression is maintained because depressed adolescents withdraw or because others find depressed teenagers unpleasant to be around. When depressed teenagers withdraw, they reduce the opportunity for developing rewarding and pleasurable activities. If depressed adolescents remain in the company of others, they may initially receive sympathy and caring concern. When the depression persists for an extended length of time, peers are likely to avoid them. Depressed adolescents tend to be perceived by peers as "downers," "bummers," or "drags." Supportive evidence for these observations comes from research with human subjects conducted by Lewinsohn and Associates (Lewinsohn and Arconad, 1981). Coyne (1976), in a research project that consisted of having people talk to depressed and nondepressed individuals, found that people who spoke to depressed patients described themselves as significantly more anxious, depressed, and hostile after the conversations and had little desire to have future interaction with the depressed person.

Summary of Depression Models

Our discussion of the psychodynamic, cognitive, learned helplessness, and behavioral models of depression indicates that depression can develop under the following conditions:

1. Real loss, characterized by death, separation, romance breakup, or major disappointments, results in lowered self-esteem, despondency, and feelings of emptiness.
2. Adolescence is a vulnerable time during which teenagers must give up the security and safety of childhood to confront the responsibilities and uncertainties of the future.
3. Unrealistic expectations of self, one's experiences, and the future.
4. Existential helplessness, learned helplessness, or deficiencies in coping responses caused by the lack of positive reinforcement.
5. Failure to resolve childhood developmental tasks leaves a residual of shame, guilt, inferiority, and self-deprecation which can be easily activated by the ups-and-downs of adolescent living.

The critical concepts used to explain depression, such as loss, negative beliefs about self, experience and the future, learned helplessness, and insufficient reinforcement, can be analyzed within a framework of psychosocial development. Developmentally speaking, depression can be viewed as an outcome or as a cause of maladaptive psychosocial development, and deficiencies in coping skills. In order to develop positive self-esteem, optimism about the future, competence, and a feeling of power and control over one's destiny, the adolescent and preadolescent psychosocial environments must provide a sufficient amount of affirmation, unconditional love, and realistic opportunities for mastery experiences. If the preadolescent psychosocial environment is lacking, a good enough pattern of nurturing and competence-building experiences young people can bring a residual of guilt, inferiority, shame, powerlessness, and fears of failure into adolescence with them. Pre-existing feelings of self-doubt, guilt, fear of the future, and hidden perfectionistic assumptions can be activated easily by the increased demands and expectations of adolescent living. When there is excess preadolescent baggage, additional rejections, losses, separations, perceived failures, or inadequacies can take on an exaggerated meaning because unresolved tensions are activated. It is difficult for adolescents to enact the reappraisal, problem-solving, and stress-reducing steps to adaptively cope with current threats of loss when they feel overwhelmed with despair, despondency, and self-deprecation. Adolescents who are not burdened by strong residuals of preadolescent doubts and fears are much freer to utilize their energies to develop the skills needed to cope with stressful situations as they arise. This might explain why many adolescents respond to heartache, setbacks, disappointments, and perceived shortcomings with the blues or mild, short-term depressions followed by resilience, while others experience persistent, self-defeating depression. Persistent adolescent depression in the absence of severe or multiple current stresses is a sign that something has gone wrong developmentally, and it can be interpreted as a disguised plea for help and support (White and Watt, 1981). In this context, persistent depression is a maladaptive outcome of defective, preadolescent psychosocial development.

At a causal level, prolonged depression can serve as a barrier to delay or slow down the completion of adolescent developmental tasks involving power, competence, and belongingness. The negative thinking of depression is sometimes a defense against exposing one's self to further risk of failure. Adolescents who feel immobilized, guilty, despondent, and fearful are not likely to seek out and complete activities that will make them feel good about themselves, their bodies, and their futures. Depression works against the risk-taking, adventure-seeking, and trial-and-error learning necessary to confront unknown challenges and uncertainties. Depression can interfere with the flexibility required to learn adaptive coping skills and conflict-resolution strategies. Adolescents who are persistently deprived of self-esteem building experiences are at greater risk when it comes to seeking relief through maladaptive coping behaviors such as drugs, sexual promiscuity, suicidal thoughts, or poorly planned runs away from home. Severely depressed adolescents are likely to get stuck in a downward cycle. The longer the depression persists, the greater the chances of additional failures, disappointments, and rejections. With additional failures, it becomes harder to motivate one's self to reach out and try again (Fuhrmann, 1986).

DIFFERENTIAL DEPRESSION RATES IN MALES AND FEMALES

Females tend to report depression experiences more often than males. Differences in male–female depression rates are generally acknowledged to be as high as 2 to 1 or even 3 to 1 (Weiner, 1980; Fuhrmann, 1986). From age 10 on, females are more likely to experience depression than males and gender differences in rates increase during the adolescent years (Weiner, 1982). Differences in male–female rates of depression are usually explained by divergent socialization practices with respect to power and control, relationship issues and affection needs, and management of feelings. Our society gives girls and young women mixed messages about power, control, assertiveness, and sexuality. If a female is assertive, competitive, power oriented, and openly acknowledges her sexuality, she runs the risk of being regarded by others as self-centered, aggressive, and seductive. If she assumes the traditional feminine role in terms of suppressing her sexuality and adopting a passive, compliant, self-sacrificing orientation, she is vulnerable to feelings of powerlessness, helplessness, and lack of fulfillment. Either choice can lead to depressive symptoms. "Going for it" can generate feelings of guilt or rejection, whereas suppression of individuality can lead to self-devaluation and feelings of inadequacy.

Interpersonal sensitivity, involvement in affectional needs and close relationships, and concern with the well-being of others are central issues in the lives of girls and women (Scharf, 1980). The plus side of interpersonal sensitivity and concerns about the feelings of others is effectiveness in people-to-people relationships. The down side of a relationship orientation is vulnerability to the hurt, pain, and loss that come with the inevitable peaks and valleys in interpersonal relationships. Loss, symbolic and real, caused by disruptions in relationships is a major cause of depression. Teenage girls are likely to experience blame and guilt when things go wrong in boy–girl relationships, especially around issues related to sexuality. If a girl gets pregnant, she is blamed for not using birth control, or for having sex in the first place. It is paradoxical that females are expected to be compliant and self-sacrificing, yet are expected to assume the responsibility and blame when things go wrong. The combination of lack of power and unrealistic beliefs about responsibility is a prominent feature of depression.

Males and females are socialized to manage feelings differently. While females are discouraged from open displays of anger and negative criticism of others, they are allowed to be in touch with and express visible signs of depression such as sadness, crying, or despondency. Suppressed, internalized, or unexpressed feelings of anger can turn inward into feelings of self-deprecation and self-condemnation. The anger-turned-inward concept is a primary factor in the psychodynamic theory of depression. Males, on the other hand, are allowed to act out or directly express feelings of anger and aggression through aggressive-competitive behavior, contact sports, and the like. Indirect expressions of anger, such as defiance of authority, fighting, and conduct disturbances, while not culturally sanctioned, are less severely punished in males than females. Males are encouraged to suppress or deny the feelings of sadness and hopelessness associated with depression. It is not masculine to cry, experience profound sadness, or admit that one feels powerless and afraid of the future. Differences in internalizing versus externalizing, or the acting-in versus the acting-out of feelings in males and females, definitely seem to be a factor in accounting for why female adolescents show more signs of depression (Kimmel and Weiner, 1985). The actual incidence of depression may be much higher than reported for males, but the tendency to engage in suppression and denial on the part of males reduces the accuracy of reported figures. Females not only are permitted to be in touch with feelings of sadness and helplessness, but also are more likely to share personal feelings with others and view going to professional counselors as a legitimate way of seeking help for depression.

DEPRESSION IN LATE AND EARLY ADOLESCENCE

Clearly discernible mood and cognitive symptoms of depression are more likely to be found in late adolescents than in early adolescents (Weiner, 1982, 1980). Late adolescents have developed the introspective, reflective, and critical self-analysis abilities necessary to experience helplessness, pervasive despondency, and negative beliefs about self, future, and one's world. Because of more extensive experiences with intimacy in peer and personal relationships, they are less resistant than early adolescents to sharing private thoughts and feelings with others. Late adolescence is a time when youths encounter self-doubt, confusion, powerlessness, and disillusionment associated with resolving the identity-related conflicts involved in defining who one is, what one wants to accomplish in the future, and what one believes in terms of personal values. Confronting these dilemmas can result in periods of stuckness, despair, drifting, alienation, or negative identity. Late adolescents sometimes withdraw from efforts to define a place for themselves in the world, avoid setting goals that might end in failure and disappointment, or take on a negative identity characterized by a blatant rejection of all values they previously internalized.

Identity disorder is a special category designated in DSM-III-R (1987) to describe youths encountering serious trouble and internal turmoil in making the identity transition from late adolescent to young adult. The essential feature of an identity disturbance is severe distress related to an inability to develop a coherent and acceptable definition of self or who one is. Uncertainty persists about a variety of issues pertaining to career choice, long-term goals, friendship and intimacy patterns, sexual behavior and orientation, religious identification, and values and group loyalties. Mild anxiety, depression, and self-doubt related to inner uncertainties are common in identity disturbances. Young people who are experiencing severe identity conflicts brought on by anger and disappointment sometimes distance themselves from family values and conventional standards by trying out oppositional patterns or temporarily taking on negative identities.

Early adolescents were thought to display depression through masked depression or behavioral equivalents such as problem behavior, boredom, restlessness, difficulties in school, social isolation, or excessive involvement in people to avoid feelings of loneliness and despair. Masked depression or behavioral equivalents were regarded as defense mechanisms that shielded true depressive feelings of hopelessness, gloom, helplessness, and excessive self-criticism from self and others. The rationale for masked depression or depressive equivalents was threefold. First, it was held that the reflective thinking and self-critical abilities of early adolescents were not sufficiently developed, therefore generating excessive negative beliefs about self, future, and experience. Second, early adolescents lacked the psychological resources to cope directly with losses in self-esteem triggered by failures, disappointments, or the dilemmas of adolescent life. Feelings of powerlessness and inadequacy were too painful to admit or share with others. Early adolescents do not realize that other teenagers struggle with the same issues. Third, early adolescents are action-oriented rather than feeling or reflectively oriented, consequently, they tend to act out their feelings rather than think or ruminate about them (Cantwell and Carlson, 1983).

In the past two decades, as noted earlier, clinicians have moved away from the masked depression or behavioral equivalents classification. The range of behaviors or symptoms associated with masked depression became too all-inclusive. By including conduct disturbances, sexual promiscuity, boredom, excessive anger, drug and alcohol abuse, delinquency, running away, and the like, depressive equivalence and masked depression were no longer definitive terms. The research of Puig-Antich (1986) has shown that the primary symptoms of depression remain stable from middle childhood to adulthood. It is generally acknowledged that there may be age-related changes in depression, but the core symptoms of despondency, loss of self-esteem, and negative beliefs are similar for adults and early and late adolescents. Through skillful interviewing and sophisticated assessment procedures, mental health workers should be able to identify the core-cognitive, mood, and behavioral symptoms of depression when they are in fact present, despite defenses or age-related changes in secondary symptoms.

DEPRESSION AND RUNAWAYS

Depressed adolescents internalize unhappy feelings and beliefs, whereas runaway adolescents act out their feelings and beliefs. Many runaways report symptoms of depression prior to running away (Gordon and Beyer, 1981). They find themselves stuck in family environments where they experience guilt, shame, low self-esteem, powerlessness, and hopelessness. Running away is an action-oriented behavior associated with adventure, excitement, or escape from an unhappy home situation. In this context, running away is a way of coping with depression. Rather than remaining in an adverse family environment, where an adolescent internalizes feelings of gloom, doom, and guilt, runaway adolescents take action or act out needs for freedom, adventure, and power. To the extent that running away ultimately leads to constructive changes in the teenager's family and personal space, depression is likely to dissipate. On the other hand, depression is likely to persist and in some cases become more severe when young people return to unhealthy home situations that resist change or when they end up in the streets for extended periods without the resources to survive. In these instances, running away is one more defeat in a somber, unhappy life.

TREATMENT AND RECOVERY

Grief and Depression

The prospects for recovery in grief and reactive depression are generally favorable. Normal grief precipitated by loss or death in close relationships usually disappears with the passage of time and completion of the emotional process of recovery. Grief seems to pass through a series of stages (Janis et al., 1969; Kübler-Ross, 1969; Kalish, 1981). The first stage is characterized by shock, numbness, emptiness, bewilderment, feeling stunned or dazed, and crying and sighing. In this stage there may be periods of denial or minimization punctuated with intermittent outbursts of anger or anguish. The second stage is one of yearning and searching for the lost figure. Adolescents report being preoccupied with thoughts and dreams of the deceased and little interest is shown in the outside world or usual activities. Teenagers may go through the motions of school and family activities, but their primary preoccupation is with memories of the lost figure. In the third stage, young people experience deep feelings of despair, loneliness, and disorganization. It is hard for them to believe that they can ever be happy again or fill the space created by the absence of the loved one. The final stage is reorganization and recovery. The adolescent gradually starts to let go, resistance to change decreases, new experiences are attempted, and the focus of life moves into the present and future. Since our definition of self is connected to people we are closely bonded to, it takes time and new experiences to redefine ourselves and fill the empty space after a period of loss.

After a few days, the overt symptoms of grief, such as crying, usually diminish to the point where the teenager can return to school or to work. The emotional pangs of grief continue for weeks or months with decreasing frequency and intensity for a period of 1 to 2 years (Kalish, 1981). The stages of grief can be repeated more than once, and the stages do not follow in the same order in all cases. Sometimes a reminder of the deceased, such as a birthday or a favorite song, can set off a wave of grief 1 or 2 years later. In addition to time, what teenagers need when they are moving through the grief cycle is patience, understanding, and emotional support. They need to be assured that they are not alone or abandoned, that there are others who care, who are willing to be there, and who are trying to understand. Teenage heartbreak follows a course similar to grief, although it is usually not as intense, pervasive, or prolonged. Psychologically healthy teenagers are resilient. In the recovery period, they realize that heartache is one of the risks of teen romance.

The majority of depressed clients can be helped (Brammer and Abrego, 1981; Rosenhan and Seligman, 1984; McCoy, 1982). Reactive depression accounts for the majority of depression cases and is the most receptive to treatment. Adolescents frequently recover from mild-to-moderate reactive depression without professional help. Recovery from reactive depression without professional help is called spontaneous remission (Weiner, 1982). In spontaneous recovery from reactive depression, a process analogous to the stages of grief probably occurs (Fuhrmann, 1986; Martin, 1977). Adolescents need time to absorb the shock of disappointment, failure, or separation, before they can return to their usual level of functioning. The recovery process in reactive depression can be complicated by guilt and self-deprecation, which is not present in grief. Chronic or endogenous depression is resistant to spontaneous recovery. The self-perpetuating quality of negative beliefs, flaw finding, and personal devaluation works against letting go of old hurts and finding pleasure and fulfillment in new experiences.

Psychotherapy with Depressed Adolescents

Three approaches to psychotherapy with depressed adolescents will be presented: (1) cognitive-behavioral, (2) client-centered—relationship, (3) psychodynamic. The primary goal in cognitive-behavioral therapy is restructuring negative beliefs and getting behavior moving toward achievable goals. Client-centered therapy is concerned with developing a client-therapist relationship based on positive regard, empathy and genuiness, and helping the client to discover personal strengths. The major objective of psychodynamic therapy with depressed adolescents is identifying, surfacing, understanding, and working through underlying feelings, hidden meanings, and intrapsychological conflicts.

Cognitive-Behavioral Therapy

Cognitive-behavioral therapy has two major components: (1) identifying and correcting distorted or irrational negative beliefs, and (2) building up a repertoire of effective, gratifying behaviors. Cognitive-behavioral therapy is an active, structured, psychoeducational approach utilizing techniques involving instruction, persuasive communication, monitoring behavior and experiences, raising activity levels, and positive self-affirmation. Therapists play an active role, and the process is centered on what's happening in the present and short-term future. Negative beliefs and erroneous thinking are gently, but firmly, challenged. When adolescents make statements to the effect that "No one cares about me," "No one will ever date me," "I always fail," or "I really look ugly," the therapist carefully questions the reasoning and evidence on which these statements are based. The client is given assistance or instruction in correcting tendencies to overgeneralize, engage in all-or-nothing thinking, maximize isolated unpleasant experiences, and operate on hidden perfectionistic assumptions. Since automatic dysfunctional beliefs and negative cognitions are thought to generate the gloom and doom of depression, the goal of cognitive-behavioral therapy is to reconstruct the client's way of thinking and appraising him/her self and experiences (Beck, 1972; Beck et al., 1979).

Adolescents are somewhat susceptible to errors in logical thinking because of inexperience and because the process of abstract reasoning is still developing. Many times depressed adolescents don't realize that their reasoning process is faulty and are not aware of the fact that other teenagers also have periods where they feel confused, despondent, frightened, and worthless. Psychoeducational and instructional approaches can facilitate the growth of logical thinking and accurate inference making from experiences.

Clients learn to replace negative self-statements with coping and rewarding self-statements. Rather than continuing with self-deprecation and feelings of helplessness, clients learn to make statements like, "I can do it if I try," "I like myself," "My mother gets mad, but I know she still loves me," "I did my best," or "I did better than last week." Mood relaxing imagery is also used, such as "I'm calm," "I feel good," "I am relaxed," or "This is going to be a pleasant evening."

The immobilization, lack of energy, and motivational deficits of depression are attacked by gradually setting up achievable goals. The behaviors involved in achieving goals are broken down into component parts. Each successive approximation is rewarded. Failure is avoided by moving from simple to complex tasks with rewards for completing each component of the task. For example, a shy, depressed adolescent who is afraid to ask for a date or attend a party might start out by imagining himself at a social gathering while in a relaxed mood, making eye contact with someone who seems friendly, initiating a conversation with planned opening statements, exchanging phone numbers, and gradually working himself up to asking for a date. After rehearsing the scene several times with the therapist and at home, the teenager would slowly enact each step in real-life situations. Clients keep a daily or weekly record of ongoing activities, pleasant events, mastery experiences, automatic thoughts, new self-statements, and the like. Adolescents and children can be taught to keep journals or diaries of their thoughts and activities (Cantwell and Carlson, 1983).

Emery, Bedrosian, and Garber (1983) recommend several modifications in using cognitive-behavioral approaches with adolescents. First, the pace of therapy is usually slower. A workable goal is only one or two treatment themes per therapy session. Second, avoid complex therapy homework assignments for adolescents who may be experiencing difficulties in school. Third, homework assignments should be specific, concrete, and achievable. Fourth, spend a considerable amount of time building a relationship and reducing threat. Fifth, tolerate some lack of compliance with treatment expectations and contracts since many adolescents don't come voluntarily to therapy. Sixth, respect the adolescent's privacy and build a collaborative therapeutic atmosphere by attempting to reach mutual treatment goals with the adolescent. Seventh, establish ongoing contact with the family so that systematic interventions can occur when needed.

Client Centered—Relationship Therapy

Client centered—relationship therapy is an outgrowth of the humanistic and self-actualization theories of Abraham Maslow (1968) and Carl Rogers (1980). In working with depressed adolescents, the primary goal in client centered—relationship therapy is to build a relationship with the depressed adolescent based on positive regard, genuineness, and empathy. The therapist tries to be caring, real as a person, and attempts to understand the client's feelings and perceptions from the client's frame of reference. The therapist provides a meaningful relationship, which to some extent compensates or temporarily substitutes for previous losses and reduces the feeling of being alone. The therapist is accepting, listens, and doesn't challenge the client's feelings of rejection, futility, hopelessness, or self-deprecation. It is sometimes easy for adults to minimize the perspective of young people when they feel upset or depressed about not making the team or getting included in a high status peer group. Through active listening, clarification, and reflection of feelings, the therapist helps the adolescent sort out the issues and get in touch with underlying feelings and potential areas of strength. Depression is usually a mixture of disappointment, internalized anger, guilt, loss, fear, rejection, and thwarted hopes and dreams the client is not fully aware of and hasn't sorted out.

In his or her verbal and nonverbal style of relating to the client, the therapist tries to communicate an attitude that is nonjudgmental, gentle, and quietly confident in the client's ability to overcome barriers to growth. The therapist is sensitive to moment-to-moment changes in the client's feelings and slowly helps the client take a fresh look at issues and conflicts associated with despair and futility.

When clients perceive that someone who is nonjudgmental cares, understands their world as they experience it, and is trying to be real with them, a gradual transformation in the feelings, cognitions, and beliefs related to the depression will start to take place. Rogers (1980) describes the beginnings of this transformation in terms of a series of tentative, subtle impressions that the individual will start to consider such as:

1. If someone cares about me, maybe I'm not so worthless, maybe I can learn to care about myself.
2. If someone is confident in me, maybe I can learn to be confident in myself.
3. If someone doesn't judge me so harshly, maybe I can learn to stop condemning myself.
4. If someone has hope for me after listening to what I feel, maybe I can have hope for myself.
5. If someone understands me, maybe I'm not so weird, confused, or alone.

The goal in client centered — relationship therapy is not to direct clients or teach them how to think and feel. The basic assumption in client centered — relationship therapy is that the drives toward growth, discovery, and actualization within the person are very strong. Adolescents do not want to be despondent, miserable, downtrodden, self-deprecating, or unhappy. To the degree that they can be involved in a therapeutic relationship where they feel appreciated, understood, and cared about, the growth drives can be unleashed in ways that allow adolescents to gain a new perspective on their experiences, beliefs, and feelings. When adolescents can gain a new emotional and psychological perspective or awareness of conflicts, they can grow free of the debilitating effects.

Psychodynamic Therapy

The goal in psychodynamic therapy with depressed adolescents is to work through the underlying pent-up feelings of anger, shame, guilt, fear, and rejection causing the depression. Working through pent-up emotions is accomplished in two ways: (1) by understanding and helping the teenager come to terms with the intrapsychological dynamics of a real or fantasy loss manifested in the belief that one is lacking in some quality essential to positive feelings about life and self, and (2) by undergoing a catharsis which permits the adolescent to ventilate or express pent-up anger, shame, fear, and guilt. In order to help the adolescent understand the indirect psychological meanings behind the depression symptoms, the therapist uses the tool of interpretation. Helplessness and hopelessness can be interpreted as disguised pleas for help, affection, and support. Constant self-criticism and self-deprecation can represent abortive attempts to expiate guilt and regain lost self-esteem. Catharsis involves working through bottled up emotions involving unresolved conflicts from previous developmental stages or intrapsychological conflicts between the past and the present, and the present and the future. Unresolved feelings of guilt, shame, fear, and self-deprecation left over from previous developmental stages can prevent the emergence of self-esteem and feelings of hope for the future.

Adolescence is a time when young people struggle with conflicts between previously internalized standards and present needs, desires, or actions. Overdeveloped standards of morality, or values inherited from parents can prevent realistic expressions of anger toward loved ones or the exploration of sexual feelings and new adventures. The guilt and shame many young people experience when their feelings or desires conflict with internalized standards can be immobilizing. Intrapsychological conflicts between the present and the future are likely to be a major feature of adolescent depression. The push toward autonomy, separation, and individuation in adolescence can activate old, dimly conscious fears, doubts, and feelings of powerlessness that need to be surfaced, understood, and resolved before the future, with its unknown promises and threats, can be confronted with a sense of hope and confidence (White and Watt, 1981).

Integrating Treatment Approaches

While approaches to psychotherapy with depressed adolescents can be differentiated for discussion purposes, there is often considerable overlap in real-life, treatment situations. The integration or overlap of psychotherapy approaches can be illustrated as a process that unfolds in a series of sequential stages.

The initial phase of psychotherapy involves building a relationship in which the depressed adolescent feels sufficient trust, safety, and comfort to open up and share personal concerns. This is usually referred to as rapport building. Rapport building is accomplished by empathy, positive regard, and some degree of genuineness on the part of the therapist. Concerns about confidentiality are discussed during this stage. The important issues from the adolescents' perspective are identified. Since adolescents are usually brought into treatment by parents or other adult authority figures, it is essential that the therapist distinguish between how the adolescent perceives the issues versus how the parents perceive the issues. Parents are usually concerned about symptoms that make them uncomfortable, such as declining school work, refusal to participate in family activities, defiance of authority, sleep and eating irregularities, drug or alcohol abuse, behavioral problems, or sexual activity. The second phase of therapy consists of sorting out the issues, deciding what is going to be worked on, and how the parents will be included. As the issues are identified and sorted out, the process of understanding and working through gets started. The third phase of therapy focuses on changing feelings of helplessness, powerlessness, self-deprecation, and immobilization by restructuring negative beliefs, planning and carrying out behavioral goals, developing positive self-statements, and discovering personal strengths. The final stage involves integration and termination. During this phase, the emphasis is on consolidating the gains, new insights, and behaviors achieved, as well as working through feelings of loss associated with ending the therapy relationship.

Clinical experience with depressed adolescents suggests that therapists, regardless of their orientation, should keep in mind three major principles of adolescent growth and development. First, psychotherapy with adolescents should be a forward-moving process. Since adolescents have four-fifths of their lives ahead of them, endless reconstruction of the past can interfere with the process of becoming and moving toward future goals. Second, adolescence is a period of rapid growth and development. Each week, adolescents are presented with a wealth of opportunities in family, peer group, school, and social interactions to receive positive feedback, try out new ideas, increase communication skills, and improve coping strategies. Therapists should capitalize on these experiences by working them in to the flow of therapy. Third, when adolescents complete therapy, they should be at a higher growth stage than when the depression started. Psychotherapy with adolescents is a growth-facilitating experience rather than merely a stress-reduction process. In the course of therapy, they should develop the coping tools they can use to actualize needs for power, competence, and belonging, and thereby reduce the likelihood of future severe depressions. Finally, the quality of the relationship between the depressed adolescent and the therapist is a critical dimension of any treatment program. By relating in a genuine, trusting, caring, and understanding manner, therapists can temporarily fill the void in the adolescent's life created by real or symbolic loss.

Case Example 4-1: Ellen, Part II

The course of psychotherapy with Ellen, the 16-year-old high school junior whose history and presenting concerns were discussed at the beginning of this chapter, followed the integrated treatment approach. Establishing a therapeutic relationship with Ellen was not difficult. She was talkative, open, and looked forward to the opportunity to sit down once a week with the therapist to share her "thoughts and feelings." In the initial stage, the therapist was

warm and gentle, listened, and occasionally summarized, clarified, or reflected Ellen's thoughts and feelings. As Ellen and the therapist sorted out her
thoughts and feelings, they agreed that the primary issues were unresolved
disappointment and loss related to her parents' divorce, general concerns
about personal worth, specific concerns about perfection as a student, daughter, and big sister, value conflicts with peers, and boyfriend–girlfriend conflicts. These concerns and conflicts generated ongoing feelings of despondency, a sense of being alone and not understood, and endless ruminations
about minor flaws. In working through her feelings of loss and disappointment surrounding her parent's divorce, Ellen was able to get in touch with a
deeper source of anger she had been unaware of. She was very angry with her
parents, especially her mother whom she held responsible for the divorce and
for not providing her with an intact family to grow up in. She was also fearful
that if something happened to one of her parents, the remaining parent would
not be able to provide a stable home for her and her younger brother. She
clung to her boyfriend because she did not want to be alone again.

The strivings for perfection were traced to her childhood. As a child, she
thought that if she could be "daddy's perfect little girl," everything would turn
out alright for her and her family. After working through the residual childhood issues and helping Ellen understand how her need to be perfect had
developed, the therapist and Ellen examined how strivings for perfection were
contributing to her despondency and low self-esteem. By always concentrating
on her flaws, Ellen was unable to appreciate her accomplishments or competencies. She quickly understood how she was setting herself up for failure. She
started to keep a daily record of negative self-statements, moods, and activities. Ellen learned to replace negative self-statements with positive self-statements, rearrange her schedule so that she would have time for fun activities,
and she slowly began to reward herself for excellence rather than for perfection. She still felt very responsible for her family and is highly motivated to
achieve. However, she recognizes that her brother, mother, and father make
choices she cannot control, no matter how perfect she tries to be. Termination
was not easy for Ellen. She felt understood, cared about, and supported by the
therapist. She admired the therapist as a person who was "straight and real."

Treatment with Antidepressant Drugs

There are mood-elevating or antidepressant drugs that seem to raise the
spirits, increase the physical activity, and improve the mental alertness of
depressed adolescents. Antidepressant psychopharmacological or psychoactive drugs are divided into two classes: tricyclics and monoamine oxidase
(MAO) inhibitors. Antidepressant drugs take 7 to 10 days to produce their
effects. The tricyclics, known by their trade names as Tofranil and Elavil,
have been used with adolescents and children without serious side effects
when properly prescribed. The MAO inhibitors marketed under the trade
names of Marplan, Nardil, and Parnat have more serious side effects. Patients may develop high blood pressure from eating aged varieties of cheese,
herring, excessive amounts of chocolate, chicken livers, or drinking beer or
wine. Since MAO inhibitors have more serious side effects, the tricyclics are
usually the first choice when antidepressant medication is recommended for
adolescents (Rosenfeld, 1985; Kaslow and Rehm, 1983). Tricyclics and MAO

inhibitors seem to work by stimulating the activity of brain neurotransmitters. The tricyclics affect the actions of two neurotransmitters, serotonin and norepinephrine. The monoamine oxidase inhibitors block an enzyme that breaks down some neurotransmitters, including norepinephrine. Since biological theories of depression are based on the belief that depression is due to a deficiency of norepinephrine and other chemical compounds at certain receptor sites in the brain, the biochemical effects of tricyclics and MAO inhibitors on the brain lend some support to this point of view. However, the evidence is far from conclusive (Clark, 1979; Sarason and Sarason, 1984).

The use of antidepressant drugs with teenagers is not without controversy. When antidepressant drugs are prescribed for teenagers, the subtle message that drugs can make one feel better is difficult to avoid. For this reason, the use of drugs with depressed adolescents should be approached with extreme caution. Once young people become convinced that it is easy to control mood and feel good with chemicals, they may start self-medicating to avoid struggling to resolve the emotional issues and psychological conflicts underlying depression. All mental health experts acknowledge that drug abuse is a major problem confronting teenagers today. Over-the-counter medications, unauthorized prescriptions, street drugs, and illegal psychoactive drugs are widely available to teenagers who want instant highs. Family physicians and mental health workers should avoid any use of medications or psychoactive drugs that might implicitly contribute to a teenager's decision to become involved in drug use as a way of avoiding the normal stresses of adolescent life.

ADAPTIVE POSSIBILITIES OF DEPRESSION

Depression, as a term, is usually associated with unhappiness or maladaptive connotations such as helplessness, hopelessness, excessive self-devaluation, and profound despondency. There are latent, adaptive possibilities in depression that often go unnoticed. Depression allows the body, emotions, thought processes, and behaviors to slow down (Fuhrmann, 1986). In the fast-paced society we live in, highly active teenagers seldom get the opportunity to slow down and reflect. To successfully resolve identity issues, existential dilemmas, value conflicts, and establish future goals, adolescents need time to reflect, ponder, and get in touch with themselves. Depression can be used as a growth signal, a signal indicating that it is time for the adolescent to slow down, reflect, and let go of or reorganize old beliefs, childhood support systems, and erroneous expectations. Depression is also a disguised communication to others that adolescents need help in the form of support, understanding, forgiving, or in working through painful, guilt-provoking feelings.

Depression provides an opportunity to get in touch with feelings of sadness. Sadness, as differentiated from the debilitating characteristics of severe guilt, shame, and hopelessness, contains an enriching emotional quality. There is a sweet side of sadness or a tender component of melancholy which can put us in touch with pleasant memories or warm feelings about past events and relationships. The Portuguese have the term *saudade*, which refers to the bittersweet side of sadness. This bittersweet side of sadness is reflected in a group of Portuguese songs called *fados* (Sansome, 1962). Those who block out feelings of sadness because of attempts to avoid depression may lose the emotional richness and renewal possibilities contained in sadness, which are important in overcoming depression.

Depression can provide young people with the opportunity to confront underlying myths of perfectability and eternal happiness. Adolescence is a time when myths and illusions need to be replaced with growth-facilitating beliefs. The myth of perfectability inhibits the growth of self-confidence, adequacy, and mastery because it leads to endless preoccupation with minor flaws. Replacing perfectability with the pursuit of excellence, doing one's best, and getting better with time and effort increases the probability for experiencing satisfaction or mastery as a consequence of one's accomplishments.

We live in a world where it is possible for teenagers to become convinced that feeling good is a constant or that happiness is eternal. The advertising world tells teenagers if they wear the right clothes, buy the right cosmetics, smile correctly, and eat certain foods, happiness and good times will be perpetual. In their first encounters with the woe, hopelessness, and self-criticism of depression, many teenagers think that because they are unhappy or downhearted something is personally wrong with them. They feel they have some defect others do not possess. To avoid coming to grips with what they perceive as personal inadequacies or environmental obstacles to feeling good, many adolescents search for pleasure in self-destructive activities such as drug or alcohol abuse, sexual promiscuity, or reckless adventurism. Teachers, parents, and counselors need to help young people confront this myth of eternal happiness. Adolescents need to understand that tragedy, loss, grief, sadness, the blues, and mild-to-moderate depression are parts of life. The goal in working with depression is not to avoid it, but to understand the adaptive possibilities of depression and assist adolescents in developing a philosophy of life that permits renewal and revitalization.

SUMMARY AND CONCLUSIONS

Depression is characterized by a profound sadness, gloom, dejection, futility, brooding, self-deprecation, low self-esteem, lack of energy, hopelessness, and loss of energy in usual activities. Mild-to-moderate depression is a fairly common experience in adolescents. Forty to fifty percent of adolescents report mild-to-severe symptoms of depression. The major symptoms of depression are divided into four clusters: mood, cognitive, behavioral-motivational, and physical-vegetative. Depression is a generic term that contains a continuum of reactions ranging from the blues and grief to chronic, severe depression. There are four major psychological theories of depression: (1) psychodynamic, (2) cognitive, (3) learned helplessness, and (4) behavioral. Females tend to report depression more often than males. Differences in male-female rates of depression were explained by different socialization practices concerning power and control, relationship issues, and affectional needs and management of feelings. Late adolescents are more likely to show clearly discernible mood and cognitive symptoms of depression than early adolescents. Late adolescents have developed the introspective, reflective, and critical self-analysis abilities necessary to experience hopelessness, pervasive dependency, and negative beliefs about self, future, and one's experiences. Late adolescents have also developed the expressive skills and peer intimacy that enables them to share personal feelings with others. Depressed adolescents internalize unhappy feelings and beliefs, whereas runaway adolescents act out their feelings and beliefs.

The majority of depressed adolescents can be helped with counseling and psychotherapy. Adolescents frequently recover from mild-to-moderate reactive depression without professional help through a process called spontaneous recovery. Severe, chronic depression is a sign that professional help should be obtained. Antidepressant drugs such as the tricyclics can be used to raise the spirits, improve mental alertness, and increase the physical activity level of depressed adolescents. The use of antidepressant drugs with depressed teenagers should be carefully controlled because teenagers may pick up subtle messages that it is acceptable to control one's mood with medications. While depression is normally associated with maladaptive connotations, there are latent adaptive possibilities in depression which often go unnoticed. Depression can be a signal that it is time to let go of dysfunctional beliefs, recover from loss, restructure relationships, or give up outdated protective systems.

SUGGESTIONS FOR PARENTS, TEACHERS, COUNSELORS, AND YOUTH WORKERS

1. Adolescence is a transition time when young people are confronted with bodily changes, increasing demands in social relationships, a higher level of competition in school and athletics, contradictions in cherished beliefs, and the responsibility for defining who they are. Lows and highs are to be expected as part of the normal course of development.
2. Grief and heartbreak are normal reactions to tragedy, loss, or separa-

tions in close relationships. Adolescents going through grief or a heartbreak will experience a sequential process of shock or numbness, emotional outbursts, and longing and emptiness while they are recovering. The best treatment for grief or heartbreak is the passage of time combined with support, understanding, and caring.

3. Excessive self-criticism, a persistent feeling of gloom and doom, eating irregularities, and a general slowing down or loss of interest in usual activities are signs of depression. If these moods, thoughts, behaviors, or physical reactions have been triggered by a specific failure or disappointment, the prospects for recovery are good. Again, be patient, understanding, and caring.

4. Persistent negative beliefs about self, future, and one's experiences should be gently challenged. Adolescents, whose logical thinking skills are still developing, may need some help in working their way out of all-or-nothing thinking, faulty generalizations, and hidden perfectionistic assumptions that lead to self-devaluative thoughts and gloom about the future.

5. Try to help young people find ways to feel good and experience joyful feelings about themselves not always based on external accomplishments. It is important for adolescents to develop a core of internal worth that will not fluctuate widely with changing circumstances or level of achievement.

6. In early adolescents, radical changes in behavior, such as withdrawal, angry outbursts, failing school grades, fighting, sexual acting out, or drug abuse may be signs of depression. Try to open up the communication channels to find out what's really happening in the teenager's private space.

7. Late adolescents sometimes experience periods of stuckness, drifting, and despair when confronted with the uncertainties of moving into adulthood. When this happens, it is a sign they may need assistance in sorting out the concerns or apprehensions preventing them from establishing a workable plan for the future.

8. When major signs of depression persist for weeks or months, despite your efforts to help, it's time to seek professional help.

9. A down-to-earth book that contains many useful suggestions for parents, teachers, and counselors working with depressed adolescents is Kathleen McCoy's *Coping with Teenage Depression: A Parent's Guide*, published by New American Library in 1982.

10. Finally, it is important that young people understand that tragedy, loss, and disappointments are inevitable life experiences. The ultimate goal is not to deny or avoid these inevitable experiences, but to help young people develop personal qualities such as resilience, revitalization, and renewal that will help them grow from disappointment and loss.

DISCUSSION QUESTIONS

1. Describe and give examples of the four primary areas in which the symptoms of depression are likely to appear.
2. Why is depression more likely to occur in late adolescence than in early adolescence?
3. Why is depression more likely to occur in female adolescents?
4. What are the major similarities and differences in the psychodynamic, cognitive, learned helplessness, and behavioral theories of depression?
5. What is the difference between fantasized or symbolic loss and real loss, and how are fantasy loss and real loss involved in depression?
6. Describe the depression spectrum. How much of the spectrum have you or close friends experienced? Discuss the circumstances surrounding these experiences.
7. Describe the cognitive approaches and client centered—relationship approaches in working with depressed adolescents. Which do you prefer and why?
8. Why is it important for adolescents and young adults to learn how to cope with tragedy, loss, grief, disappointment, and sadness?
9. How do you help friends and family cope with sadness, loss, or separations? Does it work? If so, why, if not, why not?

5
Suicide

PREVIEW

"Against all the injuries of life, I have the refuge of death" — Seneca.
"There is but one truly serious philosophical problem, and that is suicide.
Judging whether or not life is worth living amounts to considering the funda-
mental question of philosophy" — Camus (1955, p. 3).

Adolescent suicide has increased 300% in the past 30 years. Suicide is now
the third leading cause of death in adolescence and the second leading cause
of death in college students. Each year, approximately 6,000 young people
take the irreversible step of choosing the refuge of death by successfully
committing suicide. They settle Camus' fundamental philosophic problem
of being and nonbeing by choosing death. Depression is the psychological
syndrome most commonly associated with suicide in adolescents. As the
severity and duration of depression increase, suicidal thoughts are likely to
occur. It is difficult to avoid momentary thoughts of not wanting to go on
living when one feels a pervasive sense of despair, misery, helplessness, and
hopelessness. Whether or not an adolescent acts on suicidal thoughts depends on personal resilience, environmental support, and the nature and
extent of personal distress and turmoil. Death and suicide have different
historical, religious, and cultural meanings. Some adolescents may not understand the permanence of death. Four primary models of adolescent suicide are discussed: the crisis model, the long-term stress model, the motives
model, and the sociological model.

The majority of adolescent suicides and suicidal attempts are the outgrowth of a long history of personal and intrafamilial discord, dissatisfaction, and distress intensified by a recent crisis. Treatment involves immediate

crisis intervention and assessment, followed by psychotherapy to help the adolescent become reinvested in life. Every suicidal attempt, threat, or gesture should be promptly evaluated to assess the degree of risk and what can be done to increase the adolescent's motivation to live. Obviously, prevention is the best treatment for suicide. Suicide-prevention programs have three primary components. First, the dissemination of information on warning signs, dynamics, and referral sources. Second, accessible suicide-prevention and crisis-intervention facilities with 24-hour hot lines. Third, research into the causes of suicide and increasing the public's awareness of the dangers of adolescent suicide. Postvention involves mental health counseling to assist the survivors in coping with grief and loss after a successful adolescent suicide. The lasting impact of adolescent suicide on family members and close friends is discussed in the epilogue.

Case Example 5-1: Lillian

> Lillian, a 17-year-old high school junior, was initially seen for a consultation by a crisis team psychologist in a hospital emergency room after she had attempted suicide by overdosing on tranquilizers and sleeping pills. She told the psychologist she wanted to die because "it's just too hard to keep trying, no one cares . . . nothing will ever change for the better, I can't ever remember being happy." She seemed very depressed, tearful, somewhat confused, and was still experiencing nausea from the overdose of tranquilizers and sleeping pills. Lillian had been planning to commit suicide for some time. She thought about hanging, throwing herself in front of a car, and using a gun. She rejected hanging and jumping from a car, as both are too painful. Shooting was eliminated because she had no access to a gun. She decided on tranquilizers because she was able to obtain a forged prescription from a contact in her neighborhood. Lillian would not reveal the identity of her contact. On the day of the suicide attempt, Lillian cut school, wrote a goodbye note to her mother and sisters telling them not to worry about "me anymore," turned on her favorite radio music station, and took an unknown quantity of the pills. Her younger sister returned from school early, found the note, and found Lillian unconscious in a bedroom they shared. The sister ran next door where the neighbor immediately called the paramedics.
>
> Lillian remembered her childhood as a very unhappy time. Her parents were divorced when she was approximately 6 years old. Prior to the divorce, there was a considerable amount of arguing and fighting between the parents, especially when they had been drinking. When her father had been drinking, he tended to become abusive toward Lillian, her sister, who was a year older, and her mother. Early in her school history, Lillian was diagnosed as having a learning disability due to a short attention span. The psychologist who tested her said she had average to above-average intelligence, but was too preoccupied with personal issues to pay attention to the teacher or concentrate on learning her school assignments. She would get very anxious when called upon to speak in class and was teased by the other children for being timid and slightly overweight. The school psychologist recommended a period of family and individual counseling, but her mother did not follow through. Lillian

moved several times when she was in grade school. Frequent moves and changes of schools made it difficult to make friends and also exacerbated her learning problems. Lillian rarely saw her father during this period. Her mother drank excessively, but stopped drinking after she joined Alcoholics Anonymous (AA) when Lillian was about 9. Shortly thereafter, her mother married a man whom she had met at AA. The following year her younger sister was born.

Two years later, when Lillian was 12, the stepfather died suddenly of a heart attack. Her mother's world seemed to fall apart. She started drinking again, became very abusive, and accused Lillian and her older sister of causing the stepfather's death by keeping him under a lot of stress. The older sister told a school counselor about the physical abuse, and the family was referred to a psychologist for family counseling. Lillian enjoyed the family counseling sessions, but the family stopped going after about eight meetings. Following the premature termination of family counseling, her mother's drinking became more severe.

During early to middle adolescence, Lillian became sexually active. She started cutting school, running around with a predelinquent crowd, and experimenting with drugs. She ran away from home three times. After she ran away a third time, Lillian's mother sent her and her older sister to live with their natural father, who had reentered the picture. Lillian saw the move with her father as a chance to "start over and get my life on the right track." During the father's long absence, Lillian had idealized what life might be like with her father, despite her memory of the early turmoil. After about 6 months with her father, an incident occurred one weekend in which the father and two of his adult friends allegedly made sexual overtures toward Lillian's older sister. Lillian and her sister refused to remain with the father after the incident. They returned to live with their mother who continued her pattern of excessive drinking and of expressing verbal and physical abuse when she was under the influence of alcohol. Lillian and her sister were now physically stronger than their mother and would fight back until their mother backed down.

After Lillian returned to live with her mother, she became increasingly depressed and withdrawn. She started cutting school again, would sleep most of the day, and periodically used marijuana and cocaine. The one bright spot in her life was her boyfriend. She described him as "straight, understanding, and caring." He worked part-time, attended school regularly, and was thinking about going to college. Lillian clung to him as her stabilizing force. As time passed, the boyfriend began to feel overwhelmed by Lillian and her problems. The relationship ended when the boyfriend stopped coming around. Lillian thinks she drove him away by being too needy and always wanting understanding and support. After the breakup, Lillian's depression became more pervasive. Life seemed hopeless. She got "tired of struggling." She started thinking about suicide, and slowly evolved a plan. After the suicide attempt, the psychologist recommended that Lillian be hospitalized for a brief period in order to do a complete suicide evaluation and assessment, remove her from a stressful home environment, and begin the initial phase of psychotherapy.

Lillian's case illustrates several important factors in the dynamics of adolescent suicide: a long history of family and personal conflicts, escalation of stress during adolescence, progressive social isolation, deteriorating coping mechanisms, and a final precipitating stress brought on by the breakup with her boyfriend.

DEPRESSION AND SUICIDE

Depression is the psychological syndrome most commonly associated with suicidal behavior in adolescents (Petzel and Riddle, 1981; Farberow, 1985; Shaffer, 1986). It has been estimated that 40% of adolescents who either attempt suicide or experience persistent suicidal thoughts are struggling with major symptoms of depression (Greuling and DeBlassie, 1980). Within the depression syndrome, hopelessness is the symptom frequently linked to suicidal behavior. Hopelessness is a negative belief about the future, a belief that nothing can be or will be done by the individual or anyone else to change the unhappiness, misery, guilt, despondency, and perceptions of personal failure that accompany depression. In research studies, helplessness has been highly correlated with suicidal intent, the wish to die, and suicidal attempts (Kovacs et al., 1975; Lester et al., 1979; Boyer and Guthrie, 1985). In some cases, depression associated with suicidal behavior is concealed by masked depression or depression equivalence, such as rebelliousness, drug and alcohol abuse, self-destructive behavior, sexual promiscuity, restlessness, or running away (Peck, 1985).

A small percentage of suicidal adolescents may be undergoing a breakdown in reality testing characterized by disorganized and confused thought processes (Husain and Vandiver, 1984; Greuling and DeBlassie, 1980). Voices within themselves, or other unreal forces tell them to kill themselves. Occasionally, suicide will be committed by an adolescent who seems to have everything going for him or her. They are popular, have a successful future ahead, and are likable, good students from loving families. When these supposedly spontaneous, impulsive, or no-warning suicides are reconstructed, using indepth interviews with family members, teachers, close friends, ministers, therapists, and physicians, a trail of direct and indirect clues usually becomes evident. These clues might include a preoccupation with death, goodbye signs, and/or failure to recover from a loss, or feelings of rejection is some form. Suicide does not just happen; more often than not there are a series of marker events leading up to the point where the adolescent decides to take his or her life (Litman and Diller, 1985; Peck et al., 1985).

DEFINITIONS, SUICIDE RATES, AND PUBLIC AND PROFESSIONAL AWARENESS

Before continuing our discussion of adolescent suicide, it is important to define several terms that appear in the adolescent suicidal literature. Suicide or completed suicide are intentional, self-inflicted acts that result in the death of the individual. Circumstances surrounding the person's death lead to the conclusion that the person took a positive action with the purpose of ending his or her life. A suicidal attempt is a life-threatening behavior in which the intent is to jeopardize one's own life or give the appearance of jeopardizing one's life. A suicidal gesture is a superficial, nonfatal attempt at self-injury primarily designed to gain the attention of others, such as making shallow cuts on one's wrist. Suicidal threats are statements of one's intention to engage in suicidal behavior. Some writers use the term parasuicide to cover all deliberately nonfatal acts resulting in self-injury, such as deliberately overdosing on medications or poisons (Sarason and Sarason, 1984). Suicidal thoughts are ideas about engaging in life-threatening acts that can be inferred from a person's statements or behaviors. Suicidal behavior is a generic term that refers to suicidal actions, gestures, attempts, plans, threats, statements, or behaviors from which suicidal intentions and thoughts can be inferred.

Signals or clues, indicating suicidal thoughts or intentions, can be divided into four broad areas: (1) verbal; (2) behavioral; (3) situational; and (4) syndromatic (Ray and Johnson, 1983). Verbal signs refer to threats about wanting to die or statements implying preoccupation with death, such as "I just don't want to live anymore, dying would be so much easier." Behavioral signs are unsuccessful suicidal attempts or actions, such as drawing up a will, saying final goodbyes, giving away prized possessions, and secretly making suicidal plans. Situational clues refer to recent deaths or suicides of loved ones, personal failures, and breakups in romantic relationships, which may leave the person feeling empty and discouraged. Syndromatic clues are depression, hopelessness, despair, isolation, and alienation. The person feels he or she has little to live for. Syndromatic signs also occur in states of psychological disorientation, where people hear voices telling them to kill themselves.

Suicidal thoughts and behaviors can be ranked on a continuum from least dangerous to the most dangerous. Fleeting suicidal thoughts and attention-getting suicidal gestures are the least likely to be fatal. Suicidal threats, such as making serious verbal statements about suicidal plans and actual suicide attempts, are the most dangerous (Gilead and Mulaik, 1983). Experts in suicidal behavior warn, however, that all suicidal statements, threats, thoughts, gestures, or attempts should be taken seriously, since the risk of being wrong could result in an adolescent's successful suicide (Peck et al., 1985). Suicidal experts have recently uncovered a series of events they now refer to as cluster suicides. Cluster suicide is a phenomenon in which a series of adolescent suicides occur in a sequence in the same community. The suicide of one adolescent triggers another in the same geographic area. Suicide experts are not sure whether the cluster suicides are coincidental or causally linked (Doan and Peterson, 1984).

According to statistics compiled by the National Center for Health Statistics (1982), the suicide rate among 15- to 24-year-olds has increased 300% since 1950 (Thornton, 1983). In 1950, the rate of suicides per 100,000 persons in the 15- to 24-year-old category was 4.1; the rate in 1960 was 5.2 per 100,000; the rate in 1970 was 8.8 per 100,000; and the rate in 1980 was 12.5 per 100,000 (see Fig. 5-1).

Approximately 6,000 young people succeed in committing suicide annually. This breaks down to 15–18 successful youth suicides a day (United States Congress, 1986). No other age group has such a significant increase in suicide rates. Suicide is the third leading cause of death in adolescents, outranked only by death from accidents and homicides. Suicide is the second leading cause of death in college students and the ninth leading cause of death in the general population (Kimmel and Weiner, 1985). Suicide is more often the cause of death in adolescence than at any other time in life. Suicide is rarely recorded as a cause of death before age 10. It starts to increase in early adolescence and continues to increase into young adulthood (Shaffer, 1986). The actual number of adolescent suicides may be much higher than indicated in the statistics. Accidents are the leading cause of death in young people. It has been estimated that 50% or more of adolescent suicides are mistakenly classified as accidents (Blaine, 1979; Emergy, 1983). Because of the social, cultural, and religious taboos surrounding suicide, physicians certifying death may classify a suicide as an accident or certify cause of death as "undetermined" to protect the family (Schaffer, 1986). High-risk, self-destructive behaviors are difficult to classify. When an adolescent who has been mixing drugs and alcohol dies in a single car accident, is it an accident or a disguised suicide? Extreme risk-taking, constantly testing the

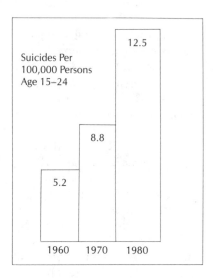

FIGURE 5-1. Youth suicide trend. (Adapted from National Center for Health Care Statistics. (1985). *Vital Statistics of the United States.* Washington, DC: U.S. Government Printing Office.)

limits of danger and flirting with doom, can lead to death whether or not it is later certified as an accident or as a suicide. There is no way to accurately determine how many fatal accidents are true suicides.

Each year approximately 1 million young people move in and out of suicidal crises or experience episodes of hopelessness and despair where suicide is considered a possible solution (McCoy, 1982). Between 250,000 and 400,000 will attempt suicide each year (Thornton, 1983; United States Congress, 1986). Fortunately, only 2% or less successfully commit suicide (Steinberg, 1985). Since one-half to three-fourths of young people who commit suicide have attempted or threatened suicide in the past, suicidal attempts and threats should be taken seriously (Hodges and Siegel, 1985).

Young women attempt suicide 4 to 8 times more often than young men, but young men succeed 4 times more often (Carlson, 1983; National Center, 1985). Males succeed more often because they use highly lethal means such as firearms, auto crashes, jumping from heights, and hanging. Females use less lethal means, such as pills or slashing wrists, which permit a higher degree of rescue. No satisfactory explanation exists to account for the differences in male–female suicidal attempts and completed suicides. Some of the reasons advanced suggest that females are more likely to ask for direct or indirect help and are less interested in highly lethal methods like hanging or shooting, which can cause disfigurement. Male suicides are more carefully planned, and males are likely to use more highly lethal means (Davis, 1983).

The dramatic rise in adolescent suicide has been called a national tragedy (Davis, 1983). Teen suicide has been the subject of numerous articles in magazines, newspapers, and professional mental health journals. The large increase in the number of articles in professional journals indicates that mental health professionals have become more interested in adolescent suicide in the past few years. Between 1900 and 1967, there were approximately 200 articles on adolescent suicide in professional mental health journals. In the one-year period 1982–1983 over 300 articles in professional mental health journals focused on adolescent suicide (Carlson, 1983).

Television has started to grapple with the sensitive topic of adolescent suicide. In 1984 CBS produced "Silence of the Heart," a trauma–drama about a 17-year-old, upper middle-class male, whose parents ignored early suicide warning signs of their son's preoccupation with poetry involving themes of death, giving away of prized possessions, rejection in social and roommate relationships, deteriorating school performance, and social withdrawal. Indirectly, the victim tried to send a message that went unheard. ABC's "Surviving," shown in 1985, is about the pain and recovery parents experience when their teenagers successfully carry out a suicide pact.

A considerable amount of debate surrounds the positive and negative effects of television dramas on adolescent suicide. On the positive side are the educational effects. Suicide trauma–dramas can highlight the causes, early warning signs, emotional despair, and critical choice points suicidal young people encounter. On the negative side is the suggestibility factor. After seeing a TV movie on suicide, some highly suggestible young people might think of suicide as the primary solution to their personal dilemmas. Studies indicate that there appears to be a link between TV, newspapers, dramas, and the increases in the number of young people taking their lives. Carstensen and Phillips (1986) report an increase of 7% in adolescent suicides in the week after major network stories having to do with suicide. Gould and Shaffer (1986) assessed the impact of TV movies on teen suicide in the metropolitan area of New York. They examined four programs that contained suicidal themes broadcast between October, 1984 and February, 1985. Their findings showed an increase in suicide after three of these broadcasts, a CBS Afternoon Special and two nighttime dramas, NBC's "Reason to Live" and ABC's "Surviving." There were no recorded suicides after the CBS drama "Silence of the Heart," which was accompanied by a discussion of suicide-prevention treatment centers and emergency hot lines.

Studies on suicide and suggestibility can be criticized on two accounts: They do not explain how the complex linkage between suggestibility and suicide operates; and those on suggestibility do not discuss the positive effects of TV programs, such as learning to recognize warning signs, increased use of suicide hot lines or counseling services, and decisions not to commit suicide after watching the effects on the survivors. Well-balanced TV programs accompanied by facts about hot lines, nonsuicidal alternatives, and counseling can have educational and preventive effects (Schacter, 1986).

Teen suicide is now part of the adolescent consciousness. Suicide themes are expressed in popular adolescent songs. "Ode to Billy Joe,"[1] a song by Bobbie Gentry about a teenager who committed suicide, was number 1 on the teen musical charts for several weeks (Davis, 1983). In "You're Only Human,"[2] Billy Joel tells teenagers not to use suicide as a way to cope with problems, to recognize that they are only human, that mistakes are part of life, and to give themselves the opportunity to get a second wind. "I Think I'm Going to Kill Myself" by Elton John and Bernie Taupin expresses suicidal intentions, how the suicidal act will be carried out, thoughts about immortality, expected grief of the survivors and an indirect plea for help (Ross, 1985):

> People rushing everywhere,
> Swarming around like flies,
> I think I'll buy a forty-four,

---

[1]ODE TO BILLY JOE by Bobbie Gentry © 1967 Northridge Music Co. Used by Permission. All Rights Reserved.
[2]"You're Only Human (Second Wind)" by Billy Joel © 1985 Joel Songs. All rights Controlled and Administered by SBK BLACKWOOD MUSIC INC.
All Rights Reserved. International Copyright Secured. Used by Permission.

Give 'em all a surprise.
Think I'm gonna kill myself,
Cause a little suicide,
Stick around for a couple of days,
What a scandal if I die.
Yea, I'm gonna kill myself,
Get a little headline news,
I'd like to see what the paper say,
On the state of teenage blues. . . .[1]

HISTORICAL, CULTURAL, AND RELIGIOUS IMPLICATIONS OF SUICIDE

The first known recorded document on suicide appeared about 4,000 years ago in Egypt. The document is known by several titles, such as *The Dispute of a Man With His Soul, The Dialogue of a Misanthrope With His Soul,* or *The Suicide* (Hatton et al., 1977). One interpretation is of a man tired of life who is trying to get his soul to accompany him to death. His soul is afraid that he will not have a blissful afterlife if he succeeds in killing himself. References to suicide appear in the Old Testament (Judges 9:53; Judges 16:25–29) and in the New Testament in the story of Judas Iscariot who commits suicide for the betrayal of Jesus Christ (Matthew 27:3–7).

A range of cultural and religious attitudes toward suicides can be found throughout history and literature. Suicide is so despised in some cultures that a person who committed suicide is not given a legitimate or sacred burial place. In other cultures, a person is praised when self-inflicted death is done for a noble cause (Davis, 1983; Sarason and Sarason, 1984). There are records of tribal cultures in which a warrior might commit suicide upon the death of the chief in order to accompany the chief to the next world, to provide him with personal services and companionship (Dublin, 1963). Most western societies attempt to prevent suicide and interfere with its completion whenever possible. The Jewish, Protestant, and Catholic religions have rules against suicide based on the biblical commandment "Thou Shalt Not Kill" (Exodus 20:13). The suicide victim has sinned against God and precluded the chance for repentance. Japan has one of the highest suicide rates in the world in the 15- to 24-year-old age group. According to traditional Japanese standards, *Hara Kari*, a form of ceremonial or ritual suicide, is an honorable death, a way one can atone for personal failure or shame brought on one's family.

On some Indian reservations in contemporary America, the suicide rate among youths is five times the national average. Cultural conflicts, circular

---

relocation from reservations to cities and back again, and the cycle of poverty, alcoholism, disease, inadequate housing, and substandard health care on the reservations are psychologically overwhelming for many Native-American youths. In seeking to define their identity and autonomy, Native-American young people face bewildering conflicts between the way of life on the reservations and the values of mainstream America. Culture shock and dislocation become part of the American Indian child's way of life very early. He or she might be removed from the security of family to attend school away from the reservation. During adolescence, a difficult choice must be made between reservation life with its limited opportunities or life in the white man's world which appears to be strange and hostile (Smith, 1980).

THE MEANING OF DEATH IN ADOLESCENCE

True suicide requires a clear understanding of the irreversibility and finality of death. The suicides of children under 10 are usually listed as accidental because young children, while they may wish to die, do not understand the permanence of death (Morgan, 1980). Between 10 and 12, preadolescents develop the abstract thinking abilities to conceptually understand the irreversibility of death. Adolescents understand the permanence of death as it pertains to others, but may have an incomplete or distorted perception of their own death (Gould, 1965). Suicidal adolescents, regardless of their general conceptual understanding of death, may think they are personally immortal. Others will die, but somehow the permanence of death will not seal them off from life. An early-adolescent female who committed suicide because of an unplanned pregnancy, left her mother a note before she stepped into a speeding train, saying she wanted to come back and care for her mother (Kraft, 1983).

Adolescence is a time when many teenagers regard themselves and their feelings, thoughts, and perceptions as highly unique. Because of what Elkind (1967) refers to as the personal fable, adolescents can create thoughts about their own immortality, special connections with God, or see death as an event that will transform the world. The actuality of death is a remote event in adolescence. One's peers are usually healthy, energetic, and looking forward to a long life. Cultural customs feed into the unreality of death by hiding the dying and the dead away from view in hospitals and memorial parks. On TV and in the movies, death is frequently violent and transient to the point that it numbs one's senses. The characters don't really die and death can be controlled by switching the channel or leaving the movie theater. Alice Cooper, a teenage rock star, used to entertain his audiences with simulated hangings. One of his avid fans, a 14-year-old boy, was apparently so stimulated by Alice Cooper's simulated hanging that he tried it himself. Unfortunately, the youth died. It cannot be conclusively determined whether or not the boy really intended to die (Rice, 1984; Adams and Gullotta, 1983).

THE PSYCHOLOGICAL AUTOPSY

A psychological autopsy is a carefully reconstructed, retrospective study of the suicide-victim's life to determine the meanings, implications, and motives for an individual's suicide. Each suicide is a complicated puzzle, the outcome of a confluence of motives, stresses, meanings, and life events. Suicide victims usually leave a trail of direct and indirect clues. The purpose of the psychological autopsy is to unravel the direct and indirect clues that make up the suicide puzzle and arrive at a sensible interpretation of the adolescent's self-inflicted death. The psychological autopsy is conducted by examining the victim's character, life-style, presuicidal crises, coping and conflict resolution strategies, developmental history, and family through interviews with those who knew the victim and the analysis of suicide notes, letters, diaries, and other personal writings (Litman and Diller, 1985).

Specific areas of the adolescent's developmental history, covered in the psychological autopsy, include the following: (1) patterns of family interaction, disruption, and coping styles; (2) peer relationships; (3) drug and alcohol abuse; (4) maladaptive behavior; (5) previous suicidal behavior and depression; (6) life-style; (7) recent stresses; and (8) ways of coping with stress. Investigators are also concerned with the adolescent's understanding of death and how he or she pictures what will happen after death, the availability of lethal means such as guns, pills, or poisons, and the adolescent's knowledge regarding how to use these means (Carlson, 1983). An extensive list of issues covered in the psychological autopsy is provided in Table 5-1. To obtain this information, extensive interviews are conducted with parents, siblings, other relatives, peers, therapists, physicians, school personnel, and others who may have known the victim. While the findings of the psychological autopsy can no longer help the victim, the information can be useful to family, friends, and mental health workers who are trying to understand the dynamics and motives of adolescent suicide.

THEORETICAL MODELS OF ADOLESCENT SUICIDE

Four primary models of adolescent suicide developed from clinical case studies, psychological autopsies, and suicide research will be discussed in this section: (1) the crisis model; (2) the long-term stress model; (3) the motives model; and (4) the sociological model.

The Crisis Model of Suicide

The crisis model depicts suicide as an emergency or crisis-oriented act brought on by an acute stress situation (Sarason and Sarason, 1984). The crisis model of suicide is similar to reactive depression. A relatively normal

Table 5-1. Psychological Autopsy Outline[a]

---

1. Identifying information for victim (name, age, address, marital status, religious practices, occupation, and other details).
2. Details of the death (including the cause or method and other pertinent details).
3. Brief outline of victim's history (siblings, marriage, medical illnesses, medical treatment, psychotherapy, previous suicide attempts).
4. Death history of victim's family (suicides, cancer, other fatal illnesses, ages at death, and other details).
5. Description of the personality and life-style of the victim.
6. Victim's typical patterns of reaction to stress, emotional upsets, and periods of disequilibrium.
7. Any recent stress—from last few days to last 12 months—upsets, pressures, tensions, or anticipations of trouble.
8. Role of alcohol and drugs in (a) overall life-style of victim and (b) his death.
9. Nature of victim's interpersonal relationships (including physicians).
10. Fantasies, dreams, thoughts, premonitions, or fears of victim relating to death, accident, or suicide.
11. Changes in the victim before death (of habits, hobbies, eating, sexual patterns, and other life routines).
12. Information relating to the "life side" of victim (upswings, successes, plans).
13. Assessment of intention, that is, role of the victim in his own demise.
14. Rating of lethality.
15. Reactions of informants to victim's death.
16. Comments, special features, etc.

---

[a]Adapted from: Shneidman, E. S. (1976). Suicide Among the Gifted. In E. S. Shneidman (Ed.), *Suicidology: Contemporary developments*. New York: Grune & Stratton, and Shneidman, E. S. (1977). The psychological autopsy guide. In *Guide to the investigation and reporting of drug abuse deaths* (Vol. 6). Washington, DC: U.S. Department of Health, Education and Welfare.

adolescent or teenager, who is functioning well, enters into a vulnerable period where a sudden drop in well-being and self-esteem is brought about by loss, failure, disappointment, or separation. The increased stress triggers a suicidal crisis. The crisis period lasts about 6 weeks, until the adolescent either resolves the situation and gets back to the precrisis level of functioning or succumbs to suicidal thoughts.

The crisis model of suicide was the traditional view of suicidal behavior proposed by the Los Angeles Suicide Prevention Center in the 1960s. Subsequent research suggests that the crisis model does not account for the majority of suicide cases in the adolescent or adult populations. Investigations conducted by the Los Angeles Suicide Prevention Center in the 1970s indicate that only a small number of adolescents were driven to suicide attempts by a single crisis episode alone. In two-thirds or more of the cases, the typical adolescent suicide or suicidal attempt was an outgrowth of a long history of dissatisfaction, conflict, and distress (Peck, 1985).

The Long-Term Stress Model

The long-term stress model of adolescent suicide, proposed by Jerry Jacobs (1971), consists of five sequential stages beginning in childhood and culminating in a conscious decision as an adolescent to commit suicide. Jacobs based his model on case histories and interviews with adolescents who had attempted suicide and a nonsuicidal control group of well-functioning young people. Progression toward suicidal attempts was an outgrowth of hopelessness, helplessness, and feelings of worthlessness, preceded by a long history of family conflicts, negative life efforts, feelings of inadequacy, ineffective coping techniques, progressive social isolation, and a final precipitating trauma signaling the end of hope. A similar model has been developed by Farberow (1985). The five stages of the Jacobs Model consist of: (1) long history of psychological turmoil and family conflict; (2) escalation of family problems and personal conflicts during adolescence; (3) progressive failure of problem-solving techniques and increasing social isolation; (4) the end of hope; and (5) justification of the suicidal act.

Stage 1: Long History of Psychological Turmoil
and Family Conflict

The family history of presuicidal adolescence is usually characterized by turmoil, conflict, marital discord, and instability. Parents have difficulties not only coping with their children and providing for the children's emotional needs, but tend to be overwhelmed by adult problems in living, such as divorce, disorganization, job stability, geographic dislocation, drug and alcohol abuse, and severe psychological distress. Parents seem unable to build growth-enhancing relationships with their children and provide the emotional security needed to build self-worth, confidence, trust, and hope. When parental loss through separation, death, or divorce occurs, it is not the loss of the parent that predisposes the child to suicide, but the lack of a caring relationship that preceded the loss (Husain and Vandiver, 1984). The absence or loss of nurturing parent–child relationships makes subsequent loss more difficult and creates questions about personal worth.

Evidence to support the observation of intrafamily turmoil and lack of supportive relationships comes from extensive research on suicidal adolescents. Hendin (1975, 1985), in a series of interviews with suicidal college and high school students, found a history of serious family problems. Garfinkel et al. (1982), in a study of 505 emergency room admissions of suicidal adolescents and children, found that their family histories showed a high percentage of psychiatric illness, alcohol and drug abuse, suicide, unemployment, and marital separations. Topol and Reznikoff (1982) assessed hospitalized suicidal adolescents, hospitalized nonsuicidal adolescents, and nonhospitalized coping adolescents. They found that the suicidal adolescents showed a more extensive history of family turmoil and distress. Psychological autopsies on 50 adolescent suicides, conducted by McIntire and Angle (1973), revealed a high degree of intrafamilial strife.

Stage 2: Escalation of Family Problems and Personal Conflicts During Adolescence

Things don't get any better for presuicidal young people during adolescence. New problems are introduced over and beyond the usual adolescent conflicts. Normal adolescent concerns regarding identity, freedom, sexuality, and values are intensified by continuing family strife. Parents and adolescents are unable to develop a relationship based upon mutual respect, two-way communication, and collaborative decision making. Conflicts center around the extreme ends of confrontation and lack of support. Parents vacillate between excessive control, verbal abuse, and psychological discipline and indifference. Consequently, the adolescent feels unappreciated, misunderstood, rejected, and may want to strike back (Jacobs, 1971; Husain and Vandiver, 1984). When things don't work out, despite one's best efforts, old feelings of self-doubt, inadequacy, and worthlessness are likely to be intensified.

Stage 3: Progressive Failure of Problem-Solving Techniques and Increasing Social Isolation

In the year prior to the suicidal attempt, the adolescent unsuccessfully tries to resolve family conflict and personal distress with a variety of adaptive and maladaptive problem-solving strategies. When the adaptive problem-solving or coping strategies do not work, behaviors become progressively more maladaptive. An adolescent might start out by trying to please parents with obedience, good grades, acquiescence, and getting rid of peers and dress styles the parents disapprove of. When these actions do not produce parental love, understanding, and support, the young person may respond with overt anger, defiance, running away, rebelliousness, school truancy, or drug use, followed by increasing signs of depression, alienation, and withdrawal from social relationships outside the family. Parents see the overt behavior problems and dramatic reversals in conduct, but are not able to understand that these adaptive and maladaptive behaviors represent attempts to cope with serious family and personal distress. Parents can only see the problems caused by the youth's disruptive behavior, whereas presuicidal adolescents, when interviewed after unsuccessful suicidal attempts, understood their actions as ways of coping with increasing distress and conflicts (Husain and Vandiver, 1984; Jacobs, 1971).

According to Caine (1978) and Farberow (1977), social isolation is one of the most important dynamic factors in teenage suicidal behavior. Withdrawal and isolation from friends and relationships outside the family is critical because the adolescent is disconnected from support systems. Since they have been unable to rely on their family for support, once the friends are no longer around, the presuicidal adolescent is increasingly alone and

alienated. Loneliness and social isolation can intensify feelings of emptiness, despondency, despair, and worthlessness, which have been building
since childhood.

Stage 4: The End of Hope

The end of hope is triggered by one last trauma or stressful event such as
an unplanned pregnancy, expulsion from school, arrest on a shoplifting or
drug charge, being sent to the other parent to live, romance breakup, or the
loss of one's last important remaining relationship. This last stressful occurrence is the final straw, so to speak, which sets into motion a chain of events
that convinces the adolescent life is hopeless. This phase is similar to the
crisis model of suicide discussed earlier. The difference is that, here, the end
of hope is the culmination of a long history of turmoil, conflict, rejection,
and disappointment, rather than a single disruptive crisis in an otherwise
manageable existence. During the end-of-hope stage, the adolescent consciously comes to the conclusion that life is no longer worth living. He or she
can no longer conceive of a fulfilling life (Forisha-Kovach, 1983).

Stage 5: Justification of the Suicidal Act

In the final stage, the suicidal adolescent goes through an internal process
in which he justifies suicide as the only viable remaining option and estab-
lishes a plan to carry out the suicidal action. It is a conscious, rational
decision of an adolescent who can see no other solution to the chronic
problems of living (Gilead and Mulaik, 1983). The young person is convinced that neither he nor anyone else can open a pathway into a fulfilling
life. The answer to Camus' philosophic question is that life is no longer
worth living, the only choice is to cross over the bridge into nonbeing.
Adolescent suicide notes often reflect the end of hope and the internal
process of justifying suicide as the only option. Notes indicate that long-
standing problems are often unsolvable and not of the adolescent's making;
the choice has been made after careful consideration and the adolescent
hopes that others will understand (Wenar, 1982).

The Motives Model

Toolan (1962), Shneidman (1976b), and others have attempted to identify
the major motivational forces underlying suicidal behavior. From their investigations, seven primary suicidal motives can be described: (1) internalization of anger; (2) suicide as a manipulative act; (3) plea for help; (4)
protection from unbearable stress and conflicts; (5) hallucinatory voices
underlying suicide; (6) need to join a deceased loved one; and (7) imitation
and suggestibility.

Internalization of Anger

The internalization of anger as a primary motive for suicidal behavior resembles the psychodynamic view of depression. An overdeveloped internal conscious and fears of rejection prevent the adolescent from expressing realistic anger, dissatisfaction, or irritability with others. The person develops a self-sacrificing, self-blaming style to avoid expressing hostility toward others, and is unforgiving of self for perceived misdeeds. The unexpressed anger or hostility ultimately turns inward into self-blame, guilt, self-contempt, and self-devaluation. Self-destruction by suicide is an attempt to punish one's self and atone for guilt and shame. The adolescent feels or thinks that "I'm so terrible, I don't deserve to live."

Suicide as a Manipulative Act

Suicide as a manipulative act is an attempt to control others, establish power, gain attention, or punish others. Adolescence is a time when young people want greater power over their lives, yet at the same time they want the attention and support of their parents, peers, and significant others. If attempts to establish power and control through straightforward communications and negotiations are unsatisfactory, young people sometimes use suicidal behavior to gain attention, to influence the behavior of others, to send a message, or to punish others (Davis, 1983).

Plea for Help

In this case, suicidal behavior is a last ditch effort to communicate to parents and others that one needs help and support to resolve conflicts. The primary goal is not death, but to send a message to parents and others that important changes need to take place before the adolescent can resume life with a feeling of hope and confidence (Farberow and Shneidman, 1961; Weiner, 1982).

Protection from Unbearable Stress and Conflict

One of the primary functions of coping strategies is to reduce conflict and pain. Suicide can be used as a way of coping with unbearable personal conflict and pain. The motive underlying suicidal behavior is to stop unendurable stress and anguish. The central goal is not the ending of one's life, but the termination of one's problems. Death is seen by the suffering adolescent as the solution to blocking out the consequences of a painful existence. Nonsuicidal coping strategies have failed, and death is seen as the final option. The individual no longer has hope that other solutions will work. The unfortunate outcome of successful suicide as a coping strategy is that it ends life (Shneidman, 1984).

Hallucinatory Voices Urging Suicide

Ten to fifteen percent of the young people who attempt suicide have been diagnosed as psychotic, or as having trouble with reality testing due to serious psychological confusion. Psychosis is a serious breakdown of thinking and of the emotional processes. Many of these adolescents hear voices representing God, the devil, or other powerful authority figures telling them to commit suicide. When teenagers are suffering from deficiencies in reality testing or the thinking and perceptual disorganization characterizing a psychotic reaction, voices telling them to commit suicide can have a compelling effect. Hallucinations, perceptual alterations, and disordered thinking can also be triggered by the excessive use of mind-altering drugs such as LSD, mescaline, or peyote (Greuling and DeBlassie, 1980; Husain and Vandiver, 1984).

The Need to Join a Deceased or Loved One

The loss of a loved one through death creates an empty emotional space that is difficult to fill. Saying the final goodbye to a cherished relationship and moving through the process of grief and recovery are not easily accomplished. Occasionally, adolescents decide to fill the void by committing suicide to join the loved one in death.

Case Example 5-2: Herb

The fiancée of Herb, a 19-year-old male college student, was killed instantly in an auto accident one evening when she was on her way home from the library with her girlfriend. At the gravesite, Herb started having feelings of wanting to join her in death. As the months went by, he was unable to move through the grief and recovery process. The feeling of wanting to join his fiancée in death became stronger. Emptiness, longing, and the thought of life without her was too unbearable. He finally decided to commit suicide by jumping off a well-known bridge. After quietly getting his affairs in order and leaving a note in which he explained his reasons for not wanting to live, he drove to the bridge, parked his car, and successfully carried out his plan.

The most famous case of young people committing suicide to join each other in death is that of Romeo and Juliet (Shakespeare, 1982). Powerful forces prevented them from being together in life, so they joined each other in death.

Imitation and Suggestibility

The imitation-suggestibility explanation of suicide states that suicidal behavior can be motivated by a need to emulate others who have committed suicide, such as entertainers or public figures, especially when these suicides are extensively covered in the mass media. In their study of suicide modeling and suggestibility, Bollen and Phillips (1982) concluded that suicide rates vary with media coverage. Front-page news stories of suicide increase suicide within the immediate geographical news distribution area. From 1977 to 1979, when 38 such stories were broadcast, 111 more suicides than expected were reported within a week after the broadcast. Bakwin (1973) noted an increase in adolescent suicide after the death of rock stars Jimi Hendrix and Janis Joplin. Two explanations have been advanced to account for these increases in suicidal behavior. First, celebrities have power and social significance to adolescents who identify with them and want to emulate them. The second explanation emphasizes the widespread publicity from media coverage and public preoccupation with celebrity suicides rather than the powerful quality of the celebrity. Other writers, such as Petzel and Riddle (1981) and Motto (1967), doubt the modeling effect as a precipitating cause of adolescent suicide. The problem in trying to document modeling or imitation effects as a result of mass media coverage of celebrity deaths is that small variations or increases in adolescent suicide rates can be due to a variety of other causes, such as changing socioeconomic conditions, seasonal effects, generalized youth alienation, and the like.

Suggestibility-modeling effects have also been investigated by examining the relationship between suicidal behavior in adolescents and prior suicidal attempts in relatives and close friends. Studies of adolescent suicides and attempted suicides have shown some support for suggestibility-modeling effects. Young people who have attempted or completed suicide were more likely to know or have been in touch with relatives or friends who have attempted suicide, shown suicidal tendencies, or spoken about possible suicidal intentions (Shaffer, 1986; Tishler and McHenry, 1982).

Imitation, suggestibility, or modeling motives do not work in isolation. The key feature in imitation and suggestibility is likely to be prior vulnerability. If an adolescent is a high risk for suicide because long-standing conflicts have been intensified by recent stresses and created feelings of hopelessness and despair, receptiveness to suggestibility at a critical moment can increase.

The Sociological Model of Adolescent Suicide

The sociological model of adolescent suicide explains the dramatic increase in suicide among young people in terms of changing social forces. Future shock, economic upheaval, changes in the job market, divorce, the decline of the nuclear family and extended family support systems, geographic dislocation and population mobility, and increasing numbers of young people due to the post-World War II baby boom have created an uncertain future for today's adolescents. Adolescents can no longer use the stable values of their elders as a foundation to develop personal standards and arrive at decisions about goals, values, and who they would like to become. Economic successes and job advancement are no longer guaranteed on the basis of hard work, future planning, and educational attainment. Adolescents are told that the pie is shrinking; if they want to get a piece of the American pie, they had better start running early, run faster than their peers, and look out for number 1. Competition is emphasized over cooperation and altruism. There is a considerable amount of pressure to measure up and excel in several activities at once, such as sports, social clubs, academics, and school politics. At the same time, adolescents are being confronted with decisions about drugs, sex, social values, and career plans at younger and younger ages without the active guidance of their elders. Many of their parents are unavailable because of family disruption, work pressures, and the dilemmas of the adult transitions.

The demands on young people have been increasing, while support has been eroding (Steinberg, 1985). The emphasis on competition and looking out for self creates a narcissistic self-centeredness that intensifies feelings of aloneness (Lasch, 1979). At a time when adolescents need to be developing a sense of power, influence, hope, meaning, and connectedness to others, many adolescents feel alone, powerless, inadequate, uncertain, pessimistic about their future, and perceive themselves as growing up in a world that offers little hope or community support. Under these conditions, disillusionment and alienation can develop.

Alienation or *anomie* is a condition that results from powerlessness, rootlessness, and social isolation. According to Durkheim (1951, first published in 1897), suicide tends to increase during times of social disruption, rootlessness, social isolation, and disintegration of moral and religious values. In his investigation of alienation and attempted suicide in adolescents, Wenz (1979a,b) found a statistically significant relationship between alienation and seven social factors: (1) lack of social contact with peers in the neighborhood; (2) conflict with parents; (3) broken romance (occurred in 33% of suicide attempts); (4) low socioeconomic status of parents; (5) inability to communicate with parents; (6) below average school performance; and (7) broken homes (occurred in 65% of suicidal attempts). Wenz suggested that the social factors are part of a circular process leading to increasing degrees of social isolation, powerlessness, loss of hope, and finally, decisions to engage in suicidal actions. Adolescent suicide is an extreme response to uncertainties, powerlessness, or lack of support experienced by young people in modern society. Alienation or anomie have also been used to account for other symptoms of troubled and distressed adolescent behavior such as running away, depression, drug and alcohol abuse, unplanned pregnancies, rebelliousness, and defiance of authority.

A second sociological explanation emphasizes population increases in the 15- to 24-year-old category as the major factor in accounting for higher rates of suicide in young people during the past 25 years. The demographic explanation assumes that a cohort group born during a baby boom will be adversely affected during adolescence and young adulthood. A cohort is a group of individuals sharing a common attribute, such as age. Cohort methods allow social scientists to follow a subpopulation across time. For example, 15- to 19-year-olds born during 1941–1945 can be compared to 15- to 19-year-olds born during 1961–1965. Larger numbers mean increased competition for jobs, admission to prestigious colleges, and entry level positions in high-status occupations (Shaffer, 1986). The increased competition creates additional stresses that are not as severe when there are more opportunities because of a smaller cohort population. The additional stress intensifies pressures created by future shock, changing values, adult–adolescent role reversals, breakups of the nuclear family, lack of extended family support systems, and the like. From about 1950 on, the period of the post-World War II baby boom, each successive cohort group of 15- to 19-year-olds appears to have had a higher suicide rate than the previous cohort group. Now that the post-World War II baby boom generation has passed through young adulthood, the suicide rate of young people seems to be leveling off and showing signs of a possible gradual decline (Sudak et al., 1984; Hendin, 1985).

The four models of suicide discussed in this section are interrelated. The crisis model focuses on the immediate causes or precipitators of stress and the individual's reaction to the emergency. The long-term stress model uses the suicidal crisis as the culmination of a long history of disappointment, failure, and lack of fulfillment ending in hopelessness intensified by recent stresses. Hopelessness, loss, and despair are primary themes appearing in all adolescent suicide models. The examination of underlying motives allows the investigator to establish the importance of specific psychosocial forces or combinations of forces in each case. The sociological model provides a broad framework to evaluate the impact of changing societal forces on the mental health needs and psychological well-being of contemporary adolescents. While there are common elements in adolescent behavior, the combination of factors at work in each case is unique. The unique motivational and psychological forces operating in any individual suicide attempt or completed suicide cannot be established without careful systematic clinical study or retrospective analysis through psychological autopsies.

SUICIDE PREVENTION

During the past 25 years, social scientists and mental health workers have identified many of the personal and family characteristics associated with adolescent suicidal behavior. This information is being utilized to develop successful prevention programs and to assess the degree of risk in individual cases in which there are signs of suicidal potential. As mentioned in the beginning of this chapter, an effective, adolescent suicide-prevention system has three major components. First, a process for disseminating clear, understandable information on the dynamics, intervention strategies and coping behaviors, referral sources, and early warning signs of suicidal behavior. Second, accessible suicide prevention and treatment facilities with 24-hour hot lines that can respond quickly in a suicide crisis. Third, research into the causes of suicide and advocacy for increased funding of research and treatment programs.

Disseminating Information and Increasing Awareness of Adolescent Suicide

In San Mateo, California, Charlotte Ross (1985) developed a suicide prevention program for high school students based on the view that: (1) students are potential victims of suicide; (2) students who are considering suicide are likely to share their thoughts and intentions with peers; (3) most of what students know about suicide and death is based on speculation, gossip, and rumor; and (4) students as confidants can be helpful as rescuers, support systems, and resource persons since they are likely to know when close friends are considering suicide.

In a survey conducted on adolescent suicide, Ross (1985) found that young people are more likely to talk to friends rather than to parents or other adult authority figures. When adolescents were asked who they would turn to if they were considering suicide, the overwhelming choice was a friend. This finding has been supported by psychological autopsies on adolescent suicides (Robinson, 1979). Adolescents feel a common bond of trust, shared needs, respect, and confidence with peers. They feel that peers will understand, maintain confidentiality, and not interfere. Conversely, adolescents considering suicide do not usually perceive adults as trusting, understanding, or empathetic. They feel adults will attempt to control the situation, and they tend to hold adults responsible for their dissatisfaction with life. Peers want to help, but often they don't know the appropriate responses, where resources are located, and how to connect troubled peers to the available resources. Since students will eventually be told about suicidal thoughts and intentions by their peers, exposure to suicide-prevention information can improve their effectiveness in the role of helpers. Peers can be helpful by increasing their range of responses, their ability to identify high risk, and their knowledge of resources. Peers are a source of education and information for each other. Dissemination of reliable information can reduce reliance on hearsay, gossip, rumor, and the speculation surrounding suicidal behavior.

A lecture-discussion format is used along with a film on adolescent suicide and informational brochures. The lecture, film, brochures, and discussion questions are designed to provide students with a greater understanding of the dynamics and motives of suicide, increase recognition of presuicidal warning signs, improve ability to respond to suicidal concerns, and disseminate information about where treatment resources are located and how to make contact with them. The discussion questions are presented in a manner that encourages empathy, dialogue, and sharing of personal experiences, coping styles, and resources. Discussion topics and strategies for dealing with loss, stress, grief, and depression, progress from mild depression to severe depression, hopelessness, despair, and consideration of suicide as an alternative to cope with unending anguish. For example, the facilitator might begin the discussion by asking the students, "Can you remember a time when you felt down? How did you handle your feelings and what did you do about the situation?" As the discussion progresses, questions introduced to get at more serious episodes of depression, suicidal thought, and suicidal behavior are followed by questions such as what was helpful or not helpful, what did other people do that was helpful or unhelpful, who did you talk to, and why did you talk to some people and not to others? The program is packaged into three to four sessions, which can be worked into the context of existing health and safety, social science, and psychology classes.

The delicate dilemmas involved in peer-to-peer confidentiality regarding suicidal thoughts or interventions are handled by discussing the implications and consequences of various alternatives. Peers reveal their innermost thoughts to each other because they believe their secrets will be safe. Disloyalty or breaking trust to protect a friend from acting out suicidal intentions can destroy a friendship. Before arriving at a final either/or juncture where the choices are telling or not telling, adolescents in the confidant role can explore a range of actions or suggestions, such as the possibility of the suicidal friend seeing a counselor, calling a mental health center hot line, or talking with a trusted adult. Troubled adolescents are often reluctant to seek help because of irrational fears surrounding the helping professions. If constructive suggestions and support fail to work with a high suicidal risk, the adolescent in the helping role then faces the choice of maintaining secrecy at the risk of losing a friend to death. Damage to friendships can be repaired, death cannot be changed. Faced with losing a friend to death, most adolescents, according to Ross (1985), would choose to break the confidentiality and seek help.

There are arguments for and against including suicide-prevention seminars in the high school curriculum. Briefly stated, the argument against holds that young people who were not considering suicide as a course of action or as a way of coping with personal turmoil, might be motivated to try suicide after hearing about it in the suicide-prevention classes. This is the suggestibility, imitation, or modeling motive. Earlier in this chapter, it was noted that the suggestibility motive as a single cause of suicide has not been substantiated. The likelihood of a student committing suicide after a discussion that includes alternatives, community resources, and available support systems is extremely low. The benefit to be gained from suicide prevention seminars for high school students far outweighs the risk.

It is generally assumed in the field of mental health that avoidance, denial, and refusal by educators and parents to face critical issues surrounding adolescent suicide are not adaptive courses of action in the long run. Ross (1985) argues that accurate information about suicide and death should be an important part of education. Students have concerns about suicide prior to any discussion of suicide in classes. Most students know some young person who has either committed suicide or attempted suicide, some students have thought about suicide themselves. Much of what students know about suicide is based on gossip, rumor, and speculation. They hear notions like suicide is a result of insanity, self-pity, or is inherited. Replacing rumors, denial, and avoidance with increased understanding based on solid information can provide students with the resources to adaptively cope with suicidal behavior in themselves and others.

Evaluations of the suicide-prevention program for students were favorable. The number of students contacting a local, suicide-prevention center and requesting help for themselves or their friends increased significantly. Other high schools requested the program, and the County Board of Supervisors commended the program for its service to the community. The State Legislature in California has established funding for pilot programs in suicide prevention for high school students, teachers, and other school personnel. To the extent that pilot programs are successful, suicide-prevention training will likely be extended to all school districts in the state (Ross, 1985; Farberow, 1985).

The suicide-prevention seminars developed by Ross can be adapted for use with teachers, counselors, school administrators, parents, and others who work closely with adolescents. Teachers, as front-line mental health workers in day-to-day contact with young people, can be instrumental in: (1) dispelling myths about suicide; (2) leading discussions on suicide and suicide-related topics such as coping with depression, despair or hopelessness; (3) conveying concern and willingness to become involved; (4) recognizing early warning signs; and (5) identifying students at risk, assessing self-destructive potential, and making referrals to appropriate mental health services (Gilead and Mulaik, 1983). Teachers, counselors, and school administrators are a vital force in determining the psychological atmosphere of the school. In a school atmosphere where teachers are concerned, empathetic, supportive, and provide students with affirmation and validation, troubled young people are more likely to feel safe in reaching out for help with suicidal dilemmas. Troubled, socially isolated presuicidal students are less likely to perceive teachers as helping agents in a school climate perceived as excessively competitive, depersonalizing, and uncaring.

The idea of the high school psychological climate as a positive force in preventing suicide among adolescents can be traced back to a Psychoanalytic Conference in Vienna in 1910 attended by Freud. Educators were concerned about the wave of youth suicides sweeping across Europe during the early 1900s. At the conference, Freud expressed the view that the high school has a responsibility to develop the kind of psychological climate that provides students with a sense of support, purpose, and a desire to live (Friedman, 1967).

Parent education in suicide prevention provides an opportunity to influence the family as a primary source of suicide prevention. Faulty family dynamics in the form of constant discord and turmoil, communication breakdowns, rejection, destructive power struggles, and a lack of supportive relationships are commonly regarded as major factors in adolescent suicide (Peck et al., 1985). Suicide-prevention programs can help parents understand the pressures operating on teenagers in and outside the family, discover ways they can improve communication and mutual problem-solving with their children, and be alert for presuicidal warning signs. A list of early warning, suicidal signs is presented in Table 5-2. Many parents see adolescence as a carefree, happy time between the dependency of childhood and the responsibilities of adulthood. It is difficult for them to understand the stresses adolescents encounter as they seek to fulfill their needs for competence, power, recognition, individuality, and belongingness.

Suicide-Prevention Centers

A suicide-prevention center is a mental health facility, which provides suicidal counseling on a round-the-clock basis. Suicide-prevention centers maintain 24-hour, telephone hot lines staffed with specially trained professional and paraprofessional counselors. Hot line counselors can mobilize crisis teams to respond to a suicidal emergency. Suicide-prevention centers are usually part of a larger network that includes hospital emergency rooms, rescue teams, runaway-youth shelters, and adolescent-oriented mental health services. Initial contact with a suicide-prevention center is frequently made by telephone calls from adolescents seeking help for themselves, their families, or their friends. The key to the suicidal hot line is the caller's need to reach out to someone and talk about troubling feelings or thoughts. Many suicidal adolescents are unable to talk to their parents because of family turmoil, poor communication, power conflicts, and lack of trust. The suicide counselor encourages the caller to ventilate his or her feelings and tries to explore nonsuicidal alternatives (Adams and Gullotta, 1983).

The first suicide-prevention center in the United States was founded in Los Angeles, California, in 1968, by two psychologists, Edward S. Shneidman and Norman L. Farberow, under a grant from the National Institute of Mental Health (Davis, 1983). The original suicide-prevention centers were

Table 5-2. Early Warning Suicidal Signs[a]

1. Preoccupation with themes of death expressed in talking or writings.
2. Expressing suicidal thoughts or threats.
3. Actual suicidal attempts or gestures.
4. Prolonged depression with attitudes of hopelessness and despair.
5. Physical symptoms of depression such as changes in sleeping patterns, too much or too little sleep, or sudden and extreme changes in weight and eating habits.
6. Withdrawal and isolation from family and friends.
7. Deteriorating school performance reflected in lower grades, cutting classes, and dropping out of school activities.
8. Persistent abuse of drugs or alcohol.
9. Major personality and behavioral changes indicated by excessive anxiety or nervousness, angry outbursts, apathy, or lack of interest in personal appearance or the opposite sex.
10. Recent loss of close relationships through death or suicide.
11. Making final arrangements, drawing up a will, or giving away prized possessions.
12. Previous suicidal attempts.
13. Sudden, unexplained euphoria or heightened activity after a long period of gloom and doom. Suicide sometimes occurs when despondency is lifting. The person feels relieved because he or she has made a final decision and now has more energy available.

[a]Adapted from: McCoy, M. (1983). *Coping with teenage depression: A parent's guide*. New York: New American Library, and Canton, P. (1985, February 18). These teenagers feel they have no options. *People Magazine*, pp. 84–87.

developed in England (Adams and Gullotta, 1983). Suicide-prevention centers have three primary goals: (1) direct services, (2) research and training, and (3) advocacy. Direct services encompass emergency treatment, outreach efforts, early detection, and 24-hour hot line counseling. Research examines the causes, dynamics, early warning signs, treatment, and prevention of suicidal behavior. The suicide-research findings are used as a foundation for updating the training of professional and paraprofessional mental health workers and increasing public awareness. In the advocacy role, suicide-prevention centers seek to increase public awareness through lectures, conferences, and the media. They also influence funding agencies and legislative bodies to provide the financial resources and support to investigate the causes, dynamics, and treatment of suicide. There are currently over 200 suicide-prevention centers operating in the United States. They are usually listed in the phone directory. Over 700 community mental health centers and runaway-youth shelters provide emergency and hot line services. If no suicide-prevention centers or emergency mental health facilities exist in your area, call the local hospital emergency room for services in the event of a suicidal crisis.

The American Association of Suicidology, based in Denver, Colorado, is an organization founded by Edward S. Shneidman (Ray and Johnson, 1983). Suicidology is a multiprofessional discipline committed to the study of suicidal phenomena and their prevention. The American Association of

Suicidology sets standards for suicide-prevention centers, serves as a clearing-house for information on all facets of suicide, coordinates legislation to develop suicide-prevention programs in schools, monitors funding agencies and research findings, and takes a leadership role in public and professional education (Canton, 1985). The American Association of Suicidology maintains an up-to-date list of suicide-prevention centers in the United States. A list of current suicide-prevention centers can be obtained by writing to: American Association of Suicidology, 2459-South Ash, Denver, Colorado 80222.

Even with the best prevention programs, there is no guarantee that adolescent suicide rates will decline in the short run. A wealthy cluster of suburban communities in Illinois experienced an increase in the adolescent suicide rates in 1978 to 1979. In a 17-month-period, 18 teenagers killed themselves — 8 by hangings, 2 by lying down in front of trains, and 18 by guns. Despite the establishment of 24-hour hot lines and suicide-prevention training programs for teenagers, mental health workers, and parents, the high suicide rate continues (*Time*, 1980).

Assessing Suicide Risk

Every suicidal attempt, threat, or gesture should be promptly evaluated. The goal of suicide assessment is to determine the seriousness of the suicidal attempt intentions, degree of risk to the adolescent's life, and what can be done to increase his or her motivation to live. Research indicates that many adolescents who successfully commit suicide discussed, threatened, or attempted suicide before the final attempt (Shaffer and Fisher, 1981). Approximately one-half of adolescents who commit suicide leave notes (Carlson, 1983). Adolescents and children who have attempted suicide are more likely to have successfully completed suicide 10–15 years later than nonsuicidal controls (Husain and Vandiver, 1984; Otto, 1972). The more premeditated the suicide, the greater the likelihood that previous attempts had been made.

Suicide assessment is usually conducted by interviewing the suicidal adolescent and his or her parents, individually and jointly. The personality, family, and psychosocial dimensions evaluated in the assessment interview include: lethality and probability of success, degree of preoccupation with suicidal thoughts and intentions, prior suicidal attempts, chronic depression, precipitating stresses, drug and alcohol abuse, presence or absence of support systems, and degree of social isolation and general mental status (Sarason and Sarason, 1984). These dimensions are outlined in Table 5-3.

High-risk adolescents tend to be characterized by lethal means, long-standing conflicts, chronic depression and helplessness, prior suicidal attempts, lack of support systems, family turmoil, poor communication, and social isolation. Low-risk adolescents tend to choose less lethal means, they

Table 5-3. Suicide Assessment Dimensions

---

1. *Lethality and probability of success.* Lethality is the degree of danger the act the person is contemplating can have or has had. Guns, crashing a speeding car into a wall, and hanging are likely to have a much more lethal outcome than superficial cuts or swallowing a small quantity of tranquilizers. Well-organized suicides planned to be carried out when no one is at home have a higher success factor than poorly organized suicidal attempts when family members are present in the home (McIntire and Angle, 1980; Boyer and Guthrie, 1985).

2. *Degree of preoccupation with suicidal thoughts and intentions.* Have suicidal thoughts, planning, and suicidal related activities become adolescent's primary interest to the extent that he or she is no longer involved in other pursuits? Is adolescent making final arrangements, writing suicide notes, or giving away possessions?

3. *Prior suicidal attempts.* Prior suicidal attempts and self-destructive behavior, especially when there has been no treatment or suicidal counseling, is a strong indicator of serious intent and future suicidal behavior (Davis, 1983).

4. *Chronic depression, hopelessness, and negative self-concept.* Chronic depression accompanied by loss of hope, powerlessness, despair, and self-devaluation are commonly associated with suicidal behavior.

5. *Precipitating stresses.* Recent loss, failure, disappointments, romantic breakups, or geographic dislocations can trigger acute depression or grief with temporary loss of hope and feelings of emptiness (Sarason and Sarason, 1984).

6. *Drug and alcohol abuse.* Adolescents who are abusing drugs and alcohol may be trying to screen out severe depression symptoms. When they are not high, feelings of hopelessness, despair, and suicide are likely to become more severe (Husain and Vandiver, 1984).

7. *Family support systems.* To what extent is family interaction characterized by turmoil, lack of support, poor communication, and rejection? Dysfunctional family dynamics are common in suicidal adolescents. To what extent has adolescent withdrawn from family and friends?

8. *Mental status.* To what extent is adolescent experiencing thinking confusion, cognitive disorganization, memory loss, hallucinations, or impaired reality testing.

9. *Other.* Debilitating illness or injuries. Some writers also list gender. Females attempt suicide more frequently than males, but males are more likely to be successful because they choose lethal methods, such as firearms (Boyer and Guthrie, 1985).

---

have good family and peer support networks, no long-term history of depression or hopelessness, and are likely to be experiencing an acute crisis brought about by loss, disappointments, romance breakup, failure, or geographic dislocation. No suicide assessment is foolproof. Not all high-risk adolescents become actively suicidal and not all actively suicidal young people fit a high-risk suicidal pattern (Weiner, 1982).

TREATMENT

Treatment objectives in working with suicidal adolescents can be separated into immediate, short-term, and long-term goals. The immediate goals are to assess the degree of suicidal risk or lethality, reduce the danger, and stabilize the situation. Suicidal adolescents often come to the attention of mental health professionals and therapists in a crisis situation involving suicidal attempts, threats, notes, or other behaviors reflecting suicidal thoughts and intentions. Temporary hospitalization should be recommended in cases where suicide assessment indicates a long history of family

conflict and turmoil, deteriorating coping strategies, progressive social isolation; feelings of hopelessness, powerlessness, and despair; availability of
lethal means, a well-organized suicidal plan, and additional recent stresses.
Hospitalization allows the adolescent to be placed in a protective and supportive environment, removes him or her from excessive external turmoil,
provides for an extended period of observation and assessment, and gives the
therapist time to build a working relationship with the adolescent and family
members (Davis, 1983; Husain and Vandiver, 1984). In cases where the
suicidal risk is minimal, adolescents should agree to a verbal contract with
the therapist to abstain from self-destructive behavior before they are permitted to return home. Parents should be made aware of this contract so
they can assist in monitoring the adolescent's behavior. The family and the
adolescent should discuss alternatives for providing support and coping
with distress until the next visit with the therapist.

Once the suicidal crisis has been stabilized, a program of psychotherapy
to work on long-term and short-term goals can be initiated. Short-term
psychotherapy with suicidal adolescents generally concentrates on the precipitating conditions that triggered the suicidal attempt or gesture. When
suicidal behavior occurs primarily as a result of loss, disappointments, or
perceived failures in the absence of a history of chronic maladaptive behavior and emotional problems, adolescents can be helped quickly and the
prognosis for recovery is favorable (Fredrick, 1985).

At the peak of a suicidal crisis, the adolescent can see only two unpleasant alternatives: (1) to go on living with unbearable anguish and psychological pain or (2) to end suffering by self-inflicted death. The role of the
therapist is to guide the process of recovery by helping the adolescent reduce
emotional distress, increase the range of choices, and improve coping strategies. This is accomplished by giving emotional support, reassessing the
suicidal motives, exploring nonsuicidal choices, and trying new coping strategies. The therapist becomes a lifeline the adolescent can count on for
support and guidance. The presence of the therapist assures the adolescent
that someone has heard his or her plea for help and is willing to respond.
The process of recovery for crisis-oriented suicidal attempts in well-functioning, psychologically intact adolescents is similar to the process of recovery in reactive depression and grief. Psychologically health adolescents who
go into a suicidal episode following the onset of severe emotional distress
account for only about one-third of the adolescents who attempt suicide
(Peck, 1985).

Two-thirds of adolescent suicide attempts appear to be the final outcome
of a long history of family conflict, discord and rejection, escalation of
emotional turmoil during adolescence, progressive social isolation, failure
of adaptive techniques, and additional recent trauma. The precipitating
incident is the last crushing blow of an otherwise unhappy and painful

existence. In these cases, the psychotherapy approach must include long-term goals as well as stabilizing and resolving the precipitating crisis. The primary goal in long-term psychotherapy with suicidal adolescents is a major reorganization of internal psychological space and the external environment. A major reorganization of the adolescent's internal psychological space and external social environment is necessary to reduce loneliness, social isolation, and family conflict, and to improve self-concept, communication skills, and strategies for resolving conflicts and stress. The complex of motives, emotions, and self-destructive thoughts underlying suicidal behavior must be brought into the open. Adolescents who attempt suicide because they feel lonely, isolated, and hopeless need to be reconnected to family and peer support systems, enabling strategies, and life-affirming experiences. Feelings of loss, social isolation, loneliness, and hopelessness can be changed by sorting out and working through the issues. New beliefs emphasizing the growth challenges of loss, positive meanings of aloneness, and personal strengths can be established, as well as new ways of coping with conflicts and satisfying needs for power, belongingness, and affirmation.

The family is an essential element in the treatment process. Suicidal behavior and suicidal attempts are not only a barometer of the adolescent's inability to cope with overwhelming stress, but also are an indication of the inability of the family and the immediate psychosocial environment to recognize or assist in resolving the adolescent's distress (Carlson, 1983).

For an adolescent whose suicidal hopelessness, isolation, and helplessness is the outcome of a long history of family conflict, rejection, and turmoil, the suicidal act is often a message to the family that he or she has been unsuccessful in communicating in other ways. Opening up the lines of communication and starting the process of mutual problem solving, support, and caring through family therapy sessions can reduce the adolescent's feeling of aloneness, despair, and rejection.

Parents and family members of suicidal adolescents are sometimes reluctant to participate in psychotherapy. They are embarrassed by the adolescent's suicidal attempt, tend to deemphasize its importance, and close ranks to prevent family secrets from being shared with the therapist. It is important for the therapist to patiently try to work through these resistances because how the family reacts will affect how the adolescent responds to suicidal thoughts in the future (Weiner, 1982). If the family refuses to be concerned or will not consider making any major changes in the way it treats the adolescent, suicidal motivation is likely to increase.

There are common features in the dynamics and treatment of runaways, depression, and suicidal adolescents. Running away and suicidal attempts are signals that the adolescent's developmental needs for power, belongingness, independence, and competence are not being met. If the signal is responded to constructively by family members and significant others, growth-enhancing changes are likely to occur. If the signal is ignored, things are likely to get worse. Chronic depression and adolescent suicidal behavior that resulted from long-standing distress and conflicts share a common element of hopelessness, despair, powerlessness, and negative beliefs about self. In view of these commonalities, similar treatment models can be used, such as psychotherapy approaches that follow a sequential course of relationship building between the adolescent and therapist, sorting out and working through psychosocial and intrapsychological conflicts and dynamics, restructuring faulty beliefs, trying out new coping styles, and consolidating growth gains prior to terminating the therapy.

POSTVENTION: SURVIVOR COUNSELING

Despite the best efforts of prevention programs and therapists, approximately 6,000 young people will continue to commit suicide annually. The relatives and close friends of the suicide victims will invariably experience the overwhelming shock, denial, disbelief, despondency, and guilt which are part of the grief process. Postvention refers to mental health counseling activities or interventions that, following the death of a significant other by suicide, assist the survivors in coping with grief and loss. Hatton et al. (1977) and Herzog and Resnik (1968) recommend that the postvention process not be limited to the initial stage of shock and grief immediately following the suicide, but should be extended to cover the entire process of mourning or bereavement.

Three stages in the postvention process have been identified: (1) psychological resuscitation; (2) psychological rehabilitation; and (3) psychological renewal. Stage 1, psychological resuscitation, involves a visit by a mental health counselor within 24 hours of the suicide. The purpose of this visit is to establish a working relationship with the survivors, help the survivors withstand the severe shock of loss, and assist the survivors in becoming aware of their emotions, such as confusion, guilt, shame, anger, or blame. Stage 2, psychological rehabilitation, begins after the funeral. The goals of stage 2 are to establish regular family meeting times and meetings with individual family members, help the family understand and work through the dynamics of grief, and deal with whatever family or individual crisis that may arise as part of the grief process. Stage 3, the renewal phase, begins around 6 months after the suicide. The goal of this stage is to complete the recovery process, set new goals for the future, and go on with life.

When a popular student commits suicide or when an adolescent commits suicide at school, shock waves are likely to reverberate throughout the student body. Students are likely to react with fear, disbelief, guilt, blame, and questions regarding death and suicide. Hill (1984) recommends that postvention programs be set up in high schools after student suicides to provide teachers and students with support, reassurance, and understanding of the dynamics of suicide and grief.

EPILOGUE. ADOLESCENT SUICIDE: THE TRAGEDY OF AN UNCOMPLETED LIFE

Statistics convey only part of the tragedy of adolescent suicide. The full tragedy of adolescent suicide cannot be understood without discussing the loss of a young life that could have been saved and the burden carried by the survivors. We have the therapeutic tools available today to help young people successfully resolve suicidal despair and hopelessness. For adolescents who commit suicide, the life cycle has scarcely begun. They leave behind an uncompleted life. With four-fifths of their lives ahead of them, adolescents who commit suicide forfeit the chance to discover their personal worth, unique potential, and nonsuicidal possibilities for resolving painful personal and interpersonal dilemmas. Suicide is a permanent negative solution that prevents more adaptive solutions from emerging. Many successful, self-actualizing, middle-aged and older adults look back on their adolescent years as a highly stressful time of struggle for meaning, values, self-worth, recognition, love, and life direction. By continuing to live, they were able to move through periods of hopelessness and discover their power to grow into psychologically healthy, productive adults (Levinson et al., 1978). Suicide would have robbed them of the opportunity to experience the fulfillment of adult growth and development. The magnitude of the crises of youth tends to diminish with age.

Adolescent suicide can have a lasting impact on family and close friends. The process of grief and recovery is likely to be complicated by guilt, shame, and self-blame. If survivor or postvention counseling is not initiated, re-crimination and self-blame can be devastating to family members and friends. Suicide is difficult to accept, but somewhat understandable in the incurable, aged, or chronically ill. Suicide in adolescents arouses feelings of waste, futility, and shame (Emery, 1983; Davis, 1983). It challenges myths of adolescence as a golden, carefree time preceding the burdens of adulthood. When adolescents die of natural causes, God, faith, or unkind existential forces can be blamed. When adolescents commit suicide, the survivors inherit the burden of blame. In his book, *In a Darkness*, a moving account about his son's prolonged struggle with life and ultimate suicide, James Wechler (1972) writes that the memories of his son's death have left an indelible imprint on the survivors for the remainder of their time on earth.

SUMMARY AND CONCLUSIONS

The premature end of a life scarcely begun is the ultimate tragedy of adolescent suicide. Adolescent suicide can leave a permanent scar on family and friends. Following a successful adolescent suicide, postvention counseling can assist the survivors in working through the shock, disbelief, loss, and guilt associated with grief. Suicide rates among young people have tripled in the past three decades. Depression is the most common psychological syndrome associated with suicidal behavior. Suicide has different religious, cultural, and historical meanings. Some adolescents may not fully understand the permanence of suicide. The majority of adolescent suicides are the outcome of a long history of dissatisfaction, personal and family turmoil, escalating conflicts during adolescence, progressive social isolation, and deterioration of coping strategies. A final crisis, which intensifies feelings of hopelessness, helplessness, and despair, leads to the suicidal act. Treatment of suicidal adolescents involves immediate intervention, assessment, and psychotherapy. Psychotherapy is geared toward helping the adolescent become reinvested in life. Every suicidal attempt, threat, or gesture should be promptly evaluated or assessed. The goal of suicide assessment is to determine the degree of risk to the adolescent's life and what can be done to increase his or her motivation to live. Research indicates that adolescents who successfully commit suicide discussed, threatened, or attempted suicide before the final attempt.

The dramatic rise in adolescent suicide and suicidal attempts challenges the myth of adolescence as a carefree happy time. Adolescence is a time of conflict and stress. Young people encounter uncertainty about themselves and their place in the world as they attempt to fulfill their needs for love, competence, power, meaning, and excitement. As society continues to grow more complex and the uncertainties and stresses confronting youth increase, the likelihood that adolescent suicide will disappear or significantly diminish in the foreseeable future is low. Since the outcome of successful suicide is permanent, effective suicidal-prevention provides the best opportunity for reducing suicidal behavior. Effective suicide-prevention programs have three major components. First, a process for disseminating information on the dynamics, intervention strategies and coping behaviors, referral sources, and early warning signs of suicidal behavior. Second, accessible suicide-prevention and crisis-intervention facilities with 24-hour hot lines. Third, increasing public awareness and funding for research. Effective prevention of suicide in youth must begin before self-destructive behavior has reached the high-risk level or causes physical harm. Congressional investigators have concluded that the funding for suicide prevention is inadequate at the state, local, and federal levels (United States Congress, 1986).

SUGGESTIONS FOR PARENTS, TEACHERS, COUNSELORS, AND YOUTH WORKERS

1. Learn the early warning signs. Adolescent suicide seldom happens all at once. Suicidal intentions are usually signaled in some way or to someone. Be aware of danger signs such as preoccupation with death, prolonged depression with hopelessness and despair, making a will or giving away prized possessions, withdrawal from family and friends, persistent abuse of alcohol or drugs, chronic risk-taking, serious accidents, and recent loss of significant others through suicide, death, or romantic breakups. (See the more extensive list of warning signs in Table 5-2).

2. Take threats, idle talk about suicide, and suicidal gestures, such as superficial cuts on wrists, seriously. It is a myth that people who talk about suicide won't do it (McCoy, 1982). The risk of being wrong is too great. Be concerned when adolescents write poems expressing death or suicide, or make statements like, "You'll miss me when I'm gone," "I'd be better off dead," "Sometimes I feel like killing myself," "You'll understand when I'm dead," or "Where I'm going, it won't make any difference."

3. When young people show early warning signs, such as those listed above, try to draw them out by encouraging dialogue about their concerns. Start off with low key questions or probes like "You don't seem very happy lately" or "You don't seem like yourself lately." Don't push too hard too quickly, listen carefully, and be supportive without offering false reassurance. Gently propose alternative solutions. Some adolescents can be inflexible in their thinking (Jensen, 1985). If you are a parent, the early warning signs may be a signal that it's time to restructure the adolescent-parent relationships in growth-facilitating directions. Don't be fooled by quick spontaneous recovery from prolonged depression. Sometimes an adolescent is at greatest risk for taking his or her life after the depression lifts. They are relieved because they have made a decision to carry out a plan for suicide and now have the energy to do so (McCoy, 1982).

4. If threats or an actual suicide attempt occurs, seek professional help. Suicide attempts that go untreated are likely to be repeated. Don't be afraid to ask for assistance or consultation. Suicide-prevention centers, emergency hot lines, and youth-shelter emergency numbers are listed in the phone directory. Family and friends can be enlisted as part of a support system (Mitchell and Resnik, 1981). If an adolescent-suicide seminar is offered in your community, take it. Encourage your spouse and your adolescent to attend with you. If you are a high school teacher, request a suicide-prevention seminar for the teachers, counselors, administrators, and students in your school district.

5. For more information on suicide, the following books and pamphlets are suggested:

Adolescent Suicide: Mental Health Challenge: Dealing With the Crisis of Suicide Pressures on Children. Public Affairs Pamphlets No. 569, 406A and 589 (Public Affairs Committee, Inc., 389 Park Ave. S., New York, NY 10016: 50 cents each).

Hide or Seek, by James Dobson (Fleming H. Revell Co., Old Tappan, NJ 07675: $9.95 hardcover).

Plain Talk About Adolescence (Consumer Information Ctr., Dept. 648J, Pueblo, CO 81009: free).

Suicide and Young People, by Arnold Madison (Seabury Press, 815 Second Ave., New York, NY 10017: $6.95).

Teenage Drinking, the No. 1 Drug Threat to Young People Today, by Robert North and Richard Orange, Jr. (Macmillan Publishing Co., Inc., 866 Third Ave., New York, NY 10022: $8.95).

DISCUSSION QUESTIONS

1. What are some of the sociological factors in modern society that might account for the dramatic rise in adolescent suicide?
2. Discuss the five-stage model of adolescent suicide. What are the major similarities and differences between the five-stage model and the crisis model? What are some of the implications of each model for treatment?
3. What are some of the primary factors that should be included in a suicide assessment interview, and why are these factors important?
4. Under what circumstances involving adolescent suicidal behavior is temporary hospitalization a sound intervention strategy and why?
5. Discuss the major immediate, short-term, and long-term treatment for psychotherapy goals in working with suicidal adolescents.
6. What is a psychological autopsy, what are its major dimensions, and how is it utilized?
7. In what way might adults and adolescents differ in the perceptions or meanings they assign to death, suicide, and personal immortality?
8. From a developmental perspective, why is adolescent suicide such a tragic event?
9. In the aftermath of an adolescent suicide, what special problems are close relatives and friends likely to face in working through the process of grief and recovery? How can they be helped?
10. List three major components of an adolescent suicide-prevention program. Why is each component important?
11. What is the major psychological syndrome associated with suicidal behavior? How are the dynamics of this syndrome connected to suicidal behavior?
12. Discuss five or six major suicidal warning signs. Why should these warning signs be taken seriously?

6
Eating Disturbances: Anorexia and Bulimia Nervosa

PREVIEW

The development of proper eating habits during adolescence is essential for the body's growth and development. Because of changes in physiological functions and the rapid acceleration of growth that takes place throughout the body, young people need a well-balanced diet of body-building foods. Once physical growth has peaked, adequate nutrition is necessary to maintain optimal body functioning and psychological well-being. Anorexia nervosa and bulimia, the two eating disorders discussed in this chapter, interfere with the body's needs for balanced nutrition. The rates of occurrence of anorexia nervosa and bulimia nervosa have increased to alarming levels among junior high, high school, and college females in recent years.[1]

Anorexia nervosa, which has been known for over three centuries, is a life-threatening, self-induced starvation syndrome characterized by the relentless pursuit of thinness and a morbid fear of fatness. As the condition progresses, weight loss increases to 15% to 25% or more of original body weight; biochemical functions such as hormonal balance, pulse and heart rate, body temperature, and the menstrual cycle can be severely impaired. The distorted image she has of her body prevents an anorexic adolescent from perceiving her emaciated state. Although bulimia nervosa has a long history, only recently has it been recognized as a separate clinical syndrome.

---

[1]The pronoun "she" will be used in this chapter because the overwhelming majority of anorexic and bulimic adolescents and young adults are female.

Bulimia nervosa, defined literally as ox hunger, is characterized by repeated cycles of binge eating and compensation for food intake by self-induced vomiting as well as laxative abuse and/or fasting in young women of non-anorexic weight. Bulimia nervosa tends to occur in late-adolescent and early-adult women, whereas anorexia is more likely to be found in early-adolescent females.

Anorexia and bulimia result from a complex interaction of cultural, biological, psychological, cognitive, and behavioral forces. It is not difficult to understand why young women in today's America are preoccupied with food, dieting, weight control, body size, and slimness. The cultural ideal of thinness as the key to success, admiration, attractiveness, and competence is constantly being projected by beauty queens, fashion models, TV actresses, and other feminine role models. Dieting has been offered, by the powerful weight-control industry, as the method to achieve the desired level of thinness. Many young women do not realize that the cultural norms for thinness as the ideal body size are incongruent with contemporary biological realities. During the past several years, the average weight level of adolescent girls has increased 5 to 6 lbs.

How young women cope with the incongruence between the biological realities and cultural pressures surrounding the pursuit of thinness depends to a large extent on the underlying psychological dynamics operating during the critical phases of early- and late-adolescent psychosocial development. The secondary sexual changes of early adolescence, which result in the beginning of the menstrual cycle and the appearance of breasts and wider hips, can be very frightening for some young women. Anorexic adolescents seem to handle the changes and uncertainties associated with early-adolescent psychosocial transitions and physical changes by exercising increasing control over dieting and food intake. Semistarvation dieting can reverse stress-producing psychosexual changes, recreate the prepubescent body, and provide a sense of power and control at the risk of ruining one's health. For most bulimic young women who have already completed the girl-to-woman body transformation, the motivation does not appear to involve reversing the development of secondary sexual characteristics. Bulimic young women have apparently resolved early adolescent psychosexual issues but seem driven to achieve the adolescent body ideal of slenderness with its connotations of sensuousness, desirability, attractiveness, and competence. Confronted with the identity, intimacy, and autonomy developmental task of late adolescence and early adulthood, bulimic young women concentrate their coping efforts on developing the culturally sanctioned, slender body image. Dieting to achieve the desired level of thinness somehow gets out of control and results in the binge, purge, and diet syndrome.

The most effective treatment programs for anorexia nervosa and bulimia combine several different strategies and approaches, including medical-nutritional, cognitive, behavioral, psychodynamic, and family therapies. Hospitalization to stabilize weight and diet may be necessary in the initial treatment phase of anorexia. Bulimics are usually more motivated for treatment and less into denial than anorexics. There are four major approaches to eating-disorder prevention: nutritional education, early detection, self-help organizations, and a reevaluation of thinness as the culturally sanctioned, ideal feminine body image. Five major eating-disorder self-help organizations have been developed in recent years. The purpose of an eating-disorder self-help organization is to provide such services as a mental health referral system, information on the causes and consequences of eating disorders, speakers for community and professional organizations, factual information and dissemination of research findings, and access to networks of physicians, parents, volunteers, peer counselors, local resources, and support groups.

ANOREXIA NERVOSA

Case Example 6-1: Clara

Clara is a 14-year-old, female eighth-grade junior high school student, who was referred to an eating-disorder clinic by a clinical social worker at a child guidance clinic. Clara was initially referred to the child guidance clinic by her pediatrician who thinks Clara may be anorexic. Clara, who is 5′3″ tall, has lost approximately 30 lbs in the past 12 months. Her original weight was 110 lbs, but she now weighs 80 lbs and wants to lose more. Clara says, "I really like being skinny." She thinks "carrying" less weight around makes her a better athlete and "looks better." She detests fat women. Her mother is slightly overweight despite repeated attempts to lose weight by exercising and dieting.

Clara has been dieting for about a year. She originally started dieting because some other girls on her gymnastic team were successfully losing weight by dieting. Clara now eats mostly salads, fruits, vegetables, and breakfast cereals. When she started dieting, her daily limit was approximately 1,100 calories. Clara thinks she is now down to about 500 to 600 calories per day. Despite her skin-and-bones look, Clara exercises daily and denies any fatigue or physical symptoms. Her physician reports menstrual irregularities. Clara does not see any need for treatment at an eating-disorder clinic. She claims her only problems are family arguments with her mother about her diet. Clara thinks her mother is "jealous" because she has been unable to lose weight and "can't stay on a diet."

Clara's parents are both professionals. Her mother is an accountant and her father is an attorney. Clara has a 19-year-old brother who is a college sophomore. Her brother is currently seeing a psychologist at the college counseling center for what Clara's mother refers to as "mild depression and adjustment problems." Clara and her brother are good students. Clara is on the honor roll, the gymnastic team, and plays trumpet in the school band. She says some of her girlfriends are experimenting with partying, sex, and drugs, but she hasn't participated in any of these activities and doesn't want to start. Her parents were separated for a year when she was in the seventh grade. They have recently reconciled. Clara thinks the separation had something to do with her father having a girlfriend, but she isn't sure. She says "nobody in my family talks about anything that's real important, except being good, staying out of trouble, and getting good grades . . . nobody knows what anybody else is really doing or thinking."

Definition, History, and Rates of Occurrence

Anorexia nervosa is a self-induced, semistarvation syndrome characterized by the relentless pursuit of thinness and a morbid, phobic-like fear of fatness (Garner and Garfinkel, 1985; Bruch, 1973). It is a life-threatening condition that results in extreme weight loss, malnutrition, and distortions of body image. No organic disease or metabolic disturbance has been identified as the cause of anorexia nervosa. Anorexic adolescents do not suffer from a loss of appetite or hunger. Instead, they starve themselves or deliberately restrict food intake in the face of severe hunger (Goldberg et al., 1980). A more appropriate term for anorexia might be the German concept of *pubertaetsmagersucht*, which connotes a leanness addiction or a leanness passion of puberty (Smith, 1984).

Literary accounts of voluntary starvation as a means of weight loss can be traced back to before the Middle Ages. In his monograph, *Fasting Girls: Their Physiology and Pathology*, written in 1879, William Hammond describes a nun in 1225 who claimed to have ingested nothing but communion in 7 years, a female saint in the 14th century whose diet was reported to consist of nothing but a little piece of apple daily, and a girl who abstained from food for 7 years (Strober, 1985). The first detailed medical descriptions of anorexia nervosa were provided by Sir Richard Morton in 1694. He documented the symptoms of an 18-year-old woman who had been suffering from self-induced starvation for 2 years. He described her body appearance as resembling a skeleton clad in skin. Her menses had ceased (amenorrhea), she was aversed to food, displayed a pattern of hyperactive behavior, and was seemingly indifferent to her malnourished state. The girl continued to lose weight and subsequently died.

Nearly 200 years later, William Gull, in 1874, and Charles Lasegue, in 1873, provided descriptions of anorexia nervosa fitting that of contemporary patients (Garfinkel and Garner, 1986). Gull, who coined the term anorexia nervosa, initially referred to the starvation syndrome as *apepsia hysterica* (Hinsie and Campbell, 1970). Lasegue used the term *anorexia hysterique*. Gull and Lasegue noted that anorexia tends to occur predominantly in early adolescent females. These young women seem to be indifferent to the emaciated condition of their bodies, take pride in severe weight loss, and resist encouragement and medical advice to resume normal eating habits. As prolonged self-starvation continues, the influence of caloric depletion results in cessation of the menstrual cycle and metabolic imbalances and can ultimately end in death, if the weight loss continues indefinitely.

During the past 30 years, the writings and clinical studies of Hilda Bruch (1973, 1978, 1982) have been instrumental in bringing the psychological, cultural, and medical issues surrounding anorexia nervosa to the attention of the professional and lay public. Her primary thesis is that anorexia nervosa represents a faulty attempt on the part of early teenage females to cope with the psychological, emotional, and psychosexual transitions of adolescence.

Anorexia nervosa is most frequently observed in early-adolescent females and young women between the ages of 13 to 20 (Crisp, 1980). This self-induced starvation syndrome, which occurs in 1% to 4% of the adolescent population, usually peaks at ages 14 and 18. Ninety to ninety-five percent of its victims are females predominantly from middle-to-upper middle-class, white families (Squire, 1983; Fuhrmann, 1986). The natural course of anorexia usually extends over a period of 3 to 4 years, but in some cases concerns about food, dieting, and thinness can last much longer (McNab, 1983). Death from the long-term effects of starvation occurs in 3.6% to 6.6% of the cases. Some studies report a death rate from anorexia nervosa as high as 22% (Maloney and Klyklo, 1983). The incidence of anorexia nervosa has increased significantly in the past 10 to 15 years. Anorexia nervosa now extends across all socioeconomic and ethnic classes, affecting a half-million females. In the past 5 years, more cases have been reported in prepubescent girls under 12 and in young women over 20 (Gilbert and DeBlassie, 1984; Halmi, 1985a). The increase in reported cases of anorexia is probably due to a combination of such factors as increased public and professional awareness, the popularity of dieting, and the emphasis on thinness in a fashion- and health-conscious society.

Twenty years ago, many parents and health care professionals didn't recognize the symptoms of self-induced starvation to create weight loss. Now high school and junior high school girls can read about anorexia in teen magazines or know of someone who has it. In the past few years, teenage girls have been steadily bombarded by best-selling diet books and media advertisements for diet aids, appetite suppressants, calorie-sparing meals, and weight-reduction plans. TV dramas and biographies of pop music stars and media personalities have emphasized the motives and dynamics surrounding the relentless pursuit of thinness through self-inflicted starvation.

Karen Carpenter, a pop singer, died in 1983 of unexplained heart failure at the age of 32. After her death, it was revealed that she had been suffering from anorexia for 12 years. Her battle with anorexia, which unfortunately she lost, appears to have been part of a larger struggle for independence, self-control, and self-determination. Cherry Boone O'Neill, Pat Boone's oldest daughter, described her 10-year struggle with anorexia in her book, *Starving for Attention*, published in 1982. At age 16, eager to set an example for her young sisters and demonstrate her self-control, Cherry attacked her weight problem with relentless determination. Through extreme dieting, aided by supplemental diet pills she stole from her mother, and 6 hours of daily exercise, she was able to reduce her weight from 140 to 90 lbs (Levin et al., 1983; Seligman and Zabriski, 1983).

Primary Characteristics

The primary characteristics of anorexia, outlined below, have remained remarkably stable during the past 100 years (McNab, 1983; Halmi, 1985a). DSM-III-R (American Psychiatric Association, 1987) criteria for anorexia nervosa are listed in Table 6-1.

1. *Significant weight loss as a result of self-imposed, semistarvation diet.* Weight is usually within normal limits prior to the onset of excessive dieting. Reduction in food consumption to 300 to 600 calories a day leading to a weight loss of 15% to 25% or greater of original body weight. Weight loss occurs at a time when the adolescent's body is growing, and she should be gaining weight. A stringent diet usually consists of food presumed to be low in calories, such as cottage cheese, salads, fruits, and vegetables. Achieving body thinness is perceived as rewarding.
2. *Intense fear of becoming obese despite weight loss.* Despite self-starvation, which has reduced their appearance to a skin-and-bones physique, anorexic adolescents constantly worry about being too fat. Anorexic adolescents refuse to maintain minimum normal body weight for age and height. Normal body weight is perceived as fat.
3. *Disturbance of body image.* Anorexic adolescents claim not to see their emaciated bodies. When looking at the mirror, instead of seeing the skin and bones others see, they are likely to see themselves as fat or over-

Table 6-1. DSM-III-R[a] Diagnostic Criteria for Anorexia Nervosa

1. Intense fear of becoming obese, which does not diminish as weight loss progresses
2. Disturbance of body image, e.g., claiming to "feel fat" even when emaciated; belief that one area of the body is "too fat" even when obviously underweight
3. Refusal to maintain body weight over a minimal normal weight for age and height; failure to make expected weight gain during period of growth, leading to body weight 15% below that expected, or weight loss leading to maintenance of body weight 15% below that expected
4. In females, absence of at least three consecutive menstrual cycles when otherwise expected to occur—primary or secondary amenorrhea

[a]Adapted from: American Psychiatric Association. (1987). *Diagnostic and statistical manual of mental disorders* (3rd ed., rev.). Washington, D.C.

weight. For example, a 70-lb, 14-year-old female is proud of what others see as her emaciated state and wants to lose more weight. She tends to overestimate her body size.

4. *Denial or failure to recognize the body's nutritional needs.* Anorexic adolescents regard themselves as being in good health despite their emaciated appearance and physical-medical symptoms. They are unable or unwilling to recognize hunger needs.

5. *No known physical illness would account for weight loss.* Common to all descriptions of anorexia is the assumption that the weight loss and excessive dieting are not being caused by any physical disease.

Personality Features and Secondary Characteristics

Favorable terms such as "the good girl syndrome," or "the best little girl in the world" (Levenkron, 1978) have been used to describe the personality make-up and secondary characteristics associated with anorexic adolescents. Teenage girls, who get caught up in the relentless pursuit of thinness through this self-starvation syndrome, have been described in the anorexia literature as concerned about others, nice, conscientious, good students, intelligent, achievement-oriented, perfectionistic, compulsive, and self-disciplined (Rice, 1978). They are generally regarded as compliant, except in the areas of dieting and weight control. In these areas, anorexic girls tend to be very defensive and stubbornly refuse advice, help, or suggestions that they need to eat to prevent further weight loss. They insist that they have the right to weigh as little as they choose, even if it means looking like a skeleton. Dichotomous, either-or thinking is likely to be apparent where weight is concerned. A girl who weighs 80 lbs perceives her failure to lose 2 lbs during the next week as a major disaster, "If I don't get down to 78 pounds, I might as well weigh 150."

Personality and life-style are organized around maintaining order and control to an almost obsessive-compulsive degree. While overly denying or minimizing hunger, anorexic adolescents may constantly be thinking about food, meticulously counting calories, collecting recipes, and engaging in elaborate preparations to cook gourmet meals for others. A 14-year-old girl will cook fancy meals for her family and only eat a few bites. Ritualistic behavior surrounding food and meals is common. Ingenious schemes are employed to give small meals of low-calorie foods, such as lettuce and fruit, an illusion of substance and variety. By slowly cutting and eating food in tiny amounts, a low-calorie meal can take an hour or more to consume (Wooley and Wooley, 1982; Halmi, 1985a). It is not uncommon for anorexics to hide small amounts of food throughout the house and frequently check to make sure it's still there (Goldberg et al., 1980). Time is usually well-organized into a highly active, demanding, tightly controlled schedule.

Exercise is often a major activity since it can be used to facilitate weight loss by burning off excess calories. Weight is constantly checked by frequent trips to the scale. The scale serves as a barometer of weight-loss progress.

Underlying the well-organized, achievement-oriented, good-little-girl personality features are likely to be deep-seated feelings of inadequacy, low self-esteem, fears of uncertainty related to adolescent transitions, and worries about loss of control. By keeping busy, staying on her diet, and showing physical stamina by constant exercise, the anorexic teenager seeks to demonstrate to herself and others that she is in control. She admires herself for being able to lose more weight than others, eat less, resist urges to overeat, and stay on top of a busy schedule. Self-control and discipline mean being able to withstand hunger pains and not depart from rigid dietary plans. She views thinness as a matter of effort, and failure to achieve the desired level of thinness means that one is personally lazy or irresponsible. She does not complain about discomfort or weight loss, nor does she see her undernourished body as ugly. Rather than viewing her ultrathin frame as unattractive, she takes pride in her body and views thinness as a sign of dietary success (Striegel-Moore et al., 1986; Garfinkel and Garner, 1982).

As adolescents become more progressively and obsessively involved in dieting and weight loss to the exclusion of other activities, a narrowing of interests is likely to occur, resulting in increasing social isolation. It is difficult to maintain normal, adolescent, social activities and peer relationships when one's sole interest is meticulous calorie counting, weight loss, and the relentless pursuit of thinness. Social isolation and loneliness reduce the opportunity to learn peer social skills and can trigger feelings of despondency in teenagers who are struggling with underlying feelings of inadequacy, low self-esteem, and doubts about self-worth. Several studies report mild-to-moderate feelings of depression, hopelessness, and suicidal ideation in adolescents who have been experiencing progressively more severe symptoms of anorexia (Garfinkel and Kaplan, 1986; Herzog, 1984).

Adverse Consequences

The relentless pursuit of thinness can have far-reaching adverse effects across several areas of adolescent growth and development: physical-psychobiological, psychosexual, cognitive, and psychosocial. If continued indefinitely, anorexia nervosa can end in death. The body's energy and chemical, physical, and hormonal systems need a sufficient supply of food to function properly. Progressive weight loss and malnutrition caused by semistarvation can arrest the menstrual cycle, delay or reverse the development of secondary sex characteristics, reduce potassium levels, upset the body's hormonal balance, lower body temperature and blood pressure, and slow heart rate and pulse to the point where there is a risk of cardiac arrest.

The longer anorexia persists, the greater the likelihood of life-threatening consequences.

Reduction of body weight below the 15% to 25% range usually causes the menstrual cycle to cease. A critical body fat composition of 23% is necessary to maintain normal menstrual function. Secondary sex characteristics, such as the hips and breasts, will decrease in size and fail to develop fully when body weight critically decreases, giving the girl's body a prepubescent look (Garfinkel and Garner, 1982).

Potassium depletion is one of the most serious side effects of anorexia. Low potassium can cause electrolyte imbalances. Electrolyte imbalances can lead to a slowing down of the heart rate and pulse, low blood pressure, and hormonal irregularities. Because the heart rate and general activity slow down, anorexic patients often complain of feeling chilled (hypothermia). Extreme weight loss reduces the amount of fat and muscle tissue the body needs to maintain heat. Hormonal changes can produce a growth of long, fine hair (lanugo) over the body (Bayer, 1984). The most common cause of death in anorexia is cardiac arrest resulting from irregularities in the heart beat caused by a low serum potassium (Levin et al., 1983). Suicide has also been reported as a cause of death in anorexia. Studies of large numbers of anorexics, followed for 4 years or longer, report death rates of 5% to 21% (Halmi, 1985a).

Alongside these injurious physical-medical consequences, there are corresponding changes in cognitive and psychosocial functions as a result of malnutrition and self-imposed starvation. The most striking cognitive features are misjudgments, self-deceptions, perceptual distortions, and even outright denials with respect to estimates of body size, acknowledgments of hunger, and a realistic concern for the deteriorating health status and optimal body functions. Despite becoming emaciated to the point injurious to their health, most anorexics think they are in good health. An 80-lb adolescent who has lost 35 lbs through extreme dieting often claims she never felt better and wants to lose more weight. Many studies report severely distorted perceptions of body size. Anorexics seem to consistently overestimate their body size, whereas others correctly perceive their skin-and-bones appearance. Hunger cues are either misread, not recognized, suppressed, or denied. A starving adolescent will claim not to feel hunger or to feel bloated after a meager meal of 150 calories (Bryant and Bates, 1985).

In the advanced stages of the disorder, many anorexics experience poor concentration, mood swings, irritability, fatigue, apathy, and sleep disturbances. Rather than attributing problems with mood, concentration, irritability, and sleep to the effects of their starvation diet and weight loss, anorexics are likely to blame themselves for a lack of discipline and self-control, which, in turn, increases their feelings of self-devaluation and despair. Lack of concentration, fatigue, and sleep disturbances can cause additional deficits in judgment, perceptual distortion, self-deception, and in the accuracy of the individual's ability to assess the injurious consequences of her relentless quest for thinness.

Distortions of body-image, the unwillingness or inability to acknowledge hunger cues, and the refusal to acknowledge the injurious effects of prolonged malnutrition created by self-starvation despite overwhelming medical and physical evidence raise questions about the degree of impairment in reality testing and cognitive reasoning. To whatever extent the impairment in reality testing and cognitive reasoning, in the final stages of anorexia, is a cause, an effect, or a combination of both, reality testing and cognitive reasoning must be improved before anorexic adolescents can be expected to return to an optimal level of psychological and physical functioning.

The cognitive-psychosocial and emotional effects of anorexia parallel those found in hunger experiments. One of the most widely known hunger experiments, sometimes referred to as the Minnesota Study, was conducted by Ancel Keys and his associates (1950) in the 1940s. The subjects for Keys's starvation experiment were 36 physically healthy, psychologically normal, young male volunteers who were doing alternative military service as conscientious objectors. For the first 3 months, the men ate normally as Keys and his associates studied their behavior and observed their psychological status and adjustment level. For the next 6 months, they were placed on a diet of one-half of their normal food consumption, which reduced their food intake to 1600 to 1800 calories a day. The average weight loss was 25% of their original body weight. Many of these men experienced poor concentration, lowered levels of alertness, intense hunger, indecisiveness, anxiety, irritability, mood swings, mild-to-moderate depression, and social withdrawal. The fact that similar cognitive, psychosocial, and emotional effects are found in anorexia nervosa suggests that these symptoms are a result of starvation and malnutrition rather than some underlying personality disorder, or that the effects of starvation can amplify preexisting personality characteristics. For example, if an anxious, insecure adolescent embarks on a starvation diet, the long-term effects of starvation could intensify her anxiety and insecurity (Garfinkel and Kaplan, 1986; Wooley and Wooley, 1982).

Dynamics, Causes, and Etiology

The relentless pursuit of thinness through voluntary starvation has perplexed parents, researchers, physicians, and mental health workers for three centuries. Why would a young female adolescent, at a critical stage in her psychosexual and psychobiological development, deliberately embark upon and stay with a food-deprivation diet that is injurious to her health, exposes her to the risk of death, impedes the proper functioning of the reproductive cycle, and reduces her body to a skin-and-bones look that reverses or diminishes the development of secondary sex characteristics, such as breasts and hips? Why would she refuse medical help and psychological assistance when it is obvious to those around her that her health and psychological well-being are deteriorating? Why does she persist in the belief that she is not hungry when she is obviously starving? Why would "the best little girl in the world" cause her family overwhelming concern, worry, and anger over her refusal to acknowledge the self-destructive aspects of her extreme dieting behavior? Why would she not compromise, at least to the point where she could voluntarily restore her weight to the minimum for her height and age? To attempt to answer these questions, we will examine the major sociocultural, psychological, and behavioral determinants that contribute to the onset and maintenance of anorexic behavior.

Sociocultural Factors

Eating behavior, dieting, and values associated with body shape and size are influenced by the cultural framework in which adolescents develop. Contemporary America is obsessed with thinness. The models and actresses presented through the mass media as the feminine ideal have a thin, lean look with a de-emphasis on secondary sex characteristics, such as breasts and hips. Sports and artistic endeavors popular with teenage females, like figure-skating, gymnastics, and ballet, place great emphasis on a lean, pre-pubescent-looking feminine body. Thinness is associated with grace, style, artistic beauty, virtue, self-control, and discipline. According to popular expressions, "thin is in," and "slenderness is next to godliness." Conversely, adolescents who are overweight or fat are perceived in negative terms. The message seems to be that "If you are fat, no one will love you." Adolescents who are overweight are viewed as self-indulgent, lacking in self-control, weak, and greedy (Steel, 1980). An adolescent female who is overweight runs the risk of being teased with names such as "moose," "tubby," "fatso," "buffalo," or "lardo." Fat is regarded as a failure to exercise sufficient discipline over eating behavior.

Dieting is being promoted as the way to achieve the desired level of thinness. The dieting industry in America is a multibillion-dollar business that seems to have the support of the medical profession, mental health workers, the insurance industry, and the media. Girls and young women are bombarded with diets from books, magazines, and TV commercials guaranteeing that all can achieve a slim, trim look in a short time and, subsequently, all of the positive consequences in the way of admiration, self-respect, and happiness that come with having a lean figure. Not only are adolescent girls being bombarded with thinness messages, but their older sisters and mothers are likely to be involved in repeated attempts at dieting and may belong to groups such as Weight Watchers. Training in anorexic psychology is being packaged and sold (Wooley and Wooley, 1982). Dieting is a very popular activity amongst adolescent females. By the time they reach 18, 80% of adolescent girls have tried dieting. Thinness has become a performance dimension in the sense that one is held personally responsible for one's weight and body shape. Changes in weight and body shape to approximate society's ideal feminine body image can be achieved by demonstrating the self-control and discipline necessary to stay with a diet until one's goals are achieved. It is virtually impossible for an adolescent female in today's society to escape from the emphasis on achieving the thin body look through dieting.

Once the cultural norms of dieting as the path to the thinness ideal have been internalized, the decision to actually begin dieting can emerge from a variety of sources. Early adolescence is a time when hormonal changes and changes in body size create weight gain and additional body fat in females. Before puberty, girls have 10% to 15% more body fat than boys. After puberty, girls have almost as much as twice the body fat of boys. The redistribution of body weight during the early adolescent growth phase generates a plumping of the features. Her new physique and shape take her further away from the cultural ideal of thinness. Many adolescent girls do not realize that the additional body weight will eventually be redistributed (Newman and Newman, 1986; Striegel-Moore et al., 1986). Family members and peers may react to early adolescent plumpness by teasing or by making not too subtle remarks emphasizing weight gain. In looking at the outlines of her shape and size in the mirror, the girl may decide that she needs to go on a serious diet in order to look more like the ideal body image projected in teen magazines. Attempts to reduce body weight by dieting during adolescent periods of increased growth are ill timed because the body requires a well-balanced diet and an increased caloric intake during periods of rapid growth.

Once dieting is initiated, the resulting weight loss has a reinforcing quality. The young woman can experience a sense of mastery, pleasure, pride, and self-control over her success in weight-reduction through dieting. Initially, others are likely to compliment her for achieving a thinner looking appearance and admire her self-control and persistence. Daily weighing can become a ritual. The scale is a filter through which the teenager can measure her success. Keeping busy and being physically active are ways to avoid thinking about hunger urges. The exercise involved in such physical activities as tennis, gymnastics, ballet, and aerobics has the added reinforcement value of burning off excess calories, thereby contributing to the overall goal of weight loss.

The cognitive or thinking patterns accompanying successful dieting behavior add a second level of reinforcement. Adolescents can make self-statements or say to themselves "When I lose five more pounds, I'll feel better," "No one will tease me when I get down to 100 pounds," or "Losing weight is good, the more I lose, the better I feel." If she cannot wish extra pounds away, she can definitely diet them away (Garner, 1986).

Understanding the cultural, behavioral, and cognitive dynamics associated with dieting as a method of achieving the ideal of thinness is not sufficient to explain the extreme dieting behavior of full-blown anorexics. Most early teenage girls who engage in dieting to achieve weight loss manage to stay within reasonable limits. Only a small minority get "carried away" to the point where their dieting becomes totally out of control. In order to understand the relentless, life-threatening, self-induced starvation dieting behavior of anorexic adolescents, we will need to examine the underlying psychological dynamics, developmental conflicts, and family interaction patterns.

Psychological Dynamics

The core psychological conflict in anorexia has been defined as the inability to adaptively cope with the developmental task involved in making the transition from preadolescence to early and middle adolescence (Strober and Yager, 1985). There are four primary developmental tasks involved in this transition: (1) forming a new body image to integrate physical changes in size and shape, (2) incorporating reproductive functions and beginning the process of conceiving of one's self as a sexual being, (3) moving closer to peers, and (4) increasing independence from parents and learning to utilize a more abstract, flexible, sophisticated problem-solving and conflict-resolution style. Physical growth and hormonal changes in the body at puberty provide a concrete signal that one phase of life is ending and another is beginning. The demands of this transition can produce uncertainty and anxiety or challenge and excitement.

The preadolescent experiences of many girls who later become anorexic have not adequately prepared them for the psychosocial challenges and biophysical transformations of early adolescence. The externally compliant, perfectionistic, conscientious, meticulous, good little girl, orderly, obedient, well-behaved personality style, which has served them well in the past, is ill-suited to cope with adolescent developmental tasks that require self-reliance, trust in self, a solid foundation of internal worth, more mature social, interpersonal and peer skills, new conflict-resolution skills, and new ways of thinking about self and body. Incorporating changes in self-concept to include a body that now goes through a monthly menstrual cycle and has secondary sex characteristics can be frightening for a girl who lacks an internal sense of personal adequacy and self-worth. Establishing individuality and greater independence from her parents requires some degree of rebellion, or at least a willingness to openly disagree with parents. Increasing the level of closeness in peer relations involves emotional sharing, intimacy, risking rejection, and tolerance for diversity. By early-to-middle adolescence, she is aware of the fact that some of her female age mates are experimenting with drugs, sex, and openly questioning or defying parental authority. Resolving conflicts with parents, peers, and siblings, and making decisions about values and future goals requires the development of problem-solving skills that make allowances for uncertainty, ambiguity, and tolerance of diversity. Part of the adolescent condition is there are no absolute, unchallengeable answers.

The psychosexual issues triggered by change in body shape, size, and physiological functions seem to pose the greatest dilemma for preanorexic, early adolescent girls. While more diffuse issues, such as individuality, independence and uncertainty about the future, can be psychologically suppressed, awareness of breast and hip growth, increased body fat, and menstruation cannot be avoided. Puberty starts earlier in girls than in boys, and the changes are more visible. Because the growth changes are more visible, pubertal growth can carry more explicit sexual messages for girls than for boys. A shapely, feminine body with its sensuous implications can attract flirtatious comments and lewd looks. Parents sometimes respond to outward signs of their daughter's sexual development with apprehension and increased protectiveness (Striegel-Moore et al., 1986). For an emotionally insecure adolescent, awareness of herself as a sexual being can be a threatening prospect.

Dieting provides a method that can reduce body size, but does not usually begin as a conscious attempt to reverse the growth of secondary sex characteristics. At a conscious level, dieting usually begins as an attempt to reduce perceived body fat. Becoming thinner represents a way of exercising choice and taking control over one's body. Success in becoming thinner creates a feeling of mastery and control. In the initial stages, dieting to achieve a slimmer look is likely to be perceived by parents as responsible behavior. Weight loss and thinness are status symbols in most female adolescent peer groups and are responded to with a combination of recognition, admiration, and, in some cases, mild envy. Thus, by achieving a noticeable degree of thinness through dieting, an adolescent girl can accomplish several developmental objectives. She can take charge of her body, win admiration from her parents, and achieve some degree of status and recognition in peer relationships.

The anorexic adolescent, however, cannot stop her dieting behavior at the point where she has achieved a reasonable amount of control, mastery, admiration, and recognition. She needs greater power and control to compensate for her underlying feelings of powerlessness, ineffectiveness, and helplessness carried over from preadolescence (Bruch, 1978). Dieting becomes a panacea through which she can confront and symbolically master adolescent challenges and demands. By extreme weight loss, she can reduce or eliminate troublesome signs of her sexual evolution, such as menses, the size of breasts and hips, and return to the security of a prepubescent body. Rather than progressing forward in her psychosexual development, she reverses the process (Romero, 1984). She can act out needs for rebellion and defiance through extreme weight loss and dieting by demonstrating very clearly, in confrontations with family members, that no one can force her to eat. Weight loss and dieting become expressions of her individuality and independence. She discovers that she can eat less than others, lose more weight, and develop greater discipline and self-control over hunger urges while competitors among her peers fall by the wayside. This discovery gives her a tremendous sense of personal affirmation, power, and distinctiveness.

As losing more and more weight through greater extremes in dieting becomes the central issue of her life, she adopts a thinking and problem-solving style congruent with her starvation goals. Within the realm of eating behavior and thinness, her thinking fails to progress from the concrete, either/or thinking of preadolescence to the more sophisticated, abstract, flexible thinking of adolescence. Her reasoning is clouded by dichotomous thinking, overgeneralization, and "catastrophizing." Gaining a few pounds is regarded as a disaster. She thinks everyone will regard her as indulgent if her weight approaches the norm for her height and age. Thinness is generalized as the primary quality for success and respect. Her obsession with weight loss helps her tune out hunger cues and ignore signs that her health is deteriorating. Control over hunger is perceived as cleansing (Wooley and Wooley, 1982). She doesn't question her conscious assumptions about the relationship between thinness and personal well-being or her covert assumptions that a postpubertal body will result in disaster (Garner, 1986).

The psychological paradox of anorexia nervosa is that dieting and weight-loss behaviors that started out as an adaptive means of coping with adolescent transitions and taking charge of one's body deteriorate into self-destructive starvation. An adaptive strategy becomes transformed into a maladaptive, life-threatening process. The golden girl gets locked into a golden cage of her own making (Bruch 1978; Wooley and Wooley, 1982). Her method of achieving self-control, mastery, discipline, and individuality becomes a prison from which she cannot escape. In her own mind, however, the dehumanizing agony of malnutrition, starvation, and body emaciation is transformed into a triumph of self-discipline and willpower. She has mastered the fear of uncertainty and loss of control without realizing that she can be destroyed by the behaviors that are the foundation of her source of power and freedom.

Family Dynamics

The family dynamics of anorexic adolescents has been studied extensively. Liebman and his colleagues (1983), in their review of the literature on family dynamics in anorexia, identified five major characteristics: (1) enmeshment, (2) overprotectiveness, (3) rigidity, (4) lack of conflict resolution, and (5) involvement of the symptomatic (anorexic) child in unresolved marital and family conflicts. Enmeshment refers to the observation that family members are highly responsive to each other. They often give the appearance of a model of success. Family members submerge individual interests to take care of each other and maintain family stability. They rarely criticize or disagree with each other, seem to follow unspoken rules of agreement, and intuitively anticipate each other's moods and needs. Parents appear to have a good marriage and are concerned about their children. Overprotectiveness is shown by a tendency on the part of parents to discourage individual initiative and autonomy in their children. Parents are very intrusive, and children are given very little privacy. The parents rigidly maintain their controls and overprotectiveness, even as the children approach the age where they should be given greater degrees of freedom and personal space. Because they rarely disagree with each other openly and tend to be overprotective, no strategy for conflict resolution is developed within the family. Conflicts are generally suppressed or denied. As a result of a lack of conflict-resolution strategies, a covert state of submerged tension chronically exists within the family. When the symptoms of the anorexic daughter can no longer be denied, her symptoms become the major focus of family interaction, thereby allowing family members to avoid dealing with other serious conflicts.

The preadolescent girl who later becomes anorexic develops her compliant, obedient, perfectionistic, good-girl style within the family. Through family interaction patterns, she learns that she is expected to please others and be cognizant of what is important to them. External behaviors that reflect compliance, niceness, achievement, and self-control are approved of, reinforced, and rewarded. The external self is developed at the expense of the internal self. She receives little experience in learning to listen to her internal, self-expressing, personal and private feelings, openly disagreeing with others, or expressing negative emotions such as anger and defiance. She is given very little in the way of opportunities to discuss how she feels about her body, the psychobiological changes she will experience, or her psychosexuality. This lack of internal awareness and familiarity in expressing personal feelings and thoughts is insufficient preparation for the personal initiative, self-reliance, interpersonal and family-conflict resolution skills, acceptance of sexuality and body changes, and willingness to express personal feelings, which will be required to master the developmental task of adolescence.

The primary conclusion that can be drawn from this lengthy discussion of consequences, causes, etiology, and dynamics is that anorexia nervosa is a multidimensional syndrome or disorder resulting from a complex interplay of predisposing cultural, individual, and family forces. While its outcome is self-destructive, anorexia starts as an attempt to cope with the adolescent developmental task of initiative, autonomy, control, and psychosexual evolution. Anorexic behavior is difficult to change because the victim is fully committed to continuing the relentless pursuit of thinness by starvation dieting, despite the concerns of others for her deteriorating health and psychological well-being.

TREATMENT

Since anorexia is a multidimensional syndrome involving cultural, biological, developmental, intrapsychic, and family factors, the most effective programs are based on an integration of medical-nutritional, cognitive, behavioral, psychodynamic, and family therapies. Primary treatment goals involve restoration of body weight, promoting normal eating habits and a realistic concept of thinness, correction of distorted body perceptions, identification and resolution of unrealistic fears and faulty beliefs, rekindling the psychosocial growth process, and the development of more adaptive strategies to cope with adolescent conflicts and covert family turmoil (Kimmel and Weiner, 1985; McNab, 1983). Treatment can be divided into three phases: medical-nutritional rehabilitation, intensive psychotherapy, including family therapy and maintenance, termination, and follow-up. Anorexic adolescents tend to be resistant to treatment. They are usually brought in reluctantly or involuntarily to health care providers by their parents. They do not perceive that anything is wrong medically or psychologically and want to be left alone. Overcoming the initial resistance is one of the critical steps in treatment, since it is difficult to make serious progress toward achieving treatment goals without the patient's active involvement and participation.

Medical-Nutritional Rehabilitation

The effects of starvation must be reversed by a restoration of normal eating patterns before the patient can benefit from intensive psychotherapy. Starvation, as noted earlier, adversely affects cognitive, psychological, and emotional functioning. Extremely emaciated anorexics cannot concentrate on psychotherapy when they are experiencing deficiencies in alertness, mood swings, irritability, fatigue, and possible obsessive preoccupations with food due to starvation. It must be clearly spelled out to the patient from the onset that weight gain is an essential condition of treatment and that extreme dieting is injurious to health and potentially fatal (Silverman, 1974; Garner and Bemis, 1985). Treatment begins with a medical and psychosocial evaluation to confirm the diagnosis (which is usually obvious from the patient's skeleton-like physical appearance and family concerns) and to determine the extent of physical and psychological deterioration.

Medical and psychosocial evaluations generally include: (1) history of development of anorexic and related symptoms; (2) methods used to achieve weight reduction; (3) current eating patterns; (4) personal, family, medical, and psychiatric history; (5) any recent changes in family or home environment; (6) previous attempts to reverse anorexic symptoms; (7) precipitating factors; and (8) complete physical examination.

The first major decision confronting the treatment team is whether the initial phase should be conducted in a hospital-based program or on an outpatient basis at home. Hospitalization is suggested if psychological deterioration is evident and the patient is experiencing life-threatening effects from malnutrition and extreme weight-loss. Psychological deterioration is indicated by suicidal thoughts and intentions, poor concentration, apathy, social isolation, and blatant denial. Dangerously low weight; lowered body temperature, heart rate, pulse, and blood pressure; and hormonal imbalances are life-threatening symptoms. A list of hospitalization signs is provided in Table 6-2. Conversely, if weight loss is not severe, body signs are stable, and the adolescent shows some insight into her anorexic behavior, expresses willingness to change, and appears to be psychologically stable, treatment on an outpatient basis should be considered (Strober and Yager, 1985; Andersen, 1986).

A weight-restoration goal of 90% of the expectant weight for the patient's

Table 6-2. Signs for Hospitalization and Outpatient Treatment in Anorexia Nervosa[a]

Signs for Hospitalization
1. Dangerously low weight loss—exceeding 25% of expected body weight
2. Lowering of body temperature, blood pressure, pulse, and heart rate
3. Low potassium and hormonal imbalances
4. Depression, suicidal thoughts, poor concentration, extreme denial, social isolation, apathy, fatigue, and impaired judgment
5. Demoralization within the family. Family exhausted from months of trying to get the patient to maintain minimum acceptable weight level, or family dysfunction due to strife or marital breakup
6. Treatment failure in the past and absence of motivation for current treatment

Signs for Outpatient Treatment
1. Weight loss does not exceed 25% of ideal weight for age and height
2. Blood pressure, pulse, heart rate, body temperature, and hormonal balance within normal levels
3. Motivation to change and willingness to tolerate anxiety involved in weight gain
4. Absence of severe depression, suicidal intention, social isolation, and difficulties in concentrating
5. Good family support and commitment to therapy
6. Ability to build working relationship with therapist

[a]Adapted from: Andersen, A. E. (1986). Inpatient and outpatient treatment of anorexia nervosa. In K. D. Brownell and J. P. Foreyt (Eds.). *Handbook of eating disorders: Physiology, psychology, and treatment of eating disorders* (pp. 333–352). New York: Basic Books, and from Strober, M. & Yager, J. (1985). A developmental perspective on the treatment of anorexia nervosa. In D. M. Garner and P. E. Garfinkel (Eds.). *Handbook of psychotherapy for anorexia nervosa and bulimia* (pp. 363–390). New York: Guilford Press.

age and height is established at the beginning of treatment and is not altered. In order to prevent circulatory overload from eating too much too early and to reduce patient's fears regarding overweight, the weight-gain diet is usually started at 500 calories above the amount necessary to maintain present weight levels. This usually amounts to about 1,500 to 2,000 calories per day. Calorie intake is gradually increased to a balanced diet of about 4,000 calories per day. Two pounds a week is considered a medically safe rate of weight gain. The majority of patients require 2 to 4 months of treatment to achieve the target weight. Patients are usually weighed once a week to assess weight gain (Halmi, 1985a; Strober and Yager, 1985).

Weight gain rather than caloric intake is the primary evaluative dimension during this phase of treatment because patients can figure out surreptitious ways to dispose of food (Bryant and Bates, 1985). Methods for assuring the patient will eat enough to gain weight range from voluntary cooperation to forced feeding. Voluntary cooperation with eating and weight gain goals is strongly encouraged. Since there are underlying developmental issues involving control and independence, it is important the patient feel she is in charge rather than being controlled by others. The consequences of her not being willing or able to take charge of her eating behavior should be carefully explained. These consequences involve a gradual escalation of external controls over eating behavior, from behavioral modification, supervision at meal times, liquid supplements and appetite stimulants to forced intravenous and tube feedings. Behavioral modification and hospital-based programs involve rewards such as TV, social interaction, letter writing, and visiting privileges for maintaining calorie intake or weight-gain goals. Supervision at mealtimes involves a nurse or attendant sitting with the patient to ensure the required amount of calories has been consumed.

If the patient is at home during the weight-restoration phase of treatment, weight-gain goals and calorie requirements should be clearly outlined to family members. Family members tend to be very cooperative during the weight-gain phase because their reasons for bringing the patient into treatment often involve anxieties about extreme dieting and weight loss (Strober and Yager, 1985).

Intensive Psychotherapy

Intensive psychotherapy with anorexic patients involves a combination of cognitive-behavioral, psychodynamic, and family therapy approaches conducted within a context of individual and group formats. Serious efforts in intensive psychotherapy cannot get underway until after the patient has gained enough weight to concentrate and think clearly (Andersen, 1986). The patient should be clearly informed that the goals of intensive psychotherapy extend beyond symptoms involving diet restoration, weight gain, and improvements of physical health status. The therapist can tell patients that in this phase of treatment they will be looking at the challenges involved in growing up, family and peer relationships, ways of fostering self-awareness, and how beliefs are acquired.

Cognitive-behavioral therapy is an excellent tool to help patients identify, understand, and reassess the faulty beliefs and misperceptions that contributed to their seemingly bizarre attitudes toward thinness, dieting, and body image. All-or-none thinking and misperceptions reflected in the belief that complete control is desirable or attainable, fat is intrinsically bad, perfection is necessary for self-fulfillment and the admiration of others, expectations of others must always be lived up to, parents are beyond criticism, and attaining the minimum weight for one's age and height is equivalent to obesity can be gently challenged, corrected, and replaced with more effective cognitive reasoning. Psychoeducational techniques are often used in conjunction with cognitive-behavioral therapy. Patients are given instruction in assertiveness, conflict resolution, problem solving, positive self-statements, relaxation, maintaining a balanced diet, health care, and stress management. Opportunities are provided to practice new behaviors within and between therapy sessions. Some therapists supplement psychoeducational techniques with readings about anorexia nervosa for patients and family members. Three excellent, highly readable books with provocative symbolism in their titles are: (1) *Starving To Death in a Sea of Objects: The Anorexia Nervosa Syndrome* by John Sours (1980); (2) *Anorexia Nervosa: Let Me Be* by A. H. Crisp (1980); and (3) *The Golden Cage* by Hilda Bruch (1978). Readings can help patients capture some of the paradoxes involved in their behavior, diminish guilt and isolation by letting them know that they are not alone, and provide an opportunity to identify with former anorexics who have recovered.

Psychodynamic therapy can help patients explore and work through the underlying anxiety surrounding psychosexual development and the uncertainties of growing up. What is preventing the patient from feeling comfortable with a mature feminine body, why is the patient's life so organized around order, control, compliance, success and perfection, and why does the patient choose to rebel in such a self-destructive fashion? These are some of the questions that can be meaningfully examined in psychodynamic psychotherapy. Looking within is encouraged to allow the patient to get in touch with authentic feelings rather than continue expressing what others want her to feel. The "I shoulds" are dismantled and replaced with genuine feelings. Recovery requires the patient change her inner image and self-concept and learn to deal directly with age-appropriate adolescent developmental issues such as autonomy, individuality, and independence, which have been arrested or delayed. Hopefully, the patient can discover a new self with new strengths that will enable her to relinquish maladaptive anorexic behaviors and the facade of the perfect little girl (Bruch, 1978, 1982).

Individual psychotherapy provides a forum in which the patient can address highly personal issues and concerns. Group therapy allows the opportunity for anorexic adolescents to share their feelings, perceptions, and attitudes with others. Denial, distorted beliefs, and minimization of self-destructive behavior can be confronted by peers. Interaction with others who have similar symptoms and dynamics decreases feelings of isolation, secrecy, and shame. Positive sharing of helpful information and successes in confronting fears can be exchanged in group settings. All forms of intensive psychotherapy with anorexics require trust building and enabling the patient to develop a sense of hope.

The purpose of family therapy is to change the patterns of family interaction such as enmeshment, overprotectiveness, rigidity, and conflict avoidance, which have contributed to the patient's anorexic behavior and maladaptive coping style. During the course of family therapy, a realignment of family boundaries should occur, allowing greater independence and freedom from family controls. A family can be viewed as a self-regulating, organizational system that has its own characteristic communication patterns, decision style, myths, ideologies, coalitions, conflicts, values, and views of adolescence. The anorexic's symptoms are evoked, reinforced, and supported by certain interactions within the family system. The therapist's role is to initiate interventions that decrease dysfunctional family patterns and improve overall family functioning which, in turn, facilitates the patient's growth (Liebman et al., 1983; Strober and Yager, 1985).

Maintenance, Termination, and Follow-Up

Maintenance refers to the patient's ability to sustain her weight gain and an adequate calorie intake on her own. Before psychotherapy is terminated, the patient should be able to demonstrate that she can maintain a balanced diet and an appropriate weight level without close supervision or weekly monitoring. Follow-up consists of developing a plan to handle possible relapses, organize a support network, join an existing support group, and arrange a timetable for periodic meetings with the primary therapist.

The prognosis for recovery in anorexia is not entirely favorable. Reviews of therapy-outcome studies indicate that after 5 years only 35% of former anorexic patients are eating normally and free of fears about body weight. Many report dietary problems such as binging, purging, laxative abuse, and discomfort when eating with others. However, most regain their menses, maintain some degree of weight gain, find employment when they become young adults, and avoid social isolation (Hsu, 1980; Maloney and Klyklo, 1983; Schwartz and Thompson, 1981). Recovery rates are very good for short-term hospitalization programs offering a combination of medical-nutritional, individual, and family therapy. The most consistent predictors of good recovery outcomes are early age at onset and symptom duration of less than a year prior to treatment (Liebman et al., 1983; Halmi, 1985a). Since treatment in the early stages of anorexia increases the probability of a favorable outcome, parents, health care providers, and mental health workers should become familiar with the early warning signs listed in Table 6-3.

BULIMIA NERVOSA

Case Example 6-2: Viviane

Viviane is a 19-year-old college sophomore who was referred to the college counseling center by a physician at the student health service. She has been binge eating and purging by self-induced vomiting about twice a week for the past 4 or 5 months. Viviane started having problems with overeating after she broke up with her boyfriend 6 months ago. She found herself overeating as a way of coping with feelings of despondency, loss, and emptiness. At the same time, she was trying to diet. She feels that she lost her boyfriend to a girl who was "prettier, skinnier, and had a great shape." She thought that by losing some weight she would look more attractive. Looking more attractive would enable her to "get and keep" a new boyfriend. Her current weight is about 5 to 7 lbs above the average for her age and height.

Viviane first got the idea of self-induced vomiting from a young woman who lived in her dormitory complex. The young woman told Viviane that she wouldn't have to worry about weight gain if she compensated for her binges by purging. After Viviane started purging, the bouts of overeating occurred more frequently. A typical binge would start out with eight to ten candy bars, a 1-lb box of chocolates, several cookies, two or three boxes of popcorn, and ice cream. She would store the nonperishable goods in her dorm room and buy the ice cream right before the binge. She would eat until she was exhausted, ran out of food, heard someone coming, or experienced stomach pain. Self-induced vomiting was accompanied by a mixture of pain and relief. The pain from vomiting gave her a feeling of relief "Because the more it hurts, the more I know I'm not going to gain weight." The binge-purge episodes were followed by renewed efforts at dieting which would only last 2 or 3 days before the binge-purge cycle would start again. Viviane is worried that her eating behavior is out of control. She feels ashamed and is afraid that others might find out about her secret binge-purge episodes.

Viviane recalls being somewhat "chubby" as a child. She was sensitive to teasing from peers about her weight. As a teenager, she has been very conscious about weight control and has struggled to keep her weight within normal limits by a combination of dieting and exercising.

Table 6-3. Anorexia: Early Warning Signs

1. Weight loss of 15%–25% or more of body weight before, during, or shortly after puberty
2. Reduction in food intake, denial of hunger, and avoidance of high-calorie foods
3. Prolonged exercising despite fatigue and weakness
4. Intense fear of gaining weight
5. Unusual patterns of handling food
6. Cessation of menstruation cycle

Definition and Primary Characteristics

The term bulimia literally means great hunger, insatiable hunger, ox hunger, or insatiable appetite. In mental health or clinical parlance, bulimia nervosa refers to a cycle of binging, followed by some form of compensation for food intake, such as self-induced vomiting, laxative or diuretic abuse, fasting, strict dieting, or excessive exercise. Bulimic individuals are usually within the normal or near-normal weight range, with frequent weight fluctuations due to the binge-purge episodes. During the binge phase, the person can consume up to 5,000 to 50,000 calories of energy-rich, tasty, fattening foods such as ice cream, sweets, junk foods, or popcorn in a period of 2 hours or less. The binge phase is usually terminated by exhaustion, self-induced vomiting, sleep, abdominal pain, running out of food, or interruptions by visitors. Self-induced vomiting, laxatives, diuretics, fasting, exercise, or severe diets are often used to reduce anxieties about weight gain, relieve painful fullness, and restore a sense of control. Between binge-eating phases, the individual is likely to attempt to maintain a strict diet of 1,000 or less calories a day and avoid energy-rich foods. While binge-purge episodes sometimes occur in individuals with anorexia nervosa, in bulimia nervosa the weight loss is not so extreme as to be life-threatening (American Psychiatric Association, 1987). DSM-III-R (1987) criteria for bulimia nervosa are listed in Table 6-4.

In bulimia, unlike anorexia, the person is aware that her eating pattern is abnormal, fears not being able to stop voluntarily, and is likely to experience self-deprecating thoughts, self-criticism, and depression about eating behavior. From a psychological perspective, the most important features of bulimia are the self-perceived loss of control over eating, a belief that the quantity eaten is excessive, and fears about gaining weight. It is not always the absolute quantity of food that is eaten, but how the episode is perceived (Fairburn et al., 1986). Once a binge episode begins, the bulimic feels a loss of control, with escalating eating behavior sometimes (or often) leading to the consumption of enormous amounts of food in a short time (Dupont, 1984; Gandour, 1984).

Table 6-4. DSM-III-R[a] Diagnostic Criteria for Bulimia Nervosa

---

1. Recurrent episodes of binge eating (rapid consumption of a large amount of food in a discrete period of time).
2. A feeling of lack of control over eating behavior during the eating binges.
3. The person regularly engages in either self-induced vomiting, use of laxatives or diuretics, strict dieting or fasting, or vigorous exercise to prevent weight gain.
4. A minimum average of two binge-eating episodes a week for at least 3 months.
5. Persistent overconcern with body shape and weight.

---

[a]Adapted from: American Psychiatric Association. (1987). *Diagnostic and statistical manual of mental disorders* (3rd ed., rev.). Washington, D. C.

There is some degree of semantic confusion in the eating disorder literature surrounding use of the term bulimia. Bulimia has two different, yet highly related meanings. First, the term bulimia has been used to describe binge-eating alone. Second, bulimia has been used to describe binge-eating coupled with compensation for food intake by such previously mentioned methods as self-induced vomiting, laxative abuse, and fasting. Further, previous DSM-III criteria did not separate these two related yet diverse behaviors, further adding to the confusion. Present DSM-III-R criteria *do* separate binge-eaters and bulimics, or women with the syndrome of bulimia nervosa. In this chapter, we use the term binge-eating to refer to compulsive episodic overeating and bulimia nervosa, or bulimia to refer to the clinical syndrome as defined by the DSM-III-R.

Rates of Occurrence

Bulimia occurs primarily in middle-class late adolescent and young-adult white females of average or near-average weight who are attending college. Research findings indicate that 90% of bulimic young people are females. The incidence of self-reported problems with binge-eating has ranged from 32% to as high as 78%. Bulimia nervosa, or binging followed by some form of compensation for food intake, appears to be much less common, with reported incidences on college campuses ranging from 1% to 14%. Binge-eating typically begins around age 18, with vomiting or purging by other means to lose weight beginning about a year later (Johnson et al., 1984; Garner et al., 1985; Bayer, 1984; Fairburn and Cooper, 1982). The average duration of bulimia is 5 to 5 1/2 years (Johnson and Pure, 1986). The number and severities of behaviors used to induce weight loss, such as vomiting, laxative and diuretic abuse, or excessive exercises, increases with the duration of bulimia (Johnson and Larson, 1982).

Studies have repeatedly shown that episodes of binging, purging, and fasting are fairly common in American young women. One-half to two-thirds of college-age females report regular binge-eating (Kagan and Squires, 1984; Gandour, 1984). A Gallup Poll conducted in 1985 found that half the women who suffer from compulsive overeating resort to extreme measures, such as fasting, strenuous exercise, laxative, or self-induced vomiting, to prevent weight gain (Gallup, 1985). Self-induced vomiting as a weight control technique is less likely to be used in women over 30 (Wooley and Kearney-Cooke, 1986). Gallup estimates that there are 2 million young women who have experienced the symptoms of anorexia or bulimia.

Like drugs, there are levels of progression and severity in bulimic behavior (Dupont, 1984). Some young women who have experimented with binging and purging once or twice during adolescence relinquish it easily. Others stuff and vomit periodically without losing control or becoming driven. A few progress to a full-blown syndrome of bulimia, with several binge-purge episodes a week. Once bulimic behavior becomes out of control, self-imposed limits on binging and purging are no longer effective. Bulimic behavior is triggered by a variety of events. The most frequently mentioned precipitating factors are stress, loneliness, interpersonal conflict, depression, boredom, developmental transitions, and tensions that build up from strict dieting attempts. Most bulimics prefer to binge at home, alone or in secret. However, in recent years, the binge-purge cycle has become more of a shared experience. Most young women now know someone who binges and purges. Adolescents teach others how to binge and purge in mutual enforcing interactions. The most frequently used purging behavior is self-induced vomiting followed by laxatives and diuretics (Striegel-Moore et al., 1986; Gandour, 1984).

Historical Notes

Although accounts of binging and purging extend as far back as the Babylonian Talmud, which was written around A.D. 400, the syndrome of bulimia nervosa was not widely known by mental health professionals or the lay public until the past 10 to 15 years (Garfinkel and Kaplan, 1986). In the late 1950s, bulimic behavior was observed in the eating patterns of a minority of obese persons (Stunkard, 1959). Later, cycles of binging, purging, and fasting were observed in anorexic patients prior to an after-weight restoration (Halmi, 1985b). Vivid portrayals of bulimic behavior and underlying psychodynamics were presented in the case histories of Ellen West (Binswanger, 1957) and Laura (Lindner, 1955). In the case of Ellen West, who went through extreme cycles of gorging, purging, exercising, and fasting, fatness was synonymous with aging, whereas slimness was equated with youth, attractiveness, and desirability. In Robert Lindner's *Fifty Minute Hour*, Laura experienced the compulsion to binge during periods of depression.

There has been a sudden and dramatic increase in reported cases of bulimia in the 1980s. *Newsweek Magazine* referred to 1981 as the year of the "binge-purge" syndrome (Adler, 1982). In 1980 the American Psychiatric Association officially recognized bulimia as a separate clinical syndrome by its inclusion in the DSM-III. Since that time, there has been a significant increase in the number of articles on bulimia published in professional journals, popular magazines, and newspapers. The upsurge of interest in bulimia in the past few years appears to be due to three interrelated events. First, lifting the veil of secrecy encouraged more closeted bulimics to come forward and seek help. Second, cultural pressures to achieve thinness have driven young women to seek methods of compensating for food intake, such as self-induced vomiting and laxative abuse. Third, the effects of imitation and modeling. The widespread frequency of binging and purging among college students has influenced others to try it (Moss et al., 1984; Kagan and Squires, 1984).

Physical-Medical Consequences

The deleterious effects of bulimia on body functions, while potentially serious, are not as immediately life-threatening as are the effects of anorexia. The major consequences of repeated cycles of binge-eating, purging, and fasting are potassium depletion and electrolyte imbalances, deterioration of tooth enamel, abdominal pains, and dehydration. The most dangerous effects of frequent vomiting or purging are depletions of potassium levels which, in turn, upset the electrolyte balance. Electrolyte imbalances can cause heart irregularities, tiredness, depression, and constipation. The gastric acid from vomiting creates dental erosion and loss of tooth enamel. The physical trauma of vomiting is responsible for abdominal pain. Chronic dehydration and loss of body fluids can come about as a result of alternating periods of dieting, vomiting, and laxative abuse (Garner et al., 1985; Mitchell, 1986). A more extensive list of physical consequences resulting from bulimia is provided in Table 6-5.

Etiology, Causes, and Dynamics

To explain why increasing numbers of late adolescent and young adult females are becoming involved in the binge-purge-diet syndrome, it is necessary to examine the mixture of sociocultural pressures driving young women to what may be for the most part unattainable goals of thinness and the underlying psychodynamics placing them at risk for losing control over bulimic behavior.

Table 6-5. Physical Consequences Resulting from Bulimia

1. Abnormally low potassium levels
2. Insufficient amount of minerals (1. and 2. together prevents effective conduction of electrical impulses through the neuromuscular system)
3. Imbalance in electrolytes
4. Cardiac arrhythmias/eventual heart damage
5. Gum recession
6. Enamel breakdown—because teeth are bathed in hydrochloric acid during the process of vomiting
7. Abrasions damaging the esophageal walls—causing extensive bleeding and occasional rupturing of the esophagus (can be fatal)
8. Chronic underhydration
9. Kidney problems
10. Infected or swollen salivary glands
11. Abdominal pains

Sociocultural Pressures Toward Thinness as the Ideal

America's obsession with thinness, weight loss, and dieting during the past two decades was reviewed in our discussion of the cultural dynamics associated with anorexia. The immense social pressures to remain thin affect people of all ages, but are more strongly applied to women. From the media, health classes, family and peers, women and girls are bombarded with messages that "Thin is Beautiful" or "No woman can be too thin or too rich." Beauty, self-worth, success, competence, and happiness in heterosexual relationships are based on achieving the ideal of a thin shape. Conversely, to be fat is to be a failure, unattractive, and lack self-control. One cannot be loved unless one is slender. The buxom, ample-breasted, large-hipped figures of the Marilyn Monroe's and Jayne Mansfield's have been replaced by the adolescent profiles of models like Brooke Shields. Most women now believe that a slender figure is the most salient aspect of physical beauty (Garner et al., 1985). Qualities such as sensuality, sexuality, attractiveness, and desirability are now being projected by thinner, more athletic, slim feminine bodies. The body dimensions of movie stars, models, beauty contestants, and *Playboy* centerfolds have been scaled down to approximate the leaner look. During the past 20 years, the contestants in the Miss America beauty pageant and centerfolds in *Playboy* magazine showed a decrease in weight for age and height and smaller bust and hip measurements. The tubular-looking figure has replaced the hour-glass figure (Garner et al., 1980; Garner et al., 1985). Unquestioning internalization of the thinness norms has led to a great deal of dissatisfaction with body image. Studies since the late 1960s have shown that most young women are dissatisfied with their bodies and want to lose weight. Statistically speaking, weight concerns and dieting are so common among women today they have become normal (Rodin et al., 1985; Mintz and Betz, 1988). Body dissatisfaction seems to increase with age. Many women within the statistically normal weight range viewed themselves as fat (Halmi, 1981; Mintz and Betz, 1986; Wooley and Wooley, 1982). A 1984 *Glamour* magazine survey of 33,000 women revealed that 41% of the respondents felt moderately or extremely unhappy about their bodies, 30% of those whose weight was below the norm viewed their weight as too high, and 80% felt they had to be slim to attract men. The majority had attempted dieting to lose weight. Weight loss was associated with pride, elation, and self-assurance. Weight gain was associated with depression, self-deprecation, and curtailment of social plans (Wooley and Wooley, 1984). Perception of body size is related to self-esteem. Young women who feel satisfied with their body image seem to have higher self-esteem (Striegel-Moore et al., 1986; Mintz and Betz, 1986).

What many young women do not realize is that while their ideal body image has grown thinner, the actual weight in women has increased. The average woman in the 17–24 age-range has become 5 to 7 lbs heavier in the last few years. The recent trend toward higher actual weight in late adolescent and young adult women is in direct contradiction to the ideal trends. The conflict between biological weight norms and cultural expectations means that many young women will ultimately be defeated by their attempts to achieve the cultural ideal of physical beauty and desirability projected in the slim body image (Garner et al., 1985; Agras and Kirkley, 1986).

The multibillion dollar weight-loss industry in America has promoted dieting as the way to achieve the desired body image and shape. There are even diets planned to accommodate binging. In the *Beverly Hills Diet*, Judy Mazel (1981) recommends a diet of semistarvation, binge-eating, and self-induced diarrhea (by eating volumes of raw tropical fruits) to compensate for binges. Every schoolgirl who has tried dieting knows that it is not easy to resist the build up of hunger urges or to avoid temptations to eat high-calorie, weight-gaining foods, such as sweets, ice cream, popcorn, pop, and junk food. Self-induced vomiting and other forms of purging offer young women a way to cope with abnormal fears of weight gain by compensating for dietary lapses and binging (Wooley and Wooley, 1982).

Sociocultural dynamics alone, however, do not completely explain why a small minority of young women go on to experience serious problems with the binge-purge-fast syndrome. All young women growing up in America are exposed to cultural images of thinness and dieting as a way to achieve the desired level of thinness. By age 18, 80% of adolescent females have tried dieting to achieve weight loss. Twenty percent or more of college-age women report episodes of binging, purging, and fasting, yet only a few experience the full-blown clinical syndrome of bulimia nervosa. To understand this small minority, we will examine the psychological dynamics underlying bulimia.

Psychological Dynamics

This section on psychological dynamics will be divided into three parts: personality characteristics, developmental dynamics, and behavioral reinforcement.

In the composite personality picture that emerges from the literature, bulimic young women are described as outgoing, socially skilled, high achieving, industrious individuals who have high needs for social approval. They seem to lack a strong internal sense of self-worth and self-directiveness. Bulimic young women tend to be preoccupied with food, weight and body size, worry excessively, and possess an exaggerated fear of becoming fat. Even when weight is normal by objective standards, they tend to perceive themselves as overweight and have a poor body image. They are aware that they have an eating problem, are distressed by their loss of control over eating, and want to receive help (Gandour, 1984; Fairburn et al., 1986). Dieting usually starts at an earlier age and extends over a longer period of time, as compared to nonbulimics (Johnson et al., 1984). A small group of bulimics seems to have problems with stealing, lying, sexual acting out, drug and alcohol abuse, and poor impulse control (Mitchell and Pyle, 1982; Striegel-Moore et al., 1986).

Depression is commonly associated with bulimia (Gandour, 1984; Johnson and Pure, 1986; Herzog, 1984). The cause-effect sequence of depression in bulimia is not clear. Clinicians are not sure to what degree the poor self-image, perfectionistic beliefs, body dissatisfaction, and doubts about self-worth, often found in the personal makeup of bulimic young women, generates depressive symptoms or to what degree depression is a consequence of guilt and self-debasement over losing control over binging, purging, and dieting. Depression can have different meanings within the binge-purge-fast cycle. Binging, purging, and dieting can be used as ways of coping with depression. These same behaviors, when used to cope with depression, can intensify depression and thereby create a vicious cycle. For example, a person might binge-eat to relieve feelings of despondency and stress. Initially, binging and purging relieve the stress. Subsequently, however, she feels more depressed because she regards herself as a failure for having given into urges to binge and feels self-loathing because of vomiting. She copes with the second level of depression by promising to go on a strict diet and never to binge or purge again, only to be defeated by the stresses of dieting, which perpetuate the bulimic-depressive cycle.

The bulimic cycle usually begins between the ages of 18 to 20. During this time frame, young women are facing the overlapping developmental task of identity and intimacy. The resolution of identity and intimacy issues involves struggling to define who she is in terms of her own uniqueness and authenticity, what she wants to do with her life, what she stands for in terms of personal values, the role of sex and intimacy in relationships, the mixture of traditional and contemporary feminine characteristics, and reorganizing the balance of autonomy and connectedness in relationship to her parents. She must also develop a flexible adaptive pool of strategies to cope with the uncertainties and challenges that lie ahead. In order to successfully resolve these identity and intimacy issues, it is essential that she possess a reservoir of inner strength and personal worth independent of external performance and appearance. Realistic acceptance of her body is important because she is going to have to live with her body for another 50–60 years. If she has failed in earlier periods of development to build an inner reserve of self-worth based on unconditional love or positive regard from significant others, she is vulnerable to basing her entire sense of worth on external accomplishments and appearances. Young women at greatest risk are those who have not developed a foundation of inner security to counterbalance the cultural images which project thinness as the only way to well-being and success. The more deeply she has internalized the cultural norms regarding thinness, attractiveness, and beauty, the greater the risk that she will be controlled by these norms (Striegel-Moore et al., 1986).

Once the slim body image becomes consolidated as her ultimate gauge of self-worth, the scale and the mirror control her self-evaluation. Beliefs attached to weight and size become the driving force in her life, taking on an almost mystical quality. Her major conflicts, fears, desires, and goals are assessed through a filter reflected in self-statements like "I hate myself now, I really look atrocious, but when I lose 10 pounds, I'll be beautiful and everything will be fine . . . I know someone will love me and want me then." Her coping style revolves around weight and size without having seriously appraised the meaning of weight and size.

Unlike their anorexic sisters, bulimic young women do not reject their sexuality or themselves as sexual beings. Rather than rejecting their psychosexual evolution, they perceive the essence of their femininity, attractiveness, and desirability in the achievement of the culturally sanctioned body image. They have never really questioned the cultural norms associated with the slender, ideal shape and have built their expectations and values around "looking good" and pleasing others (Boskind-White and White, 1983; Gandour, 1984). The pursuit of thinness is congruent with their ideal of sexual attractiveness. Through cultural conditioning, these young women have been encouraged to turn to dieting as a means to achieve weight-control goals. For a young woman whose major source of self-esteem is tied up in her body image, dieting is a serious, stressful endeavor. Her coping strategies become increasingly centered on concerns with dieting, weight control, and fears about weight gain. She is likely to worry constantly about gaining weight, deprive herself unnecessarily of fattening but enjoyable foods, and vigilantly count calories. As the stresses involved in dieting and her fears of not achieving the desired body image build up, she runs the risk of beginning the bulimic cycle.

The internalized cultural norms and underlying developmental dynamics set the stage for eliciting bulimic behaviors. Once the psychological and cultural-foundation factors or antecedent conditions are in place, the binge-purge-fast cycle can be triggered by a variety of precipitating stressors, such as loss or separation, inability to cope with the daily problems of living, inability to lose weight despite continuous dieting, teasing by friends about weight gain, unresolved developmental conflicts, romance troubles, depression, loneliness, and anxieties about the future. At the next stage in the process, the binge-purge-fast cycle becomes self-reinforcing, each behavior having a symbolic meaning and reinforcement value within the cycle.

Binging and eating large quantities of food forbidden because of restrictive dieting are initially experienced as pleasurable or stress-reducing. Binging can provide a release from the rigors and monotony of dieting and provide temporary escape from current problems and distraction from depressive moods. The delayed response to binging is more likely to have a negative tone, such as guilt, remorse, self-criticism, and depression, because of perceived failure in maintaining dietary behavior. Purging by vomiting or laxative abuse often begins as a way to resolve the conflict posed by the terror of weight gain on the one hand, and appetite buildup or desires to eat restricted foods on the other (Garner, 1986). Vomiting, while sometimes painful, can be experienced as cleansing, because it nullifies the weight-gain outcome of binging. Secondary effects of vomiting are self-disgust and self-loathing. Purging is followed by renewed attempts at dieting, which are usually more severe and restrictive because fasting symbolizes repentance and a firm self-control. Adopting more and more restrictive dieting rules increases the likelihood that the person will be unable to religiously stay within the boundaries of the rules. Either-or thinking feeds into the binge-purge process because minor lapses in dietary controls are perceived as major failures that lead to self-statements such as "Now that I've proved that I'm a failure by eating one scoop of ice cream, I might as well eat the whole quart." The breakdown in self-control over eating is gradual. It usually takes about 9 months after dieting is instituted for bulimic behaviors to approach full-blown proportions. Since binging and purging, for the most part, are still socially unacceptable, the behaviors remain secret, reducing the possibility of help (Dupont, 1984).

In the final analysis, the bulimic syndrome is the outcome of unquestioned internalization of culturally sanctioned body-image norms (which are biologically unattainable for most young women) without the counterbalancing effects of a genuine sense of intrinsic personal worth. To achieve the impossible dream of the ideal body image, a dietary process is set into motion which cannot succeed because the ultimate body-image goals are biologically unattainable. The dietary process, also culturally sanctioned, has its own pitfalls in the way of food deprivation, hunger buildup, and desires to sample the forbidden foods. These pitfalls can trigger the binge-purge more restrictive dieting cycle. Bulimia is an adaptive-maladaptive paradox. Pursuing culturally sanctioned goals by socially approved methods of dieting results in a maladaptive pattern of binging, purging, and fasting, undermining self-worth, competence, and feelings of desirability, the very qualities that diet-purge eating behaviors were designed to enhance.

TREATMENT

Psychotherapy with bulimia nervosa has four primary goals: (1) elimination of the binge-purge-diet cycle; (2) improving coping strategies and restructuring faulty beliefs about body image and self-worth; (3) resolving late adolescent or early adult developmental tasks involving identity, autonomy, and intimacy; and (4) increasing self-esteem. Treatment programs combine several different techniques and approaches in a multidimensional strategy that includes group therapy, one-on-one therapy, psychoeducational lectures, homework assignments, and follow-up. Except in cases where there are serious health problems, severe depression, or suicidal risk, treatment normally takes place on an outpatient basis. In comparison with anorexia, prognosis is generally more favorable. Bulimic young women usually come into treatment voluntarily and are highly motivated to change. They no longer consider their dietary chaos as adaptive behavior and recognize that their symptoms have built up to the point where they are out of control. As a group, bulimic young women are bright, well educated, and resourceful. While they may experience relapses and resistances when it comes to giving up old beliefs and behaviors related to body image and dieting, they are struggling to move to a more adaptive level of coping with troublesome conflicts.

Treatment can be divided into three phases (Fairburn, 1981; Wilson, 1986). Phase 1 is an assessment of eating behaviors and psychological development to establish a realistic weight level, develop an eating plan, monitor eating behavior and eating-related thoughts, and psychoeducational lectures. Eating-disorder assessment inventories and standardized interviews are utilized to help establish baseline data on eating habits, dieting, binging, and purging and to provide relevant case history information concerning psychosocial development. The realistic weight level is set at 10% below the highest weight prior to the onset of the eating disorder or at what is now being referred to as the "set point." The set point is the usual body weight one achieves without extreme fasting or overeating. It tends to remain stable over time, despite variations in calorie intake (Garner et al., 1985). To normalize eating patterns, a meal plan is developed where the patient has three to four nutritionally well-balanced meals a day totalling 1,500 to 2,000 calories. The goal is to make eating consistent, mechanical, and sufficient to prevent the build-up of hunger urges. Desires to eat forbidden foods are handled by working these foods gradually into the diet in small amounts. The rationale is that after prolonged periods in which daily calorie intake is stable and biologically and psychologically satisfying, intense urges to binge will decrease. Relearning or reregulating eating behaviors and eliminating dieting allow food intake to be determined by internal signals of hunger and satiety. The patient is informed that dieting is not consistent with treatment to reduce binging and purging.

Eating behaviors are closely monitored in phase I. Patients are required to keep a daily record of foods eaten, the time of day and location of binge-purge episodes and accompanying thoughts, feelings, and stress levels. These thoughts and feelings are discussed during therapy meetings. Patients are encouraged to handle urges to binge and vomit by techniques involving interruption, distraction, delay, and response-prevention, such as going for a walk, calling a friend, watching TV, or waiting 15 minutes before starting through the responses that culminate in binging or purging (Wilson, 1986). Many patients report significant reductions in binge-purge symptoms after a short period of self-monitoring and regular meals (Kirkley, 1985). Psychoeducational interventions consist of instruction and lectures on bulimia and related eating disorders, feminist issues, body image, coping behavior, relaxation techniques, life-cycle development, family systems, relapse prevention, and assertiveness training. The lectures are designed to dispel the myths many bulimic women have internalized about dieting, body image, weight regulation, and self-worth. One of the biggest myths is that it is possible to recover from bulimia while still dieting and occasionally vomiting (Garner et al., 1985).

Phase II involves restructuring faulty beliefs regarding body image, femininity, personal worth, dieting, developing more effective problem-solving and coping skills, and working through unresolved developmental conflicts. Unexamined, dysfunctional beliefs about the relationship between the ideal slender body and success, beauty, competence, desirability, and sexuality are replaced with self-affirming beliefs based on internal worth and discovery of personal values and assets. The person is encouraged to look within to find the true source of personal power rather than to unattainable cultural ideas. One of the major problems of bulimia is how womanhood is constructed. Historically, physical appearance has been a primary characteristic in evaluating womanhood. In reexamining this definition of womanhood, bulimic young women need help and support in learning to accept their bodies without negating themselves for not achieving the culturally sanctioned slender body. Bulimic coping styles and thought patterns need to be replaced with adaptive problem-solving skills and functional reasoning. Overgeneralizations about weight are questioned and patients are provided with a wider range of coping skills, such as assertiveness training, relaxation techniques, communication skills, guided imagery, conflict resolution, and problem-solving skills (Fairburn et al., 1986; Wooley and Kearney-Cooke, 1986).

Phase III involves consolidating treatment gains and maintaining positive changes. Patients are provided with specific guidelines on how to handle difficulties in the future. One relapse or setback doesn't mean treatment was a failure or that one is a bad person. A list of support groups that can provide companionship and information is made available, and a periodic check-in schedule is worked out. Treatment is usually conducted over a period of 5 months.

The treatment history of bulimia is too brief to venture a conclusive statement about effectiveness. Wilson (1986) and Kirkley and associates (1985) report positive outcomes in studies using a combination of cognitive, behavioral, nutritional, and general therapy principles. Binging and purging was significantly reduced, and patients reported improved ability to cope with stress, depression, and conflict.

ANOREXIA AND BULIMIA NERVOSA: A MIXTURE OF OVERLAPPING SYNDROMES

The lines of demarcation between the syndromes of anorexia and bulimia cannot always be clearly drawn. In 1976 Marlene Boskind-Lodhal coined the term bulimarexia to highlight the similarities between anorexia and bulimia (Boskind-White and White, 1983). A related term is Hilda Bruch's (1973) thin–fat people. Bulimia nervosa was originally described as a variant of anorexia nervosa (Russell, 1979). Both bulimics and anorexics share a preoccupation with dieting, food, and exaggerated fears of gaining weight. Differences between anorexia and bulimia are listed in Table 6-6.

Bulimia may exist concurrently with anorexia, subsequently, or as a separate syndrome with different psychological roots (Smith, 1984). Several studies indicate that 35% to 50% of anorexics display symptoms of bulimia, such as binge-eating and purging by vomiting or laxative abuse (Fairburn and Garner, 1986; Garner et al., 1985). Many bulimics have been anorexic in the past or alternated between anorexia and bulimia at different points in time (Gandour, 1984). These findings have led mental health workers and clinicians to identify two groups of anorexics: restrictor anorexics and bulimic anorexics. Restrictor anorexics maintain a relatively steady pattern of excessive dieting to achieve weight-loss goals. Bulimic anorexics exhibit periodic episodes of binging and purging in the course of pursuing weight-loss goals by dieting (Strober, 1986). Bulimic anorexics as compared to restrictor anorexics are likely to be older, sexually active with bouts of promiscuity and abstinence, outgoing, and admit more frequently to awareness of strong hunger. Many have been involved in abusing street drugs or alcohol, steal-

Table 6-6. Differences Between Anorexia Nervosa and Bulimia

Anorexia

    Often denies problem (may pride herself on her weight loss)
    Exhibits significant weight loss
    Usually maintains rigid control of eating
    Turns away from food to cope
    Has difficulty in accurately assessing body size

Bulimia

    Recognizes abnormal eating pattern
    Usually within 10 to 15 lbs of normal body weight
    Often feels loss of control of eating
    Likely to be older and more outgoing
    Turns to food to cope
    Has less difficulty with accurately assessing body size

ing, and give histories of impulsive behavior, depression, and mood swings (Garfinkel and Garner, 1982). Restrictor anorexics report fewer sexual experiences, greater introversion and anxiety, and extreme self-denial and self-control (Garfinkel and Kaplan, 1986).

To further complicate the diagnostic picture, bulimic and anorexic behavior, separately and in combination, are appearing with increasing frequency among adolescents and young women on junior high, high school, and college campuses. The popularity of binging, purging, and dieting in college communities and the glamorization of anorexia as the "good girl syndrome" (Leven Kron, 1978) has generated a rash of what Hilda Bruch (1986) refers to as "me-tooism" imitations of disordered behaviors. The me-tooers are young women who are drawn into the orbit of disordered eating behavior by imitation, modeling, or publicity. A generation ago, it was much easier for an anorexic adolescent to regard herself as a unique person whose originality gave her special powers of control and discipline over dieting. Today young women teach each other to diet, binge, and purge. Those who develop disordered eating behavior know others who have tried it or started after watching TV programs and reading magazine articles. Disordered eating behavior tends to be less severe and transient in teenagers and young adults who are experimenting or imitating as part of a fad. In these cases, the personality dynamics, etiology, and causes are likely to be quite different. By not distinguishing less severe, transient forms of eating disorders from full-blown clinical cases, inflated research surveys can create the impression that severe eating disorders have reached epidemic proportions, which may not be a true reflection of the actual picture.

The Eating Continuum

Some writers conceive of a spectrum of eating disorders (Andersen, 1983; Squire, 1983) in which eating behavior, weight concerns, dieting, and purging can be classified along an eating continuum or arc that ranges from normal eaters at one extreme to anorexics at the other extreme. The eating continuum described by Squire (1983) is shown in Figure 6-1. The psychological disturbance tends to become more severe as one moves along the continuum (Mintz and Betz, 1988). Beginning on the left-hand side are normal eaters and dieters. Normal eaters and occasional dieters are content with their bodies as they are, eat when they are hungry, and stop eating when they are full. They may occasionally cut back on meals for a few days after holidays, or other occasions when their calorie intake has been excessive. Normal eaters and occasional dieters tend to stay the same weight for years without becoming extremely concerned. Normal eaters and occasional dieters are followed by noncompensatory bulimics on the continuum. Noncompensatory bulimics are overweight-to-obese people (see Box 6-1, p. 214 for

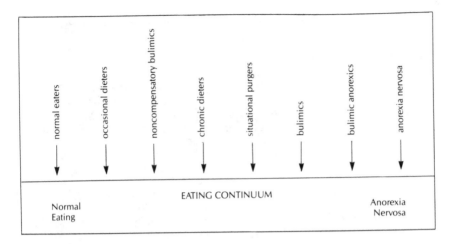

FIGURE 6-1. Eating continuum. (Adapted from Squire, S. (1983). *The slender balance.* New York: Pinnacle Books.)

brief description of obesity) who periodically go on binges but don't try to compensate for binge-eating with consistent purging, fasting, or exercise. Their weight remains high, but stable. At the center of the continuum are the chronic dieters. To the right of the center are the situational purgers, such as models or actresses who may compensate for occasional binging with self-induced vomiting or laxatives. They are not particularly obsessed with weight and do not feel disgusted with themselves after occasional binge-purge behavior. Next on the continuum are traditional bulimics whose weight is within the normal range. They regularly engage in binge-purge-diet episodes. Bulimics are followed by two subgroups of anorexics. Bulimic anorexics reduce weight through food denial, but regularly binge and then purge through the use of laxatives, diuretics, appetite suppressants, or self-induced vomiting. The other half of the anorexics at the far extreme right fit DSM-III-R (1987) criteria for anorexia. They have weight losses of 15% to 20% of their original body weight from prolonged fasting, they feel fat, deny their emaciation, and want to lose more weight. A number of similar eating continuums have been proposed.

Only a small number of females between puberty and old age fit into the normal eater's category. In one study, it was found that only 32% of 643 college women surveyed could be classified as normal eaters (Mintz and Betz, 1988). Susan Squire (1983) regards this group as fortunate and lucky since most women are concerned about their weight and eating patterns. What is not fully understood at this time is how or which women will move along the continuum from normal eating and unconcerned-with-

---

Box 6-1

OBESITY

Obesity, as opposed to simple overweight, is comonly defined as a condition in which the individual's weight is 20 to 25% above the norm for age and height. Additional weight is primarily fat rather than muscle. Obesity is not listed as a separate disorder in DSM-III (1980). Obesity is more prevalent in girls than boys, possibly because boys are generally more physically active (Dusek, 1987). Obesity is a future health risk. Sixty to eighty percent of obese teenagers will become obese adults (Fuhrmann, 1986; Maloney and Klykylo, 1983). Chronically obese people are more susceptible to heart disease, high blood pressure, and soreness of joints. Obesity can interfere with physical and social activities. Adolescents who are excessively overweight can become easily exhausted, which makes it difficult for them to participate in sports that require a great deal of running or moving about. Obese adolescents are often the victims of social stigma. Obese figures have been described by grade school children as stupid, lazy, and dirty. Peers ridicule obese teenagers with names such as "buffalo," "lardo," or "whale." Even professionals rank figures of obese people as less desirable (Garner et al., 1985). Internalization of negative stereotypes can create a poor self-concept. Obesity is generally the result of a combination of internal and external factors, such as hereditary characteristics, endocrine irregularities, low activity level, or eating too much. Treatment for obesity involves a combination of medical, nutritional, behavioral, cognitive, psychodynamic, and family approaches. The cure for obesity is elusive. Only 10% of obese adolescents will outgrow overweight without treatment, and many of those who enter treatment will have relapses (Kimmel and Weiner, 1985). Overweight in some people may be a natural condition that cannot be changed over the long-term by treatment.

---

weight to relentless concerns about dieting, overeating, and weight loss (Striegel-Moore et al., 1986).

Eating Disorder Assessment

Mental health clinicians and researchers use structured interviews and eating-disorder assessment instruments to evaluate eating behaviors, weight concerns, body-image perceptions, dieting, and purging, which occur along the eating continuum. Two of the most widely used eating-disorder assessment instruments are the *Eating Attitudes Test* (EAT) and the *Eating Disorder Inventory* (EDI). The Eating Attitudes Test is a 40-item self-report questionnaire that measures such factors as food preoccupation, fears of weight gain, drive for thinness, vomiting and laxative abuse, dieting, and clandestine eating (Garner and Garfinkel, 1979). The Eating Disorder Inventory, a 64-item self-report questionnaire, provides information on eight cognitive-behavioral dimensions or subscales relevant to anorexia and bulimia, i.e., drive for thinness, bulimia, body dissatisfaction, ineffectiveness, perfectionism, interpersonal distrust, introceptive awareness, and maturity fears (Garner et al., 1983). The drive-for-thinness scale assesses preoccupation with weight loss, dieting, and the pursuit of thinness. The bulimia scale indicates habitual binging that may be followed by urges to engage in self-induced vomiting. Body dissatisfaction reflects displeasure with body shape and size. Ineffectiveness represents an awareness of general feelings of inadequacy, insecurity, worthlessness, and not being in control of one's life. Perfectionism, a characteristic theme in anorexia and bulimia, is associated with expectations for superior performance and dichotomous reasoning with respect to success and failure. Interpersonal distrust, characterized by a reluctance to form close relationships, has been identified as a major feature in anorexia. Deficiencies in introceptive awareness, expressed as an inability to recognize internal hunger signals and personal needs, has been identified as a feature of anorexia. Maturity fears or an underlying wish to return to the security of preadolescence has been referred to as the root cause of anorexia. Items from the bulimia and body dissatisfaction subscales of the EDI are listed in Table 6-7.

Table 6-7. Items from the Bulimia and Body Dissatisfaction Subscale of the Eating Disorder Inventory (EDI)[a]

Bulimia

    I eat when I am upset.
    I stuff myself with food.
    I have gone on eating binges where I have felt that I could not stop.
    I think about binging (overeating).
    I eat moderately in front of others and stuff myself when they're gone.
    I have the thought of trying to vomit in order to lose weight.
    I eat or drink in secrecy.

Body Dissatisfaction

    I think my stomach is too big.
    I think my thighs are too large.
    I think my stomach is just the right size.
    I feel satisfied with the shape of my body.
    I like the shape of my buttocks.
    I think my hips are too big.
    I think my thighs are just the right size.
    I think my buttocks are too large.
    I think my hips are just the right size.

[a]Adapted from: Garner, D. M., Olmstead, M. P., and Polivy, Jr. (1983). Development and validation of a multidimensional eating disorder inventory for anorexia and bulimia. *International Journal of Eating Disorders*, 2, 15–34.

Eating Disorder Prevention

There are four major approaches to eating disorder prevention: nutritional education, early detection, self-help organizations, and reevaluation of thinness as the culturally sanctioned ideal feminine body image.

Proper eating habits during adolescence are essential for the body's growth and development. It is important to educate young women, parents, teachers, and others who work with adolescents that chronic dieting, binging, and purging can be injurious to one's health. Because of the rapid acceleration of growth taking place throughout the body during adolescence, young people need a well-balanced diet of protein, vitamins, iron, and other body-building foods. Once physical growth has peaked, adequate nutrition is necessary to maintain optimal body functioning and psychological well-being. Inadequate nutrition, binge eating, and purging can interrupt the menstrual cycle, reduce stamina and concentration, and interfere with heart rate and hormonal balance. Young people need to be provided with opportunities to discuss the conflicts they encounter as they try to balance nutritional needs, biological realities, and cultural demands for thinness. In New England, a professional group toured prep schools and colleges with a show called *Food Fright*. The themes in the performance were based on the experiences of two of the actresses with eating disorders. After each performance, the cast would join the students for a discussion on dieting, eating, binging, purging, and related topics. The message to the students was that they were not alone in their struggles with anorexic and bulimic behaviors (Seligman and Zabriski, 1983).

Early detection increases the opportunities for successful treatment and recovery. Parents, physicians, health educators, counselors, peers, mental health professionals, and others who come into contact with young people should be taught to recognize the early warning signs of anorexia and bulimia. Warning signs are usually signaled by excessive weight loss and dieting; lack of concern about weight loss; abuse of appetite suppressants, laxatives, or diuretics; secret vomiting and binging alternating between binging and fasting; intense fear of gaining weight; and abdominal pain, sore throats, disturbed gastrointestinal functioning, or menstrual irregularities. Be available to talk to young people when these signs are noticed. If the symptoms persist, seek professional help.

Five major eating disorder, nonprofit self-help organizations have been developed in recent years. The National Association of Anorexia Nervosa and Associated Disorders, Inc., (ANAD), the oldest self-help organization, is only 12 years old. ANAD has set up chapters on 36 college campuses. The purpose of an eating disorder self-help organization is to provide such services as a mental health referral system, information on the causes and consequences of eating disorders, speakers for community and professional organizations, literature, research monitoring, dissemination of factual information about treatment approaches, and access to cooperative networks of physicians, parents, volunteers, educators, peer counselors, nurses, local resources, and support groups. Another self-help group, The National Anorexic Aid Society, maintains a list of support groups offered around the country. Support groups are usually free of charge or charge a small fee to cover operating expenses. Support groups are not designed to replace treatment by professionals but serve as a mutual assistance adjunct to therapy for family members and young women recovering from anorexia and bulimia (Rubel, 1984; McNab, 1983). Addresses of the five major eating disorder self-help organizations are provided in Table 6-8.

Finally, a national effort must be mounted to counteract the symbolic association of thinness with competency, success, desirability, femininity, attractiveness, and sensuousness. It is biologically impossible for most young women to achieve the slender body image projected by models, actresses, and TV stars. Everyone is not going to be thin. Some young women are going to have a wide-body look, with large hips and ample breasts, no matter how much exercising, purging, or dieting they do to reduce body size. Adolescent females should be encouraged to discover inner qualities and personal characteristics they can feel proud of rather than use body size as the sole measure of self-worth. The Women's Movement has made signifi-

Table 6-8. Eating Disorder Self-Help Organizations[a]

American Anorexia/Bulimia Association, Inc. (AABA)
133 Cedar Lane
Teaneck, New Jersey 07666
(201) 836-1800

Anorexia Nervosa and Associated Disorders, Inc. (ANAD)
P.O. Box 271
Highland Park, Illinois 60035
(312) 432-8000 (ext. 3307) or (312) 831-3438

Anorexia Nervosa and Related Eating Disorders, Inc. (ANRED)
P.O. Box 5102
Eugene, Oregon 97405
(503) 344-1144

Bulimia, Anorexia Self-Help, Inc. (BASH)
522 North New Ballas Road, Suite 206
St. Louis, Missouri 63141
(314) 567-4080

National Anorexic Aid Society, Inc. (NAAS)
P.O. Box 29461
Columbus, Ohio 43229
(614) 895-2009

---

[a]Adapted from: Rubel, J. A. (1984). The function of self-help groups in recovery from anorexia nervosa and bulimia. *Psychiatric Clinics of North America, 7*(2), 381–393.

cant strides, during the past two decades, toward opening up a wider range of economic, educational, legal, occupational, and life-style choices for women. The movement now needs to turn its attention to encouraging the mass media to offer a wider range of acceptable feminine body types. Companies such as Command Performance, a nationwide chain of hair salons, should be publicly commended for their efforts to reduce the connection between beauty and thinness. Command Performance directed its advertising agency to stop using skinny models in its print and TV ads because images of ultrathin models might be subtly encouraging anorexic behavior (McNab, 1983).

SUMMARY AND CONCLUSIONS

Anorexia nervosa and bulimia are eating disorders that share a common fear of weight gain, preoccupation with food and dieting, and an exaggerated concern with body size and shape. Anorexia, a life-threatening syndrome that usually occurs in females during early adolescence, is characterized by the relentless pursuit of thinness, self-induced semistarvation dieting, significant weight loss, a distorted perception of body image, and a lack of concern about the deleterious physical and psychological consequences of malnutrition and weight loss. Bulimia, which literally means ox hunger, tends to occur in late-adolescent and young-adult females of normal or near normal weight. The primary symptoms are repeated cycles of binge-eating, purging by self-induced vomiting or laxative abuse, fasting, strict dieting, and/or excessive exercise. Bulimic young women are generally aware of the discomforting aspects of their behavior and are receptive to help, whereas anorexics tend to resist treatment. The causes, etiology, and dynamics of anorexia and bulimia involve a multidimensional complex of sociocultural, psychological, biological, cognitive, behavioral, and nutritional factors. Young women are bombarded from early childhood with images of thinness as the cultural ideal. Thinness is associated with competence, beauty, discipline, desirability, and success. The powerful, multibillion dollar weight-loss industry promotes dieting as the way to achieve the desired level of thinness. Young women who attempt to cope with the developmental tasks of early and late adolescence by concentrating on excessive dieting and weight reduction place themselves at great risk. The maladaptive consequences of anorexia and bulimia are not only potentially injurious to physical health, but create additional psychological stresses that impede the resolution of body image, sexual identity, intimacy, and autonomy development tasks.

In addition to adequate nutrition, two of the most important areas of therapeutic and preventive interventions in bulimia and anorexia nervosa involve psychological and cultural factors. At the psychological level, young women need to be equipped with the tools needed to adaptively cope with the psychological and psychobiological developmental tasks of early and late adolescence. Major transformations in the body, signaling the evolution of one's sexuality, combined with expectations for greater independence and more mature peer relationships, can be frightening for a young woman who lacks a solid inner foundation of self-worth and confidence. In late-adolescent females, profound dissatisfaction with body image, because one's body does not approximate cultural ideals of thinness, can impede the resolution of identity, intimacy, and autonomy issues.

At the cultural level, the ideal of the slender body as the key to success, competence, attractiveness, and desirability needs to be changed to allow young women the opportunity to discover inner qualities of personal worth. Thinness has been oversold to the point where young women are even afraid to be in the normal weight range or slightly above the normal weight range. Despite the claims of the diet industry, most women are biologically destined to be slightly heavier than the thinness profiles projected by models, movie actresses, and TV personalities, regardless of what weight-reduction programs they try. The Women's Movement, which has accomplished significant legal, economic, and social gains over the past two decades, must now turn its attention to liberating young women from the tyranny of the slender body ideal. Girls need to be taught at an early age to base their self-esteem on internal worth rather than on external accomplishments or appearances. We need to teach girls to discover the beauty within and listen to the internal voice of their own being (Gilligan, 1982). Emphasis, in feminine socialization, must shift from physical appearances to concerns with who one is and what one stands for with respect to such ideals as fair play, reciprocal love for self and others, and appreciation of one's humanness. Someone once remarked that the emphasis in female socialization in America is focused on the body at the expense of the soul.

SUGGESTIONS FOR PARENTS, TEACHERS, COUNSELORS, AND YOUTH WORKERS

1. The importance of balanced nutrition and proper exercise for optimal body functioning should be taught at home and in school. Teenagers should understand that weight and body size are determined by age, height, and a biological set point rather than by popular images of thinness. Most bulimics and anorexics have a variety of misconceptions about dieting, weight regulation, and nutrition and do not understand the discrepancies between biological realities and cultural values regarding thinness.
2. Be careful about encouraging young people to lose weight. Make sure the adolescent who needs to lose weight knows you are primarily concerned

about her health. It is important for adolescents to know they are cared about and respected by those close to them, regardless of their weight.

3. If an adolescent wants to begin dieting, find out why and whether she really needs to lose weight. Many young people think parents will love and respect them more if they lose weight.

4. If weight-loss is indicated, the diet or nutritional program should be supervised by a health care specialist. The weight-loss program should include a physical examination, a reasonable weight-loss plan, a realistic weight goal, and a weight-maintenance diet once the weight-loss goals have been achieved.

5. Encourage young people to discuss the conflicts and uncertainties involving values, body image, sexuality, sex role identification, and the success they are encountering in the process of growing up. Help them learn to feel good about themselves and to develop a sense of internal worth independent of their achievements and physical appearance. Avoid driving them to excel beyond their capacities.

6. Recognize the early warning signs of eating disorders. Excessive weight loss and dieting; lack of concern about significant weight loss; repeated episodes of binging, purging, and fasting; dissatisfaction with body image; and an intense fear of gaining weight are signs that should be taken seriously. Consult professional help if these signs persist.

7. If your club or professional organization needs speakers, literature, resource people, or general information about eating disorders and problems, contact one of the eating disorder self-help organizations.

8. References for additional readings are provided below. These references can be utilized not only by parents, teachers, and youth workers, but also might provide helpful information to young women who are victims of anorexia or bulimia.

a. S. H. Heater. (1983). *Am I Still Visible? A Woman's Triumph Over Anorexia Nervosa*. White Hall, VA: Betterway.

b. B. P. Kinoy and Associates. (1984). *When Will We Laugh Again?* Irvington, NY: Columbia University Press.

c. S. MacLeod. (1982). *The Art of Starvation*. New York: Schocken.

d. C. O'Neill. (1982). *Starving for Attention*. New York: Continuum.

e. A. Rumney. (1983). *Dying to Please*. Jefferson, NC: McFarland.

f. S. Squire. (1983). *The Slender Balance*. New York: Putnam.

g. M. B. White. (1983). *Bulimarexia: The Binge Purge Cycle*. New York: Norton.

DISCUSSION QUESTIONS

1. What are the major early warning signs of anorexia, what is likely to happen medically and psychologically if anorexic behavior continues, and why are anorexic adolescents resistant to treatment?

2. Why is anorexia sometimes referred to as the "golden girl" or "good girl"

syndrome, and how might the use of such terms unwittingly increase the popularity of anorexia?

3. What is behind the increasing rates of anorexia and bulimia, and why is bulimic behavior in such abundance on college campuses?

4. What are the major developmental tasks confronting young women in early and late adolescence, and how can unresolved developmental tasks contribute to the evolution of anorexic and bulimic behaviors?

5. How does the cultural emphasis on thinness and weight loss contribute to the development of anorexia and bulimia? Why are American women obsessed with thinness as the ideal body image, and what can be done to make a wider range of body types acceptable?

6. What is the so-called contradiction or incongruence between biological realities and cultural ideals in women's weight and body size? Why is this contradiction important in the dynamics of anorexia and bulimia?

7. Explain the role of body image-distortion in anorexia as a defense mechanism or protective device.

8. Discuss anorexia and bulimia in terms of adaptive and maladaptive coping.

9. What are the similarities and differences between anorexia and bulimia?

10. Explain the progressive development of symptoms in anorexia and bulimia in terms of cognitive models and behavioral reinforcement theory.

11. Treatment programs for anorexia and bulimia usually combine several approaches. Describe four of the major approaches, methods, and goals for each approach.

12. Describe four major approaches to eating disorder prevention. Which one do you think is the most promising and why?

7
Schizophrenia

PREVIEW

Schizophrenia is a pervasive psychological disorder characterized by severe disorganization and distortion in thinking, feeling, and perception. The primary signs of schizophrenia are grossly disordered thinking, poor reality testing and perceptual distortions, diminished capacity to form close relationships, progressive involvement in fantasy, impairment in emotional expressiveness, and deterioration from previous levels of adaptive functioning.

Throughout the 20th century, two broad categories or dimensions of schizophrenia have been observed. These categories have been labeled *process* and *reactive schizophrenia*. In process schizophrenia, there is a slow, gradual onset of symptoms, poor psychosocial adjustment prior to the active phase, lack of any clear precipitating stressors, a family incidence of schizophrenia, and low recovery rates. Reactive schizophrenia is characterized by the sudden onset of symptoms precipitated by major stresses, good psychosocial adjustment prior to the onset of symptoms, little or no family history of schizophrenia, and high recovery rates. The search for the causes of schizophrenia has baffled investigators for more than 100 years. Researchers have examined how underlying biogenic and psychogenic predispositional factors interact with the stresses of late adolescent-young adult development to activate the schizophrenic breakdown.

Treatment of what is now known as schizophrenia has changed significantly in the past 40 years. From the middle of the 19th century to the development of the antischizophrenic drugs in the early 1950s, schizophrenic patients were confined in large, state-run custodial institutions for years, sometimes for the remainder of their lives. The development of the phenothiazine derivatives or antischizophrenic drugs revolutionized the treatment of schizophrenia and paved the way for the community mental health movement and deinstitutionalization in the 1960s and 1970s. Antischizophrenic drugs seem to have a calming effect and reduce disruptive thought processes, confusion in speech and emotions, agitation, and withdrawal. Since the introduction of antischizophrenic drugs, the length of hospital stay has been reduced from years and months to weeks and days. The contemporary treatment of schizophrenia involves a mixture of hospitalization, antischizophrenic drugs, psychosocial therapy, and family intervention.

Treatment can be divided into two phases, the acute phase and aftercare. The goal of the first or acute treatment stage, which usually takes place in a hospital setting, is to reduce disruptive symptoms, reestablish contact with reality, and improve psychosocial functioning. The goal of the aftercare phase is to assist the patient's continuing recovery in the community and facilitate his or her reentry into the mainstream of school, work, vocational preparation, and social interaction. The aftercare phase has been impeded by the lack of adequate community-based services. The comprehensive system of community-based support services, vocational rehabilitation and transitional housing anticipated by the community mental health movement, and deinstitutionalization did not materialize. Consequently, many recovering schizophrenics have fallen through the cracks. They are found wandering the streets of urban America, living in substandard housing, not taking their medication, and are often caught up in a revolving door between the hospital and the community. Families have been called upon to assume a major role as care providers in the aftercare phase. Family intervention programs are being developed to assist families in their role as aftercare providers.

The two main forms of prevention in schizophrenia are early detection and relapse prevention. Early detection involves being alert to early warning signs and initiating a program of evaluation and treatment. The key elements in relapse prevention are adequate family intervention and comprehensive community-based support services to fill the gaps created by deinstitutionalization.

Case Example, 7-1: Ashley

Ashley is a 19-year-old female, high school graduate who was admitted to the psychiatric unit of a general hospital for diagnosis and evaluation after showing signs of bizarre behavior, disorientation, confused thinking, and poor reality testing. Her mother had observed Ashley scooting across the floor at home in the nude. Ashley told her mother that she was trying to "get the dirt out of my pee-pee . . . a boy put some dirt in my pee-pee." Ashley confused the admitting physician with a former boyfriend, tried to kiss him, and asked him to marry her. She was disoriented with respect to date, time, where she was, and her date of birth. She told the doctor that she had been born "three months ago." The next day during the psychological evaluation, she confused the psychologist with her high school counselor and cheerleading coach. She asked the psychologist if she could try out for the cheerleading squad and demonstrated several cheerleading routines in his office. She also asked the psychologist if she could kiss him.

Ashley's mother traced the beginning of Ashley's confusion, disorientation, and difficulties in reality testing to the breakup of a romantic relationship several months earlier. The mother felt that Ashley had misinterpreted the nature of the relationship. Ashley perceived it as a committed, long-term relationship, whereas her male friend saw it as a casual coworker relationship. When Ashley discovered that she was pregnant, the boy made it clear that he did not want to marry her or continue the relationship. He encouraged her to have an abortion. He subsequently quit working in the fast-food restaurant where they met, cut off all contact with Ashley, and moved to another community. Despite all evidence to the contrary, Ashley insisted that he would marry her and made elaborate wedding plans. Her mother repeatedly had to cancel orders for bridal dresses, invitations, flowers, and church reservations only to discover that Ashley was making new arrangements a few days later.

When Ashley was no longer able to deny the reality that a wedding would not take place, she became increasingly isolated and withdrawn. She would spend hours in her room playing with dolls and talking with imaginary companions about Christmas parties, Thanksgiving dinner, birthday parties, Halloween, and "ghosts and goblins." She refused to have an abortion, but after much back-and-forth discussion with her mother and mother's minister, she agreed to give her baby up for adoption a few days after its birth. After giving up the baby for adoption, Ashley's behavior continued to deteriorate. She showed very little interest in personal grooming or hygiene, seldom went outside the home, and spent most of the day playing with dolls and talking with her imaginary companions. She told her mother that she heard voices telling her "to do bad things."

DEFINITION AND RATES OF OCCURRENCE

Schizophrenia is a pervasive psychological disorder or psychosis characterized by severe disorganization and distortion in thinking, feeling, and perception. The distinguishing signs of schizophrenia are a breakdown in reality testing, deterioration of adaptive behavior, and a decline in cognitive, interpersonal, and integrative functioning. The confusing, eccentric, peculiar, hard-to-understand behavior, and expressive patterns of schizophrenia are often labeled by lay people as bizarre, weird, crazy, insane, or madness. The term schizophrenia was coined in 1911 by Eugen Bleuler, a Swiss psychiatrist, to replace the earlier term, dementia praecox. Bleuler derived the word schizophrenia from two Greek terms, *phren* meaning mind and *schizen* meaning to split. The splitting of the mind Bleuler refers to is the disorganization and fragmentation of thinking, feeling, and perceptual processes rather than the dual or split personality that occurs in the Jekyll-and-Hyde syndrome (Davison and Neale, 1982; Torrey, 1983).

Schizophrenia occurs in one out of every 100 Americans. There are currently 2 million diagnosed schizophrenics in the United States. One-hundred thousand new cases are added each year and 600,000 diagnosed schizophrenics receive some form of mental health treatment annually. Schizophrenia occurs equally in males and females. Schizophrenia occupies more hospital beds than any other medical or psychiatric condition and more hospital beds than cancer, heart disease, arthritis, and diabetes combined (Goldstein et al., 1980; Kimmel and Weiner, 1985). The estimated cost of schizophrenia, in terms of hospital and mental health fees, lost wages, and social security and welfare benefits for the disabled, is between $10 and $20 billion annually. Schizophrenia is the most expensive of all chronic disorders because it often strikes young people at a time when they are just beginning their wage-earning years. Schizophrenia can prevent young people from completing late-adolescent and young-adult developmental tasks, ruin a promising future, and force young people to become dependent on their families or on public services for much of their adult life.

Schizophrenia was once called adolescent insanity because three-fourths of all cases begin in the 16- to 25-year-old age group (Herbert, 1982). The high-risk age begins at 17 and continues into the early twenties. The age of onset for females is about 5 years later. After the peak onset period in late adolescence and early adulthood, the rate of occurrence declines. The first appearance of major schizophrenic symptoms is uncommon after age 30 and rare after age 40 (Jensen, 1985; Holzman and Grinker, 1974; Fuhrmann, 1986).

PRIMARY SYMPTOMS

The primary symptoms of schizophrenia appearing in the literature are: (1) disordered thinking; (2) poor reality testing and perceptual distortion; (3) social isolation, diminished capacity to form relationships, and progressive involvement in fantasy; (4) impairment in emotional expressiveness; and (5) deterioration from previous levels of adaptive functioning. DSM-III-R (American Psychiatric Association, 1987) criteria for schizophrenia and subtypes of schizophrenia are listed in Tables 7-1 and 7-2.

1. *Disordered thinking.* Disordered thinking, or what is frequently referred to as a thought disorder, is a core feature of schizophrenia. Schizophrenic adolescents and young adults have trouble putting together a logically coherent train of thought others can follow. Thoughts, ideas, and images are often communicated in a vague, confused, rambling manner. A 19-year-old, male schizophrenic gave the following response when he was

Table 7-1. DSM-III-R (1987) Criteria for Schizophrenia[a]

A. At least two of the following symptoms:

   1. Bizarre thinking and delusions. Thoughts that are blatantly untrue, such as the person's brain is being controlled by a TV station or others are broadcasting one's thoughts.

   2. Grandiose, religious, nihilistic, or persecutory delusions.

   3. Prominent hallucinations such as voices conversing with each other or one voice keeping a running commentary on the patient's thoughts and behaviors.

   4. Prominent hallucinations on several occasions, with the content of words having no apparent relationship to depression or elation.

   5. Incoherent thinking, marked loosening of associations, illogical thinking, or marked poverty of content of speech if associated with at least one of the following:

      a. Blunted, flat, or inappropriate affect

      b. Delusions or hallucinations

      c. Catatonic or other grossly disorganized behavior

B. Deterioration from previous level of functioning in areas such as work, social relations, self-care, or failure to achieve expected level of development.

C. Duration: Continuous signs of the disorder for at least 6 months at some time during the person's life, with some signs at present.

D. During the early or prodromal phase and the residual phases, at least two of the following, are not due to a mood disturbance or drug abuse: social withdrawal, digressive vague speech, illogical thinking and loosening of associations; peculiar, odd behavior; grossly disorganized behavior or blunted, flat, or inappropriate affect.

   The symptoms of schizophreniform disorder are similar to schizophrenia, except for duration. In schizophreniform disorders, the symptoms of schizophrenia are present, but must not last longer than 6 months.

[a]Adapted from: American Psychiatric Association. (1987). *The diagnostic and statistical manual of mental disorders* (3rd ed., rev.). Washington, DC: American Psychiatric Association.

Table 7-2. Subtypes of Schizophrenia[a]

   DSM-III-R (1987) recognizes five subtypes of schizophrenia: (1) hebephrenic-disorganized; (2) catatonic; (3) paranoid; (4) undifferentiated; and (5) residual.

   Disorganized or hebephrenic schizophrenia is characterized by excessive silliness, giggling and laughing, incoherent speech, and inappropriate affect.

   Catatonia is indicated by rigid posture, refusal to talk, disturbed motor behavior such as immobility, rocking back and forth, and violent outbursts.

   In *paranoid schizophrenia* the central features are either systemized, grandiose or persecutory delusions without grossly disorganized behavior or bizarre thinking.

   Undifferentiated or simple schizophrenia is used to designate persons who show symptoms of several subtypes and a general lack of interest in the world around them.

   The *residual category* is used for schizophrenics who have recovered but still show some symptoms.

[a]Adapted from: American Psychiatric Association. (1987). *Diagnostic and statistical manual of mental disorders* (3rd ed., rev.). Washington, DC: American Psychiatric Association.

asked how he would go about finding his way out of a forest if he were lost in the daytime: "The forest is such a beautiful place. The sun shines at an angle near the moon. Many great battles of good and evil have been fought in the forests. It is a shame that evil forces are allowed to live in the forest and spoil God's sacred gifts. Forests can be scary at night when evil forces are all around. If your mind isn't careful, they will get inside your head and control you like they did me. The last battle of good and evil will be fought in the forest." Underlying the disconnected, rambling, schizophrenic communication style is a breakdown in cognitive filtering and integrative mechanisms. The end result is a looseness of mental associations. Irrelevant thoughts intrude into the flow of ideas to impede the person's ability to maintain a set mental direction or stick to a topic (Herbert, 1982).

2. *Poor reality testing and perceptual distortions*. Several examples of poor reality testing and perceptual distortions appear in Ashley's case. Although she was 19 years old, she stated that she had been born only 3 months ago. She confused the psychologist and psychiatrist with her boyfriend. She heard voices telling her "to do bad things" and carried on conversations with imaginary companions. At times during the psychological evaluation, she thought she was in the high school counselor's office or that she was trying out for the cheerleading team.

Hallucinations, delusions, and loss of ego boundaries are the most common forms of poor reality testing and perceptual distortions in schizophrenia. Hallucinations are sensory perceptions appearing in the absence of appropriate reality stimuli. Schizophrenics often hear voices talking back to them, which those around them cannot hear, or they see things that aren't really there. The majority of schizophrenic hallucinations are unpleasant voices talking to them or even groups of voices carrying on several conversations (Torrey, 1983). Nonschizophrenic people occasionally experience powerful perceptual images in the absence of appropriate reality stimuli, but usually they are aware that these perceptions are part of their imagination rather than real events. Most people do not mistake these experiences for objective reality, and they can usually turn them on and off when they wish.

Delusions are an extreme form of faulty beliefs the rest of society, including members of one's peer subculture, would regard as extreme misinterpretations or misrepresentations of reality. Delusions, ideas of reference, and hallucinations are often connected in schizophrenic thinking. A schizophrenic patient may believe the eye movements and hand gestures of actors and actresses on television programs control the voices in his head and are part of a plot to insert thoughts in his head or spy on his thoughts through a mini-television camera placed inside his head by drug agents. Through ideas of reference, the patient attributes personal significance to events that in fact have no relationship to himself or herself (White and Watt, 1981). Other delusional beliefs involve paranoid suspicions, thought insertion, thought withdrawal, thought broadcasting, and the insertion of feelings or impulses by outside forces. Schizophrenic individuals erroneously believe that others are plotting against them, controlling their thoughts, broadcasting their thoughts to the external world, stealing their thoughts, or introjecting powerful feelings such as anger or sexual urges. Delusional beliefs seem to defy correction. Most late adolescents and young adults have developed a reasonable amount of skill in role-taking and in assessing personal predictions. They can see an event from a variety of perspectives and reassess their beliefs as new information becomes available. Delusional beliefs are trapped in a single perspective. The person refuses to acknowledge different perspectives and new evidence. The world, as he or she sees it, makes sense, no matter how bizarre his or her beliefs appear to others.

Loss of ego identity refers to distortions in self-perception. The sense of self that gives each of us our uniqueness is grossly disturbed (Shapiro, 1981). The line between personal boundaries and the external world becomes blurred. Oceanic or cosmic experiences eradicate definitive personal parameters, and depersonalization impairs the integration of identity and creates a sense of diffusion. Sometimes, schizophrenic teenagers and young adults confuse themselves with God or claim to be famous people, such as rock stars or actresses.

3. *Social isolation, diminished capacity to form close relationships, and progressive involvement in fantasy.* It is difficult to concentrate on interpersonal relationships and external affairs when internal concerns in the forms of hallucinations and delusions are demanding one's attention. Many adolescent and young-adult schizophrenics become increasingly preoccupied with internal psychological concerns, daydreams, and fantasies to the point where they withdraw from active participation in external events and close relationships. Friends describe them as preoccupied, spaced out, or off in their own world. Their withdrawal and social isolation occur during a developmental time frame when they are expected to become more involved in intimate relationships and occupational preparations for adult life. Some writers believe that schizophrenic withdrawal is partly a defense mechanism to protect the individual from further hurt and disappointment in the external world (Laing, 1965).

4. *Impairment in emotional expressiveness.* The signs of emotional impairment in schizophrenia are affective flatness or blunting, grossly inappropriate emotional expressiveness, and unpredictable, poorly controlled emotions. In affective flatness or emotional blunting, the individual shows little or no emotion at all. The tone of speech is monotonous and there is very little facial expressiveness, regardless of what the person is saying or what is going on around him. A 19-year-old, unemployed college dropout, who had been living alone in the woods near a university campus, wanted to sell his eyes to the medical school "so I can get money to eat." While relating this

request, he seemed very emotionally detached, expressionless, and spoke in a slow monotone. Recovering schizophrenic patients have described affective flatness as feeling empty inside (Torrey, 1983). In inappropriate affective responses, there is a noticeable incongruence between emotional expressions and the context of ideas. The person may laugh uncontrollably while talking about a very sad, tragic event in his or her life. Sudden, unpredictable changes in affect can lead to poorly controlled outbursts of anger. This explosive, volatile, unpredictable characteristic of schizophrenic behavior can be frightening to those around a patient. While the emotional flatness, inappropriateness, and unpredictability strike the outside observer as strange or pathological, it should be remembered that the schizophrenic person's emotional, expressive style is likely to be influenced by compelling internal psychological concerns, such as voices, delusional beliefs, and unresolved personal issues (Boffey, 1986).

5. *Deterioration from previous level of adaptive functioning.* Deterioration from previous levels of adaptive functioning tends to show up in areas of daily functioning, such as school, work, grooming, and peer and family relationships. Others notice that the person is no longer able to stay on top of things or follow through on assignments. Volitional actions or self-initiated, goal-directed behaviors are interrupted (Coleman et al., 1984).

Personal descriptions of schizophrenia tend to confirm the confused thought processes, perceptual distortions, withdrawal, emotional impairment, and adaptive deterioration. Recovering schizophrenics describe fierce battles, going on inside their heads, between imaginary and real forces. Unresolved conflicts become draining. The mind divides and subdivides on a topic, until one feels totally disorganized and ambivalent. In withdrawn states, schizophrenics are sometimes hiding from imaginary demons that have invaded the bodies of friends and family members. The person may want to speak out, but nothing comes out. Self-boundaries become vague, and others cannot be trusted because they are perceived as having joined forces with the persecutors. The body can be depersonalized into a machine which feels disconnected from the world (Schizophrenic, 1986; Green, 1964).

THE COURSE OF SCHIZOPHRENIA

Schizophrenia seems to involve a course or sequence consisting of three phases: the prodromal, the active, and the residual phase. In the prodromal or early phase, there is either a slow, insidious onset of symptoms or a rapid deterioration of psychosocial functioning. The term prodrome comes from the Greek word *prodromos*, which means running before or signs that serve as a warning or premonition of events to come. In the active or acute phase, the primary symptoms of schizophrenia are prominent. Distortions in reality testing, confusion and disorganization in thinking, and difficulties in emotional expressiveness are usually quite visible. During this phase, former schizophrenics report that they cannot think straight, long-forgotten memories surface in a distractive fashion, and ideas, thoughts, and perceptions emerge faster than they can be sorted out, assimilated, or organized. The internal filtering system that protects us from being overwhelmed by personal and external events seems to break down. Words and familiar sights and sounds take on strange, idiosyncratic meanings. Expressed emotions seem unrelated to the topic at hand, or no emotions are expressed at all. Unknown forces issue orders, steal thoughts, or give orders to engage in forbidden actions. Communication with others is often a jumble of vague, confused talk, unrelated emotions, or senseless, repetitive talk. In the residual or recovery phase, the florid symptoms recede, but some aspects of schizophrenic psychosocial deterioration are likely to remain. Many schizophrenics in the residual stage are withdrawn, isolated, apathetic, and have trouble resuming active participation in school, work, and social activities outside the home. Others fade in and out of reality with good contact one day only to be wrapped up in confusion and perceptual distortions a few days later (Goldstein et al., 1980; Bootzin and Acocella, 1980).

Prospects for Recovery

At the beginning of the 20th century, the prospects for recovery from schizophrenia were surrounded by an aura of pessimism. According to the thinking of that time, schizophrenia started in adolescence or early childhood and followed a predetermined, downhill, ever-worsening course through the remainder of the life cycle. In the past 20 years, the prospects for recovery have brightened. Five major studies in progress show that over the long run, two-thirds of persons diagnosed as schizophrenic improved to the point where they could live in the community with only minor assistance (Turkington, 1985). Other studies, including one by Manfred Bleuler (1978), the grandson of Eugen Bleuler, indicate that 25% to 33% of schizophrenics recover fully, 10% to 15% remain severely disturbed, and 50% to 60% show some improvement but may require hospitalization periodically (Stephens, 1978; Torrey, 1983). After 5 years, the disorder does not show further signs of deterioration, and many patients recover spontaneously over the course of several years.

The earlier schizophrenia occurs, the less the likelihood of complete recovery. Weiner (1982) and Kimmel and Weiner (1985) estimate that only 23% of adolescent schizophrenics fully recover without any relapses, 40% to 60% are readmitted for further hospital treatment within 2 years, and 25% show improvement with periodic relapses and tend to require continual residual or hospital care. Six factors influence recovery: (1) age at onset; (2) gradual as opposed to sudden onset; (3) premorbid adjustment; (4) degree of psychological deterioration; (5) family attitude; and (6) number and frequency of schizophrenic episodes.

The prospects for recovery are better for older adolescents and young adults than for younger adolescents or when the onset of symptoms is sudden rather than gradual. Schizophrenic episodes brought on by identifiable life stresses or developmental crises remit more quickly than schizophrenic episodes precipitated by vague, obscure factors. Young people whose premorbid adjustment or psychological functioning was relatively normal prior to the onset of schizophrenia have a better chance for complete recovery than those with poor premorbid adjustment. The greater the degree of deterioration in thought processes and psychosocial functioning, the less the likelihood of complete recovery. Frequent relapses are contraindicative of recovery. A person who has had only one or two acute schizophrenic episodes in 2 years has a better chance of recovering than one who has experienced several episodes. Finally, the family's attitude is important in the recovery process. A hostile, rejecting family attitude is likely to impede recovery, whereas a responsive, caring attitude tends to enhance recovery (Forisha-Kovach, 1983; Goldstein and Doane, 1982).

Historical Notes

The symptoms of madness in the form of thought confusion, distorted reality testing, hallucinations, and delusions extend as far back as the Old Testament and appear in literature, art, and philosophy throughout the world. There is a continuing controversy among scholars and mental health experts over whether these symptoms represent schizophrenic disorders (Shapiro, 1981). The first recorded clinical case of what is now known as schizophrenia was observed in 1860 by a Belgian psychiatrist, Benedict A. Morel, in a 14-year-old boy. The boy, who had been a brilliant pupil, became withdrawn, apathetic, forgot most of what he had known, and talked of killing his father. Morel labeled the condition as *demence precoce*. Demence or dementia refers to mental deterioration, *precoce* or praecox means beginning at an early age. Emil Kraepelin, a German psychiatrist, adopted the term dementia praecox in a paper he presented to the Congress of Southwestern German Psychiatry in Heidelberg in 1898. Kraepelin described dementia praecox as a severe mental disorder that began early in life (in adolescence) and followed a slow, irreversible course of progressive mental deterioration (Davison and Neale, 1982).

Eugen Bleuler, who coined the term schizophrenia in 1911 as a replacement for dementia praecox, broke with Kraepelin on two major issues. He thought that schizophrenia did not always begin in adolescence nor did schizophrenia always follow a slow, irreversible, downhill course of deterioration. Some schizophrenics recovered, some improved with periodic re-lapses, and some followed the slow, downhill course of progressive mental deterioration. During the later stages of his career, Kraepelin (1919) changed his views about the inevitability of progressive psychological deterioration in schizophrenia. By the eighth edition of his book in 1919, Kraepelin stated that 14% to 19% of schizophrenics recover (Shapiro, 1981).

Bleuler was a brilliant theoretician. His classic description of schizophrenia in terms of the 4 A's—association, autism, affect, and ambivalence—is still used in mental health textbooks today. The central feature of schizophrenia is a thought disorder caused by a looseness of mental associations. The loosening results in a lack of connection between ideas and an inability to follow a concentrated mental set. Thinking loses its purposeful direction. Autism refers to progressive involvement in fantasy, hallucinations, and delusions while withdrawing from reality and concerns in the external world. Affect is flat, inappropriate, or explosive. Ambivalence refers to indecisiveness, hesitance, or uncertainty. The person tries to go in several directions at once. What comes out is a confusing mixture of thoughts, communications, and emotions, or a psychological blockage in which the person seems unable to initiate or carry out goal-directed behaviors (Bootzin and Acocella, 1980; Shapiro, 1981).

Process and Reactive Schizophrenia

Throughout the 20th century, two broad categories or dimensions of schizophrenia have emerged. The first category, as depicted in the early writings of Kraepelin, is marked by a slow gradual onset, poor premorbid (prior to the onset of symptoms) psychological adjustment, and follows a downhill course of deterioration throughout the life cycle. The second category, which appears in the writings of Bleuler and Adolph Meyer (1906) and was later acknowledged by Kraepelin, is characterized by a rapid onset of symptoms, adequate premorbid psychosocial adjustment, and a high probability of recovery. These two categories, labeled as process and reactive schizophrenia, are the two extreme dimensions along a schizophrenic continuum rather than mutually exclusive syndromes (see Fig. 7-1).

Process and reactive schizophrenia differ in terms of psychosocial adjustment prior to the onset of schizophrenic symptoms (premorbid adjustment),

Reactive	Mixed	Process
Short-term	Process-Reactive	Chronic
Good premorbid		Poor premorbid

FIGURE 7-1. Schizophrenia continuum.

age at onset, suddenness of onset, precipitating events, and family history (White and Watt, 1981). In the middle of the continuum is a mixed reactive-process schizophrenic syndrome characterized by partial recovery and periodic relapses. At the reactive end of the continuum, schizophrenia has a sudden onset precipitated by major stress; good premorbid adjustment at home, school, work, and in peer relationships; older age at first appearance; little or no history of schizophrenia in the family; and high recovery rates. Reactive schizophrenia has also been known as schizophreniform psychosis, and short-term, good premorbid, and atypical schizophrenia. Process schizophrenics show an early onset (first diagnosis prior to age 25), poor premorbid psychosocial history; lack of any clear precipitating factors; slow, gradual onset of symptoms; high family incidence of schizophrenia; and low recovery rates. Synonyms for process schizophrenia are poor premorbid, chronic, typical, and nuclear schizophrenia. Follow-back studies of schizophrenia, looking at school records and other psychosocial information, indicate that process schizophrenics show greater social isolation, have fewer friends, and tend to show signs of eccentric or schizotypical behavior in childhood and early adolescence (Kimmel and Weiner, 1985; Weiner, 1982). After 5 years, 80% to 90% of reactive schizophrenics are rated recovered or improved as compared to 50% to 60% for process schizophrenics (White and Watt, 1981; Stevens, 1978).

ETIOLOGY, CAUSES, AND DYNAMICS

The search for the causes of schizophrenia has baffled investigators for over 100 years. A comprehensive explanation of schizophrenia must answer two questions: Why does schizophrenia peak in late adolescence and early adulthood, and what are the root causes of schizophrenia? To answer these questions, researchers have examined how underlying psychogenic and biogenic factors, when combined with the complexities of late-adolescent and young-adult psychosocial development, can lead to major breakdowns in integrative, affective, perceptual, and cognitive functioning. In this section, we discuss the major biogenic and psychogenic models of schizophrenia and the complexities of late-adolescent and young-adult development, which can contribute to the development of schizophrenia.

Why Does Schizophrenia Emerge in Late Adolescence and Early Adulthood?

To complete the psychosocial developmental tasks of late adolescence and early adulthood, young people must develop new cognitive, interpersonal, and emotional skills. They are expected to resolve the incongruity between beliefs in the home and the external world, integrate divergent aspects of self into a coherent identity; formulate values and strategies for achieving goals; define themselves as sexual beings; develop communication styles effective in family, work, school, and personal relationships; and achieve a greater sense of intimacy and authenticity in relationships with others. No one can offer young people a perfect blueprint to help them accomplish these tasks. Some degree of risk, uncertainty, and independent action is inescapable. They can no longer be shielded by the protective, structured environment of childhood. The key to resolving late-adolescent and early-adult expectations involves developing a higher level of integrative and organizational skills. To successfully organize a series of complex developmental tasks and maintain a goal-directed orientation, young people must develop a more-advanced level of logical sophistication, conceptual clarity, imaginativeness, and the capacity to anticipate events so that they can plan ahead.

The challenges of late adolescence and early adulthood can be very demanding and stressful, if the cognitive, emotional, integrative, and expressive foundational structures are weak because of psychological or psychobiological deficiencies in preadolescent growth. The individual may be overwhelmed by the demands placed on his or her resources. The strain created by the emotional and psychological overload causes a breakdown in the individual's ability to synthesize, respond, and maintain self-boundaries. The breakdown in the ability to synthesize and integrate, which is at the core of schizophrenia, prevents the individual from being able to organize thoughts, feelings, and perceptions in a coherent manner. The schizophrenic experience is an extreme example of identity diffusion wherein the individual either temporarily or permanently loses a clear sense of self (Holzman and Grinker, 1974).

Schizophrenics subjectively describe the course of a schizophrenic break as starting with what they perceived as an unresolvable conflict or impasse before the actual breakdown. Reaching identity or developmental impasses is not unusual in late adolescence and early childhood. After feeling there was no way out or nowhere to turn, many schizophrenics report finding themselves in a frightening state in which they were unable to think, feel, or recognize familiar people and objects. It was as if some alien force propelled them into another state where the world became a bizarre place. They could no longer distinguish clear boundaries between themselves and the rest of the world. Rene Nee, the teenage schizophrenic patient in Marguerite Sechehaye's (1968) *Autobiography of a Schizophrenic Girl*, confused herself with a doll. Other patients have reported seeing themselves in different bodies (Goldstein et al., 1980; Torrey, 1983).

Most adolescents and young adults are confronted with developmental conflicts and impasses, yet only 1% or less become schizophrenic. To understand why some young people lack the foundational cognitive, integrative, emotional, and expressive resources to cope with the transition into adulthood, we will examine the predispositional biogenic and psychogenic factors that increase the risk or vulnerability to schizophrenia.

Biogenic Theories of Schizophrenia

The biogenic theory of schizophrenia looks for the underlying predispositional factors or causes of schizophrenia in the individual's biochemical and inherited genetic structure. Kraepelin (1898, 1919) was one of the early proponents of a biochemical theory of schizophrenia. He thought that schizophrenia was a metabolic disorder caused by toxic chemicals or poisons moving through the bloodstream to the brain. In his autointoxication or sex intoxication theory of schizophrenia, Kraepelin believed that since schizophrenia usually came after puberty, the sex glands might be producing an unfavorable chemical state that affected the central nervous system. Carl Jung also favored a toxic chemical theory. Jung predicted that an X or unknown biochemical factor would someday be found to explain schizophrenia (Herbert, 1982; Davison and Neale, 1982).

The Biochemical Model
In the past three decades, researchers have concentrated on the brain and central nervous system as the site for abnormal biochemical functioning in schizophrenia. The line of reasoning for a brain or central nervous system-based biochemical theory of schizophrenia has evolved from the following interrelated assumptions and observations (Coleman et al., 1984; White and Watt, 1981):

1. Schizophrenic-like reactions can be created by hallucinogenic or psychomimetic drugs. Consciousness-altering or mind-bending drugs, such as LSD, mescaline, and peyote, produce thinking confusion, hallucinations, and other perceptual distortions and feelings of depersonalization.
2. Hallucinogenic drugs affect the chemical balance of the brain's regulatory centers and are similar in structure to chemical compounds, such as dopamine, normally found in the brain.
3. Dopamine is a neurotransmitter known to be involved in the normal functioning of the brain and thought to play an important role in emotions and attention.
4. Antischizophrenic drugs, such as the phenothiazines, reduce the level of dopamine in the brain. These drugs seem to work by blocking the brain's receptor sites for dopamine. Reducing the activity of parts of the brain that use dopamine to transmit neural impulses seems to reduce schizophrenic symptoms.
5. Furthermore, certain drugs like L-dopa and amphetamines (speed), which increase the level of dopamine, can intensify symptoms in schizophrenics

when given in high doses and produce schizophrenic-like symptoms in nonschizophrenics.

Following this line of evidence, many researchers suspect that excess dopamine is the cause of some forms of schizophrenia. The dopamine hypothesis holds that schizophrenia is caused, in part, by biochemical abnormalities in the brain, which result in an excess of dopamine activity in certain brain pathways. Other chemical compounds in the brain, which are being investigated, are serotonin and norepinephrine. At this stage of development, there are two flaws in the biochemical theory of schizophrenia. First, excess dopamine or other abnormal chemical compounds do not consistently show up in the blood or urine samples of all schizophrenics. Second, the appearance of excess dopamine or other suspected chemical compounds in the blood and urine samples of schizophrenics may be due to a third factor, such as excess coffee-drinking or cigarette-smoking, poor institutional diets, or the inactivity that occurs as a result of withdrawal. Excess dopamine could also be a result of the emotional and cognitive changes in schizophrenia, rather than the cause of the aforementioned changes. Despite these criticisms, however, the evidence for the biochemical theory as one of the major causes of schizophrenia is sufficiently promising to warrant continued investigation.

The Genetic Model

Many biochemical theories of schizophrenia assume a genetic influence. The predisposition to schizophrenia is thought of as an inherited error of brain metabolism leading to the biochemical defect. The tendency of schizophrenia to run in families is used as evidence to support the conclusion that there is a genetic transmission of the biochemical abnormalities in the brain. Family, twin, and adoptive studies show there is a relationship or concordance between having a schizophrenic parent and the likelihood of developing the disorder (Torrey, 1983; Davison and Neale, 1982). The incidence of schizophrenia is higher among relatives of schizophrenics than among people in the general population. Two related people are concordant for a particular characteristic, such as schizophrenia, if both share the particular characteristic or if neither manifests it. The more closely two people are related, the more likely they are to be concordant for schizophrenia.

The rate at which schizophrenia occurs in the general population is 1%, or 1 chance in 100. Children of one schizophrenic parent, on the other hand, have a 10% chance of developing schizophrenia, whereas children of two schizophrenic parents have approximately a 40% chance. In identical twins who share the same genetic structure, there is a 40% chance the second twin will develop schizophrenia if one twin manifests it. If schizophrenia were perfectly correlated genetically, the concordance rate for schizophrenia in identical twins would be 100%, since they share an identical genetic structure. The concordance rate for nonidentical twins is around 10% to 15%, which is about the rate for nontwin siblings. The concordance rate for schizophrenia among relatives has been supported by over 70 studies (Kimmel and Weiner, 1985; White and Watt, 1981).

The genetic concordance rates hold up in children of schizophrenic parents who are adopted. Research done in Denmark indicates that children of schizophrenic parents, reared by nonschizophrenic adoptive parents, show an increased likelihood of developing schizophrenia (Kety et al., 1975). The concordance for adoptive children of chronic schizophrenics was higher than the rate of acute schizophrenic natural parents. This indicates that chronic or process schizophrenia may be more genetically transferable than episodic or reactive schizophrenia.

In recent years, investigators have followed high-risk children to examine the development of schizophrenia and other disorders. In high-risk research, children who are at a higher than average risk for developing schizophrenia, such as the children of schizophrenic parents, are identified early and followed by researchers for a period of several years (Garmezy, 1978). This way, the development of schizophrenia and other maladaptive behaviors can be studied in the prodromal phase. Mednick and Schulsinger (1968) followed 207 high-risk children whose mothers were process schizophrenics. When compared to low-risk children of nonschizophrenic mothers 10 years later, a higher proportion of the high-risk children showed signs of schizophrenia and other maladaptive behaviors. Twenty of the high-risk children had already suffered a major psychological breakdown (Schulsinger, 1976). Other high-risk studies of schizophrenia are currently in progress (Asarnow and Goldstein, 1986).

At this point in its development, genetic research is open to criticism in three areas. First, no specific genetic defect or schizophrenic gene has been found. It is believed that a pool of genes may contain the predisposition potential for schizophrenia, but what they are and how they lead to schizophrenia is not known (Schmeck, 1986). Second, the concordance among family members for schizophrenia is far less than 100%. Eighty to ninety percent of schizophrenics do not have schizophrenic parents. Even in the case of identical twins, identical genetic structure does not totally account for schizophrenia. Third, by the time young people have become schizophrenic, they are usually in adolescence or early adulthood. They have spent close to two decades living in a psychosocial environment that has significantly influenced how they define themselves, experience the world around them, express themselves, and integrate thoughts, feelings, and ideas.

The strength of the genetic model is its assertion that the biochemical predisposition or vulnerability to schizophrenia is inherited rather than schizophrenia itself. This assertion leaves the door open for investigators to examine the role of psychogenic factors in the development of schizophrenia, such as the quality of social learning, the communication, and the emotional interaction that takes place in the family psychosocial environment. The future of genetic and biochemical research is very promising. New technologies that will assist researchers in resolving genetic mysteries and probing the complexities of the brain are being developed. Gene splicing and other new tools of molecular biology are enabling researchers to find and trace gene products. Computer-enhanced pictures of the brain, produced by PET (position emission tomography) scanners, allow investigators to view biochemical processes as they actually work inside the brain and other organs of the body (Roark, 1985).

The Psychogenic Model of Schizophrenia

The psychogenic theory of schizophrenia holds that the appearance of schizophrenia is the result of growing up in a family environment characterized by excessive distortions in communication, a hostile, confused or ambivalent emotional climate, and destructive marital interactions. Faulty social learning during childhood creates the basis or predisposition for the thinking-confusion, distorted perceptions, and emotional impairment that later becomes manifested in schizophrenia. Even when the schizophrenic breakdown has a sudden onset, the underlying vulnerability involving defective patterns of thinking, communication, and emotional expressiveness has a long history. The psychogenic view of schizophrenia has been championed by Eugen Blueler (1911), Harry Stack Sullivan (1953, 1962), Frieda Fromm-Reichmann (1948), and Gregory Bateson and his associates (1956). Families that seem to foster the development of schizophrenia are called schizophrenogenic families (Rosenhan and Seligman, 1984; Fromm-Reichmann, 1948).

Interpersonal communication in the context of family life is a key element in the socialization process. Experiences in interpersonal communication within the home provide the child with an orientation to language, shape the child's thinking structures and emotional expressive style, and establish the child's initial approach to human relationships. According to psychogenic theorists, communication in schizophrenogenic homes is characterized by a vague, fragmented, ambivalent, contradictory quality. Gregory Bateson (1956) tried to capture the essence of preschizophrenic parent–child communication in his double-bind theory. Bateson's double-bind theory grew out of Harry Stack Sullivan's work on the importance of interpersonal communication in psychosocial development. In double-bind communications, the child is continually confronted with mutually contradictory messages from the parent. One message denies the other, placing the child in a no-win situation. The child is not allowed to discuss the contradictions. The double messages, usually involving an appeal to come closer yet stay away, occur continuously over a period of many years. A mother invites a child to kiss her while assuming a cold, rejecting posture. A father encourages self-reliance, yet subtly maintains power and control. A teenager who is recovering from a reactive schizophrenic breakdown is visited by her mother in the hospital. The mother seems happy to see the young woman. When the daughter appears in the waiting room, mother embraces her then steps back and says, "Your makeup is overdone, you look like a whore." Either way a child responds to a double-meaning parental message is likely to result in censure or disapproval (Walrond-Skinner, 1986).

Habitual exposure to double meanings; paradoxical communications; and mutually incompatible ideas, feelings, and demands during the formative years when children are dependent on parents for survival, nurturance, and approval can generate fear, confusion, and withdrawal. Under these conditions, it is difficult for children to develop a stable sense of reality, to understand what they should think or do, what they should feel, what is really expected of them, and how to feel comfortable in close relationships (Kimmel and Weiner, 1985). A similar process is called mystification by Laing (1965). Children can internalize the confusion and contradictions to the point where they become unsure of their own feelings and thoughts, or selectively tune out stress-producing parts of messages. In families where the communications are vague and amorphous, children learn to imitate the vague, amorphous style in sharing their thoughts and feelings.

In other seriously disturbed schizophrenogenic families, children get caught in a crossfire of open hostility between their parents, which ends up being directed at them. The parents try to get the children to take sides in marital conflicts. When the child sides with one parent, he or she ends up being rejected by the other parent (Lidz, 1975). Pseudomutual relationships between parents also confuse children. In pseudomutual relationships, parents give the outward appearance of genuine caring while covertly experiencing a considerable amount of hostility towards each other (Wynne and Singer, 1963a,b).

Children are not equally affected by negative emotions and distorted communications in schizophrenogenic families. In some families, a particular child may become the focal point of double-bind communications and hostile emotions. In other families, one child may not be able to sort out double meanings or cope with hostility, whereas his or her siblings can figure out adaptive ways of coping with family confusion (Walsh, 1985).

Repeated exposure to negative emotions, double-meaning messages, fragmented communications, or no-win interpersonal interactions can have two detrimental, long-term effects on the child's psychosocial growth. First, the contradictions, ambivalences, confused meanings, and hostility are likely to become reflected in the child's own thinking and feelings. The parents, as role models, are deficient tutors for learning how to organize and express thoughts, emotions, and perceptions (Coleman et al., 1984). The child learns maladaptive ways of thinking and communicating by being exposed to distorted models of family interaction. Second, the child may learn to withdraw from unpleasant external realities by retreating into wish-fulfilling fantasies. Since the external world, as represented by the family, offers very little in the way of personal affirmation or validation, the child creates an internal reality of his or her own choosing. Withdrawal is a defense mechanism or coping strategy the child erects to insulate himself from further hurt and pain. According to Laing (1965) and Frieda Fromm-Reichmann (1948), this defensive withdrawal is the underlying core of the schizophrenic experience. Behind the schizophrenic mask of craziness is a real person, with inner hopes and aspirations, who is afraid to come forward because the external world is filled with constant frustrations and devaluations.

A number of studies have shown a relationship between negative parental emotional expressiveness and deviant communication and the appearance of schizophrenia in offsprings (Goldstein and Doane, 1982; Lewis et al., 1981). Michael Goldstein and his colleagues at UCLA (Goldstein, 1985; Goldstein and Doane, 1985) have conducted a 15-year study on 50 moderately mal-adapted children from intact families, who showed signs of progressing toward schizophrenia. For the children who later manifested schizophrenic symptoms, parents interacted with them in ways that showed higher communicative deviance and negative expressed emotion. Parents communicated with their children in vague, confusing language, lost track of what they were discussing, expressed harsh criticisms, and seemed distant in interpersonal interactions. The disturbed patterns of communication and emotional interaction preceded the onset of schizophrenia.

The psychogenic model of schizophrenia is open to criticism in two areas. First, many children grow up in homes where there are negative emotions and vague, confusing communication, yet the overwhelming majority of these children do not become schizophrenic. Conversely, some children who grow up in seemingly warm, nurturing homes where there are clear patterns of communication do become schizophrenic. A valid psychogenic theory of schizophrenia would allow investigators, who had knowledge of the antecedent conditions, to predict which children would become schizophrenic before the actual appearance of schizophrenia. Second, most of the psychogenic studies of schizophrenia involve retrospective analysis. After schizophrenia has developed in late adolescence and early adulthood, researchers look backward to try to pinpoint the causative psychosocial factors. What researchers cannot determine from retrospective analysis is whether parental expressive and interactive styles are a cause or a result of schizophrenic behavior. Parents may react to eccentric or odd behavior in children with hostile emotions and distorted communications that, in turn, create a vicious cycle. Even when parental evaluations are conducted before symptoms of schizophrenia appear, there is still the possibility that the parent's critical or detached manner could have been shaped by subtle signs of strange, odd, or atypical behavior in the child (Kimmel and Weiner, 1985).

Obviously, the psychogenic model cannot fully explain and predict schizophrenia. Like the biogenic model, the strength of the psychogenic model is in its assertion that psychosocial factors can increase the vulnerability, disposition, or risk for the subsequent development of schizophrenia. Many contemporary experts adopt the view that schizophrenia is the result of a series of interactions between predisposing psychological and biological factors exacerbated by the developmental crises of late adolescence and early adulthood (Kimmel and Weiner, 1985). This is an example of the diathesis-stress model in which the diathesis or vulnerability can be created by either environmental or biogenic conditions, or a combination of both. The problem ahead is to figure out how the psychological environment interacts with heredity and the biochemical functions of the brain to produce the schizophrenic experience.

Both psychosocial and biological predispositional factors are important causative agents of schizophrenia, but neither is sufficient by itself. Evidence at present seems to suggest that the genetic-biochemical component may be stronger in process or chronic schizophrenia, where there is an early, gradual onset with greater potential for continuous deterioration. Conversely, in reactive or short-term schizophrenia, where there is a sudden onset precipitated by definitive stresses and a higher probability of complete recovery, the psychogenic component is likely to be the major determinant (White and Watt, 1981).

TREATMENT

Treatment of what is now known as schizophrenia can be divided into three phases: the institutional phase, the deinstitutionalization phase, and contemporary treatment approaches. Contemporary treatment approaches of schizophrenia involve a mixture of hospitalization, antipsychotic drugs, psychosocial therapy, family intervention, and aftercare.

The institutional phase of schizophrenia started in the early 19th century with the opening of the first insane asylums in America and lasted until the early 1970s. Prior to the 19th century, madness or insanity was surrounded by religious beliefs. People who displayed schizophrenic symptoms such as thinking confusion, bizarre behavior, reality distortions, hallucinations, and delusions were thought to be possessed by demons or other evil spirits. Madness was a sign that God's will had been violated, especially in the area of sexual taboos governing masturbation. The cure for madness or devil possession involved religious rituals such as exorcism and witch hunts. The mentally ill were persecuted, forbidden to appear in public, and often placed in jail for violating religious taboos (Shapiro, 1981).

Political and humanitarian reforms, beginning in the early 19th century, led to the creation of institutions for the care of persons suffering from severe mental disorders. From 1850 to 1925, the number of insane asylums or state-run psychiatric hospitals increased rapidly. They soon developed into large custodial asylums, where little of what today would be called treatment occurred. Patients were warehoused in a custodial system with several hundred other severely disturbed persons. They often remained in custody for several decades, sometimes a lifetime, with only minimal contact with their families. It must have been very frightening for psychologically disturbed young people to be involuntarily removed from their homes, sent to a strange place with hundreds of confused, dysfunctional people, and held there for several years. Long-term confinement in custodial institutions was congruent with Kraepelin's pessimistic belief that dementia praecox or schizophrenia followed a lifelong course of progressive psychosocial deterioration. The state used the vague legal doctrine of *parens patriae* to justify prolonged involuntary confinement. Under the doctrine of parens patriae, the state has the right to act as an authority for persons who are disabled, or who cannot take care of themselves. The belief that alien forces were responsible for bizarre, eccentric, or insane behavior persisted until well into the 20th century. The early psychiatrists in America were called alienists to symbolize their emphasis on ridding the patient of alien internal forces (McGill and Lee, 1986; Torrey, 1983).

Three innovations that took place between the late 1930s and the early 1950s shifted the direction of large state-run psychiatric institutions from custodial institutions toward treatment hospitals: (1) electroconvulsive therapy; (2) antischizophrenic drugs; and (3) milieu therapy.

Electroconvulsive therapy (ECT) was developed by Cerletti and Bini in 1938 (Davison and Neale, 1982). Electroconvulsive therapy is also known as electroshock therapy (EST) or shock therapy. It is administered by applying an electric current of between 70 and 130 volts, for a fraction of a second, through electrodes attached to the patient's head. The electrical current creates a seizure, followed by a period of unconsciousness. After the patient sleeps for a few minutes, he or she wakes up in a much clearer, stable, calm mood. Today, patients are given a muscle relaxant to prevent injuries from uncontrollable thrashing of the body during the seizure. Prior to the use of muscle relaxants, many patients suffered injuries during the seizure. The rationale for ECT is uncertain. Some mental health workers in the past believed that since epileptics rarely suffered from schizophrenia, they could cure schizophrenia by creating seizures (Sackeim, 1985).

Electroconvulsive therapy now occupies only a minor role in the treatment of schizophrenia. It has largely fallen into disrepute because of a number of controversial issues. First, many patients report side effects involving memory loss, learning difficulties, and thinking confusion. The severity and length of cognitive disruptions vary with each individual, how the procedure is performed, and how many times it is repeated. Repeated exposure to ECT can cause brain damage in animals and may have similar effects in humans. Second, ECT is perceived by many professional and lay people as cruel and barbaric. In the movie, *One Flew Over the Cuckoo's Nest* (Kesey, 1962), ECT is depicted as a punitive way of controlling unruly patients. Third, there is some question regarding whether it really works. In many cases, even after several shock treatments, the original symptoms return (Sackeim, 1985; Cimons, 1985). Most hospitals require a special review before ECT can be administered. In California, approval for shock therapy must be granted by a review panel. The city of Berkeley, California outlawed the use of ECT in a local referendum in November, 1982. The referendum was later reversed by the courts (Torrey, 1983).

Beginning in the 1950s, antischizophrenic medications or drugs replaced electroconvulsive therapy as the basic treatment in schizophrenia. Antischizophrenic drugs are also known as neuroleptics, major tranquilizers, and antipsychotic drugs. Two of the most widely known antipsychotic drugs, thorazine and stelazine, are members of a class of drugs called phenothiazines. Antipsychotic drugs seem to have a calming effect on schizophrenic patients. The vividness of hallucinations, delusions, and thinking confusion is reduced. Disordered thought and speech becomes more intelligible and patients are less agitated, violent, fearful, and withdrawn. By reducing disruptive symptoms, antipsychotic drugs have the overall effect of making patients more manageable and receptive to other forms of psychosocial therapy. Antischizophrenic drugs appear to work by blocking the transmission of dopamine in brain cells. Some patients suffer side effects such as involuntary muscle movements, tremors of hands and feet, rigidity in neck muscles, stiffness, restlessness, and slurred speech. These side effects can usually be handled by altering the dosage or shifting to another phenothiazine derivative (Bootzin and Acocella, 1980).

The antischizophrenic drugs were discovered by accident, in France in 1952, by Deschamps and Laborit. They noticed that phenothiazine drugs, which were used to induce sleep, created a sense of serenity. They encouraged Delay, a psychiatrist, to try the phenothiazine drugs with his schizophrenic patients. The dramatic result quickly spread throughout the world (Delay and Deniker, 1952). Antischizophrenic drugs revolutionized the treatment of schizophrenia and opened the door for a new generation of researchers to examine biochemical correlates of schizophrenia in the brain (Herbert, 1982). Withdrawn, volatile, confused, dysfunctional schizophrenic patients are now more manageable and receptive to psychosocial rehabilitation. Physical restraints and locked wards are rarely needed. Mental health workers can concentrate more of their efforts on growth-facilitating experiences rather than on confinement and custodial care. The length of hospital stay has been reduced from years and months to weeks and days. In a study conducted in 1967 in West Germany, the average length of stay for hospitalized schizophrenics, between 1929 and 1931, was 1,033 days. After ECT was introduced, the length of treatment was shortened to 353 days. When drugs became part of the treatment program, the length of stay was reduced to 113 days. Now 80% to 90% of hospitalized schizophrenic patients are discharged within a few days or, at most, several weeks (White and Watt, 1981; Coleman et al., 1984).

A word of caution should be mentioned about the use of antipsychotic drugs with schizophrenic late adolescents and young adults. Antipsychotic drugs will not provide them with the psychosocial skills they need to cope with the demands of living. While antischizophrenic drugs are thought to be nonaddictive, young people should not be encouraged to become dependent on these drugs as their only form of treatment. Active participation in new learning experiences is required to complete the age-appropriate developmental task involving intimacy, identity, and autonomy.

The third innovation involved in the shift of custodial institutions to treatment hospitals was the development of milieu therapy. In milieu therapy, the hospital is organized as a transitional living center rather than a long-term custodial institution. Every effort is made to treat the patients with respect and consideration as adults or as late adolescents in the process of becoming adults. Patients are encouraged to actively participate in social, recreational, cultural, and rehabilitative experiences. The hospital ward becomes a therapeutic community in which patients participate in the decision-making process, rather than a custodial unit in which they are treated like children. The philosophy of milieu therapy is based on the principle that institutions are social systems that can be growth facilitating or growth inhibiting. Much of the apathy, withdrawn, and child-like behavior of schizophrenic patients in the old custodial institutions may have been due to the institution itself, rather than the ultimate downhill course of schizophrenia. Incarcerating young people for years in a large, poorly run state hospital with nothing to do all day probably contributed as much to their ultimate debilitation as the schizophrenic disorder (Jones, 1953; Goldstein et al., 1980; Greenblatt et al., 1957).

The Deinstitutionalization of Schizophrenia

Deinstitutionalization is a broad concept referring to the goal of treatment schizophrenic patients in the community. Where large state-run hospitals were once the major source of treatment or confinement for schizophrenic patients, hospitalization is now used primarily to stabilize the patient during the acute phase. Once the patient's symptoms have been stabilized with antischizophrenic drugs, they are returned to the community. Only 20% of schizophrenic patients are now living in mental hospitals and very few spend their entire lives there (Care and Treatment I and II, 1986). The average length of hospital stay is now down to around 8 to 15 days (Mosher et al., 1986). After the power of modern antipsychotic drugs was discovered, four subsequent events in the 1960s and 1970s contributed to the growing momentum for deinstitutionalization: (1) the community mental health movement; (2) changes in the laws regarding mental patients; (3) budgetary constraints; and (4) doubts about the efficacy of hospital treatment.

In 1963 President John F. Kennedy signed into law a bold new piece of legislation to create a comprehensive system of community-based mental health centers. These new community, mental health centers were designed to replace the old, state hospital system with new therapies, in flexible treatment centers located near the patient's home community. Two thousand centers were needed, but only 700 were ever built (McGill and Lee, 1986). In the aftermath of the Civil Rights Movement, civil liberties advocates successfully supported legislation to prevent patients from being hospitalized for prolonged periods against their will and to ensure their right to adequate treatment. In most states, patients 18 and over can no longer be held over 72 hours on an involuntary commitment, without a court order. At the end of 72 hours, the family or the hospital must file a petition in the court asking for a longer term of confinement. The justification for involuntary confinement is clear evidence that the patient is a danger to self or others because of grave disabilities. Patients now have a right to adequate treatment and the right to refuse treatment. In cases in Florida, Alabama, and the District of Columbia, the courts have ruled that patients have a right to adequate treatment. If they are being confined in custodial hospitals that do not provide adequate care, the hospital must make arrangements for treatment or discharge them. In most jurisdictions, patients confined in state hospitals can no longer be required to accept treatment or medication, except in emergency situations in which there is likelihood of injury to self or others (Morganthau et al., 1986; Torrey, 1983).

Deinstitutionalization was fueled by the growing fiscal conservatism and cost-containment of the 1970s and 1980s. Facing shrinking, social service budgets, states could save money by reducing the cost of long-term care in state-run hospitals. The deinstitutionalization movement had a broad base of support in the legislative, public, and professional communities. Eradicating the debilitating effects of long-term custodial confinement, providing adequate community-based treatment, and reducing expenditures were all laudable objectives. The sad reality, however, is that deinstitutionalization has failed in many ways to reach its ideal goals. The community-based mental health system, supported by a network of treatment centers, foster homes, halfway houses, and rehabilitation services, did not fully materialize. Funding, which was supposed to follow the patients from the state hospital system to the community, got lost in the bureaucratic maze. In some cases, understaffed, community mental health centers preferred to work with less disturbed young people or were not equipped to provide the long-term interventions required by schizophrenic patients. Consequently, many young patients either fall through the cracks or become part of a revolving door of admission, discharge, relapse, and readmission. Within a year following discharge, 45% of schizophrenic patients were readmitted to hospitals. Many patients live in substandard, one-room hotels, or have become part of the roaming army of homeless Americans (Coleman et al., 1984). It is estimated that one-third of America's 3 million homeless people are mentally ill schizophrenics (Morganthau et al., 1986). On the streets, they stop taking their medication, lose contact with their support system, may get into trouble with the law, and are vulnerable to physical abuse and exploitation.

There is now a growing consensus among mental health workers and family members of schizophrenic patients that the pendulum has swung too far in the direction of deinstitutionalization. Patients who need treatment cannot obtain it because there are no facilities available or because they refuse to see the need for treatment. Authorities are reluctant to hospitalize patients, who need treatment, against their will because of the risk of law suits and the lack of facilities. There is a need to reassess how low-cost, effective treatment can be provided for schizophrenics without violating their civil liberties. There are times when patients incapable of taking care of themselves may need to be hospitalized for several weeks, yet do not meet the exact legal requirements for being grossly disabled or a danger to self or others.

Contemporary Approaches to Treatment

Contemporary treatment approaches for schizophrenia involve a mixture of hospitalization, antischizophrenic drugs, psychotherapy, and family interaction. Treatment can be divided into two phases: the acute and the aftercare phase. The goal of the first or acute stage is to reduce disruptive symptoms, reestablish contact with reality, and improve psychosocial functioning. The goal of the aftercare phase is to assist the patient's continuing recovery in the community. The acute phase treatment usually takes place in a hospital setting. Since deinstitutionalization is now a reality in most sections of the country, aftercare has become the primary focus of treatment in schizophrenia. The length of hospital stay is likely to be determined by financial, rather than clinical, considerations.

The Hospital Phase

In public psychiatric hospitals, the length of stay is generally 30 days or less. In free-standing, private psychiatric hospitals, the hospital phase of treatment may continue for 6 months to a year depending on the patient's insurance coverage (Mosher, 1986; Goldstein et al., 1980). Hospitalization is indicated when the young adult's or adolescent's behavior is out of control, when the family can no longer tolerate the stress of living with the patient and no other suitable temporary living arrangements are available, and when a thorough evaluation, with laboratory tests, is needed to rule out the presence of drugs or other medical illnesses. Ruling out street drugs and illegal substances is an important part of diagnosis, since drugs such as speed, LSD, PCP, peyote, and other substances can induce symptoms resembling schizophrenia (Weiner, 1982).

Reducing disruptive symptoms is accomplished through a combination of antischizophrenic drugs and psychosocial therapy. The psychotropic drugs decrease thinking-confusion, stabilize emotions, and diminish withdrawal. Behavior therapy and psychoeducational interventions are used to improve social interaction, communication, and personal hygiene. Patients are expected to be responsible for personal hygiene and grooming; participate in recreational, occupational, cultural, and other therapeutic activities on the living unit; and keep individual appointments with therapists and case workers. Appropriate behavior is systematically reinforced with rewards, such as approval, extra television privileges, outings, and token economies that can be used to purchase personal items at the hospital canteen. Training in social skills is utilized to help patients learn how to send and receive clear, straightforward communications, sort out their thoughts before speaking, maintain eye contact while speaking, and modulate voice intonation and facial expressions. Behavior therapy and social-skills training are based on the assumption that schizophrenic patients need systematic practice in learning how to focus and attend to what others are saying in their presence, express friendly feelings, handle brief conversations, stand up for their rights, and understand the cues involved in social interaction. Many patients have forgotten these skills, and some fail to master them in the first place (Bootzin and Acocella, 1980). Most experts on schizophrenia believe that intensive, individual psychodynamic therapy is contraindicated, especially in the early stages of working with schizophrenic patients and their families (Torrey, 1983). Because intensive psychodynamic therapy surfaces emotionally stressful conflicts, it can work against the goal of stabilizing the patient. Increased stress is likely to aggravate thinking-confusion, disrupt emotional stability, and increase the patient's fear of making contact with others. Supportive individual therapy is recommended. The goal of supportive individual therapy is to slowly build a close relationship the patient can use as a bridge to reality. Building a close relationship reduces social isolation and withdrawal. It usually requires a considerable amount of skill, patience, and sensitivity for therapists to build close, trusting, working relationships with schizophrenic patients. Part of the schizophrenic experience is a withdrawal into craziness to protect one from further hurt and disappointment. Beneath the mask of craziness, however, they may be longing for someone who will be patient, understanding, and help them through their times of unreality (Laing, 1965; White and Watt, 1981). A successful therapeutic relationship for a schizophrenic patient can be a healing experience that provides an opportunity to test the realness of their ideas and feelings in a trusting, caring relationship. The therapist–patient relationship in schizophrenia also has a practical side. The therapist can be a source of help and support in connecting the patient to resource people who will guide him through the aftercare phase. Prior to discharge, the patient needs to have someone available who can provide assistance in dealing with the bureaucratic maze of community agencies, housing programs, social security and disability benefits, vocational rehabilitation, and the like.

Aftercare

The major goals of aftercare are to continue the stabilization process started in the hospital phase; to facilitate the patient's reentry into the mainstream of school, work, vocational preparation, social interaction; and to encourage renewed interest in completing the late-adolescent, young-adult developmental tasks. As a result of deinstitutionalization, the job of providing aftercare has fallen increasingly on the family. Most late-adolescent and young-adult schizophrenics return home, either temporarily or for long-term living. In light of this trend, there is renewed interest in helping family members learn to cope with recovering schizophrenic relatives. For years, mental health professionals criticized the disturbed schizophrenogenic family as the major cause of patients' psychological breakdown. Now there is a growing consensus that family members can become effective care providers in the aftercare phase, with proper training, counseling, and support (Goldstein and Doane, 1982). Family intervention begins while the patient is still in the hospital, and continues when the patient reenters the home environment. It is important for the family to talk over their feelings about resuming the responsibility for the patient before he or she leaves the hospital. Family members are understandably concerned, frightened, or angry about the patient's potential for crazy, eccentric, and unpredictable behavior. Nothing in their lives has prepared them to cope with the sometimes bizarre behavior of schizophrenia. How do you live with a person who talks back to imaginary voices or refuses to go into the kitchen because the microwave oven controls the voices and communicates with them through hidden microwaves? Family intervention in schizophrenia is not geared toward resolving past family conflicts or assessing blame for the patient's condition. The goal of family intervention in schizophrenia is to establish a clear, practical set of guidelines for living with patients, which can be administered in a firm, fair, caring fashion. Family members need down to earth advice on communication and problem solving, the mechanics of everyday living, the nature and causes of schizophrenia, recognizing early warning relapse signs, and developing a family support network (McGill and Lee, 1986).

Communication should be brief, clear, and unambiguous. Since the patient may still be recovering from a thought disorder and auditory hallucinations, clear, simple messages have a better chance of being understood. Complex directions should be avoided. If the patient has a series of chores to do everyday, she should be encouraged to do them one at a time. Parents and other family members should not try to argue patients out of their delusional beliefs. If the patient thinks that persons on TV are sending special persecutory messages, he or she does not have to watch TV. A simple, predictable, daily routine should be established, which includes personal hygiene, chores, meals, snacks, and recreation. Periods of withdrawal should be accepted, since the patient may be trying to cope with confusing internal experiences. Patients should be given as much autonomy and independence as they can handle. Autonomy and independence are age-appropriate development tasks. Problems should be solved one at a time as they arise, rather than waiting until crises build up. Sex and drugs are delicate issues. Both are part of the late-adolescent-young-adult life-style and should be approached carefully. Illegal drugs are contraindicated when patients are taking prescribed medication and should be discouraged with recovering schizophrenics who have a history of spacing out when they are under the influence of alcohol or drugs (Walsh, 1985; Torrey, 1983).

Parents and siblings need to be given some instructions that will help them understand the nature, causes, probable course, and treatment of schizophrenia without provoking guilt or assigning blame. They need update information on how schizophrenia is subjectively experienced and may need to reassess their long-term achievement goals for the patient. It is vitally important that family members accept their role in monitoring anti-schizophrenic medication. Failure to continue the prescribed course of medication can reactivate the original schizophrenic symptoms. Parents need to be taught to recognize early warning signs, signaling the beginning of a relapse, and need to know the side effects of medication. The buildup of symptoms to their original level can usually be handled by reevaluating the medications or by a brief return to the hospital to give the patient time to stabilize. Finally, family members must learn how to take care of themselves and not to try to accomplish everything alone. Too much self-sacrifice can lead to resentment and burnout. The social stigma attached to schizophrenia often prevents families from reaching out to family support networks and mental health organizations willing to help.

Many families have done an outstanding job as primary care providers for their recovering schizophrenic offspring. Their schizophrenic relatives have bloomed in the world outside the hospital and successfully resumed school, work, and psychosocial development. For other families, the presence of a recovering schizophrenic in the home has been a nightmare. They feel they have been victimized by the system and have not been provided with sufficient backup services. Tensions have become magnified within the home to the point where other family members show signs of deterioration. They feel anger and resentment toward the patient for not being able to take care of personal hygiene, follow through on household duties, control bizarre behavior, and maintain an integrated level of social functioning without periods of withdrawal and confusion. The decision to reintegrate a recovering schizophrenic family member into the household should not be made lightly. Mary Ellen Walsh (1985), whose son is a recovering schizophrenic, suggests that patients are likely to do better in a relaxed, accepting, nonjudgmental family atmosphere, where the recovering schizophrenic is fairly high-functioning and capable of resuming activities outside the home and the family is willing to use outside help, such as support groups, rehabilitation counseling, and follow-up centers. Conversely, home care is not likely to work where there is marital and family discord, a critical, hostile, and judgmental family attitude, frightened family members, and/or younger family members who feel their lives are being disrupted. This is especially true if the former patient is still grossly disturbed.

Several studies reviewed by Falloon and his associates (1984) and McGill and Lee (1986) indicate that the emotional climate of the home decisively affects recovery and relapse rates. Schizophrenic patients who returned to homes where the emotional climate was characterized by hostility, criticism, intrusive overprotectiveness, and distorted communications were four times more likely to return to the hospital. In a highly critical, hostile home environment, 50% to 58% of the patients returned to the hospital within 9 months to a year, whereas in homes low in hostility, criticism, intrusive overprotectiveness, and distorted communications, only 13% to 15% returned to the hospital. Furthermore, when highly critical, hostile, intrusive families were given psychoeducational training in family management techniques, there was a much lower relapse rate.

Many recovering late-adolescent and young-adult schizophrenics do not live at home during the aftercare phase because their families cannot or will not assume the burden of taking care of them. For these young people, finding a suitable alternative home placement, halfway house, or transitional living center is a difficult task. They often end up in substandard rooming houses, board and care homes, and single occupancy hotels, or they roam the streets until they get into trouble with the law and are forced to return to the hospital. Without supportive therapy or supervision, they are likely to stop taking their medications, increasing the probability of a relapse. To fill the void in suitable aftercare placements, several alternative living programs have been developed, such as The Training for Community Living Program in Madison, Wisconsin, Green Door in Washington, D.C., Fellowship House in Miami, Florida and Fountain House in New York City (Torrey, 1983).

Fountain House has more than 100 centers throughout the world. It provides a comprehensive package of aftercare services to recovering schizophrenics such as supervised housing, vocational training, job placement, education, social skills training, and emotional support. Its clients are referred to as members rather than patients. Fountain House recognizes that reentry into the world of work, school, and social relationships can be frightening for people who are still experiencing a residual of withdrawal, confused thinking, hallucinations, and delusions. Job-training starts with a graduated reentry program with each step requiring less supervision and more individual responsibility. In the beginning members start out working at the central Fountain House center by helping in the office or kitchen, answering the phone, operating the switchboard, or working on the newsletter. The next step is transitional employment where they share an entry level job outside Fountain House with another member for 4 hours a day. Fountain House has contracted with a number of local employers to fulfill certain jobs, so a job is usually available. If members cannot make it to the job, a Fountain House staff member does the job for them so the job will remain with the agency. While recovering patients are reentering the work world, they are provided with social skills training and how to budget money, get to work on time, get along with their coworkers, converse with others, maintain personal hygiene, and follow directions (Walsh, 1985).

Several problems need to be addressed before we can improve the success rate in working with young schizophrenics in the aftercare phase. First, family members need to be provided with a stronger comprehensive network of support services and training to assist them in their role as aftercare providers. Second, the number of suitable alternative home placements or transition living centers needs to be increased. Third, short-term crisis centers need to be developed where patients can go for a few days when their symptoms intensify or when the family needs temporary relief from the daily strains of aftercare. Last, we need to recognize that there are two classes of symptoms in schizophrenia. The more vivid symptoms such as thinking confusion, hallucinations, delusions, bizarre behavior, and inappropriate emotional responses are responsive to antischizophrenic drugs and supportive therapy. The second set of symptoms, sometimes referred to as negative symptoms, such as deficiencies in sustained achievement motivation and effort, apathy, inertia, emotional flatness, indifference, and social withdrawal are more difficult to treat. Without the sustained motivation necessary to complete educational or vocational goals and the ability to sustain long-term intimate relationships, young schizophrenics who never fully recover are vulnerable to the so-called downward, social-class drift cycle (Schmeck, 1986; Boffey, 1986).

PREVENTION

The two major forms of prevention in schizophrenia are early detection and relapse prevention. Early detection involves being alert to early warning signs and initiating a program of evaluation and treatment. The following early warning signs indicate that schizophrenia may be emerging (Walsh, 1985):

1. Dramatic changes in communication and organization of thought processes. A person who was formerly logical and coherent now talks in a vague, rambling manner. Communications are disconnected and seem to have no beginning or end.
2. Frequent oceanic, cosmic, or depersonalization experiences. Individual loses a sense of personal boundaries.
3. Auditory hallucinations. Person hears voices, or family hears person talking to voices that aren't there.
4. Delusional beliefs connected to voices or beliefs that others are controlling one's thoughts. Adolescent or young adult may believe that actors on TV are controlling voices with hand signals, or vague forces are inserting, broadcasting, or stealing thoughts.
5. Emotional flatness, volatility, or extreme inappropriateness in a young adult or adolescent who previously has seemed emotionally normal.

Approximately 50% or more of recovering schizophrenics will require rehospitalization within a year. With adequate follow-up, the relapse rate can be cut to 12% to 14%. The two key elements in relapse prevention are strengthening family intervention services and developing a comprehensive community-based support system to fill in the gaps created by deinstitutionalization. Several family intervention models are being developed and evaluated at various locations, such as UCLA, University of Pittsburgh, London, University of Southern California, and The Menninger Foundation in Topeka, Kansas (McGill and Lee, 1986). The family intervention models involve a psychoeducational course of training, for family members and professionals, consisting of:

1. Support for family members and exploration of feelings regarding schizophrenia.
2. Clarification and information about schizophrenia, including how schizophrenia is experienced subjectively.
3. The role of antischizophrenic drugs and the importance of compliance with medication programs.
4. How to manage difficult symptoms and what to do about socially embarrassing behaviors and disclosure of schizophrenic disorder outside the family.
5. Relapse prevention and rehospitalization by early identification of the symptoms.
6. Crisis management and assessment and referral to emergency treatment teams.
7. Stress reduction strategies, problem solving, and how to deal with family burnout and resentment.
8. Adjustment of expectations concerning achievement and social functioning. Balancing overprotectiveness and independence.
9. Assuring continuity of care.

In their book on family care of schizophrenia, Ian Falloon and his associates (1984) discuss a comprehensive psychoeducational program for mental health clinicians who want to learn how to conduct family intervention workshops and training programs for families with schizophrenic members. Family support groups and self-help organizations, like the National Alliance for the Mentally Ill (AMI), are working to strengthen family support networks and educate the public on the need for a more comprehensive community-based system of services for recovering schizophrenics. AMI was founded in Madison, Wisconsin in September, 1979. Three hundred representatives from 80 family support groups met to form a coalition that became AMI. AMI is a nationwide advocacy organization with over 25,000 members in 300 chapters in state and local areas. AMI assists families with schizophrenic members by exchanging information on treatment and financial resources, voluntary and involuntary hospitalization procedures, places for recovering schizophrenics, problems they are encountering with schizophrenic relatives, and the sharing of common experiences and information. They lobby for legislation affecting schizophrenia; work with state, federal, and local agencies to strengthen the community network of services; and provide the public with current information on the etiology, causes, and treatment of schizophrenia. The address of the AMI national office: National Alliance for the Mentally Ill, 1200 15th Street N.W., Suite 400, Washington, DC 20005; (202) 833-3530. They will provide, upon request, information regarding AMI chapters in your area and other items of interest.

SUMMARY AND CONCLUSIONS

Schizophrenia is a pervasive psychological disorder that strikes one in every 100 Americans, three-fourths of all cases begin in the 16- to 25-year-old age group. The primary symptoms of dementia praecox or schizophrenia have been known for over 100 years. Bleuler's classic description of schizophrenia in terms of the 4 A's, association, autism, affect, and ambivalence, is still used in today's textbooks. At the core of the schizophrenic experience is a fragmentation of cognitive, emotional, and integrative processes characterized by disorganized thinking and communication, distorted perceptions, emotional impairment, and poor reality testing. Revolutionary changes have occurred in the theory and treatment of schizophrenia. Theories of schizophrenia have advanced from the prescientific theories of devil possession and early scientific, sex gland secretion biological models to the sophisticated biochemical and psychogenic models of today. Treatment of schizophrenia has progressed from exorcism and warehousing of schizophrenic patients in large, state-run custodial institutions to a combination of brief hospitalization, antischizophrenic drugs, psychosocial therapy, family intervention, and community-based aftercare.

Two exciting and demanding challenges lie ahead in the research and treatment of schizophrenia. First, a stronger network of community-based services must be developed to fill the gaps in the aftercare phase created by deinstitutionalization. Family members need to be provided with support and training to become more adequate aftercare providers, and the number of suitable alternative home placements or transitional living centers needs to be increased. Short-term crisis centers need to be developed to provide families with temporary relief from the burdens of aftercare and where patients can go for a few days when their symptoms intensify. Second, an integrated theory of schizophrenia, which combines the biological and psychogenic models, needs to be developed. Schizophrenia is a complex disorder that cannot be sufficiently explained by single factor biological, psychosocial, or adolescent and young-adult crisis models. It is the relationship or interaction between these factors that needs to be understood, as does the manner in which the interaction between these factors influences the process-reactive continuum of schizophrenia.

SUGGESTIONS FOR PARENTS, TEACHERS, COUNSELORS, AND YOUTH WORKERS

1. Early detection is one of the best ways to prevent schizophrenia from becoming severely debilitating.
2. If your son or daughter is acting bizarre, hearing voices, or talking back to voices; having trouble distinguishing personal boundaries; showing

signs of grossly confused thinking and perception; and expressing inappropriate emotions, emotional flatness, or extreme withdrawal, these symptoms should be promptly evaluated by a qualified mental health professional.

3. Make sure the evaluating team does a thorough screening for illegal drug usage. Street drugs or mixtures of street drugs, such as speed, LSD, PCP, peyote, and mescaline, can cause symptoms closely resembling schizophrenia.

4. If the diagnosis is schizophrenia, try not to panic or become excessively pessimistic. Once your son or daughter starts a treatment program of antischizophrenic medications, supportive therapy, and resocialization training, the more florid symptoms will probably clear up in a short time.

5. The aftercare or posthospital phase is the most critical stage of treatment. The decision regarding whether your son or daughter should return home during the aftercare phase should be made only after careful deliberation involving the patient, family members, and treatment team.

6. If the decision is for the patient to return home, take advantage of any family intervention training programs that might be offered in your area, lay out a clear, simple daily routine involving expectations for personal hygiene, taking medication, household chores, and keeping therapy and rehabilitation appointments.

7. It is important for family members to take care of themselves emotionally, physically, and psychologically; burnout from too much self-sacrifice can cause resentment, which is detrimental to the patient and family.

8. Get in touch with a local chapter of AMI or other support groups. They can help the family get connected to a network of mental health and financial resources, support services, and other families who are facing similar problems. It helps to know that you are not alone, others are willing to provide assistance.

9. If the decision is made not to return home, National Alliance for the Mentally Ill or other support groups can help you find a suitable alternative home placement. Visit the alternative home placement personally, talk with the residents and supervisory personnel, and find out if the placement offers experiences conducive to growth and rehabilitation.

10. Finally, you may have to reassess your expectations regarding the pace at which former academic, occupational, and social goals can be achieved. Although schizophrenia is a complex condition, often requiring long-term supervised guidance, many recovering schizophrenics, with time, patience, and support, can successfully cope with the problems of living and subsequently live a fulfilling life.

The following are some books that might be helpful in expanding your understanding of schizophrenia.

Awakenings: Organizing a support advocacy group. (1982). Washington, DC: National Alliance for the Mentally Ill.

Green, H. (1964). *I never promised you a rose garden.* New York: New American Library.

Hatfield, A. (1982). *Coping with mental illness in the family: The family guide.* Washington, DC: National Alliance for the Mentally Ill.

Sechehaye, M. (1968). *Autobiography of a schizophrenic girl.* New York: New American Library.

Torrey, E. F. (1983). *Surviving schizophrenia: A family manual.* New York: Harper and Row.

Walsh, M. E. (1985). *Schizophrenia: Straight talk for families.* New York: Warner Books.

Wasow, M. (1982). *Coping with schizophrenia: A survival manual for parents, relatives and friends.* Palo Alto, CA: Science and Behavior Books.

DISCUSSION QUESTIONS

1. Describe the primary symptoms of schizophrenia and relate the primary symptoms to Bleuler's 4 A's. What was the core feature of schizophrenia according to Bleuler?

2. What is meant by the terms process and reactive schizophrenia, in what way do process and reactive schizophrenia differ in terms of onset, prodromal features, etiology, treatment, and recovery?

3. Explain the two major components of a biological model of schizophrenia and how they are interrelated. What are the strengths and weaknesses of the biological model?

4. In terms of developmental tasks, what is there about the demands of late adolescence and early adulthood that renders young people more susceptible to schizophrenia than older adults?

5. What is the psychogenic theory of schizophrenia, what is meant by the term schizophrenogenic family, and how has disordered communication in schizophrenic families been explained?

6. Trace the three major developments in the treatment of schizophrenia since the beginning of the 20th century and explain the custodial model of treatment.

7. What is meant by the term deinstitutionalization with respect to schizophrenia? What were the major social forces that created deinstitutionalization, what are the advantages and disadvantages of deinstitutionalization, and how can the disadvantages be corrected?

8. Compare and contrast the major forms of prevention in schizophrenia.

9. Why is the role of the family so important in aftercare? What are the essential elements of a family-intervention training model, and what features would you look for in an alternative home placement?

8
Drug Use and Abuse

PREVIEW

This chapter discusses the major questions surrounding the use and abuse of psychoactive drugs among young people, such as: Why do young people begin taking drugs? What is the extent of drug use among young people? What drugs do they use? What are the motives, patterns, and circumstances underlying drug use? What is the difference between use and abuse, and how can drug-abuse habits be changed or prevented? Psychoactive drugs are natural and synthetic substances that can be used to induce changes in moods, thoughts, feelings, and behavior. Included in this definition of psychoactive substances are eight common classes of drugs: alcohol, marijuana, stimulants, depressants, cocaine, hallucinogens, heroin, and inhalants. The experimental and social-recreational use of psychoactive drugs among young people seems to be part of the rites-of-passage in America. Annual surveys of drug use among high school seniors conducted by the University of Michigan (Johnston et al., 1986) indicate that over 90% of late adolescents have tried alcohol, 58% have experimented with either marijuana or other illegal drugs, 4% use marijuana daily, 4.8% use alcohol daily, and 37% participate in heavy drinking at parties. The use of psychoactive drugs by teenagers cannot be understood without examining the role of chemical substances in American life. We live in a society that bombards teenagers with messages of instant relief from anxiety, boredom, restlessness, and stress through alcohol and drugs. Parents drink and take prescription and nonprescription drugs. Drugs are glamorized and associated with being sexy, masculine, feminine, and grown-up. It takes no great feat of the imagination to understand how emulation, modeling, and teenage curiosity could lead to experimentation with drugs and alcohol.

Adolescent drug use can be classified into five motivational patterns forming a continuum from mild-to-moderate then to severe. The dividing line between use and abuse is characterized by frequency, intensity, or quantity of drugs consumed, degree of preoccupation with drugs as part of one's life-style, and maladaptive consequences resulting from drug use. Drug abusers frequently use drugs in large quantities, tend to be preoccupied with drug use, and often experience conflict with friends, family members, and school authorities regarding their drug use. Most adolescents are not high-frequency, high-intensity drug users. They experiment with drugs periodically or use chemical substances in a social-recreational context with their friends.

Four major factors are associated with drug abuse: (1) sociocultural, (2) family interaction, (3) peer relationships, and (4) personal characteristics. The consensus among drug experts is that substance abuse results from the interaction of several factors rather than one factor alone. As the number of risk factors increases, the likelihood of extensive drug use increases. Treatment programs for adolescent drug abusers are based on a combination of behavioral, medical, cognitive, psychodynamic, and psychoeducational approaches integrated within a context of individual, group, and family therapy. Drug-treatment programs for adolescents have two primary objectives: (1) to either significantly reduce the frequency and amount of substances consumed, or to completely eliminate the use of psychoactive substances; and (2) to help adolescents develop the social-competency tools to build a drug-free life-style.

Drug-abuse prevention is based on the rationale that anticipatory measures can be taken in advance to control the abuse of drugs by adolescents. There are two broad categories of drug-abuse prevention: (1) drug education and (2) social-policy prevention. Antidrug education seeks to create values, attitudes, and behaviors conducive to abstinence or moderation in drug use by moral persuasion, dissemination of factual information, and social competency promotion. Social-policy prevention is oriented toward creating legislation, restricting a supply of drugs, and developing community standards for the appropriate use and nonuse of drugs. To be effective, it is essential for drug-prevention programs to have a strong base of support among teenagers. Attempts to indoctrinate teenagers or to force them to abstain from using chemical substances by employing scare tactics have been largely unsuccessful. There are no simple solutions to the problem of drug-abuse prevention. To be successful in the long run, drug experts, school administrators, parents, and youth workers must enlist the active participation of young people in defining standards for appropriate drug use and nonuse, finding drug-free alternatives to feel good, elated, or mellow, and coping with the stresses of growing up.

Case Example 8-1: Jerry

Jerry is a 16-year-old male who was brought into an inpatient, adolescent drug-treatment center by his parents. His parents gave him the option of entering the drug-treatment program or being "thrown out of the house." His parents were concerned about excessive alcohol and drug use, and escalating conflicts in family, school, and interpersonal relationships. At age 13, Jerry started drinking and smoking pot with his older brother and brother's friends. He now drinks several six packs of beer a week, smokes marijuana two to three times a day, and snorts cocaine once or twice a week. Jerry has also experimented with speed, LSD, and mescaline. He has been arrested twice for alcohol-related incidents, and is currently on suspension from school for marijuana possession after he had been repeatedly warned not to bring drugs on campus. Jerry says he decided to enter the drug-treatment program "because I need help, I'm doing drugs and I can't control it, I'm burning out, drugs are ruining my life." Jerry feels he needs drugs because "they help me through my bad times and make me feel better." He admits to four or five blackouts when using combinations of drugs and alcohol, but denies any history of seizures or hallucinations. He feels depressed when he isn't using, and hasn't been successful in three attempts to stop using drugs on his own. His school grades have deteriorated, and Jerry is frequently absent from school. Most of his friends are heavy drug users.

STATEMENT OF THE PROBLEM

This chapter is about the use and abuse of psychoactive drugs by young people in America. Why do young people begin taking drugs? What is the extent to which young people take drugs? What drugs do they use? What are the motives, patterns, and circumstances surrounding their use of drugs? What is the difference between use and abuse, and how can drug habits be changed or prevented? These are the major questions this chapter will attempt to answer. Psychoactive drugs are natural and synthetic chemical substances that can be used to produce changes in mood, thought processes, feelings, and behavior. The eight most common classes of psychoactive drugs used and abused by adolescents and young adults are: alcohol, marijuana, stimulants, depressants, hallucinogens or psychedelics, cocaine, heroin, and inhalants. Tobacco, which in a broad sense can be technically classified as a psychoactive drug, will be reviewed separately (see Box 8-1 on page 260). Drugs is a generic term that refers to psychoactive substances, including alcohol, capable of altering perceptions, moods, thoughts, and behavior. Synonymous terms are substances, chemical substances, and psychoactive agents.

The experimental and social-recreational use of psychoactive drugs and

---

Box 8-1

TOBACCO

The nicotine contained in tobacco is a psychoactive stimulant drug that increases the activity of the heart and central nervous system. Regular smoking over an extended period of time can increase the risk of heart disease, lung cancer, emphysema, and bronchitis and can shorten the lifespan. While there has been a general decline in the number of youths who smoke, large numbers of youths continue to smoke despite the surgeon general's warning that smoking can be dangerous to one's health. Over one-half of junior high school students and two-thirds of all senior high school students have smoked cigarettes on one or more occasions (Rice, 1984). Approximately 18.7% of high school seniors smoke daily (Johnston et al., 1986). The number of female teenagers who smoke regularly has increased in recent years. This has been attributed to greater independence and autonomy. Parental influence, peer pressure, and suggestive advertising appear to be the major reasons why young people start smoking. Cigarette smoking is depicted as masculine, feminine, sexy, powerful, independent, and romantic. Smoking-prevention programs based on scare tactics do not seem to work. The most effective programs begin with early adolescents or preadolescents; appeal to positive themes, such as personal pride, self-control, and achievement; present the health consequences in a straightforward manner, and teach positive ways to say "no" to pressures to smoke (Rice, 1984).

---

alcohol by young people appears to be part of the rites-of-passage from childhood to adulthood. While statistics indicate that some forms of drug use are declining or remaining stable, the percentage of adolescents who have tried drugs remains substantial. The most extensive data about the use of drugs by teenagers comes from annual surveys of approximately 15,200 high school seniors, conducted by the University of Michigan Survey Research Institute (Johnston et al., 1986). According to the University of Michigan data, over 91.3% of teenagers have tried alcohol, 57.6% of the students surveyed reported trying illegal drugs at some time, and 37.7% used an illegal drug other than marijuana. The percentage of students who used marijuana dropped from a peak of 51% in 1979 to 38.8% in 1986. Major drug usage trends are shown in Figure 8-1. The daily use of marijuana fell from a high of 11% in 1978 to 4% in 1986; 4.8% of the students admitted to daily alcohol use and 37% participated in heavy drinking, usually at parties. Drunk driving and related fatalities are 50% more common among adolescents and young adults than among other drivers (Steinberg, 1985). Auto accidents are the leading cause of death among teenagers.

Responses to recent University of Michigan surveys indicate that students are showing greater caution about the use of marijuana. In the 1986 study,

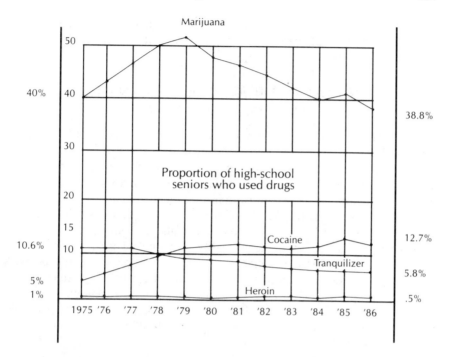

FIGURE 8-1. Youth drug trends. (Adapted from Johnston, L. D., O'Malley, P. M. & Bachman, J. G. (1986). *Use of licit and illicit drugs by American high school students, 1975–1984.* Ann Arbor, MI: University of Michigan Survey Research Institute.)

more than 71.3% saw potential harm in using marijuana, up from 62.8% in 1983. In the 1985 study, almost 60% listed potential harm as reasons for quitting marijuana. Approximately 13% of those surveyed had experimented with cocaine as compared to 9% in 1976; 82.2% of the students were aware of the harmful effects of cocaine, yet only 34% saw much risk in experimenting with it. The much-publicized drug, crack, a new form of smokable cocaine, barely seems to register on the statistical charts (Duffy, 1986).

Most students reported they had little difficulty in obtaining drugs. Drugs are usually given to students by friends, purchased from classmates, or bought using phony prescriptions and fake identification cards. Drugs can be found on most high school campuses. What troubles many drug counselors is that the age at which young people first start to experiment with drugs is drifting downward. A student drug survey conducted by the National Parents Resource Institute for Drug Education in conjunction with *Family Circle* magazine indicates that 6%, or over 500,000, sixth- to eighth-grade children have experimented with marijuana and 2% used it at least once a

week; over one-half million 10- to 13-year-olds admitted to getting drunk
once a week and 1% of sixth- to eighth-graders, or about 100,000 have used
cocaine (Mann, 1985).

THE ROLE OF DRUGS IN AMERICAN LIFE, CULTURE, AND HISTORY

The use of psychoactive drugs and alcohol by teenagers cannot be understood without examining the role of chemical substances in American life,
history, and culture. Society sends young people mixed messages about the
use of psychoactive drugs. On the one hand, we live in a society that bombards us with promises of serenity and instant relief from anxiety, boredom,
restlessness, and stress through alcohol and drugs. The use of drugs and
alcohol is glamorized in movies, advertisements, and music as a way to
gain acceptance, have fun, enhance beauty, and increase sensuousness. Using psychoactive drugs is associated with adventure, partying, and being
grown-up. It is also associated with being sexy, masculine, and feminine.
Overt and covert messages—i.e., "do drugs" messages—are sent out in popular songs, slogans, and on T-shirts and decals. Studies estimate that 43
million Americans have tried marijuana and 16 million are regular users
(Howlett, 1986). Drugs are commonplace in factories, offices, and high
schools. The philosophy of "better living through chemistry" is widely accepted. During a drug-sting operation in the Silicon Valley, a high-tech
suburb located near San Jose, California, police found that 90% of the
work force were using psychoactive drugs (Martz, 1986). Millions of adult
Americans spend billions of dollars annually on alcohol, over-the-counter
prescription drugs, and under-the-counter, illicit or street drugs, such as
marijuana, amphetamines, barbiturates, hallucinogens, cocaine, and heroin. Under these conditions, it is not surprising that most teenagers experiment with drugs and alcohol. Social learning of psychoactive drug use
comes about through modeling, imitation, and curiosity.

On the other hand, millions of dollars are spent annually by school
districts, civic groups, churches, and youth organizations encouraging
young people to abstain from using drugs, to say "no," or to only use drugs
moderately in social situations. It is difficult for teenagers to draw the line
between use and abuse when parents use tranquilizers to control anxiety,
sedatives to help them sleep, and liquor to relax them after work; yet, they
condemn teenagers for smoking pot or taking downers to cool out.

The contradictory "do—don't do" drug messages young people encounter
are symptomatic of deeper value conflicts in American society regarding
how actualization, fulfillment, insight, satisfaction, wisdom, and serenity
should be achieved. One pathway to fulfillment and self-actualization is
through delayed gratification, hard work, planning, organization, pro-

longed effort, and disciplined, logical thinking. The other pathway is through instant gratification and fulfillment facilitated by psychoactive drugs. As each new psychoactive drug is introduced, its proponents claim it holds the instant key to a major aspect of fulfillment, insight, serenity, wisdom, adventure, or actualization. The conflict is not about the end goals of self-actualization, but the means to achieve it (Musto, 1986; Cross and Kleinhesselink, 1980).

While many polls conducted during the past 20 years have identified teen drug use as a major health problem or social issue, the widespread use of drugs among youths did not begin in the 1960s, and is not restricted to youth. Youth is part of a larger society that has been developing into a drug-oriented culture for many years. The search for well-being and perceptual enrichment through natural and synthetic chemical substances is well-documented in American history (Conger and Petersen, 1984; Gullotta and Adams, 1982). Liberal amounts of opium and psychoactive substances were contained in home remedies and patent medicines prior to 1900. Coca cola, a popular beverage recommended as a remedy for a number of ailments, contained the stimulant coca when it was first introduced in 1886. Coca has since been replaced by caffeine. Morphine dependence and alcoholism were common after the Civil War, and opium was used liberally by Chinese workers during the westward expansion of the railroad. In 1893 the Indian Commission examined the long-range effects of marijuana use.

Society has attempted to control the use of psychoactive drugs and alcohol by young people and adults through a combination of legislative acts, law enforcement, medical supervision, education, and moral persuasion. There are legal restrictions on the sale of alcohol to minors. Since the passage of the Pure Food and Drug Act in 1906, and the Harrison Narcotics Act of 1916, the government has periodically passed laws restricting the sale of hallucinogens, heroin and other opiate derivatives, and cocaine. Most other psychoactive drugs cannot be legally purchased without a medical prescription. The most widely known attempt at legal control was the 18th Amendment to the Constitution, which unsuccessfully sought to prohibit the sale, manufacture, and consumption of liquor in the United States from 1919 until it was repealed in 1933. From early in this century to the present, educators, parents, and religious leaders have relied on moral persuasion in informing young people of the dangers associated with drug use to prevent them from using psychoactive substances. Despite these efforts, the use of alcohol and other psychoactive substances among young people and adults remains substantial. There are three lessons that can be drawn from past failures to control the use of psychoactive substances. First, people seem to have a need to seek pleasant perceptions, serenity, excitement, and instant relief from stress through chemicals. Second, as long as this need exists, people will find a way to legally and illegally obtain psychoactive substances to satisfy this need. Third, drug entrepreneurs are willing to take the risk involved for the opportunity to make the high, financial profits that can be derived from the sale of drugs to adolescents and adults.

PSYCHOACTIVE DRUGS COMMONLY USED AND ABUSED BY ADOLESCENTS

The drugs most commonly used and abused by teenagers can be grouped into eight categories: (1) alcohol, (2) marijuana, (3) depressants, (4) stimulants, (5) cocaine, (6) hallucinogens, (7) heroin, and (8) inhalants. In the following section, these drugs will be discussed in terms of their descriptive properties, chemical composition, source of origin, psychological effects, street names, popularity of usage, and legality (see Box 8-1 for a brief discussion of tobacco).

1.   *Alcohol* is the number one psychoactive drug used by teenagers. Over 90% of young people will have tried alcohol by the time they graduate from high school. Alcohol is a central nervous system depressant formed by fermenting sugar with yeast spores. In varying degrees of distillation or concentration, this colorless, inflammable liquid is a major ingredient of beer, wine, and liquor. The results of alcohol consumption are fairly predictable. In moderate amounts, alcohol releases inhibitions. People become more relaxed, talkative, and sociable. Disinhibition produces feelings of well-being, of pleasant emotions, and of expansiveness. In heavy amounts, the intoxication and sedative effects of alcohol become more pronounced. Speech becomes slurred, motor coordination is impaired, and judgment, memory, and perception are distorted. Finally, a stupor is reached. Long-term heavy drinking can damage the liver, heart, and brain. The amount of alcohol in the bloodstream is called Blood Alcohol Concentration or Content (BAC), and is represented by percentages. A blood-alcohol percentage of .10, which represents 6 ounces of alcohol consumed in 2 hours, produces pronounced intoxicating effects in most people (Schumer, 1983; White and Watt, 1981). Driving under the influence of alcohol is one of the major causes of death among teenagers. Most states forbid the sale of alcohol to persons under 21. Teenagers work around these restrictions by using phony identification cards, getting older friends to purchase liquor for them, finding lenient liquor store clerks, and having permissive parents.

2.   *Marijuana* is the second most popular drug among teenagers. By the time they graduate from high school, 48.7% to 53.1% of young people will have tried marijuana (Johnston et al., 1986). Marijuana, also known as pot, weed, and grass, is made from the dried leaves of the hemp plant, cannabis sativa. The cannabis sativa is a durable plant that grows wild or is cultivated in nearly every region of the world. The principal psychoactive ingredient in

marijuana is THC (delta-9-tetrahydrocannabinol). The amount of THC determines how strong the effects will be. The strength of today's marijuana is as much as 10 times stronger than the marijuana used in the early 1970s when the THC content of marijuana rarely exceeded 10% (Gullotta and Adams, 1982). Marijuana is usually smoked in the form of cigarettes called joints. Hash or hashish is another substance derived from the cannabis plant. Hashish is usually stronger than crude marijuana with typical samples containing 15% to 20% THC. Hashish can be smoked in a glass pipe. A typical marijuana-high produces feelings of relaxation, contentment, and inner satisfaction. Higher doses of THC produce perceptual enrichment and changes in body awareness. Marijuana is not considered to be physically addictive, but there is controversy regarding potential harmful effects of long-term usage. Some observers believe there is no conclusive evidence that long-term use of marijuana causes permanent physical, behavioral, or emotional damage. Others feel that lung damage can result from the long-term use of marijuana (Conger and Petersen, 1984). In medical research, marijuana is being used experimentally to reduce eye pressure in glaucoma and to control nausea in cancer patients receiving chemotherapy. Under federal law, the sale and distribution of marijuana is illegal. Many states have decriminalized marijuana so that possession of small amounts of marijuana for personal use is no longer considered a criminal offense.

3. *Depressants* are a class of synthetically produced sedative-hypnotic psychoactive substances that have a slowing down effect on the body and central nervous system. Approximately 10.4% of teenagers have used depressants (Johnston et al., 1986). Two major categories of depressants, or "downers," as they are referred to in the drug culture, are barbiturates and tranquilizers. Barbiturates and tranquilizers produce calmness, sedation, euphoria, and relaxation. Large doses can slur speech, slow reflexes, and cause poor motor coordination. Sedative-hypnotic drugs are used medically to induce sleep, control high blood pressure, reduce anxiety, and as a relaxant before and during surgery. Barbiturates, often called barbs, downers, red devils, or yellow jackets, are sold under the brand names of Seconal, Nembutal (phenobarbital), and Amytal in pill and tablet form. Brand names for tranquilizers include Valium, Miltown, Equanil, Tranxene, and Placidyl. Metaqualone, also known as quaaludes, ludes, or quads, is a powerful sedative-hypnotic drug that enjoyed popular recreational use in the 1970s (Wilford, 1981). It was medically prescribed to reduce anxiety during the day, and to facilitate sleep at night. In recent years, methaqualone has been brought under strict federal controls. Although most sedative-hypnotic drugs are not addictive, heavy use over a prolonged period of time can cause increased tolerance and psychological dependency. Depressants taken in combination with alcohol and other drugs can be dangerous. The fact that the sale and distribution of sedative-hypnotic drugs is controlled by federal

law does not prevent high school students from being able to purchase them illegally on campus, or from neighborhood drug vendors.

4. *Stimulants*, or "uppers," are psychoactive drugs that speed up the central nervous system to produce varying degrees of arousal, alertness, and euphoria, depending on the dosage. About 23.4% of adolescents have tried stimulants (Johnston et al., 1986). Stimulant users describe the effects as a rush of excitement that restores energy and elevates mood. Amphetamines are a major group of stimulant drugs. Other classes of stimulant drugs include caffeine and cocaine. Amphetamines include drugs such as benzedrine, dexadrine, and methadrine (speed). In the drug culture, amphetamines are referred to as crystal, white crosses, pep pills, diet pills, bennies, uppers, dexies, speed, crank, and meth. Amphetamines have been used medically to treat mild depression and fatigue. As appetite suppressants, amphetamines have been useful in the treatment of obesity. Amphetamines are synthetically manufactured and are usually taken orally in the form of tablets and capsules. They can also be injected under the skin or directly into the vein. Excessive use of amphetamines can create a pattern of highs, followed by lows that necessitate additional doses of amphetamine to cope with the lows. Some adolescents use uppers to counteract the effects of downers or alcohol. This up-down cycle is extremely hard on the body and medically dangerous. High doses of amphetamines can create restlessness, anxiety, and distortions in reality testing. Speed runs of several days duration can cause disorientation and psychosis in extreme cases. Low-priced look-alike amphetamines, manufactured by street laboratories, sometimes contain harmful mixtures of toxic substances. The Food and Drug Administration has warned physicians to curtail the widespread medical use of amphetamines because of the drug's addictive potential and adverse side effects (Cross and Kleinhesselink, 1980).

5. *Cocaine* is a dangerous, illegal, seductive, addictive, psychoactive stimulant drug that produces a powerful sense of arousal, euphoria, excitement, and well-being. Cocaine is derived from the leaves of the coca bush, which grows in the Andes mountains of South America (Schumer, 1983). It usually comes in the form of a powder that can be sniffed, snorted, smoked, or injected. For centuries, cocaine was used as an anesthetic. Street names for the drug include snow, blow, flake, and gold dust. Cocaine abuse is the fastest-growing drug problem in America among adults and young people. The number of adolescents who have tried it has nearly doubled from 9% to 16.9% in the past 11 years (Johnston et al., 1986). Cocaine was once known as a rich man's drug, but in recent years a worldwide glut of cocaine has brought prices down to within reach of high school students. Cocaine travels in seconds to the pleasure centers of the brain. Its effects are felt immediately and last for 15 to 30 minutes. Laboratory animals conditioned to press a bar to receive doses of cocaine continue bar-pressing until they are ex-

hausted, ignoring food, water, painful electric shocks, and willing sex partners. The newest form of cocaine is a deadly street drug called crack or rock cocaine (Morganthau, 1986a,b). It is smokable, cheap, and highly addictive. Crack is made by mixing cocaine with baking soda to create a paste that is 75% cocaine. The conversion process is simple and can be performed in any kitchen. Once the paste hardens, it is cut into tiny chips that resemble small pieces of soap. Single doses of crack sell for $10 to $15. Crack is purer than sniffable cocaine and produces an instant, euphoric high that lasts 20 to 30 minutes. The euphoric high is followed by a feeling of depression. Within 2 weeks, the cycle of ups and downs created by using crack can cause a chemical dependency. Overdose deaths due to cardiac arrest can occur when cocaine is injected, smoked, or even snorted.

6. *Hallucinogens*, or psychedelic drugs, are illegal psychoactive substances that act on the central nervous system to release a store of elaborate, colorful fantasies; they alter perceptions, emotions, self-awareness, one's sense of time, and levels of consciousness. Under the influence of hallucinogens, colors take on a more brilliant, vibrant look, objects change shapes, and music takes on a richer sound. Hallucinogens have been referred to as mind-bending, mind-altering, mind-blowing, and psychomimetic drugs because they are capable of producing loss of personal boundaries, distortions in reality testing, confusion, and depersonalization. Approximately 9.7% of teenagers have experimented with hallucinogens (Johnston et al., 1986). Psychedelic drugs, such as mescaline, peyote, LSD, and PCP, are derived from natural and synthetic sources (Wilford, 1981). Mescaline and peyote are derived from the peyote tax plant that grows naturally in Mexico and in the southwestern part of the United States. Mescaline has been used for a religious ritual of the Native American Church of the Southwest.

The most widely known hallucinogenic drug is LSD, a semisynthetic drug produced from the fungus found in the seeds of rye and other grass plants. LSD is a colorless, odorless substance sold on the streets in tablets, capsules, or occasionally in liquid form. It is usually taken by mouth. LSD was first used in the laboratory to study experimentally-induced psychotic life conditions or psychomimetic states. It became very popular with young people during the youth revolution of the 1960s. Its proponents believed that LSD could create deeper levels of self-awareness, personal growth, and transcendent consciousness. In recent years LSD has fallen into disfavor. It is associated with bad trips, emotionally upsetting experiences, panic, flashbacks, and psychological damage. Many young people who used LSD repeatedly lost control of their perceptions, felt they were falling apart, and could not maintain an integrated sense of self and reality. Phenecyclidine or PCP, also known as the monster drug and angel dust, was originally developed as an animal tranquilizer in the 1950s. Its unpredictable effects on humans range from pleasant, dream-like experiences to volatile, assaulting paranoid states.

Teenagers under the influence of PCP have engaged in unprovoked attacks on others and exposed themselves to unnecessary dangers. Judgment becomes severely distorted, and overdoses can cause convulsions, coma, and death. PCP is usually smoked or snorted.

7.   *Heroin*, classified as an addictive narcotic drug, is produced from the opium poppy plant that flourishes in the Middle East and in Southeast and Southwest Asia. Heroin is known on the streets as smack, horse, H, and junk. Only 1.1% of teenagers have experimented with heroin, and most have only used it one or two times. Opium is a dark, gummy substance extracted from the juice of unripe seed pods of the opium poppy. Morphine, the chief active ingredient in opium, is produced as a bitter, white, odorless powder. Heroin is derived from morphine in a simple chemical process. Codeine, another opium derivative, is often used in cough syrups as an analgesic to relieve mild body aches and pains. Methadone and meperidine (Demerol) are synthetic opiates.

Heroin is usually injected into the vein, but can be snorted or injected under the skin. It produces a rush of pleasant, calm, detached feelings that last about 4 hours. Heroin users have described the feeling as being at peace with one's self in the world. Heroin is more addictive than other drugs, such as cocaine, because its effects are stronger and last longer. Withdrawal from the prolonged use of heroin is very painful, physically and psychologically. The classic (cold turkey) symptoms include nausea, running eyes and nose, chills, spasms, muscle aches and pains, anxiety, and a powerful craving for more heroin. The sale and distribution of heroin in the United States is illegal. Morphine is used medically to relieve pain. Extensive research in Great Britain has demonstrated the pain-killing properties of heroin, especially in dying cancer patients suffering from intractable pain. In 1987 the United States Senate was considering a bill that would allow the experimental use of heroin as a pain killer for terminal cancer patients (Kilpatrick, 1987).

8.   *Inhalants*. Low doses of the vapors of solvent fumes from a variety of products, such as glue, gasoline, paint thinner, cleaning fluid, and fingernail and furniture polish, can produce a euphoric high when inhaled (Conger and Petersen, 1984). To create the psychoactive effects, these substances are usually placed in a paper or plastic bag, or on a rag and deeply inhaled while held over the mouth and nostrils. The use of inhalants is dangerous. Deep-breathing of high doses of vapors can cause intoxication, loss of consciousness, poisoning, breathing difficulties, and brain damage. Most people do not think of inhalants as psychoactive substances because they were never intended to be used as drugs. Approximately 15.9% of adolescents have experimented with inhalants (Johnston et al., 1986). The typical inhalant abuser is a junior high school male who does not have access to other psychoactive agents. Older youths have access to other drugs and tend

to realize the dangers inherent in using solvents. The most popular new inhalants are amyl nitrate (poppers) and butyl nitrate, which produce highs that last from several seconds to a few minutes (Dacey, 1986).

MOTIVES AND PATTERNS ASSOCIATED WITH DRUG USE

Young people use psychoactive drugs for a variety of reasons and combinations of reasons including: stress reduction, escaping from unhappiness, self-improvement, becoming one of the crowd, rebellion, curiosity and adventure, searching for spiritual enlightenment, enhancing sensual experiences, personal enjoyment, relieving boredom, mood control, boosting one's spirits, and/or the need for immediate gratification.

Drug use can be classified into five motivational patterns: (1) experimental, (2) social-recreational, (3) circumstantial-situational, (4) intensified, and (5) compulsive (Rice, 1984).

1. Experimental drug use involves the short-term, low-frequency use of psychoactive substances where curiosity, adventure, and trying something new and exciting are the primary motives. The majority of teenagers first try drugs out of curiosity in a spirit of adventure-seeking and mild rebellion.

2. In the social-recreational use of drugs, the motives are usually to share pleasurable experiences with friends and become one of the crowd. Teenage society is a peer-oriented culture; therefore, young people are motivated to do what their friends do. Most young people are introduced to drugs by their friends.

3. The circumstantial-situational use of drugs is motivated by a need to achieve a mood or mental effect in a specific situation, e.g., using stimulants to stay awake while studying, tranquilizers to relax during school exams, sedatives to induce sleep, or marijuana to be cool at a party.

4. Intensified drug use involves the long-term use of drugs to escape from the daily stresses and problems of living. Drug use becomes an habitual part of the adolescent's life-style.

5. Compulsive drug use is high-intensity, high-frequency drug use of long-term duration motivated by the desire to maintain the drug high or the enjoyable psychological effects. The person's life-style revolves around drugs, and one's primary goal is to continuously experience the effects of individual drugs and combinations of drugs. Withdrawal from drugs is likely to be accompanied by physical and psychological discomfort. Without drugs, life seems empty and gloomy.

These patterns of drug use form a continuum from mild-to-moderate to severe. On the mild-to-moderate end of the continuum are the experimental and social-recreational users. The occasional, mild use of drugs among young people is not uncommon. The majority of young people have tried either alcohol or marijuana on one or more occasions. They typically drink or smoke pot with their friends on weekends, don't progress beyond the occasional use of soft drugs, and drug use does not interfere with overall psychosocial adjustment. Toward the middle of the continuum are the circumstantial users. Although these young people can be classified as moderate users, they run the risk of becoming dependent on drugs to get them through troublesome situations. The use of drugs to handle troublesome moods or such situations as exams, interaction with the opposite sex, depression, or social situations can prevent them from exploring drug-free alternative ways of coping. At the other extreme of the continuum are the intensified and compulsive drug users. These adolescents regularly abuse drugs, cannot get along without them, and may not remember what life was like without drugs.

The dividing line between the use and abuse of drugs is characterized by the frequency, intensity, or quantity of drugs consumed, by preoccupation with drugs as part of one's life-style, and by maladaptive consequences resulting from the use of drugs. Drug abusers frequently use drugs in large quantities over an extended period of time; they tend to be preoccupied with drug use, often to the exclusion of other activities; they experience conflicts with family, friends, and school authorities regarding drug use, and are likely to become anxious and physically uncomfortable when they cannot obtain drugs. Conversely, occasional or mild users can cope with life without using drugs. Despite the public attention focused on the teen drug problem, the majority of teenagers fall into the user rather than the abuser category. They occasionally have a few drinks, or smoke pot with their friends at parties and social gatherings. The problem is not teenage drug use, but teenage drug abuse. DSM-III-R (American Psychiatric Association, 1987) categories for drug-related disorders are described in Table 8-1. Addiction was the term formerly used to characterize young people who habitually or compulsively abuse drugs. Drug addiction has been replaced by the term drug or chemical dependence. There is no universally agreed upon definition of what constitutes chemical dependency. Chemical dependency is often used to indicate psychological and physical symptoms accompanying withdrawal from habitual drug use. Physical symptoms of withdrawal are general discomfort, nausea, and dizziness. The body can build up a tolerance or a need from the compulsive use of certain drugs to the point that withdrawal produces physical symptoms. Psychological signs of withdrawal from chronic drug use are restlessness, anxiety, hyperactivity, and depression. The term drug abuse is currently used by most mental health workers and counselors to refer to the compulsive, habitual use of drugs. Other frequently used drug terms are listed in Table 8-2.

Polydrug abuse is used to describe teenagers who are abusing several

Table 8-1. DSM-III-R Drug-Related Disordersa

DSM-III-R recognizes two major categories of drug-related disorders: (1) psychoactive substance-induced organic disorders, and (2) psychoactive substance-use disorders.

1. *Psychoactive substance-induced organic disorders* refer to a range of psychobiological disorders that can be created by the toxic effects of psychoactive chemicals in the body and central nervous system. For example, extensive use of alcohol and other substances can cause memory loss, vitamin deficiencies, brain damage, amnesia, psychosis, and flashbacks.

2. *Psychoactive substance-use disorders* refer to maladaptive behaviors and consequences resulting from the regular use of psychoactive drugs. Psychoactive substance-abuse disorders can be divided into two categories: psychoactive substance dependence, and psychoactive substance abuse. Psychoactive substance dependence is characterized by behavioral, cognitive, and emotional difficulties in school, work, and interpersonal functioning, which come about through continued drug use. For example, an adolescent who uses marijuana everyday falls behind in his school work, gets suspended by school authorities, withdraws from family and social relationships, and ends up in trouble with his parents. He spends a great deal of time and effort trying to obtain drugs. Attempts to stop using voluntarily are unsuccessful. Drug tolerance levels increase, and he shows withdrawal symptoms. Increasing tolerance is evidenced by the need for increasing amounts of a drug to produce the desired effect. Withdrawal symptoms refer to such symptoms as tremors, anxiety, stress, and cravings when the drug is not available.

Substance-abuse disorder is a residual category of maladaptive drug use indicated by either: (1) continued use of psychoactive substances, despite knowledge of having a recurring or persistent educational, occupational, social-interpersonal, or physical problem caused by excessive use of drugs, or (2) continued use of a drug in situations where it is physically hazardous. For example, a high school student repeatedly drives his car while intoxicated, or a college student misses school because of frequent weekend cocaine binges. There are no other symptoms.

---

aAdapted from: American Psychiatric Association. (1987). *Diagnostic and statistical manual of mental disorders* (3rd ed., rev.). Washington, DC: American Psychiatric Association.

drugs, or who frequently consume various mixtures of street drugs during the course of a day. For example, a polydrug-using teenager might smoke pot before and after school, take stimulants to stay awake during school, mix alcohol and pot in the evening, and add cocaine and hallucinogenic drugs on weekends. Teenagers have very little trouble spotting the extremes of drug abuse. The "stoners" and "loadies," as excessive drug-abusers are called in many high schools, are fairly easy to point out. The chronic high-intensity, high-frequency drug users tend to hang out with each other and form their own network (Huba et al., 1979). The kids who don't use, or who occasionally drink or smoke pot on weekends are also fairly well-known. The dilemma for many teenagers and, for that matter, many adults is where to draw the line between use and the beginning of abuse.

PERCEIVED DRUG EFFECTS

Many young people who engage in mild-to-moderate use of psychoactive drugs tend to perceive the effects in positive terms (Cross and Kleinhesse-link, 1980). From a personal-experiential or phenomenological perspective,

Table 8-2. Drug-Related Terminology

---

1. *Burnout* refers to the disorientation, sluggishness, confusion, and possible memory loss resulting from the heavy, long-term use of amphetamines and hallucinogenic drugs.
2. *Crash or crashing* refers to coming-down from a speed or cocaine high. Coming-down is frequently accompanied by withdrawal into sleep or depression.
3. *Decriminalization* involves reducing penalties for drug possession from felonies to misdemeanors, or to a civil offense, like a traffic ticket, when small amounts of the drug are involved. Marijuana has been decriminalized in many states.
4. *Flashback* involves the involuntary reappearance or reexperiencing of LSD-induced feelings and perceptions weeks or months after the last LSD consumption. Flashbacks can be very frightening and can last from seconds to several minutes.
5. *Illegal drugs* are psychoactive substances which, if possessed or sold, can lead to a felony conviction. Substances in this category are heroin and other opium derivatives, hallucinogens, cocaine, and the more powerful stimulants and depressants. The distribution of these substances is controlled by federal law. Controlled substances are generally referred to as hard drugs. Alcohol and marijuana are considered soft drugs.
6. *Mainlining* involves intravenously injecting drugs directly into the vein.
7. *Slamming* involves injecting speed, cocaine, or heroin.
8. *Skin popping* refers to injecting drugs under the skin.
9. *Overdose* is a heavy level of drug consumption resulting in a loss of consciousness, possibly leading to convulsions and the risk of death as a result of respiratory failure.
10. *Tolerance* means a person has to have larger and larger doses of drugs to create the same effect. Tolerance occurs when people use the same drug on a regular basis.
11. *Trip* refers to the feelings, thoughts, and perceptions one experiences while under the influence of LSD or other hallucinogenic agents. A "bad trip" is a frightening experience that results in panic and terror.

---

adolescents and young adults cite four positive drug-induced effects: (1) identity-related and coping effects, (2) inhibitory-disinhibitory effects, (3) involvement in peer relationships, and (4) perceptual enrichment, creative thinking, and spiritual transcendence. Many young people feel psychoactive drugs calm their anxieties so that they can critically examine previously internalized beliefs without feeling guilty. One of the identity-related adolescent transitions involves questioning rigid law-and-order beliefs internalized during childhood. Adolescent living demands a flexible range of emotional responses. Engaging in new adventures sometimes requires loosening up one's inhibitions; at other times it is necessary to control powerful emotions, such as anger. Many young people use drugs to enhance sexual experiences. Studies indicate that a majority of young women used alcohol or other psychoactive drugs during their first sexual encounters (Cross and Kleinhesselink, 1980). As noted earlier, drugs are part of the youth culture. Young people want to be part of the crowd or the gang. They don't want their friends to think they are afraid or "chicken." Some young people feel that psychoactive drugs help them experience a broader vision of life, deeper insights into themselves, and increased artistic appreciation. Under the influence of mind-expanding drugs, they can transcend the constrictions and demands of day-to-day reality in order to achieve a global consciousness, a higher sense of personal fulfillment, and harmony with the universe. Formerly unavailable or suppressed thoughts become accessible, providing thinking with a fresh, new, creative perspective.

These perceived drug effects correspond to major adolescent development tasks. The risk of using drugs as a tool for personal growth and coping is one of self-deception. Young people can come to believe that drugs are helping them master growth tasks involving values, peer relationships, identity, and discovery when, in fact, drugs are actually impeding their growth. Youth who don't have the resources or self-confidence to actively master developmental challenges are vulnerable to believing that drug-induced experiences can substitute for psychosocial competencies that can only be developed through persistent effort.

NONDRUG HIGHS

The proponents of nondrug-induced highs believe that psychoactive drug effects, such as feeling good, self-knowledge, spiritual transcendence, excitement, creativity, discovery, and serenity, can be produced without using chemical substances. Nondrug activities and interests that many people experience as rewarding, enriching, joyful, exciting or relaxing are: (1) physical fitness and exercise, (2) personal growth, (3) loving relationships, (4) fascination with ideas and the pursuit of excellence, and (5) religious involvement.

Joggers and other athletes report feelings of joy and calmness when the body reaches a peak-performance level. Self-knowledge and personal expansion can be achieved through growth groups and psychoeducational experiences that provide the opportunity for self-exploration, feedback, stress reduction, and improving psychosocial competency in a supportive environment. Loving relationships and romantic encounters can create feelings of joy, rhapsody, and enchantment. The search for intellectual clarity and scientific understanding can produce a fascination with ideas and symbols. Evangelical and "Born Again" religions can be a source of spiritual and emotional fulfillment. Eastern religions offer meditation as a tool to pursue serenity, transcendence, and oneness with the universe.

If drug-free experiences can produce joy, excitement, serenity, self-knowledge, and spiritual awareness, why do young people continue to use psychoactive drugs? There are at least three answers to this question. First, the effects of alcohol and drugs are immediate. Drug-free pursuits usually require prolonged effort and delayed gratification. Self-knowledge or physical fitness is not something that occurs instantly. Second, there are no guaranteed outcomes with real-life adventures and challenges; real-life involves risk and setbacks. The joys of love can be followed by the pain of breaking up. There is no guarantee that prolonged intellectual or scientific effort will result in creative achievement. Third, adult society seeks to define and control what is considered an acceptable drug-free alternative. Adults seem to want young people to stay away from nontraditional religions, and from exciting ideas that challenge the status quo. They want young people to restrain their sexual enjoyment. Adults give young people double messages. They tell young people to look for drug-free alternatives, but what adults really mean is to look for drug-free alternatives of which they approve. Limiting one's search for joy and fulfillment to activities approved by adults takes away some of the excitement, discovery, and adventure that are essential parts of the passage through adolescence.

FACTORS ASSOCIATED WITH DRUG ABUSE

In this section, the major factors associated with drug abuse will be discussed. The four major factors that have consistently emerged in the adolescent drug-abuse literature are: (1) social cultural factors, (2) family interaction, (3) peer relationships, and (4) personal characteristics. Drug abuse is defined as the compulsive, high-intensity use of large quantities of psychoactive substances; preoccupation with seeking, obtaining, and consuming drugs; and adverse psychosocial consequences as a result of drug behavior. Any psychoactive substance, including alcohol or marijuana, can be abused. Young people who are heavily into the drug scene often abuse more than one drug. Habitual consumption of more than one drug, as noted earlier, is referred to as polydrug abuse. Compulsive high-intensity drug use is often accompanied by increased levels of drug tolerance and deteriorating adjustment in school, family, and peer relationships. Larger quantities of drugs must be consumed to produce the desired mood and mental effects, and it becomes difficult for the person to withdraw from drug use without professional help (Wilford, 1981).

It is virtually impossible for teenagers in our society to avoid some degree of exposure to drug use. Psychoactive drugs are glamorized in movies, television dramas, music, and advertisements. Drugs, especially marijuana and alcohol, are part of the youth culture. As a result of a combination of social learning experiences, including exposure, curiosity, modeling, imitation, and peer reinforcement, it is statistically predictable that the majority of teenagers will sample psychoactive drugs on one or more occasions. Only a minority of young people will progress from the experimental and social-recreational use of drugs to drug behaviors that could be labeled as abuse. As young people progress from use to abuse, identifiable family factors, peer relationships, and personal characteristics are likely to take on greater importance.

The two family factors that correlate with adolescent drug use are regular drug use by one or more family members, and inadequate parenting. Teenagers who abuse drugs are likely to have at least one parent who regularly uses alcohol, tranquilizers, sedatives, or illegal drugs such as marijuana or cocaine. While parental influence is greater for alcohol than marijuana in predicting patterns of teen drug use, parents act as a role model in setting standards for use and abuse (McDermott, 1984). Parents who abstain from alcohol and other psychoactive substances, or use them only occasionally, seldom have children who abuse drugs. Parents who regularly use alcohol, sedatives, tranquilizers, stimulants, and other substances are sending a message to their children that such behaviors are acceptable. Drug counselors are now seeing the second generation of drug abuse in some families. Some parents who have continued to use marijuana since they were adolescents in the 1960s introduce their children to marijuana and other soft drugs. They rationalize that these drugs are not harmful, and they want their children to learn to use drugs under proper adult supervision. Supplying young people with drugs for any reason is a high-risk endeavor, since young people may decide on their own to exceed the boundaries set by their parents. When parents try to set limits after the fact, adolescents can always reply with "How can you tell me what to do when you smoke pot all the time?"

The quality of parent-child interaction is an important correlate of adolescent drug abuse. Teenage drug abusers tend to come from homes characterized by family turmoil, absence of mutual decision-making, insufficient warmth and caring, poor communication, and lack of mutual respect (Glynn, 1984; Kandel, 1985). The worst parental combination appears to be parents who model regular alcohol and drug use, and fail to provide a nurturing, supportive environment for their children to grow up in (Kimmel and Weiner, 1985).

Peer influence on behavior reaches a peak during adolescence. Peers provide the social context in which drugs are used. Most young people are first initiated into marijuana and other illegal drugs by their peers. Young people who are heavily into such drugs as marijuana, stimulants, psychedelics, and cocaine tend to hang out with other young people who abuse drugs (Kandel et al., 1978; Brook et al., 1986).

Drug abuse can be a cause or a consequence of peer relationships. Since adolescents tend to emulate peer behavior and seek reinforcement from their peers, frequent drug use by friends often influences one's own level of drug use. On the other hand, once teenagers start to abuse drugs, they tend to seek out others who are high-frequency users. Peer relationships among high-intensity drug users are likely to revolve around drug-related activities rather than around close, emotional bonding. Drugs become the center of peer activities to the exclusion of other interests. Compulsive high-frequency adolescent drug users can find themselves overtly or covertly excluded from the mainstream of peer activities. Young people who abstain from drugs, or only use them occasionally, may not want their reputation tainted by hanging around with "stoners" and "loadies."

The personality factors commonly associated with adolescent drug abuse are deficits in psychological adjustment and psychosocial competency. Several studies indicate that, as a group, adolescent drug abusers are likely to show signs of low self-esteem, anxiety, depression, restlessness, rebellion, predelinquent behavior, impulsivity, and a lack of focus or diffusion that goes way beyond the usual search for identity (Lettieri, 1985; Gullotta and Adams, 1982). As drug use progresses from social-recreational to compulsive daily use, a process of self-deception seems to set in and drug tolerance increases. While greater quantities of drugs in various combinations are being consumed, the individual continues to believe that drug use has not progressed beyond the social-recreational level. They may admit to occasionally needing a boost or to "cool out," but vigorously deny any drug dependency or abuse. They maintain that they are in control or point out that others are abusing drugs more severely. The greatest danger of adolescent drug abuse is that drugs can become a substitute for learning to cope with the inevitable demands, frustrations, and challenges of living. Mastery of adolescent development tasks requires an active struggle to learn to overcome setbacks. One of the most important developmental tasks of adolescence is acquiring a flexible range of coping behaviors and problem-solving strategies. High-frequency, high-intensity drug-using adolescents are vulnerable to an increasing reliance on drugs as a coping tool without realizing the maladaptive consequences of their behavior (Conger and Petersen, 1984).

Drugs become a panacea for coping with depression, tuning out unpleasant feelings, and raising low self-esteem. What started out as a pleasure-seeking adventure turns into an escape from time-consuming responsibilities and sustained goal-directed efforts requiring delayed gratification. Rather than producing pleasure, drugs are used in a self-medicating fashion to avoid the emptiness, pain, and suicidal thoughts that arise when one is not using, eventually creating a vicious cycle. The more drugs interfere with learning drug-free adaptive behaviors, the more ill-prepared young people are to handle the frustrations and conflicts of living. And, the less able they are to handle the conflicts of living, the more vulnerable they are to a greater reliance on drugs. Consequently, young people who have been abusing drugs for an extended period of time are usually behind their agemates in psychosocial development in such areas as conflict-resolution skills, social conduct, school performance, and interpersonal relationships. Giving up drugs creates stresses they are unable to cope with, so they continue to rely on drugs. At this point, professional intervention usually is necessary to help young people discover drug-free alternatives for coping. Once young people become dependent on drugs, it is difficult for them to change without help.

While the adolescent who is abusing drugs is prevented from engaging in an honest reappraisal of drug behavior by self-deception and denial, others, such as family members, former friends, and teachers, are likely to notice the deterioration in interpersonal relationships, school performance, social conduct, and choice of peer relationships. In the rare instances in which they briefly admit to the painful reality of increasing drug-related personal and social frustrations, they are likely to project the blame onto others. The family turmoil cited in many studies as a cause of adolescent drug abuse can be regarded as a consequence of drug abuse in many cases. Parents and other family members are likely to be frustrated and angered not only by the adolescent's heavy use of drugs, but also by failing school grades, truancy, household thefts for money to buy drugs, not following through on attempts to stop using, involvement with drug-oriented peers, and the emotional roller coaster of highs and lows associated with mixtures of drugs.

There is a growing consensus that teenage substance abuse results from the interaction of several factors, rather than from one single factor acting alone. As the number of risk factors increases, the likelihood of extensive drug use increases. For example, a teenager with low self-esteem, who is involved with peers and parents who are heavily into drugs, is more likely to abuse drugs than is a self-confident teenager whose parents and peers abstain or only use psychoactive substances occasionally. Different factors may be more important in different stages of drug use. The decision to experiment with drugs is no doubt heavily influenced by peers and sociocultural factors, whereas the transition from occasional use to abuse is more influenced by personal characteristics and psychosocial competency factors (Lettieri, 1985; Gullotta and Adams, 1982).

Denise Kandel and her associates (1985) propose a stepping-stone theory of substance abuse in which substances such as beer and wine are the gateway or entry drugs. From gateway drugs, the progression is to hard liquor, marijuana, and ultimately to other illicit drugs. Role models, beliefs, and values are likely to be different as one progresses toward more serious levels of substance abuse. The weakness in the gateway theory is that very few adolescents progress from alcohol and marijuana use to regular abuse of cocaine, psychedelic drugs, stimulants, or heroin.

Some theorists add a biological dimension to the correlates of adolescent drug abuse. They generally cite the work of Goodwin (1976), which suggests that alcoholism runs in families. Biological theorists assume there is an inherited vulnerability to drug abuse that takes on greater significance when combined with high-risk social, peer, and personal factors. While biological theories of adolescent drug abuse are not highly specific at this time, the general reasoning is that drug abusers have a genetic hypersensitivity or a metabolic deficiency that results in the overuse of drugs and alcohol as methods of calming themselves down or boosting themselves up (Holden, 1985).

TREATMENT

Drug-abuse warning signs that suggest a need for professional intervention are listed in Tables 8-3 and 8-4. Treatment programs for adolescent drug abuse are based on a combination of behavioral, medical, cognitive, psychodynamic, and psychoeducational approaches integrated within a context of individual, group, and family therapy. In one way or another, most drug treatment programs address the major sociocultural, family, peer, and personal factors that contribute to adolescent drug abuse. A variety of treatment facilities and programs are available; these include hospitals, mental health centers, school, church and youth center drug-counseling programs, free clinics, halfway houses and youth homes, Alcoholics Anonymous and Narcotics Anonymous, and private practitioners. In California and several other states, teenagers can legally obtain drug counseling without parental consent. Local mental health centers, crisis and teen hot lines, school counselors, physicians, ministers and mental health professionals can usually provide a list of referral sources. The National Association of Parents for Drug Free Youth has established a toll free hot line (1-800-554-KIDS) you can call for sources of help if you need assistance with an adolescent who is having trouble with drugs or alcohol.

Hospitalization should be considered in cases where: (1) adolescents have unsuccessfully tried to quit or stop abusing drugs on their own several times, (2) teenagers have been unsuccessful in outpatient programs, (3) there has been an overdose, or where dangerous mixtures of street drugs and alcohol are being used that could cause an overdose, (4) symptoms such as suicidal thoughts, flashbacks, and bad trips are frequent, (5) medical attention is necessary to control severe discomforts and psychological and physical ef-

---

Table 8-3. Drug Abuse Warning Signs

Parents, youth workers, teachers, and teenagers who may need to refer young people to drug treatment programs should be alerted to the following warning signs that indicate substance abuse is progressing from the social-recreational level to serious abuse. Additional warning signs are presented in Table 8-4.

1. Extreme mood swings, periods of euphoria followed by periods of depression, irritability, or calmness and passivity.
2. Slurred speech, staggering, confusion, and general appearance of being spaced out or drunk without visible signs of drinking.
3. Presence of drug paraphernalia such as pipes, pill boxes, straws, spoons, and clothing such as belt buckles and T-shirts with drug themes, or leftover evidence of marijuana, stimulants, barbiturates, or cocaine.
4. Deterioration of school performance, lack of interest in school activities, and a shift away from mainstream friends.
5. Thefts of money by the adolescent, missing liquor, forged checkbook entries, and missing objects in the house, which could be sold for money.
6. Blatant denial when confronted with above evidence.

Table 8-4. Drug Abuse Warning Signs: Questions for Youth and Parents

Questions for Youth	Yes	No
1. Do you lose time from school due to drinking or drugs?	☐	☐
2. Is drinking or using drugs affecting your reputation?	☐	☐
3. Do you drink or use drugs to escape from study or home worries?	☐	☐
4. Do you feel more at ease on a date when drinking or using drugs?	☐	☐
5. Do you borrow money or do without other things so you can buy liquor or drugs?	☐	☐
6. Have you lost friends since you started drinking or using drugs?	☐	☐
7. Have you started hanging out with a heavy drinking or "using" crowd?	☐	☐
Questions for Parents		
1. Is your liquor supply dwindling?	☐	☐
2. Has your child's personality changed noticeably?	☐	☐
3. Do you hear consistently from neighbors, friends or others about your child's drinking or questionable behavior?	☐	☐
4. Does your child turn-off to talks about alcohol or drugs?	☐	☐
5. Do you find obvious signs like a stash of bottles, pot, pills, or drug paraphernalia around the house?	☐	☐

If the answer to any of the questions for parents of youths is yes, it is a warning sign that drugs may be becoming a problem. If the answer to several questions is yes, you can assume a problem with drugs or alcohol exists.

fects of withdrawal, (6) behavior is out of control as indicated by failing school grades, truancy, stealing to obtain drugs, and blatant denial or running away when confronted with evidence of drug abuse, and (7) family members are emotionally drained from the roller coaster of mood swings, social conduct problems, and arguments that accompany drug abuse. Hospital-based programs generally last 6 to 8 weeks with a 3- to 4-month follow-up. One of the primary advantages of hospital-based programs is that withdrawal from drugs can be conducted under supervised conditions and monitored by urine samples. Under these conditions, doubts, deceptions, and outright lies about continued drug usage are eliminated. Intermittent testing for drug usage can be conducted in outpatient programs, but 24-hour, day-to-day supervision in a drug-free environment is not possible in outpatient programs.

Drug-treatment programs for young people have two primary objectives: (1) to significantly reduce the frequency and amount of drugs consumed, or to entirely eliminate the use of psychoactive substances altogether; and (2) to assist the adolescent to develop the psychosocial competencies, tools, and mastery experiences to lead a drug-free life-style. The first goal is objective and behavioral. The amount and frequency of drugs consumed can be observed, charted, and measured. No one can force an adolescent to abstain from using drugs. However, once a person has developed a history of drug abuse, he or she should strongly consider abstinence as a goal in view of the fact that a potential risk or a vulnerability for future abuse exists. The assumption underlying the second objective of improving psychosocial competency is that young people equipped with the tools or resources that enable them to feel good about themselves, to actively confront the challenges of growing up, to seek positive solutions to interpersonal and intrapersonal conflicts, and to plan ahead, will be less likely to engage in future drug abuse.

Drug treatment can be divided into three phases. The initial phase involves confronting resistances to treatment, establishing motivation, and setting goals for personal growth and future drug use. The second phase involves working through intrapersonal and interpersonal conflicts, which can be both a cause and a consequence of drug abuse. Psychoeducational learning experiences are utilized in phase two to improve psychosocial competency. Phase three, the aftercare or follow-up phase, consists of developing and carrying out a plan to maintain treatment gains and to prevent relapse into drug abuse. Family participation is encouraged in all three phases of treatment. Both hospital and nonhospital programs follow a similar sequence. Phoenix House, a special residence treatment home for adolescent drug abuse, is described in Box 8-2.

Adolescents usually are brought into treatment by their parents, who are exhausted from dealing with drug-abuse problems. In many cases, parents have been required to seek treatment by school authorities or juvenile officials because of social conduct problems or deficiencies in school conduct, including being apprehended using drugs on the school campus. Young people who are forced into drug-treatment programs, by parents or other adult authority figures, often show considerable resistance in the form of denial, deception, externalization of blame, and minimization of drug abuse. They claim their parents are overacting, making their lives miserable, and are trying to limit their freedom and fun; "all the kids around here get high, my parents drink, so why can't I smoke a little pot once in a while."

An effective way of handling initial resistance is through peer confrontation in group sessions. Since peers further along in the treatment program have already been through the process of denial, deception, and externalization of blame, they have the credibility based on real-life experience, which is helpful in breaking through the resistances to honest self-assessment. With honest self-assessment, adolescents can begin to examine the role of drugs in their lives, evaluate the positive and negative consequences of drug use, look at the factors that led them into drug use, admit there is a problem, and consider making a commitment to stop using. Internal motivation is the most important element in drug treatment. Until young people accept responsibility for their behavior and gradually make a commitment to

Box 8-2

PHOENIX HOUSE: A RESIDENTIAL TREATMENT CENTER FOR ADOLESCENT DRUG ABUSE

Phoenix House is a long-term group home or residential treatment center for young people who have an extensive history of drug abuse. The treatment approach of Phoenix House is based on the milieu of the therapeutic community model. Treatment generally lasts up to 12 months. Phoenix Houses are operated by the Phoenix House Foundation headquartered in New York. Six treatment centers in New York and four in California are part of over 100 residential centers in the United States based on the therapeutic community model. The Phoenix House Foundation operates the largest number of residential drug-treatment facilities for adults and adolescents in America. The first Phoenix House was opened in 1967. Phoenix House uses a combination of group pressure, psychotherapy, support, and peer counseling to help young people recover from drug problems, rebuild their shattered self-esteem, and cope with the pain and fears that caused them to return to drugs. In an environment of openness, trust, caring confrontation, and continual self-evaluation, young people learn to believe in their competence and value as human beings. A level system based on behavioral reinforcement (similar to the one used in many hospital drug-treatment programs) is used to facilitate gradual reentry into the larger community. In the beginning of the program, residents have very few privileges. As they progress through the stages of treatment and demonstrate that they can handle responsibility, their privileges and outside activities increase. The success rate is 85% for young people who stay a whole year. For those who leave early, against medical advice, the rate of success falls below 20%. Many Phoenix House residents have unsuccessfully tried short-term treatment programs in the past (Wilford, 1981; Brown, 1987).

change, very little in the way of positive growth is likely to occur. For most young people, the negative consequences of family conflict, peer rejection, social conduct problems, depression, guilt, and mood swings far outweigh the feel-good effects of drugs.

By the time young people enter treatment programs, drug abuse is not the only major problem. In addition to drug abuse, they usually are experiencing family turmoil, have low self-esteems, and possess unresolved feelings of anger, shame, guilt, and self-blame. They may also be experiencing peer conflict and rejection; a deteriorating school performance; and in some cases, trouble with juvenile authorities. These issues need to be sorted out and priorities established in terms of how the issues should be addressed. A comprehensive medical examination should be included in phase one. Young people who are high-frequency, high-intensity drug users may be suffering physical side effects and nutritional deficits caused by poor eating habits.

The lethargy and reduced mental and physical energy, which often appears in young people who have been abusing drugs, may be partly due to a lack of balanced nutrition and exercise.

Phase two can be considered the work phase or recovery phase. There are two major objectives in phase two: (1) to work through the issues that have contributed to substance abuse and resolve the adverse consequences of family, personal, and social conflicts that have come about as the result of drug abuse; and (2) to initiate new learning and growth experiences.

Feelings of inadequacy and inferiority, residuals of guilt, shame, fear, and anger from preadolescent experiences and from underlying motivations contributing to drug abuse can be identified, brought to the surface, and worked through in individual, group, and family therapy. Effective family therapy can create a more nurturant climate at home, and can allow the family to function as a mutual support system. The adverse consequences in family, peer, and school relationships, which have been created as a result of drug behaviors, generate additional stresses that often intensify drug use as a way of coping. To break the maladaptive cycle of coping with stress by escaping into drugs, new conflict resolution skills, problem-solving strategies, and ways of viewing self need to be developed.

New learning and growth in psychosocial competency are facilitated by exposing the adolescent to a planned sequence of psychoeducational experiences. The psychoeducational approach is designed to clarify values, to improve communication, coping, and problem-solving skills, to establish goals and a sense of direction, to increase awareness of cues that trigger drug use, to build support systems, to explore nonchemical highs, and to develop stress-reduction methods, such as progressive relaxation and meditation. Lectures that realistically and accurately discuss the psychological and pharmacological effects of the major psychoactive drugs are presented. Old beliefs about the necessity of using drugs to feel good about self, to create excitement and adventure, and to block-out unpleasant feelings can be replaced with new self-statements and beliefs that eliminate the necessity for drugs as part of one's life-style. Drug-free alternatives for feeling good, relaxing, or pursuing adventure can be substituted for chemical substances. New behaviors and beliefs are practiced and rehearsed in role plays, psychodramas, and real-life experiences. Young people are provided with the opportunity to publicly commit themselves, in group sessions, to nondrug use or nonabuse, and to hear testimony from others struggling to resist peer pressures and personal desires to resume old drug-abuse habits. Reinforcement for change from significant others strengthens new behaviors. Some programs incorporate the 12 steps of Alcoholics Anonymous (AA) into the growth and recovery process. The 12 steps, which are the guiding principles of AA's "one day at a time" philosophy for continuing sobriety and growth, have been adapted for young people and are shown in Table 8-5.

Table 8-5. The Twelve Steps of AA[a] Adapted for Young People

1. We admitted we were powerless over alcohol—that our lives had become unmanageable.
2. We came to believe that a Power greater than ourselves could restore us to sanity.
3. We made a decision to turn our will and our lives over to the care of God, as we understood Him.
4. We made a searching and fearless moral inventory of ourselves.
5. We admitted to God, to ourselves, and to another human being the exact nature of our wrongs.
6. We were entirely ready to have God remove all these defects of character.
7. We humbly asked Him to remove our shortcomings.
8. We made a list of all persons we had harmed, and became willing to make amends to them all.
9. We made direct amends to such people wherever possible, except when to do so would injure them or others.
10. We continued to take personal inventory and when we were wrong, promptly admitted it.
11. We sought through prayer and meditation to improve our conscious contact with God, as we understood Him, praying only for knowledge of His will for us and the power to carry that out.
12. Having had a spiritual awakening as the result of these steps, we tried to carry this message to alcoholics and to practice these principles in all our affairs.

aAdapted from: Nelson, D. D. & Nolan, J. T. (1983). *Young winners' way: A twelve step guide for teenagers.* Minneapolis, MN: Comp Care Publications. Inquiries should be addressed to Comp Care Publications, 2415 Annapolis Lane, Minneapolis, MN 55441, or call toll free 1-800-328-3330.

Setbacks or relapses are most likely to occur in the aftercare or follow-up stage, especially with adolescents who have participated in hospital-based programs. Growth does not always follow a straight line, and setbacks can be expected. During the work or recovery phase, adolescents have the ongoing support of staff members and other patients who are at various stages of recovery. Without this ongoing support, many adolescents eventually start abusing drugs again when they hang around with their old friends and at familiar hangouts. To avoid drug-abuse relapses, it is necessary to plan ahead. Good aftercare-planning has three components: maintenance of a support system, recognition of relapse warning signs, and the development of a relationship with a primary resource person. Adolescents who want to continue nonabusive drugs need to be connected with a support system that encourages and provides reinforcement for drug-free living. Reinforcement for continuing growth or sobriety and validation of one's self as a person can come from others who have gone through drug-abuse programs, are not ashamed of past problems with drugs and alcohol, and are trying to meet the challenges of growing up without abusing drugs. Organizations such as AA and Tough Love, youth centers, teen hot lines, and drug-abuse programs can usually connect teenagers to long-term aftercare support groups.

Some of the early warning relapse signs adolescents need to be taught to recognize are being dishonest with one's self, justifying or rationalizing how one can resume using drugs frequently without abuse, drifting back to old drug-abusing peers, expecting life to be perfect and becoming depressed or angry when it isn't, and denying that one has to worry about drug abuse anymore. Finally, young people in the aftercare phase need to develop a relationship with a resource person, counselor, or therapist they can meet with periodically to discuss the concerns of growing up, and who will be immediately available if an emergency arises. It may be necessary for some young people to go through the treatment program a second time to make a genuine commitment to resolve drug abuse and to improve the chances of success.

PREVENTION

Drug-abuse prevention is based on the rationale that anticipatory measures can be taken in advance to control the use and abuse of drugs by adolescents. There are two broad categories of drug-abuse prevention. The first seeks to create values, attitudes, and behaviors conducive to abstinence or moderation in drug use by moral persuasion, dissemination of factual information about the effects of drugs, and social competency promotion. The goal is to reduce the demand for drugs among young people as consumers. This approach is similar to a consumer education or informed decision-making model and has been labeled drug education and preventive drug education. The second approach is oriented toward controlling drug use by legislative mandate and law enforcement, restricting the supply, manufacture, and sale of chemical substances, and by developing clear community and social standards defining the appropriate use or nonuse of drugs. This approach has been called social-policy prevention (Bell, 1985).

Preventive Drug Education

Three major drug education strategies have been utilized during this century: (1) moral persuasion, (2) dissemination of factual knowledge, and (3) social competency promotion. The first approach which was popular early in the century and continued until the 1960s featured a combination of moralizing, scare tactics, and persuasion. Young people were admonished to refrain from using psychoactive drugs because they were dangerous. Drugs caused moral decay and were injurious to physical and mental health. No attempt was made to distinguish between soft drugs, such as marijuana and alcohol, and hard drugs, such as heroin. All drugs were considered to be a social menace. The message delivered in numerous lectures, pamphlets, and films, such as "Reefer Madness," an antidrug film produced in 1936, was that the first drink or the first marijuana cigarette could start an adolescent on the road to ultimate physical, psychological, and moral deterioration (Martz, 1986). The moral persuasion approach has been discredited for several reasons. Young people who were experimenting with drugs quickly discovered that one drink or marijuana cigarette did not inevitably lead them to moral and physical deterioration. Exaggerated claims of danger create a credibility gap between adults and young people, which can lead to ridicule and rejection of adult advice about drugs that are really dangerous. College students now regard films such as "Reefer Madness" a social comedy rather than serious dialogue about the menace of drugs. Other young people pay no attention to adults who tell them that drugs like PCP and crack are, in fact, dangerous. Scare tactics can backfire and create the opposite effects. Efforts to instill a fear of drugs by heightening excitement can activate risk-taking and adventure-seeking behaviors. Part of the passage through adolescence is seeking new adventures and confronting the unknown. Lastly, attempts to deceive young people by presenting personal moral beliefs as objective evidence is likely to increase the generation gap regarding attitudes towards drugs (Jones and Bell-Bolek, 1986).

The second approach to drug education consists of disseminating factual knowledge about the psychological and pharmacological effects of drugs. This approach assumes that young people who are aware and knowledgeable about the health, legal, and psychological consequences of drug abuse and who care about their health and future will be less likely to experiment with drugs (Jones and Bell-Bolek, 1986). The factual knowledge approach was widely used in high schools, from the mid-1950s until the late 1970s, as part of social studies, and of health and safety classes. In many school districts, drug-abuse education was mandatory. Few students were able to pass through the public high schools during this period without some form of drug education. No convincing evidence has been presented that teaching students about the pharmacological properties and the mind and mood effects of psychoactive drugs reduces or eliminates use and abuse. Some studies suggest that simplified pharmacological courses for high school students can have unintended or, in some cases, reverse effects. Students find their curiosity is aroused and want to try out the mood and mind effects of drugs. Students who were already using drugs were unaffected (Hanson, 1980). By the time students reach high school, many have already started to experiment with drugs, and often know more about certain drugs than their parents or teachers. They are more likely to listen to their peers or to form attitudes about drug use from their own experiences rather than from what they hear in a classroom. This suggests that drug-education programs designed to foster attitudes and beliefs by presenting information should begin prior to high school, possibly as early as the fifth grade. Preadolescents are starting to get pressures to use psychoactive substances, but they are at the age where heavy use is not common and their beliefs are still somewhat pliant (Rice, 1984).

Social Competency Promotion

The social-competency approach to drug education, which came into vogue in the 1980s, moves beyond fear arousal and the dissemination of pharmacological information. Social-competency promotion incorporates the best of what appears to work in humanistic education and adolescent drug-treatment programs. Learning by discovery, active participation, modeling, personal commitment, and peer support are emphasized. Young people are given the opportunity to define their needs and goals, and to talk about what drugs mean to them rather than being told what they "should" do, or what drugs "should" mean to them. Through group discussions, role plays, lectures, psychodramas, and other psychoeducational activities, young people are provided with opportunities to increase their skills in positive risk taking, problem solving, coping, decision making, and conflict resolution; they are taught methods of stress reduction and relaxation, communication, and of restructuring their negative beliefs; they are shown ways of developing supportive relationships and drug-free alternatives for feeling good, serene, or confident, ways of saying no without condemning others who use, and ways of defining their own level of use or nonuse of drugs. Young people are not told not to take drugs. The social competency promotion approach is built on the assumption that if young people feel good about themselves and are equipped with the resources to accomplish their goals, they will make responsible decisions about drug use. Self-confident, resourceful young people who have positive relationships with others are less likely to engage in the maladaptive use of drugs and are not likely to need drugs to control negative moods, such as depression.

LeCoq and Capuzzi (1984) have developed a social competency-prevention program consisting of eight sessions, which can be utilized as part of a high school program of drug-abuse prevention. The program is not designed to totally prevent drug use but to facilitate the building of skills identified as helpful to adolescents at the point of making choices regarding substance use and abuse. Students learn to identify and modify coping behaviors, take the responsibility for personal decisions and behavior, integrate values into behavior and daily decision making, focus on long-term goals, and identify patterns of responsible drug use and drug abuse.

In the first session, students attempt to achieve a consensus on what is meant by the terms responsible drug use and drug abuse. The instructor defines terms like self-disclosure and feedback. The homework assignment is to identify environmental pressures to use drugs. In the second session, students discuss environmental pressures to use and how they responded. The instructor provides information on how thoughts, feelings, and behaviors are connected and how behavior flows from inner thoughts and feelings. Students are asked to identify good and bad sources of feelings and how they cope with them. The homework assignment is to monitor good and bad feelings and how they are handled. In the third session, guided imagery and other relaxation techniques are introduced. Students discuss how they coped with positive and negative feelings; they then discuss other ways feelings could have been handled. The homework assignment is to identify major goals. During the fourth session, the discussion focuses on the concept of responsibility for personal choices, and the giving away and keeping of decision-making power. In the fifth session, students identify situations in which they retained power and decision-making responsibility, and situations in which they gave it away. Coping with blame is discussed, and the transactional dyads of "I'm OK-You're OK, You're not OK-I'm OK," etc., are introduced. The sixth session concentrates on enhancing communication and listening skills. Sessions seven and eight focus on self-concept building, strength bombardment, progress toward goals, and how chemical substance use or abuse will hinder goal achievement.

Some social competency programs employ many educational devices: they enlist the aid of student body leaders; they hear testimonials from students who have been habitual users in the past; they appeal to young people to take pride in themselves, and to believe that they can have fun and accomplish their goals without abusing chemical substances; they role-play situations in which parents are trying to justify their drug use, while at the same time forbidding their adolescents to use drugs; they encourage students to make contracts, clearly spelling out the conditions under which they will and will not use drugs, and they prepare adolescents to cope with dysfunctional families (Weisheit, 1984).

Public appearances by celebrities, TV commercials, antidrug messages in teen music, and parent education have also been included in adolescent drug-prevention programs. Growing numbers of athletes, rock stars, actresses, actors, and television personalities are trying to get antidrug messages out to young people. Some of these public personalities have had problems with drugs, some have not. Youth heroes and celebrities are powerful socialization agents whose life-styles and behaviors are frequently emulated by young people. Their visible participation in messages deglamorizing drugs, or announcing that it's okay to say no to drugs, is likely to have an impact on young people who are starting to experiment with drugs. The National Council on Alcoholism and other civic organizations are urging television and radio stations to balance the glamorous, upbeat presentation of alcohol and other psychoactive substances with health, safety, and "say no" messages. Media messages, such as telling young people not to let an intoxicated friend drive home, or how to have fun without using substances, raise consciousness and remind adolescents that there are other alternatives.

The family can be utilized as a key intervention force in adolescent drug-abuse prevention. Although peers have a strong influence on the day-to-day behavior of adolescents, the family, as a primary socialization agent, has an enduring influence that begins long before adolescence and continues into adulthood. Parenting styles as well as family attitudes and behaviors with respect to use and abuse of alcohol and other psychoactive substances, are an important determinant of adolescent substance abuse. The Parent Power Movement of De Kalb County in Georgia, which arose as a result of parental frustration with teenage drug abuse, recommends six principles parents should follow in monitoring teen drug use: (1) parents should ban together in combatting teen substance abuse; (2) parents need to become aware of the frequency, types, and effects of psychoactive substances their children are using; (3) adolescents should be aware of their parents' drug-monitoring activities; (4) parents need to settle on a common set of parental guidelines, and present a united front for behaviors, such as curfews, school attendance, behaviors at rock concerts, etc.; (5) parents should build strong relationships with their children, and share parenting experiences with other families; and (6) parents should take a firm stand on the use and misuse of alcohol and other psychoactive substances (Gullotta and Adams, 1982).

Family Circle magazine (Mann, 1985) recommends that family members take a Drug Buster Pledge promising that family members: (1) will talk openly about the harmful effects psychoactive substances have on the physical, social, and mental health of family members, and that they will continue to share the information with each other, (2) will help each other cope with pressures from adults and young people to use illegal drugs, (3) will talk openly about pressures to try drugs at parties and do something to help others who are in danger of drug or alcohol dependence, (4) will make a commitment to avoid illegal drug use and follow a rule of no use of alcohol by family members under the state's legal drinking age, except on those occasions specified as permissible under state law (e.g., religious ceremonies), and (5) will listen and help if anyone in the family has problems with drugs or alcohol, without getting angry, and will do whatever is necessary to stop any member of the family from using chemical substances excessively. Other prevention programs focus on parenting skills, especially parents of elementary and junior high school students; these skills include communication, active listening, family problem solving, participation in childrens' activities, and expressions of love and interest.

One of the ironic outcomes of the increased awareness of drug abuse among children and teenagers is that young people are starting to turn parents in to law-enforcement authorities for drug abuse. This has created a dilemma for drug-prevention experts and drug-abuse counselors since they're not quite sure they want kids turning in their parents to the police for using illegal drugs, such as cocaine and marijuana. Some young people think their parents' use of illegal drugs is cool and emulate them, others are upset, frightened, and confused by their parents' behavior. More and more, teachers conducting drug-abuse classes are facing questions such as, "My parents use cocaine, what should I do about it?" As they tentatively work their way through this family mine field, drug counselors are suggesting that young people concerned about their parent's drug use seek drug hot lines, relatives or family friends, health care professionals, or try to talk to their parents diplomatically to let them know they are concerned (Beck, 1986).

Social Policy on Prevention

The social policy approach to prevention is designed to control drug use, through legislation and law enforcement, by restricting the sale, manufacture, and distribution of chemical substances, and by developing clear social standards and rules that define the appropriate use or nonuse of drugs. The social policy approach rests on two assumptions: (1) restricting the manufacture, sale, and distribution of drugs will affect the consumer, and (2) the use and abuse of psychoactive substances can be changed by instituting rules and standards that restrict the conditions or places where drug use or abuse can occur.

Law enforcement has not been a highly successful approach to controlling adolescent drug use. Beginning with the passage of the Pure Food and Drug Act in 1906, state and federal governments have passed a variety of laws restricting the sale and use of liquor and other psychoactive substances. All but eight states forbid the sale of alcohol to persons under 21, and no state permits the commercial sale of marijuana. Despite these laws, most young people have experimented with marijuana or alcohol. College administrators have been unsuccessful in their attempts to control the drinking behavior of students under 21. A medical prescription is required for the purchase of controlled substances, such as powerful stimulants, depressants, and barbiturates; yet, most of these substances can be easily purchased on high school campuses. Drug busts by police are periodically conducted on high school campuses, using youthful-looking undercover agents. After the controversy surrounding the bust subsides, most students return to their original levels of use or abuse, but connections for drug purchases are not easily established. Peter Du Pont, the former governor of Delaware, who was a candidate for the 1988 Republican presidential nomination, has called for mandatory drug testing of all high school students (Duffy, 1986; Mashek, 1986). His rationale is that if states can require vaccinations for children before they enter school, they can require drug testing while they are in school. From time to time, police and governmental officials announce major crackdowns on drug pushers, growers, manufacturers, and suppliers. Elaborate publicity campaigns are mounted in the media announcing tougher penalties for violators, the burning of marijuana fields, and tougher border surveillance to reduce the quantity of cocaine entering the United States. Despite these efforts, the flow of street drugs does not show any sign of disappearing.

Family, school districts, community groups, and peer networks, acting alone or in concert, can develop social policies, rules, and standards defining the appropriate and inappropriate use of psychoactive drugs. For example, a high school district could initiate a policy prohibiting the use of alcohol, marijuana, or other substances on the school bus or in the school building. Parents, school administrators, student body leaders, and peers could agree that use of drugs or alcohol would not be permitted at school dances, athletic events, or extracurricular activities. A family might permit alcohol to be served at family holiday dinners or festivities, but not at teen parties. The rules set the boundaries for what is acceptable and unacceptable substance use.

Once the rules are formulated and clearly communicated, the stage is set for three consequences. First, users can be warned when they are approaching the boundary line. Second, teenagers who cross the boundary line can be given assistance in the form of counseling and guidance. Third, debate is likely to be stimulated among members of the designated group. Prohibiting drugs at school functions or testing high school athletes for substance abuse encourages debate among students about the pros and cons of drugs and may cause some students to think seriously about the role of drugs in their life. For the rules to be successful in the long run, the target group must explicitly and implicitly support the rules (Bell, 1985). If no consensus exists in support of the rules, young people will continue to use and abuse substances. For example, many college students, both those under 21 and those over 21, do not support rules prohibiting students under 21 from drinking at campus-related functions. Therefore, students freely violate the rules. Prohibition of alcohol in the United States is a classic example of a policy that did not have support in the population. In time, Prohibition became a worse social problem than the alcohol it prohibited.

The War on Drugs, initiated by President and Mrs. Reagan in 1986, contains elements of traditional drug education, social competency promotion, and social policy prevention (Duffy, 1986; Dolan, 1986). The Reagans' national crusade to create a drug-free society included a promise of stricter enforcement of existing laws, severe penalties for violations, and new legislation to control the supply and distribution of illegal substances. Mrs. Reagan's "Just Say No" program concentrates on drug prevention in children 7 to 12 years of age by using a combination of social competency promotion, drug education, peer pressure, and willingness to make a public commitment to abstain. The philosophy of the "Just Say No" program is that younger children can be diverted from substance use by building a peer culture and a community consensus that supports not using. Young people are taught specific skills that help them to feel good without using drugs

(Adams et al., 1985). No systematic evaluation of the effects of the War on Drugs has been conducted.

There are no simple solutions to the problem of drug-abuse prevention. To be successful over the long term, drug prevention programs must build a consensus among young people regarding standards for use and abuse. To think that the experimental and social-recreational use of alcohol and marijuana can be completely stopped is unrealistic. As long as adults continue to model legal and illegal drugs for recreational and coping purposes, young people will emulate their behavior. Reducing drug abuse, however, can be accomplished by using social learning principles that involve modeling, active participation, peer reinforcement, and the relevance of behavior to personal goals. This is how drug use is learned; therefore, the same process can be used to prevent drug abuse.

For example, LSD was very popular among young people in the 1960s. Turning-on to psychedelic trips was the in thing. Psychedelic trips held the promise of deeper insights, peace, fulfillment, and transcendence. Over time, young people learned the disastrous consequences of bad trips, flashbacks, and burnout. There is now a negative attitude toward LSD in the youth culture, and little reinforcement for seeking discovery, adventure, or fulfillment by taking acid trips. Consequently, the abuse and recreational use of LSD has declined significantly. The central issue here is that once young people perceive a drug as dangerous, or that it no longer fits into their posture of being cool or sociable, they begin to back away from it. Statistics indicating downward trends and leveling-off effects in the use of marijuana and other drugs suggest that young people may be having second thoughts about drug involvement (Musto, 1986; Johnston, 1985).

When perceptions emerge, from direct experience, modeling, peer reinforcement, and personal discovery, that certain behaviors are not acceptable or congruent with one's goals, they are likely to be believed and thereby influence future drug behavior. Youth drug experts need to concentrate on helping young people discover, through peer support, role modeling, and active participation in goal setting, that abusing drugs is not cool, that it can interfere with reaching goals, and that it may cause rejection by peers. Antidrug beliefs cannot be forced on young people, explicitly or implicitly; they must perceive that abusing drugs is not in their best interest and is not supported by the peer culture.

SUMMARY AND CONCLUSIONS

Psychoactive drugs are natural and synthetic chemical substances that can be used to alter moods, thought processes, feelings, and behavior. The eight most common clusters of psychoactive drugs used and abused by teenagers are alcohol, marijuana, stimulants, depressants, hallucinogens or psychedelics, heroin, and inhalants. The experimental and social use of drugs by young people in America appears to be part of the rites-of-passage. Over 91.3% of late adolescents have tried alcohol, 58% have experimented with marijuana or other illegal drugs, 4% use marijuana daily, 4.8% use alcohol daily, and 37% participate in heavy drinking at parties.

Society sends young people conflicting messages about the use of psychoactive drugs. Teenagers are bombarded with messages of instant relief from boredom, anxiety, restlessness, and stress through alcohol and drugs. Drugs are associated with adventure, curiosity, and fun, and are glamorized as sexy, masculine, feminine, and grown-up. Conversely, millions of dollars are spent annually on prevention programs that urge young people to abstain, to say "no," and to exercise constraint. Adolescent drug use involves a mixture of motives: curiosity and adventure, becoming one of the crowd, personal enjoyment, enhanced sensuousness, mood control, and the search for spiritual enlightenment. Five patterns of adolescent drug use have been identified: (1) experimental, (2) social-recreational, (3) circumstantial-situational, (4) intensified, and (5) compulsive. These patterns form a continuum from mild-to-moderate and then to severe drug use. The dividing line between drug use and drug abuse is determined by frequency, intensity or quantity of drugs consumed, degree of preoccupation with drugs as part of one's life-style, and maladaptive consequences. Adolescent drug abusers frequently use drugs in large quantities, tend to be preoccupied with their use, and are often in conflict with family, friends, and school authorities as a result of their drug use.

The four major factors commonly associated with drug abuse are: (1) sociocultural, (2) family interaction, (3) peer relationships, and (4) personal characteristics. The consensus among drug experts is that substance abuse results from the interaction of several factors, rather than from one factor alone. As the number of risk factors increases, so does the likelihood of drug abuse. Drug treatment programs for adolescents have two primary objectives: (1) to completely eliminate substance use or to significantly reduce the frequency and amount of drugs consumed, and (2) to help adolescents develop the psychosocial competency tools to lead a drug-free life.

Drug-abuse prevention is based on the rationale that anticipatory measures can be taken in advance to control the abuse of drugs by adolescents. There are two broad categories of drug-abuse prevention: (1) drug education and (2) social policy prevention. Drug education seeks to create values, attitudes, and beliefs conducive to abstinence or moderation by moral persuasion, by dissemination of factual information, and by social competency promotion. Social policy prevention is oriented toward enacting legislation, restricting the supply of drugs, and developing community standards for use and nonuse.

Attempts to indoctrinate teenagers or to scare them into drug abstinence have been largely unsuccessful. Rules and standards are not likely to be successful in the long run, unless there is a supportive consensus within the target group. Beliefs and standards about drug use and consumption patterns cannot be mandated by adults. Values, beliefs, and standards are internalized and owned by young people who arrive at them through dialogue, modeling, active participation, direct experience, and peer reinforcement. Once young people believe that certain drugs are dangerous, or that it is in their best interest to control their use of psychoactive substances, they will behave accordingly. To build the kind of consensus essential for reducing adolescent drug abuse, adults need to involve young people in an active dialogue regarding appropriate standards for use and nonuse so that their beliefs will be reflected in the planning and implementation of drug-prevention programs.

The adolescent drug problem in America cannot be resolved without confronting adult drug use and abuse. No amount of drug prevention can disguise the fact that adults in our society use and abuse excessive amounts of legal and illegal psychoactive substances. As long as adults continue to model the use of psychoactive substances as a way of seeking fun, companionship, serenity, stress reduction, pain relief, and fulfillment, young people will follow their example. It is the adults who are not sure whether psychological well-being and fulfillment should come through hard work, delayed gratification, struggle, and pain, or through instant gratification provided by psychopharmacology. While there may be no clear solution to this dilemma, it is a question that must become part of the ongoing debate on adolescent drug use and abuse. The answer is not in the quick fixes offered by periodic "wars" on drugs. Telling the truth about legal and illegal drug use will work, in the long run, far better than hypocritical overstatements about the dangers of drugs by self-righteous adults. The challenge before us as teachers, mental health workers, parents, and drug experts is to develop an open discussion between the generations that will allow a rational, honest dialogue to take place on the use and abuse of drugs.

SUGGESTIONS FOR PARENTS, TEACHERS, COUNSELORS, AND YOUTH WORKERS

1. As a parent, do not wait for a crisis to develop before initiating discussions about drugs. Since drugs are a part of the adolescent culture and also a part of adult society, sooner or later your child is going to have an encounter with drugs. Discussion should begin prior to adolescence, and should allow for an honest exchange of ideas and standard-setting.
2. Learn to recognize the early warning signs of drug abuse, such as mood swings, drug paraphernalia, appearing drunk without traces of an odor of alcohol, deteriorating school grades, a change from mainstream to

unconventional peers, thefts of objects that can be converted into cash, missing liquor, and the like. Additional signs are listed in Tables 8-3 and 8-4. Have a frank discussion with the adolescent about these signs, and be prepared to initiate referral to a drug counselor.

3. Parents and young people should try to attend at least one program on drug prevention together. This is a good way to open up a continuing dialogue, not only about drugs but about other important parent–adolescent issues, such as coping skills, sex, drug-free alternatives for feeling good, goal setting, problem solving, decision making, and caring.

4. As a parent, reassess your use of alcohol, prescription drugs, and nonprescription drugs. What kind of model are you setting for feeling good, coping, and controlling moods through chemicals?

5. If you are a teacher or a counselor, find out what kind of drug prevention or treatment programs exist in your school, agency, or community. If you can find the time, get involved. One of the best ways to become more knowledgeable about teen drug problems and how you can help, is through active participation.

6. Personal competency, family support, and peer reinforcement are three of the factors associated with adolescent drug abuse. What can you do to help young people feel more secure, more able to cope with the demands of adolescent living, and more willing to use drug-free alternatives in peer interaction?

7. There is no guarantee that your child will not become involved in experimenting with drugs at some point in time. Keep the lines of communication open, be patient, and try to encourage responsible decision-making.

8. Suggestions for starting a parent drug prevention group or for developing a drug prevention program in your community can be obtained from (a) National Federation of Parents for Drug Free Youth, P.O. Box 57217, Washington, DC 20037 — Telephone: 1-800-554-KIDS, and (b) National Institute on Drug Abuse, P.O. Box 2305, Rockville, MD 20852.

9. The Will Rogers Institute has a series of booklets on the effects, composition, motives, treatment, and consequences of psychoactive drugs. You can obtain these free booklets by writing to Will Rogers Institute, 785 Mamaroneck Avenue, White Plains, NY 10605 — Telephone: 914-761-5550 or 212-931-1211.

10. The following readings are recommended for those who wish to learn more about adolescent drug abuse and how to cope with it:

(a) 800 COCAINE, by Mark Gold, M.D., founder of the nationwide 800-COCAINE hotline. Send $2.95, plus $1 for postage and handling, to: Bantam Books, Inc., 666 Fifth Ave., New York, NY 10103.

(b) *Getting Tough on Gateway Drugs: A Guide for the Family*, by Robert L. DuPont, Jr., M.D., founding director of the National Institute on Drug Abuse and president of the American Council for Drug Education. Send $13.50, plus $1.75 for postage and handling, to: American Council for Drug Education, 5820 Hubbard Dr., Rockville, MD 20852.

(c) *Marijuana Alert*, by Peggy Mann. Send $10.95 for paperback, plus $1.90 for postage and handling, to: McGraw-Hill, Dept. PL, 1221 Ave. of the Americas, New York, NY 10020.

(d) *Not My Kid*, by Beth Polson and Miller Newton, Ph.D. Send $2.95, plus 75 cents for postage and handling, to: Avon Books, 1790 Broadway, New York, NY 10019. Attn: Lorraine Buckley.

DISCUSSION QUESTIONS

1. What are some of the major value conflicts in American society underlying the adolescent drug problem, and how do these conflicts influence the use and abuse of drugs?

2. What are the major psychological, pharmaceutical, and legal differences between the so-called soft drugs and hard drugs?

3. What are some of the motives teenagers give for initiating drug use, and describe the major patterns of drug use? Explain the major factors associated with the habitual high-frequency, high-intensity use of drugs.

4. Describe three or four ways of feeling good, serene, and joyful, or of experiencing a sense of discovery and fascination that can occur without drugs. Why are nondrug alternatives not appealing to many adolescents?

5. Describe some of the major warning signs that signal an adolescent may be abusing drugs. How should parents deal with concerns involving the abuse of drugs by one of their children?

6. Explain the major phases and goals of an adolescent drug treatment program. Why is aftercare such a critical phase of treatment?

7. Discuss the rationale underlying the three major drug education approaches. What are the strengths and weaknesses of each approach, and what sorts of revisions would you suggest for each approach?

8. What is social policy prevention, what is the key element in making it work, and why do adolescents need to be included in social policy prevention decisions?

9. Explain drug use, abuse, treatment, and prevention from a perspective of social learning theory and psychosocial competency.

10. The issues, conflicts, and controversies surrounding adolescent drug use and abuse have been with us for some time and will exist in the future. Why are these issues, conflicts, and controversies so persistent?

11. Discuss the major factors that should be taken into consideration in planning and implementing a drug-prevention program for high school students.

9
Juvenile Delinquency

PREVIEW

Juvenile delinquency is a legal term used to designate lawbreaking by minors. Each year between 4% and 5% of American teenagers, or approximately 1,300,000, are referred to the courts for suspected offenses other
than traffic violations. Most referrals to court are usually made by the
police. Approximately twice as many young people come into contact with
the police for suspected offenses; most are ignored, counseled, or released
without being arrested, or are diverted to community agencies for a variety
of services.

Juvenile delinquency is a much more complicated, ambiguous phenomenon than the seemingly straightforward definition of lawbreaking by minors
suggests. Delinquency does not have a single meaning; it covers a wide range
of behaviors from running away to murder. A clear picture of the scope of
delinquent behavior cannot be derived from simple statistics on arrest records or juvenile court cases because of the many kinds of delinquency. There
are status as opposed to nonstatus offenders, occasional versus repeat offenders, major offenders versus minor offenders, hidden versus recorded
delinquents, arrested delinquents as opposed to counseled and released or
diverted delinquents; and those adjudicated by the court and labeled delinquent. Much adolescent lawbreaking is episodic, transitory, and minor.
Some degree of rebellion, testing the limits, and experimenting with behaviors that violate adult rules are expected parts of the process of establishing
independence and autonomy.

At one time or another, delinquency has been attributed to urbanization,
working mothers, aggressiveness, too little or too much punishment, peer

influence, rebellion, unresponsive schools, too much television, poor impulse controls, and community disorganization. The list could be expanded indefinitely. Most of the essential factors correlating with serious, repeat delinquency can be incorporated into two major theories of delinquency: a psychological and a sociocultural theory. According to the psychological theory, delinquent behavior is symptomatic of an emotional disturbance that comes about as a result of unresolved conflicts in psychosocial development. Sociocultural or sociogenic theories assume that delinquent behavior evolves from a normal social learning process through reinforcement, imitation, and identification with antisocial role models and influences. The psychological-emotional disturbance view of delinquency was popular from early in the 20th century to the 1960s. The therapies derived from the psychological view are concerned with working through underlying feelings, motives, thoughts, and conflicts. The sociocultural model currently in vogue emphasizes treatment approaches that focus on reinforcing prosocial behaviors and making social systems more responsive to the needs of the individual.

The juvenile justice system is an umbrella term for the major organizational structure society has put in place to deal with juvenile offenders. The juvenile justice system consists of the police, juvenile courts, community-based programs, and custodial institutions or homes. The first juvenile court was founded in Illinois in 1899. The original purpose of the juvenile court was to guide and rehabilitate rather than to punish youths or lawbreakers. The juvenile justice system has a wide range of options in determining what happens to young people accused of delinquent behavior. Youths apprehended or cited for misconduct can be ignored, counseled and released, referred to community agencies, arrested and detained, placed on probation, or adjudicated and sent to custodial facilities. A storm of criticism of the juvenile justice system has led to a series of reforms and counter-reforms over the past 20 years. On one hand, youths now enjoy a greater range of legal rights. On the other hand, there is greater concern for protecting the public, and one's responsibility and accountability for his or her behavior and its consequences.

Some experts on delinquency are involved in prevention. A number of prevention programs across the country are demonstrating that it is possible to ward off delinquency by spending money ahead of time to teach prosocial behaviors and to work with key socialization systems and primary social groups, such as the family, peer groups, educational systems, and community action programs.

Case Example 9-1: Reggie

Reggie is a 16-year-old high school dropout who was placed in a locked, juvenile correctional institution for a period not to exceed 9 months. Reggie's custodial placement was the result of a juvenile court petition in which he was charged with breaking and entering, robbery, and parole violation, offenses in which he admitted involvement. Reggie first started getting into trouble with the juvenile authorities at age 12 when he was accused of assaulting two women during a "purse-snatching" incident. He was diverted to a family counseling program and required to perform 80 hours of community service. Reggie's father is an accountant and his mother is a teacher in a college of fashion and design. Reggie describes himself as a "bad ass." He claims to have committed numerous illegal acts the police don't know about. He thinks his parents believe that hanging around with the wrong people is the source of his many difficulties with established authority and the law. As an elementary and junior high school student, Reggie was constantly involved in fighting, defiant of school authorities, and occasionally truant. He was good at sports, but seemed to lack the discipline to practice and cooperate with his teammates and coaches. He wanted to do it his way, or he would quit. By the time Reggie entered high school as a 14-year-old, ninth-grader, he had been back in juvenile court for offenses involving theft, destruction of property, and unauthorized use of an automobile. After a reasonably good attendance period in his first semester of the ninth grade, Reggie stopped attending school on a regular basis. He spent most of his time hanging out with youths, 2 to 3 years older, who were known to the police and juvenile courts as delinquents. As a tenth-grader in a continuation high school, Reggie briefly participated in a work-study program on the advice of his counselor, but did not stay with it. The following summer, Reggie and his friends broke into an appliance store and stole several color TVs, tape recorders, and portable radios. When he was apprehended and brought before the juvenile court, the judge stipulated formal probation with counseling, restitution, community service, and no further lawbreaking. Five months later, Reggie was arrested on charges that led to his present confinement.

SCOPE OF THE PROBLEM

Juvenile delinquency is a legal term used to designate lawbreaking by minors (Gold and Petronio, 1980). In 32 states, minors are legally defined as persons under the age of 18; in 12 states, under 17; and in 6 states, under 16. Juvenile delinquency ranges from major felonies to minor misdemeanors but also involves status offenses. Status offenses, such as running away, truancy, and purchasing liquor, are only violations of the law because of the person's age and legal status as a minor. Juvenile delinquency is a social problem that has received a considerable amount of attention in our society. The public is bombarded with newspaper headlines, magazine articles, and television documentaries about the costs and dangers of delinquent behavior. Polls indicate that most Americans think there has been steady and alarming increase in juvenile crime (Galvin and Polk, 1983). Despite the drama and alarm juvenile lawbreaking has created, actual rates of delinquent behavior have been declining or holding steady since the mid-1970s. After an over 250% increase between 1950 and 1974, the rates of juvenile court cases have stabilized in recent years (Krisberg and Schwartz, 1983).

As mentioned earlier, each year between 4% and 5% of America's teenagers, or approximately 1,300,000, are referred to the courts for suspected offenses other than traffic violations. Referrals to the juvenile court are usually made by the police (Flanagan and McCloud, 1983). Again, approximately twice as many young people come into contact with the police for suspected offenses; most are ignored, counseled, and released without being arrested or are diverted to community agencies for a variety of social services. The juvenile justice system is like a funnel, with the number of juveniles decreasing at each stage of processing and decision making. For those arrested or referred to the court, approximately 50% are handled without formal adjudication through a process called intake, which usually results in outright release. Adolescents are released to parents with recommendations for counseling, diverted to community agencies, or placed on informal probation. Formal adjudication, which in the juvenile court is equivalent to a trial in adult court, can result in formal probation or detention in custodial facilities (Gibbons and Krohn, 1986).

Less than 5% of the 2 million or more youths who annually come into contact with the police for alleged violations of the law, end up in custodial facilities. In 1985 there were 88,414 young people in short-term and long-term juvenile custodial institutions, such as training schools, group homes, and camps in the United States (U.S. Census Bureau, 1987).

Most adolescents who break the law are neither serious nor repeat offenders. Of juvenile arrests, 60.9% are for misdemeanors rather than for serious offenses such as assault, rape, armed robbery, robbery, and arson. The more serious the public regards the behavior, the less teenagers are likely to engage in it. Status offenses, curfew violations, running away, and violations of liquor laws account for one-fifth of adolescent arrests, whereas disorderly conduct, vandalism, drunkenness, and other minor violations of the law account for another 30% (Flanagan et al., 1982). The small group of young people who engage in violent crimes, such as rape, homicide, armed robbery, assault, and arson, are likely to be repeat offenders. Juvenile lawbreaking increases with age and peaks between 14 and 17 (Adams and Gullotta, 1983).

Low-income, minority urban youths are more likely to be arrested than their Anglo, middle-class suburban counterparts. Arrest records for male teenagers are much higher than arrest records for females. The official rates of male-to-female delinquency, which used to run as high as 4 to 1 or 5 to 1, are now closer to 3 to 1 (U.S. Census, 1980). Males commit more than twice as many violent offenses and are more likely to be involved in crimes against property, whereas females are more likely to be apprehended for status offenses, such as sexual promiscuity, running away, incorrigibility, curfew violations, and truancy. The popular notion that crimes committed by adolescent females are becoming more serious is not supported when status offenders are removed from the statistics (Sarri, 1983). The lesser involvement of females in delinquent behavior is usually explained by greater constraints during the socialization process for females and, except for sexual misconduct, a more permissive attitude on the part of juvenile officials. Police and juvenile officials are more willing to handle minor female offenses by counseling and release, rather than process them into the juvenile court system.

Juvenile delinquency is a much more complicated, ambiguous phenomenon than the seemingly straightforward picture presented above suggests. Official records do not reveal the vast amount of hidden delinquency, variations in arrest and enforcement procedures between different legal jurisdictions, nor do they reveal the reasons underlying the higher arrest rates for low-income, urban minority youths. Mild forms of delinquent conduct and lawbreaking are commonplace among teenagers. Self-report studies, confidential interviews, and questionnaires have demonstrated that 80% to 90% of young people engage in delinquent behavior that never comes to the attention of the police or juvenile authorities and thus does not become part of official juvenile delinquency statistics (Gibbons and Krohn, 1986; Gold and Petronio, 1980).

The 1967 Presidential Commission on Law Enforcement and Administration of Justice, estimated that 90% of persons committed at least one act as an adolescent that could have brought them to the attention of juvenile authorities had they been apprehended. Other self-report studies confirm this observation. Under anonymous or confidential conditions, most people will admit to one or more actions, such as teenage sexual behavior, minor shoplifting, using a motor vehicle without the owner's permission, purchasing or consuming alcoholic beverages, experimenting with drugs, curfew violations, and occasional truancy. A list of self-report questions is provided in Table 9-1.

James Short and F. Ivan Nye (1958) carried out a series of studies on hidden delinquency involving several thousand high school students. The overwhelming majority of respondents admitted to one or more delinquent acts. Youths incarcerated in training schools were more likely to be involved in serious misconduct than youths not in custody. Jay Williams and Martin Gold (1972), using a national probability sample of 847 boys and girls between the ages of 13 and 16, found that 88% of their sample admitted to one or more delinquent acts and only 20% had any contact with the police. Relatively few of these young people had been involved in serious or repeated delinquency.

Much of hidden delinquency and, for that matter, officially recorded delinquency by young people is transitory, episodic, and situational. Some degree of rebellion, testing the limits, and experimenting with behaviors that violate adult rules, is to be expected as part of the process of establishing one's independence and autonomy. Adolescence is a time of sorting out

Table 9-1. Delinquency Self-Report Questions[a]

The following questions pertain to activities you did when you were a juvenile, before 18 years of age in most states. It is a general set of questions to be used in estimating the presence of juvenile delinquency. Take the test. Keep in mind that the questions refer only to what you did as a juvenile.

Current Age _____   Sex: Male _____   Female _____

1. Disobeyed your parents, defying them to their face.
       Yes _____ No _____
2. Stole something from a store (shoplift).
       Yes _____ No _____
3. Ran away from home overnight without your parents' permission.
       Yes _____ No _____
4. Stole a car, even if you just drove it around and abandoned it.
       Yes _____ No _____
5. Drove a car before you had a license or learner's permit.
       Yes _____ No _____
6. Took money or other valuables from a person by using force or the threat of force.
       Yes _____ No _____
7. Broke into a building and stole something.
       Yes _____ No _____
8. Defaced, damaged, or destroyed property that did not belong to you or your family.
       Yes _____ No _____
9. Drank alcoholic beverages without your parents' knowledge or permission.
       Yes _____ No _____
10. Had sexual intercourse with someone of the opposite sex (if not married at the time).
       Yes _____ No _____
11. Used illegal drugs, such as marijuana, LSD, cocaine.
       Yes _____ No _____
12. Skipped school without a valid or legitimate excuse.
       Yes _____ No _____

---

[a]Adapted from: Sanders, W. B. (1981). *Juvenile delinquency: Cause, patterns and reactions.* New York: Holt, Rinehart & Winston.

values, questioning existing community norms, and discarding, at least temporarily, previous values and roles that required unquestioned obedience to adult dictates. Furthermore, adolescents have a greater probability of violating the law than do adults, because they are covered by two sets of regulations, status offenses, and nonstatus offenses. A great deal of adolescent misbehavior, such as occasionally cutting school, staying out beyond curfew, minor vandalism, discovering sex, experimenting with alcohol and soft drugs, small thefts, and running away, has a quality of excitement, adventure, and curiosity. Many delinquent acts are committed in groups, in a social-recreational context. Peer group approval is an important determinant of behavior standards and values during adolescence (Riemer, 1981; Covington, 1983). While adults may not admit it publicly, a certain amount of "hell raising" is expected from adolescents and is generally tolerated, unless it crosses the boundary into serious delinquency such as assault, homicide, robbery, rape, or arson.

To further complicate the delinquency picture, there are variations in arrest and enforcement policies in different police districts and, for that matter, within different neighborhoods in the same police district. In some police districts, minor offenders, status offenders, and first offenders are usually counseled and released. In others, the same youths are cited and diverted to community social service agencies. In still other districts, almost all offenders, regardless of the nature of the alleged lawbreaking, are arrested, booked, taken into custody, and referred to juvenile court. Differential diversion, arrest, booking, and referral procedures make official arrest statistics suspect. For example, arrest records are higher for low-income minority urban youths, especially Black males (Gibbons and Krohn, 1986).

Does this mean that minority youths commit more juvenile crime, or are the reported differences in arrest records a reflection of police attitudes toward race and poverty? When a middle-class, suburban white youth takes a car without the owner's permission, it may be regarded as an adolescent prank. When a Black urban male does the same thing, it is likely to be called car theft. Whether or not one is arrested seems to depend on the perceptions and social values of the arresting officers, reputation of the parents, and the manner in which the juvenile interacts with the police.

Many sociologists challenge the perception that low-income minority youths actually commit significantly more juvenile lawbreaking than do higher-income, nonminority youths (Zober, 1981; Gold and Petronio, 1980). The self-report studies reviewed earlier indicate that unreported delinquency is common among all groups of adolescents. Higher-income, white youths and their parents have more resources at their disposal to keep them out of the clutches of the juvenile justice system, such as attorneys, private psychotherapists, boarding schools, psychiatric hospitals, and politically sensitive juvenile authorities. When the class and race bias seemingly inherent in juvenile arrest statistics is taken into consideration, the differences in minor offenses between groups, for the most part, disappears. The remaining data suggest, however, that minority, low-income males are more likely to be repeat offenders and more likely to be involved in serious crimes, such as assault and robbery (Carey and McAnany, 1984).

To summarize briefly, juvenile delinquency is not easy to define. Delinquency covers a wide range of behaviors from purchasing liquor, to promiscuity, to murder. A clear picture of the scope of adolescent delinquent behavior cannot be derived from simple statistics on arrest records or on juvenile court cases because of the many kinds of delinquency. There are status as opposed to nonstatus offenders, occasional versus repeat offenders, minor versus major offenders, hidden versus recorded delinquency, arrested delinquents versus those counseled and released, diverted delinquents, and those adjudicated by the courts and labeled delinquent.

One way to reduce the ambiguity, complexity, and social class bias inherent in different definitions and statistical reports of delinquent behavior is to think of delinquent behavior as spread across a continuum ranging from extreme overconformity to repeated involvement in serious lawbreaking and complete rejection of conventional standards. Based on estimates from numerous studies and analyses of several definitions of delinquent behavior, Ruth Cavan and Theodore Ferdinand (1981) devised the conformity-delinquent continuum shown in Table 9-2, which defines delinquent behavior regardless of variations in law enforcement standards and statistical reporting procedures.

To the far right of the continuum, in areas G and F, are young people who always follow the rules and value extreme goodness. They are likely to be excluded from social activities because their overconformity and extreme goodness make peers nervous. Next to the extreme conformist on the continuum, are the overly conscientious young people, in area E, who avoid misbehaving, are eager to please, and worry excessively over misbehaviors and mistakes. In areas D and C are the teenagers who usually follow the rules but occasionally engage in mild misconduct, status offenses, or episodic delinquency such as shoplifting, marijuana use, truancy, unauthorized automobile use, or theft of small items from work. They do not perceive themselves as delinquents, and their behavior is within the limits generally tolerated by the community. At the far left of the continuum are the status offenders and serious delinquents. The status offenders and minor delinquents are likely to come to the attention of juvenile authorities and youth guidance agencies for runaways, drug use, stealing, truancy leading to school suspensions, sexual promiscuity, and open defiance of adult authority. Their behavior is beyond the tolerance level of the community. They are moving toward a delinquent life-style and the outer limits of mainstream behavior. Because they are at risk for moving into a delinquent life-style, these young people are referred to as early delinquents, predelinquents, or high-risk teenagers. At the extreme left, in area A, are young people who have adopted a delinquent life-style. Only 2% to 3% of American youths fall into this category. They engage in serious, repeated antisocial behavior, which by anyone's definition would be considered delinquent or criminal, such as armed robbery, homicide, assault, major property disturbances, arson, and rape. In a strictly formal sense, the term delinquency can be applied to the behavior of these young people. They are serious, career-oriented lawbreakers.

The teenagers in areas A and B account for most of the young people referred to juvenile courts and subsequently assigned to informal probation, formal probation, and custodial facilities. They are generally known to social service agencies, police officers, and juvenile court officials. Sociocultural and psychological theories of delinquency, which will be discussed in the next section of this chapter, are most likely to apply to the high-risk and delinquent young people in areas A and B. The overwhelming majority of young people fall into the middle of the continuum, in areas C,

Table 9-2. Conformity-Delinquency Continuum[a]

	A Contraculture (delinquent)	B Extreme underconformity	C Minor underconformity	D Normal conformity	E Minor overconformity	F Extreme overconformity	G Contraculture (extreme goodness)
Public attitude	Condemnation; "hard core"	Disapproval	Toleration without approval	Tolerance with approval	A sissy by peers; valued by adults	Extreme overconformity; a real "goody two shoes"	Extreme goodness; seen as saintly
Public reaction	Rejection; school expulsion; commitment to correctional school	Police warnings; school suspension; referrals to social agencies	Disciplinary action by parents or school	Indifference; acceptance; mild reproofs	Some isolation by peers; positive regard by adults	Major social isolation by peers; adults are somewhat uncomfortable	Total isolation by peers; too good to be true by adults
Child's attitude toward public	Rejects values of D	Wavers between acceptance and rejection of D values	Accepts values of D; feels guilt	Accepts values of D; feels no guilt	Anxious to please	Extremely anxious to please adults; avoids own age group	Avoids all contacts with peers

	Self-concept of delinquent	Confused self-concept; marginal to D and A	Views self as misbehaving nondelinquent	Conforming nondelinquent	Anxious and somewhat tense	Never really enjoys anything; living means working hard	Pretends to be an adult; a non-adolescent
Child's attitude toward self							
Examples	Indiscriminate murder	Manslaughter in fight	Negligent homicide	Somewhat careless but no danger to others	Avoids misbehaving Too conscientious Excessive worry over any mistakes	A teacher's pet; assignments always perfect; attendance always perfect; one error is regarded as a catastrophe; upset by an A – grade	Avoids all worldly pleasures May join an isolating religious cult
	Armed robbery; burglary	Larceny of valuables	"Borrowing" to use; pilfering	Minor pilfering			
	Rape; serious sex deviations; promiscuity; prostitution	Promiscuity; minor sex deviations	Extensive normal sex relations	Occasional, normal sex relations			
	Drug addiction	Occasional use of drugs	Smoking marijuana only	Smoke tobacco only			

aAdapted from: Cavan, R. S. & Ferdinand, T. N. (1981). *Juvenile delinquency* (4th ed.). New York: Harper & Row.

D, and E. They generally do not come to the attention of the courts or police officers and should not be considered delinquents. Their behavior is within the tolerance range of the community, even if some of their misconduct technically violates the law. If they are apprehended by the police or brought to the attention of the courts, minor episodic or transitory behavior usually is involved. They are generally counseled and released to their parents, or diverted away from the juvenile justice system into community social service programs. The misconduct of these young people is part of the normal adolescent passage. The misconduct usually occurs only once or twice and should not be labeled delinquent.

PSYCHOLOGICAL AND SOCIOCULTURAL THEORIES OF DELINQUENCY

Juvenile delinquency has been associated with multiple factors. At one time or another delinquent behavior has been attributed to aggressiveness, a low IQ, inadequate parent–child interaction, unresponsive schools, too much television, divorce, working mothers, interethnic conflict, urbanization, too little punishment, too much punishment, changing adult morality and values, adolescent rebellion, poor nutrition, reinforcement of deviant standards, overactive autonomic nervous system, physical build and size, and poor impulse control. The list could be expanded indefinitely. Most of the essential factors that correlate with delinquent behavior can be incorporated into two major theories of delinquency: a psychological theory and a sociocultural theory. Psychological theories look for the source of delinquent behavior in unresolved emotional conflicts. Sociocultural theories assume that delinquent behavior evolves from a normal, social learning process through reinforcement, modeling, imitation, and identification. Psychological and sociocultural theories are best understood as attempts to account for serious, repeated adolescent misconduct or lawbreaking, rather than the transitory, episodic, minor transgressions that can be expected as a normal component of adolescent experimentation, curiosity, and adventure-seeking.

A third theory of delinquency, the biogenic model, searches for the causes of delinquency in biochemical factors that result from brain damage, genetic inheritance, heightened autonomic nervous system activity, chromosome deficits, or inadequate nutrition (Mednick, 1985). The specific links between biological factors and delinquent behavior have not been clearly spelled out and are difficult to isolate and test. The biogenic model of delinquency is actually a biosocial or psychobiological model, since environment and psychosocial factors determine the extent to which biological potentials are activated. Crude biological determinism has been supplanted by theories stressing the interaction between biological factors and psychosocial experiences (Gibbons and Krohn, 1986). For example, minimum brain damage can make it hard for a child to pay attention in school. Because the child is unable to concentrate on her school work, she falls behind in her studies and develops a learning disorder. If the learning disorder is not properly treated, school failure can lead to low self-esteem and cause the child to look for positive reinforcement and peer activities outside the school environment. The child's peer group then becomes other low-achieving young people who have already started drifting toward delinquent behavior. In this case, minimum brain damage is not the sole or even a major cause of delinquent behavior. The minimum brain damage sets-up the risk factor, which had to be followed by a chain of psychosocial and environmental events to have a delinquent outcome. Environmental interventions, such as special learning programs with understanding, support, and building self-esteem could easily break up the process. In the next section we will discuss the psychological and environmental factors that shape delinquent behavior, whether or not a biological component is present.

Psychological Theory

According to the psychological theory, persistent, serious delinquent behavior, such as robbery, assault, and crimes against persons and property, is symptomatic of an emotional disturbance that results from unresolved conflicts in psychosocial development. Continuing parent–child turmoil and insufficient emotional support prevent the successful resolution of preadolescent psychosocial tasks involving the development of trust, intimacy, self-worth, impulse controls, and the internalization of parental rules and values. Parental rules and values are assumed to correspond to mainstream standards. Deficiencies in internalizing parental values, or super-ego development, and poor self-control can ultimately lead to what Erikson (1963, 1968) refers to as negative identity. Delinquent young people with a negative identity attempt to emulate or act out all of the roles presented to them as undesirable, bad, or dangerous by parents and conventional society. They define themselves by identifying with what they are least supposed to be. The delinquent life-style is a defense mechanism, or coping strategy used to suppress feelings of doubt, shame, and fear that one will not be able to reach the goals expected of one. Many young people rebel by questioning the relevance of parental values, testing the limits, and experimenting with minor misconduct, but they manage to stay within limits that can be tolerated by the community. Negative identity represents the extreme case of rejecting parental and mainstream values. Young people with a negative identity, who are labeled by the society as bad or delinquent, often seek each other out as associates. Their relationships are based more on their mutual rejection of society's norms than on closeness, trust, and intimacy. Their rejection of mainstream standards and society's rejection of them creates a delinquent subculture in which young people band together for recognition and reinforcement. Recognition and support reinforces the negative identity and delinquent life-style (Zober, 1981; Covington, 1983). A moderate degree of support for the psychological theory of delinquency comes from numerous research studies indicating that lack of warmth, marital strife, family disharmony, rejection, and hostility are common in families with delinquent children (Adams and Gullotta, 1983). Longitudinal studies conducted by Sheldon and Eleanor Glueck (1950) with delinquent boys and Konopka's (1966) research with institutionalized delinquent females, suggest that a lack of affectionate patterns in the home and inadequate parenting result in hostility, arrested psychosocial maturity, and deficits in empathy, which end up being acted out in delinquent behavior. Children who become delinquent as adolescents get stuck in the childhood stages of impulsive behavior and preadolescent moral development. Parents who lack a mutually caring, trusting relationship with their children may be unable to engage in effective discipline or teach social norms in a consistent, affectionate manner (Fischer, 1983; Shamsk, 1981). The work of Patterson (1981), Hirschi (1969) and Craig and Glueck (1963) indicate that parents of delinquent children, compared to parents of nondelinquent children, are more likely to engage in erratic supervision, inconsistent and inappropriate discipline, and are less likely to know where their children are when they are not at home or in school, and who they are with. Parents of delinquent children seem to lack positive family management skills and problem-solving strategies. When misbehavior occurs, parents lean heavily on aversive discipline. They are likely to holler and threaten but do not follow through or back up their warnings with clear rules and predictable punishment for rulebreaking. A national survey of 1,725 youths, 11 to 17 years old, reported by Delbert S. Elliott, found young people without close family bonds were more likely to become involved in delinquency than adolescents with close family relationships. Once young people who lacked close parental bonding started to experiment with delinquent behavior, they were more likely to continue if they developed ongoing associations with a peer group of delinquent adolescents (Hurley, 1985).

The psychological view, which depicts persistent, serious delinquent behavior as an emotional disturbance caused by unresolved childhood conflicts, was popular from early in the 20th century until the 1960s. Since the core of the unresolved conflict was inside the delinquent, the therapies derived from psychological theory emphasized a psychodynamic approach. The goal of treatment or rehabilitation involved uncovering and working through the suppressed motives, feelings, and perceptions underlying delinquent behavior. The emotional disturbance-psychodynamic therapy approach to delinquency was incorporated into a quasi-medical model that, in practice, consisted of a case study, diagnosis, and rehabilitation or therapy plan. The emotional disturbance-case study-rehabilitation model was championed by William Healy (1915), a British-born, American-trained psychiatrist. Dr. Healy worked with the Juvenile Psychopathic Institute which was affiliated with one of the early juvenile courts in Chicago. In 1917, Healy left Chicago to become director of the Judge Baker Foundation's Child Guidance Clinic in Boston. Successive generations of juvenile mental health professionals were trained in the emotional disturbance-rehabilitation view. Each group passed it along, until it became standard practice for working with delinquents processed by the courts (Carey and McAnany, 1984).

During the past 20 years, the emotional disturbance view of delinquency has come under a storm of criticism. Critics contend the model is conceptually weak, not supported by research evidence, and that psychodynamic therapies do not work effectively in changing delinquent behavior (Gibbons and Krohn, 1986). Psychological-emotional disturbance theories do not clearly explain the linkage between parent–child turmoil and subsequent delinquent behavior. Many young people have conflicts with their parents, yet only 2% to 3% turn out to be serious, repetitive delinquents. Some critics view the diagnosis of emotional disturbance as a way of putting pathological or illness labels on behaviors parents and adults disagree with. Young people can reject conventional values of their parents and become involved in alternative life-styles without necessarily being emotionally disturbed. Refusal to adhere to parental values or mainstream standards cannot automatically be interpreted as evidence of an emotional illness. Prior to the 1970s, many young people were labeled as delinquent by the juvenile justice system for such status offenses as defiance of parental authority, running away, being sexually active, experimenting with alcohol, associating with immoral persons, and refusing to attend school on a regular basis. In some cases, behavior such as running away or defiance of parental authority can be healthy responses to an oppressive home situation. Values at variance with conventional standards can also be developed in a normal social learning process through associations with peers and community role models adhering to alternative life-styles. There are families in which the parents themselves model deviant behavior.

The cause-effect sequence in measurements of negative identity and turmoil in parent–child relationships can be confounded by the point in time the assessments are conducted. Young people who feel they have been unfairly processed and detained by juvenile courts are likely to be angry, bitter, powerless, and disillusioned with community values, not because of unresolved childhood turmoil but because they feel they have been treated unjustly by the system. Evidence of parent-child turmoil, obtained after young people have been adjudicated and placed on probation or in institutions, may be the result of the child's behavior rather than the cause of delinquency. Finally, the psychodynamic therapies have not shown promising results in reducing delinquent behavior. Delinquent young people coerced into psychotherapy are usually not highly motivated to change their lifestyle. To the extent that they are street-wise, they know how to manipulate the system, "play it cool," and simulate reassessment of their values without having any serious intentions of changing.

Sociocultural Theories

Sociocultural or sociogenic theories of delinquency begin with the assumption that delinquent behaviors can be acquired through a normal process of social learning involving reinforcement, exposure, modeling, imitation, identification, and suggestion. Sociologists have observed a strong relationship between teenage delinquency and social class, which persists after corrections have been made for bias and discrimination on the part of arresting officers and juvenile officials. Young people who grow up in low-income, high-crime, deteriorating urban neighborhoods of America's large metropolitan areas have a higher probability of becoming involved in a delinquent way of life than their suburban counterparts. According to sociocultural theory, the higher rates of delinquency for low-income, urban young people can be explained by the cultural transmission of deviant values, differential economic and social opportunities, unavailability of socially approved routes to success, insufficient exposure to mainstream learning experiences, and weak institutions in disorganized neighborhoods. Delinquent young people are socialized into values, norms, and beliefs that support illegal activities. They want the same goals as nondelinquent adolescents in terms of status, money, recognition, and their share of the good life as depicted in movies, but go about attaining these goals in ways considered unacceptable by the standards of mainstream society. The sociocultural view assumes that most delinquent young people are not emotionally disturbed; they are psychologically normal teenagers whose lawbreaking behavior is a learned response acquired in the process of socialization. They resort to delinquent behavior because legitimate avenues to socially approved goals are not readily available. Three sociocultural theories will be discussed: (1) the social control-social disorganization perspective; (2) strain theory; and (3) subcultural deviant-cultural transmission theory (Carey and McAnany, 1984).

The social control-social disorganization perspective is based on the assumption that within each of us is the potential to engage in lawbreaking behavior. We refrain from serious lawbreaking because of the social constraints and controls society has established. Cultural norms place limits on behavior and the appropriate means for satisfying needs, desires, and impulses. Society's controls operate, and are enforced through institutions such as the church, school, social groups, community organizations, and the family. These groups discourage lawbreaking and delinquent behavior by young people. In low-income, deteriorating urban neighborhoods, social institutions are weak, disorganized, and ineffective. When established institutions no longer have power to control behavior, young people are free to behave as they please. They are attracted to delinquent behavior because it is exciting, adventurous, and can be financially rewarding (Redner et al., 1983).

Walter Reckless (1961, 1967) modified social control-social disorganization theory to include two sources of control or containment influenced by social learning, outer containment and inner containment. Outer containment is the power of society to confine the individual's behavior within acceptable limits. The power of outer containment is determined by the individual's ties to others, the consistency to which prosocial behavior is reinforced, and the integration of the individual into established social institutions, such as the family, school, church, and other social groups. Inner containment refers to the self and personality characteristics, such as self-control, frustration tolerance, goal orientation, coping skills, internalized conscious, and retention of norms. Internal control is a psychological dimension that refers to the individual's willingness to follow conventional social norms through self-control, whereas outer containment focuses more on the behavior-shaping or reinforcing aspects of the external world. According to Hirschi (1969), the extent to which social controls are effective depends on the degree of bonding to mainstream groups. The degree of bonding is determined by the strengths of one's attachments, beliefs, involvement, and commitments. Teenagers who are strongly bonded to prosocial groups are less likely to engage in persistent delinquent behavior. When strong bonds do not exist, the likelihood of deviant behavior is much higher (Thompson and Dodder, 1983).

The strain theory assumes that all youths want to achieve power, money, recognition, and status. The key concepts in the strain theory are blocked opportunity and frustration (Merton, 1957; Cloward and Ohlin, 1960). In economically disadvantaged urban slum areas, unemployment, poverty, institutional racism, inferior schools, and a general lack of equal opportunity act as barriers to goal achievement. In many low-income, minority urban areas, the high school dropout rate is around 50%; another 20% may be functionally illiterate when they graduate. Young people in rundown, economically disadvantaged neighborhoods do not take school seriously because they don't believe they can get a job with the skills they are being taught, or they don't feel confident they have the ability to master the skills (Rossman, 1981). How can these young people compete for jobs in a highly technical and literate society? Delinquency is created by the frustration of not being able to achieve power, money, status, and recognition by legitimate means. When young people perceive a large discrepancy between middle-class goals and their ability to achieve these goals by following conventional pathways, alienation increases. Society loses its power to regulate behavior because its regulations are no longer perceived as relevant or worthwhile. The key issue is the youth's perception that he or she is shut out or that the means to achieving socially acceptable goals are not available. It is important that young people believe they have a stake in society. If youths doubt that hard work, future planning, self-control, delayed gratification, education, and conformity to mainstream values will pay off, they face a dilemma that is not easily resolved. They can conform and keep trying despite the disadvantages and lack of opportunity, or they can turn to crime as a solution, lower their goals, retreat into drugs, and rebel, seeking opposing goals (Jensen, 1985). In high-crime urban barrio and ghetto neighborhoods, the choice is frequently crime. Crime, as opposed to work, is the more accessible form of economic activity. Young people can make money by stealing, robbery, burglary, prostitution, and selling drugs. Those who defy the system and get away with it, or who are tough enough to survive in custody when they get caught, are often admired and, unfortunately, emulated.

The choice of delinquent activities or illegal means to achieve success is likely to be reinforced by peers and associates. The norms of many low-income urban peer groups run counter to the values of mainstream society. Illegal behaviors are reinforced by recognition, status, intimacy, and protection. The peer group or gang sets the standard. Status is measured by how successful adolescents are in committing illegal activities and staying out of jail, or how well they survive when they are placed in correctional facilities. Delinquent, gang activity is a form of social protest against the frustrations triggered by barriers to legitimate pathways to financial and occupational success. Social reappraisal of personal beliefs and experiences is a critical factor during adolescence. Adolescence is a time when young people become aware of inequities in society and blocked opportunities. This awareness can cause young people to question the conventional values they were taught in childhood by their parents. The traditional beliefs preventing delinquent behavior no longer seem relevant and are replaced with values more congruent with one's daily experiences and peer relationships (Covington, 1983).

The subcultural deviant-cultural transmission perspective focuses on the role of deviant subcultures in transmitting antisocial norms as part of the socialization process. In every large city there are delinquent subcultures in which successive generations of young people are socialized into illegal behaviors as part of the normal process of growing up. Young people adopt a deviant life-style from close associations with delinquent role models and groups that provide reinforcement for behaviors that violate traditional social norms. Sutherland and Cressy (1978) suggest that American cities are characterized by different levels of social organizations and adherence to conventional norms. Within the same area of a city, youths can be exposed to definitions of behavior, beliefs, values, and norms favorable to and those unfavorable to violating the law. If the individual is exposed to an excess of definitions favorable to violating the law, he or she is more likely to become involved in criminal and delinquent actions.

All young people who grow up in high crime, economically disadvantaged ethnic areas of the inner cities do not become involved in a delinquent way of life. Some develop strong prosocial self-concepts and values as children through positive family interaction. As adolescents, they find ways to seek out others, inside and outside of the family, who can provide them with the support and mentoring they need to keep searching for a viable pathway into the mainstream. Although social scientists and delinquency experts have extensively studied young people who adopt antisocial life-styles, very little is known about how prosocial young people from economically disadvantaged, ethnic neighborhoods successfully master the obstacles at each critical stage of psychological development.

The psychological and sociological theories of delinquent behavior are similar to the DSM-III-R (American Psychiatric Association, 1987) classification of solitary-aggressive and group-type conduct disturbances listed in Table 9-3. The source of solitary-aggressive conduct disorders or delinquency is likely to be in the troubled psychological development of the child, whereas group delinquency is often the result of a social learning process involving reinforcement and emulation of delinquent role models. Neither psychological theory nor sociocultural theory alone explains the spectrum of delinquent behaviors. Each theory is valid in some cases. A thorough case history is necessary to determine which theory best explains any individual pattern of adolescent delinquency. Sociocultural and social learning models of delinquency have become increasingly popular in recent years, while the preference for the psychological disturbance model has been declining. The current generation of social scientists, juvenile justice officials, and delinquency counselors believe that the major advantage of the sociocultural-social learning model is its emphasis on overt behavior rather than on vague underlying feelings, motives, thoughts, and conflicts. Therapy and treatment approaches derived from the sociocultural model focus on reinforcing prosocial behavior and changing social systems rather than on working through internal psychological dynamics.

While many social scientists reject the emotional disturbance view of delinquency because of its mental illness and psychopathological implications, it should be pointed out that maladaptive consequences to self and others can result from delinquent behavior, regardless of whether its source is troubled emotions or normal social learning. Psychological and physical injuries to others are often the outcome of robbery, assault, rape, and crimes

Table 9-3. DSM-III-R (1987) Conduct Disorders[a]

The term conduct disorder is used to describe the behavior of adolescents who show evidence of a repetitive pattern of actions that violate the rights of others and major age-appropriate social norms and rules. Behavioral pattern is usually exhibited in the family, at school, and with peers. Stealing and aggression are common. Adolescents with conduct disorders frequently steal, destroy property, and may engage in physical confrontations with victims during robberies, purse snatchings, muggings, or extortions. Physical violence in the form of rape or assault and, in some cases, homicide, may take place in the later stages of conduct disturbances. Lying, shoplifting, school truancy, and cheating in games and school work are common. Running away may occur. Although the adolescent may project an image of toughness, self-esteem is usually low. Angry outbursts, low frustration tolerance, irritability, and reckless behavior are frequent characteristics. School achievement in reading and language skills is below the expected ability and age level.

Specific criteria for the diagnosis of conduct disorder include at least three of the following during a period of 6 months:

1. Stealing without confrontation by the victim on more than one occasion
2. Running away from home overnight twice, or one runaway without returning
3. Frequent lying
4. Deliberate fire-setting activity
5. Frequent truancy from school, or for older adolescents absence from work
6. Breaking into houses, cars or buildings
7. Destruction of property and vandalism
8. Cruelty to animals
9. Forcing another person into sexual activity
10. Using weapons in fights on one or more occasions
11. Initiates physical fights often
12. Steals with confrontation of the victim in muggings, purse snatchings, extortion, armed robbery, and the like
13. Physical cruelty toward people

DSM-III-R recognizes three conduct disorder subtypes:

1. *Group type.* Essential feature of group type is that conduct problems occur primarily as a group activity with peers. Physical aggression may or may not be present.
2. *Solitary aggressive type.* Major feature of the solitary aggressive type is the predominance of aggressive physical behavior toward adults and peers initiated by the adolescent, which is not part of a group activity.
3. *Undifferentiated type.* Undifferentiated type has mixtures of both group type and solitary aggressive type.

[a]Adapted from: American Psychiatric Association. (1987). *Diagnostic and statistical manual of mental disorders* (3rd ed., rev.). Washington, D.C.

against property. In some cases, death results from gang violence or unintended homicides during armed robberies. Young people who persist in serious lawbreaking will eventually have limits placed on them by the courts. Placement in custodial institutions restricts personal freedom and psychosocial growth. Confinement with other delinquents leads to further reinforcement of an antisocial life-style which, in turn, increases the likelihood of further lawbreaking behavior and additional confinement. If delinquent behavior continues past the age where the state no longer considers the individual a minor, a police record can interfere with future job opportunities. Lack of involvement in school and vocational training because of a delinquent way of life can prevent young people from developing the basic reading and math skills they will need to be marketable in an increasingly technological labor force.

INTERVENTIONS: THE JUVENILE JUSTICE SYSTEM, PSYCHOSOCIAL THERAPY, AND PREVENTION

The Juvenile Justice System

History and Philosophy

In the next three sections we will discuss the organizational structures, treatment procedures, and prevention programs developed to cope with juvenile lawbreaking. The juvenile justice system is an umbrella term for the major organizational structure society has put in place to deal with juvenile offenders. The juvenile justice system consists of the police, juvenile courts, community-based programs, and custodial institutions and homes. The first juvenile court was founded in Illinois in 1899 to provide for court hearings and judicial processes for juveniles separate from the trials of adult offenders (Binder, 1983). From the beginning, three types of youths were subject to the jurisdiction of the courts: (1) dependent and neglected children who were victims of parental abuse or abandonment; (2) young people who committed offenses that were defined as violations of adult criminal laws; and (3) status offenders defined as young people who violated laws that only applied to minors. Status offenses included such behaviors as associating with immoral persons, wandering the streets at night, young women riding about in cars unchaperoned, engaging in sexual relationships, purchasing alcohol, defying adult authority, running away, and truancy. Dependent and neglected youths have been referred to as CINS, PINS, and YINS— Childrens, Persons, or Youths in Need of Services—respectively. By 1945 juvenile courts had been established in all states. The courts have retained broad jurisdiction over these three groups, although a number of reforms have been enacted to differentiate status offenders and dependent and neglected youths from young people alleged to have violated adult criminal laws (Gibbons and Krohn, 1986; Schlossman and Wallach, 1978).

Creation of the juvenile justice system was inspired by humanitarian social reformers, youth advocates, and child guidance workers interested in removing young people from the punitive philosophy and adversarial style of the adult criminal justice system. The emergence of juvenile court became one of the cornerstones in the development of adolescence as a psychosocial and legal reality in America. Based on advances in child psychology and adolescent development, the early reformers believed that wayward young people still in the formative stages of their development were not as psychosocially mature or as responsible as adults. Therefore, they should be guided and rehabilitated rather than punished. The legal justification for the juvenile courts was provided in the doctrine of *parens patriae*. Under the doctrine of parens patriae, the state has the authority to guide and control the behavior of young people when parents cannot or will not assume responsibility. The judge, in the juvenile court, was to function as a kindly but firm parent whose responsibility was to guide the child away from misconduct and toward behaviors that would enable him or her to become a productive citizen. Safeguards used in adult courts to guarantee fairness and due process, such as presentation of charges in writing, cross-examination of witnesses, and the adversarial relationship between attorneys for the client and the prosecution, were not necessary because the goal of all parties was not to contest guilt or innocence but to determine what was needed to assure the minor's proper growth. Furthermore, it was asserted that legal processes were difficult for young people to understand and would only confuse them. The court adopted a quasi-medical model, which meant that youths brought to the attention of the courts were to be psychologically and socially evaluated, diagnosed, and treated. Delinquency was thought of as an emotional disturbance or psychiatric illness that should be examined, diagnosed, and rehabilitated by mental health and social service specialists (Gold and Petronio, 1980; Wenar, 1982).

Embedded within the philosophy of the juvenile court were assumptions that would not be challenged until the 1960s: First, adults have the legal and moral right to establish and control the social conduct of young people in areas beyond criminal law, such as sexual behavior, personal friends and associates, obedience to parents, hours they can be outside the home at night, use of alcoholic beverages, and school attendance. Second, young people can be protected and properly guided by the juvenile courts without the essential legal rights guaranteed under the Constitution and Bill of Rights.

How the System Works

The juvenile justice system has a vast range of options in determining what happens to young people accused of delinquent behavior. The police are the initial point of contact for most young people who enter the juvenile justice system. Complaints can also be filed by parents, schools, community agencies, citizens, and victims. Once a complaint is filed or the youth is apprehended or arrested, police officers and juvenile court officials have a wide latitude in determining each of the following options and outcomes (Binder, 1983; Kirk, 1980).

1.   The offense can be ignored. The police officer can decide that no further action is warranted.

2.   Counsel and release. The arresting officer or juvenile official can let the youth go with a warning and caution about future behavior.

3.   The juvenile can be released to the parents, who are counseled about the consequences of future misconduct.

4.   The case can be referred directly to the community mental health facilities or social services for family counseling and crisis intervention.

5.   The minor can be taken into custody or turned over to a special juvenile court officer, who is sometimes referred to as a probation officer. The juvenile officer or intake division conducts a preliminary hearing to determine whether an offense was committed or a convincing reason existed to bring the youth to the attention of the courts. At this point, the case can be dismissed; the youth can be placed on informal probation with certain conditions, such as counseling and no further arrests, or, after careful investigation, a petition can be filed in the juvenile court for a formal hearing. Fifty percent of the cases that come to the attention of the juvenile court are disposed of during the intake phase, without referral for a formal hearing.

6.   A formal court hearing consists of two parts: an adjudication phase and a disposition phase. In the adjudication phase, which is similar to a trial in an adult court, the evidence supporting the allegations is presented. If the evidence is sufficient to support the alleged offenses, the juvenile is determined to be delinquent (guilty), and the petition is upheld. The case then enters the disposition phase. The finding of delinquency creates the legal basis for the court to assume control or jurisdiction over the juvenile's life. In the disposition phase, the court selects the guidance program, living arrangements, and therapy approach most likely to rehabilitate the adolescent. In the predisposition phase, which is the interim period between adjudication and disposition, a psychosocial evaluation is conducted to determine the strengths and weaknesses of the adolescent and the appropriate recommendations for treatment. Factors such as support systems, school achievement, prior offenses, future aspirations, family turmoil, and types of peers are considered. Disposition outcomes can include outright release, referral to community programs, informal probation, formal probation, placement in a group home, or confinement to a custodial institution. Only about 5% of delinquent youths are confined to custodial institutions. The range of disposition outcomes, utilized by the juvenile court, is listed in Table 9-4. Youths confined to custodial institutions are generally serious, repeat offenders who have been involved in crimes such as robbery, assault, homicide, rape, arson, burglary, and the destruction of property.

The flow of decisions and options in the juvenile justice system is illustrated in Figure 9-1. In some states, only the prosecuting attorney can petition the courts for a formal hearing. Over the years, the juvenile court has developed its own vocabulary. A petition is filed on behalf of a child, rather

Table 9-4. Dispositional Outcomes Utilized by the Juvenile Court

1. Detention (in county facility)
2. Private institutional placement (residential programs)
3. Commitment to state training schools
4. Commitment to residential, mental health facility
5. Commitment to residential center for mentally retarded
6. Commitment to state department of social services
7. Residential ranches and camps (court-operated)
8. Halfway houses
9. Group homes
10. Temporary shelter homes
11. Foster homes
12. Independent living status
13. Residential vocational training center
14. Vocational training programs
15. On-the-job training programs
16. Educational tutorial programs
17. Community work projects
18. Restitution programs
19. Essay-writing assignments
20. Individual probation—formal or informal
21. Volunteer big brother, big sister
22. Drug education programs
23. Referral to youth clubs
24. Referral to community mental health agencies
25. Referral to day-care treatment programs
26. Referral to youth protection programs
27. Counseling programs
28. Wilderness training
29. Parent training and family mediation
30. Social skills training
31. Fear and shock therapy

than a complaint issued against him or her; initial hearings or intakes are used rather than arraignments; the adolescent is adjudicated and found to be delinquent, rather than tried and convicted; a petition is supported in place of guilt, disposition replaces sentencing, and rehabilitation replaces punishment (Gibbons and Krohn, 1986; Binder, 1983).

Critique and Reforms

Major criticisms of the juvenile justice system have led to a number of significant reforms in recent years. After reviewing the criticisms of the juvenile justice system, we will discuss the reforms that have taken place during the past 20 years. The five major criticisms of the juvenile justice system can be described as follows: (1) insufficient protection of the rights of young people; (2) arbitrariness; (3) deleterious effects of labeling and processing by the system; (4) sophisticated youth can beat the system; and (5) too much emphasis on rehabilitation rather than personal responsibility and protection of the public.

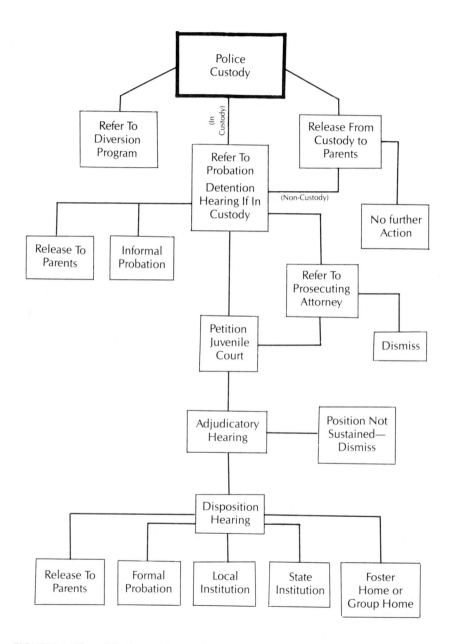

FIGURE 9-1. Flow of decisions in the Juvenile Justice System. (Adapted from Binder, A. (1983). "The juvenile justice system and juvenile offenders: An overview. *The counseling psychologist,* 11(2), 65–68.)

1. *Insufficient protection of the rights of young people.* Young people, as a protected class, have often been harmed by a system where treatment, under the guise of rehabilitation, has sometimes been harsh and punitive. The best interest of the child has frequently been used to correct behavior that is unacceptable to adults, rather than a criminal violation of the law. Many teenagers have been judged to be delinquent and sent to state-run custodial institutions on the basis of evidence that would be insufficient to convict an adult. One of the best examples of failure to protect the rights of young people and harsh treatment based on insufficient evidence is the case of Gerald Gault (U.S. Supreme Court, 1967), which eventually became a landmark Supreme Court case in 1967. In 1964 Gerald Francis Gault, a 15-year-old Arizona teenager, was given a 6-year sentence in a state-run industrial school for participating in making lewd phone calls to a female neighbor. The maximum legal penalty in Arizona for adults guilty of a misdemeanor involving the use of vulgar, abusive, or obscene language was a fine of $5 to $50 or a few months in confinement. When Gault was taken into custody and placed in a detention facility, his parents were at work. No attempt was made to reach them to inform them of their son's whereabouts, and no charges were presented in writing. When the hearing was held, Gault was not represented by an attorney, the complaining witnesses did not testify, and no transcript or recording was made of the hearing. Gault admitted to placing the call and making some of the lewd remarks. He was returned to the detention home, and at a subsequent hearing was committed to the state training school.

2. *Arbitrariness.* Because the system does not have adequate guidelines for determining conditions under which youths accused of lawbreaking are released outright, counseled and released, referred to community agencies, arrested and detained, placed on probation, or adjudicated and sent to correctional facilities, a certain amount of ambiguity, inconsistency, and arbitrariness pervade the system. Minority youths from low-income urban neighborhoods complained they are harassed and arrested by the police for minor offenses that would be ignored or treated lightly in suburbia. Historically, young women have been treated harshly by the juvenile courts for engaging in behaviors that violate traditional morality. Young women who in the past defied parental authority, ran away from home, associated with so-called immoral persons, or engaged in sexual activity were often labeled as incorrigible and sent to correctional facilities for indefinite stays (Schlossman and Wallach, 1978). There are also countless stories of juveniles detained and physically abused in adult jails while awaiting hearings on minor charges; young people do not have the option of being released on bail.

3. *Deleterious effects of labeling and processing by the system.* Youths arrested, detained, booked, and processed through the juvenile justice system for minor misconduct or status offenses are more likely to become

future lawbreakers than youths ignored, counseled and released, or referred to community social service agencies. Labeling noncriminally oriented youths as delinquent and treating them as such by locking them up and placing them on probation for behavior such as running away, defiance of parental authority, sexual behavior, and school truancy creates a self-fulfilling prophecy. Youths treated as delinquent and placed in close association with other delinquents by order of the court eventually come to behave as delinquents. Once the delinquent label is reinforced and internalized, youths tend to act out the role. The further youths progress into the arena of the juvenile justice system, the greater the likelihood of future arrests or recidivism. At the most extreme end of the spectrum, youths placed in locked custodial institutions have a 70% chance of being re-arrested after their release. Rather than rehabilitating youth, confinement in correctional institutions seems to have the opposite effect. The imposition of punishment perceived as harsh or unjust tends to further alienate teenagers from conventional standards and subjects them to sexual and physical exploitation by stronger inmates. Training schools are often a breeding ground for future criminal behavior. In juvenile correctional centers, young people can refine their criminal skills. Placing juveniles in an environment with repeat offenders exposes them to influences that reinforce a delinquent way of life. Negative attitudes toward the police, institutions in which they are confined, and the juvenile justice system that placed them there, work against rehabilitation and increase delinquent self-identification (Zober, 1981; Weiner, 1982; Conger and Petersen, 1984).

4.   *Sophisticated youths can beat the system.* Sophisticated, street-wise young people know how to maneuver their way around juvenile officials, probation officers, social workers, judges, and counselors (Prescott, 1981). While the founders of the juvenile justice system may have believed that youth could not understand the complexities of the legal system, many young people have the conceptual skills to not only understand the system but to manipulate it to their advantage. Gangs often use younger members to commit homicides and other serious crimes because they know the system will be lenient. A 15-year-old, involved as one of the trigger men in a drive-by slaying of a rival gang member, remarked to his friends after getting a 6 months sentence to a juvenile facility, "I knew I wasn't going to get no big time behind a scene like that . . . I'm too young, my mama's on welfare, and my daddy ran away from my mama." Tough, urban youngsters do not seem to be afraid of confinement to institutions. They perceive confinement as a test of their wits and masculinity. They know how to "play it cool," "work the program," manipulate the structure, and simulate participation in therapy and educational programs.

5.   *Too much emphasis on rehabilitation rather than personal responsibility and protection of the public.* The emotional illness-rehabilitation par-

adigm of delinquency has not protected the public or rehabilitated serious repeat adolescent lawbreakers. Psychological treatment such as psychotherapy, group work, and counseling has not proved effective with young people whose commitment to criminal behavior is reinforced by social learning. Under the banner of rehabilitation, dangerous juveniles are prematurely released from custody to inflict further harm on the community. In leaning toward protection and rehabilitation of youths, the juvenile justice system has not sufficiently emphasized personal responsibility for one's actions nor regard for the rights of others (Galvin and Polk, 1983).

As a consequence of unfavorable evaluations and criticisms, several major reforms in the juvenile justice system have been recommended by numerous task forces, special commissions, legislative enactments, and legal groups, including the American Bar Association, the Children's Legal Defense Fund, the Office of Juvenile Justice and Delinquency Prevention and the 1967 President's Commission on Law Enforcement and the Administration of Justice (Carey and McAnany, 1984; Ruterman and Hughes, 1984). The reforms and counter-reforms represent a mixture of conservative and liberal trends. On one hand, juveniles now enjoy a greater range of legal rights. Hard-core offenders are separated from status offenders, minor offenders, and dependent as well as neglected juveniles. In keeping with the principle of treatment by using the least restrictive alternative, more emphasis is being placed on nonintervention, nonjudicial alternatives, and handling young people outside the juvenile justice system through community service projects, restitution, and family counseling. These reforms have been described as the four D's: diversion, decriminalization, deinstitutionalization, and due process (Armstrong and Altschuler, 1982). On the other hand, there is a much greater concern for protecting the public and more emphasis on personal accountability and responsibility for the consequences of one's behavior. Almost all states have passed laws making it easier for people over the age of 15 to be tried as adults for violent crimes, such as murder, and have stipulated a variety of crimes that can result in juveniles being sent to locked facilities. Rehabilitation has not been forgotten, but the best interest of the child must be balanced against the need to protect society from dangerous teenagers. Psychodynamic-reconstructive psychotherapy approaches have been replaced by treatment paradigms focusing on reinforcing prosocial behaviors and providing young people with the social skills and technical competencies they need to succeed in mainstream society.

The decisions of the United States Supreme Court in the case of Gerald Gault (U.S. Supreme Court, 1967) ushered in a new era in the legal rights of juveniles. Juvenile courts now resemble adult courts in terms of the constitutional rights granted to young people. The court declared that the Bill of Rights and constitutional guarantees of due process and equal protection under the law be applied to minors. Specifically, the court ruled that juveniles have the following rights: (1) right to be informed of the charges against them in writing; (2) right to be represented by an attorney; (3) right to face witnesses and accusers and cross-examine them; (4) right to remain silent and refrain from making self-incriminating statements; (5) right to a transcript of the proceedings; and (6) the right to a review by an appeals court. The court did not grant bail, jury trials, or open the proceedings of the juvenile court to the public. In a sense, the court rescued young people from the injustices of the juvenile justice system by providing procedural safeguards. Justice Abe Fortas, in writing the court's majority opinion, concluded that under the old system, juveniles inherited the worst of both worlds. Their rights were not protected, and they were often subjected to cruel punishment by juvenile officials who were supposed to be looking out for their welfare. Far from creating chaos in the courts, many young people have shown that they have the conceptual skills to understand legal complexities and are interested in participating, with their attorneys, in defending themselves against alleged offenses (Gross and Gross, 1977; Gold and Petronio, 1980).

Recommendations from the Juvenile Justice Standards Project of the American Bar Association (Institution of Juvenile Administration, 1977), President Johnson's 1967 Commission on Law Enforcement and the Administration of Justice (President's Commission, 1967), and the Juvenile Justice and Delinquency Prevention Act of 1974 as amended in 1977, support the separation of status and nonstatus offenders in detention facilities, the utilization of the least restrictive treatment alternative to prevent further progression into the juvenile justice system network, diversion or filtering status and minor offenders out of the juvenile justice system's structure, and the employment of nonjudicial alternatives whenever possible. In practice, this has led to the increasing use of a process known as diversion and small community-based homes rather than large institutional facilities for youths in custody. In one state, state training schools were shut down completely (Carey and McAnany, 1984; Gibbons and Krohn, 1986).

Diversion is a method of filtering status offenders, first-time offenders, and minor offenders out of the juvenile justice system. Nonjudicial, community-based alternatives are substituted for further processing into the juvenile justice system (Binder and Geis, 1984). The rationale underlying diversion is that much of the juvenile misconduct coming to the attention of police and the courts is transitory, episodic, and does not involve harm to self or others. Diverting youth out of the juvenile justice system avoids the stigma of being labeled "delinquent," and prevents exposure to the corrosive effects of associating with hard-core delinquents. In theory, diversion programs should concentrate on providing youths with positive experiences that facilitate psychosocial growth, identification with prosocial values, and a sense they have something positive to contribute to the community. Typical diversion programs involve family counseling, individual and group counseling, crisis intervention, enhancement of parenting skills and discipline, community services and restitution, volunteer work, guided recreational and outdoor experiences, psychoeducational experiences to promote responsibility, power, competence and belonging, employment, educational guidance, and the like. Diversion can be instituted at any stage after the juvenile is reported or a complaint has been issued.

Diversion, which became popular in the 1960s and 1970s, is not a panacea. Its critics charge that diversion is not really new, is not uniformly administered within the same jurisdiction or across jurisdictions, and that diversion programs have not been shown to be consistently effective in reducing further delinquency or recidivism (Polk, 1984). From the beginning of the juvenile justice system, nonjudicial alternatives have always been available. Police and juvenile authorities have always had the option to counsel and release, and refer suspected juvenile offenders to community social services. The lack of uniform guidelines for diversion in many districts prevents objective choices in terms of who is included or omitted. Diversion programs have been accused of favoring middle-class white youths while continuing to route low-income minority youths through regular channels of the juvenile justice system. Despite these criticisms, Binder et al. (1988) conclude that diversion is worth continuing. While diversion hasn't been consistently successful in reducing delinquent behavior or improving social adjustment, the diversion programs have generally met the criteria of diverting youth from the juvenile justice system into less coercive alternatives that were more interested in meeting the client's needs than traditional approaches within the juvenile justice system.

The population of juveniles in custodial institutions has declined sharply in the past two decades. In 1974 Dr. Jerome Miller, Commissioner of the Massachusetts Department of Youth Services, surprised the juvenile justice community by closing down the state's ten custodial training schools, which housed more than 1,000 juveniles. When Dr. Miller took over as the Commissioner of Youth Services in 1969, he was appalled by the conditions in the state's youth reformatories and training schools. Recidivism rates were as high as 40% to 70%, and very little was taking place in the way of what could be called rehabilitation. Deinstitutionalization moved, in three phases, from awareness of the need for institutional change to attempts at reform, to treatment in community-based group homes and privately run residential facilities in place of institutions (Binder et al., 1988; Gibbons and Krohn, 1986). In group homes and small residential facilities housing only 4–24 young people, the staff can devote more time to rehabilitation, social skills development, and behavior changes. Residents have a larger investment in what happens in the home and have more opportunities to participate in management decisions and group problem-solving. Young people living in the community in open, residential facilities can interact with nondelinquent teenagers in school, work experiences, and social activities. Most delinquent young people do not need to be locked up for the protection of the community, and confinement in state training schools has not reduced future delinquent behavior. Even young people facing serious charges can be worked with in nonsecure settings, if the facilities are well run and staffed by highly competent people.

On the conservative end of the delinquency reform continuum, several states have initiated programs in which the primary emphasis is on responsibility, accountability, proportionality of sentencing, and predictable consequences of delinquent behavior. In 1977 in the state of Washington, a new juvenile law went into effect explicitly defining protection of the public and punishment of juvenile lawbreakers as the major purpose of the juvenile justice system in that state. All status offenders and many minor offenders will be diverted out of the juvenile justice system and handled by community agencies. Serious, repeat juvenile offenders must be sent to institutions, judges no longer have a choice. Those who score above 110 on a point system that takes into consideration age, severity of current lawbreaking, and previous record are automatically committed to an institution. Those who score below 110 will be required to perform community services and make restitutions. If they fail to live up to the sentencing agreement, they can be locked up in an institution for 30 days (Sherrill, 1979).

The controversies surrounding the liberal and conservative trends in the juvenile justice system reforms are by no means resolved. What is clear at this point in time is that status and minor offenders are being diverted out of the juvenile justice system, whereas more serious chronic offenders are being assigned to institutions for a determinate period. While there is still some reluctance on the part of the juvenile justice-system professionals to endorse the concepts of punishment and retribution, there seems to be a general consensus that guidance, rehabilitation, and treatment involve learning to accept blame, responsibility, and accountability for one's actions and that the public has a right to be protected from dangerous juveniles.

Psychosocial Therapy

Psychosocial therapies are treatment approaches designed to change the feelings, values, behaviors, attitudes, and coping styles of delinquent and predelinquent young people so as to reduce the probability of serious lawbreaking in the future. Psychosocial therapies are utilized across all levels of the juvenile justice system from diversion and probation to group homes and locked custodial institutions. Ninety to ninety-five percent of young people referred to the courts are treated in community-based noncustodial programs. Major changes, corresponding to the reforms and counter-reforms in the structure and function of the juvenile justice system, have taken place in psychosocial treatment approaches in the past 20 years. There has been a shift away from psychiatrically oriented treatment models that focus on emotional disturbance, diagnosis, and working through childhood conflicts to intervention approaches that emphasize growth, behavioral change, new social learning, and active responsibility for choices.

The early therapists, counselors, and case workers were concerned with intrapsychic conflicts, feelings, motives, and thoughts. The goal was understanding troubled young people and working through the internal emotional disturbances which were the source of delinquent behavior. Efforts to rehabilitate juvenile offenders using traditional psychopathology, psychotherapy models were largely unsuccessful. Major reviews of therapy and rehabilitation studies using traditional methods, conducted by Romig (1978) and Lipton et al. (1975) indicate very little in the way of significant treatment effects. Using various forms of recidivism as a criterion — parole violations, re-arrests, and reincarceration — there were few significant differences between those who received treatment and those who did not. Part of the failure of traditional therapies may have been due to the lack of motivation on the part of the clients, inexperienced therapists, lack of commitment by the institution to rehabilitation goals, the resistance of hard-core delinquents to change their life-style, and the reinforcement of delinquent behavior outside of therapy by antisocial peers (Conger and Petersen, 1984).

Contemporary psychosocial interventions are characterized by a spirit of experimentation and trial and error. Current theoretical models emphasize human growth and the development of strengths, as opposed to clinical psychopathology. Rather than working through underlying conflicts, the goal is to open up a range of options and alternatives so the adolescent will be less dependent on delinquent behavior. Prosocial behavior is enhanced through social learning, behavior modification, and skill building. Adequate psychosocial development means power, competence, usefulness, and a sense that worthwhile alternatives are available to achieve success. Socially appropriate behavior is enhanced by direct rewards, i.e., approval of behaviors such as completing school work, responsible management of freedom, work and employment experience, and positive social interactions. Young people are not perceived as helpless victims of internal psychological forces or external social forces; they are perceived as active agents who can meaningfully participate in their own development when opportunities for new learning are provided.

Behavior and social learning growth-paradigms involve a variety of formats that can be used with street gangs, individually or in family, group, and institutional settings. Primary techniques include token economies, behavioral contracting, modeling and role-playing, goal-setting and systematic reinforcement. Behavior and social learning techniques have the advantage of being straightforward, communicable, easily understood by staff members, and target behaviors can be reliably identified. Six formats utilizing social learning and behavioral methods to enhance psychosocial growth with delinquent youth will be reviewed: (1) restitution and community service; (2) family intervention; (3) token economies; (4) fear, emotional shock, and avoidance training; (5) wilderness training; and (6) social skills training.

Restitution and community services are attempts to teach responsibility and accountability by direct or symbolic repayment of the victim in thefts and crimes against property. Repayment can develop an appreciation of how lawbreaking impacts others. The payment should come from the adolescent rather than the parent. Some restitution programs arrange face-to-face reconciliation meetings between the juvenile and the victim. If the youth is unemployed or too young to have a work permit, symbolic repayment can be made through community service. Work in hospitals, preschools, homes for the elderly, community beautification projects, and other places where labor makes a positive contribution to the community, can help convince delinquent youth that they have something of value to provide and hopefully increase their sense of belonging and social bonding to the community (Fuhrmann, 1986; Dacey, 1986).

Family interventions based on social learning and behavioral models emphasize parental monitoring of children's behavior, mutual problem solving, noncoercive methods of control, reinforcing positive behavior, contracts clearly stating specific rules, expectations, and consequences for violations, as well as learning to negotiate, and, finally, emphasis on listening and developing a spirit of individual and collective responsibility for conflicts that create stresses among family members. Many delinquent children lack clear household rules and expectations. When they are away from home, their parents generally don't know where they are, who they hang out with, and what they are doing. Transgressions are handled inconsistently. Parents shout and holler but don't follow through with firm, consistent, predictable discipline. Parents are taught to monitor their children's behavior more closely, how to deal with deviant behavior decisively but firmly, and how to negotiate mutual contracts that involve privileges, responsibilities, rewards, and penalties (Patterson, 1981; Redner et al., 1983).

Token economies have been used in group homes like Achievement Place and the National Training School for Boys in Washington, D.C. A token economy is a behavioral reinforcement system in which positive behavior is rewarded by tokens, points, or chips that can be exchanged for privileges, services, or rewards. Inappropriate behavior results in a lack of points or, in some cases, a loss of points. Achievement Place is a group home for delinquent and predelinquent youths, started in Kansas in 1967. Several Achievement Place homes now exist around the country. Achievement Place homes are located in the community, and residents are 6–8 boys between the ages of 12 and 16 who are under the 24-hour supervision of two surrogate parents. The residents attend school in the community. The surrogate parents work with the youths and their natural parents as teachers and counselors. The boys can earn reinforcement points for keeping up with current events, cleaning their room, getting along with others, helping with household chores, keeping up with school work, and neat appearance. Points are lost for sloppiness, poor grammar, aggressive behavior, lying, stealing, cheating, not doing one's school work, and the like. Points can be cashed in for a reward, such as weekend passes, early release, watching TV, telephone calls, snacks, and money. Achievement Place generally exhibits positive results. Two years later, recidivism rates were lower compared to boys who were placed in traditional training schools or boys assigned to probation with no special psychosocial treatment. Ninety percent of the Achievement Place boys were still in school 3 months after treatment, compared to 9% of the training school boys and 37% of the probation boys (Phillips, 1968; Fixen et al., 1976).

A similar token economy program was instituted at the National Training School for Boys in Washington, D.C. where 41 boys, ages 14–18, had been sent for violations of federal law involving such offenses as car theft and crimes against property. Points were earned for working on programmed academic courses, taking tests, regular attendance at lectures and discussions, studying, passing tests with high grades, and prompt attendance. Boys who participated in the program acquired better study skills, showed greater improvement in seven academic areas than did public school students, and, after discharge they stayed out of trouble longer than did comparable groups for 2 years after discharge. By the third year after discharge, however, re-arrest rates approached the norm (Cohen and Filipczak, 1971).

Fear, emotional shock, and avoidance training were the primary techniques used in a program called Scared Straight, which gained nationwide attention from a television documentary in 1979. Groups of delinquent boys and girls were brought to Rahway State Prison in New Jersey where they were confronted for several hours in a hostile, angry manner by hard-core inmates. They were told about the sexual assaults, brutality, and beatings awaiting them in prison if they continued their delinquent way of life. The program was initially successful. Delinquent youths who participated in the program were less likely to be involved in delinquent activity in the immediate period following the program than were youths not exposed to the Rahway experience. Later follow-up, however, suggested that the initial success rate was not maintained (Finckenauer, 1982; Lundman, 1984).

In wilderness training programs such as Outward Bound, urban delinquents are taught outdoor survival skills, teamwork, and trust in self and others. To develop survival skills in the outdoors, youths must learn how to climb rocks and high cliffs, plan ahead, cook meals, ration supplies of water, and make decisions. By confronting challenges, pushing themselves hard, continuing the course, and teamwork, young people learn self-sufficiency, discipline, and the competence that comes from sticking with a difficult task until it is finished. In one study, delinquent youths who participated in survival training had lower recidivism rates for a year after the program, but five years later the initial success had decreased (Blake, 1977; Kelly and Baer, 1971).

Training in social skills facilitates psychosocial development by increasing competence in interpersonal interactions, conflict resolution, problem-solving, resisting peer pressures to engage in delinquent behaviors, and managing a wide range of life situations, such as applying for a job, dating, and confronting new social experiences. Social skills are taught by modeling, role-playing, rehearsal, feedback, and practice in real-life situations. Goldstein et al. (1980) has developed a social skills training package for adolescents, which includes beginning social skills, advanced social skills, skills for dealing with feelings, alternatives to aggression, skills for coping with stress, and planning skills.

Despite the innovations brought about in recent years by the behavior and social learning models, the psychosocial treatment of delinquent behavior has not been consistently more successful in the long run than age and maturity, ignoring most nondestructive delinquent behavior, or counseling and releasing status offenders and youths accused of minor misconduct. The major criticisms of social learning and behavior therapy treatment programs are the lack of transfer to real-life situations and the failure to maintain initial successes for extended periods after the treatment has been completed. More attention needs to be paid to how to help young people and their parents generalize the results of restitution and community service, token economies, social skills training, survival training, shock therapy, and the like to real-life situations. A longer period of follow-up is necessary to see what support services are needed to maintain and reinforce new prosocial behaviors. Additional opportunities must be opened for delinquent youths from the inner cities. It is difficult to sustain prosocial behaviors when pathways to future success are blocked and delinquent behavior is reinforced by the social context of crime, poverty, and urban decay.

Psychosocial treatment is often too little, too late. Programs need to begin earlier before the ages of 15 and 18 when young people are at a higher risk for becoming involved in a delinquent way of life. Perhaps traditional psychotherapies, which rely on insight, self-understanding, and working through underlying emotional disturbances, have been abandoned prematurely. Some young people may need a period of personal exploration and uncovering before they are ready to incorporate new prosocial learning into their everyday behavior. Recidivism or future lawbreaking as a criterion for evaluating the effectiveness of psychosocial therapy is too constricted. Arrest data, as noted earlier, and self-reports of lawbreaking are not reliable measures of delinquent behavior. Other criteria, such as self-concept, interpersonal effectiveness, and getting and holding a job, are very important components of social adjustment and should be used to decrease reliance on recidivism as the sole outcome measure.

Prevention

The purpose of prevention is to identify potential delinquents and help them learn to cope more effectively with the challenges and demands of the adolescent passage. Delinquency-prevention programs have adopted many of the behavioral and social learning techniques and approaches discussed in psychosocial treatment. Delinquency prevention is based on the assumption that all young people have the potential to become productive adults. To actualize this potential, the social environment must be responsive to psychosocial growth needs and provide young people with the tools and support systems they need to internalize nondelinquent values and behaviors. Treatment and prevention interventions can be distinguished by the point in time at which they occur. Therapy or treatment is aimed at identified delinquents, whereas prevention is directed at predelinquents, mild offenders, and so-called high-risk youths who indicate a propensity toward delinquent behavior. Primary prevention programs seek to assist young people before they come to the attention of the juvenile justice system. Secondary prevention is concerned with preventing early delinquents and status offenders from progressing further into the juvenile justice system. There is considerable overlap between treatment and primary and secondary prevention. The target group of prevention programs can be the community or subgroups, and specific individuals within the community (Weisheit, 1984).

A variety of projects across the nation are demonstrating that it is possible to head off delinquency by spending money on prevention. Mental health professionals and delinquency-prevention researchers have been working with key social systems and primary socialization groups, such as families, peer groups, educational systems, and neighborhoods (Hurley, 1985). The Chicago Area Project, which utilizes a community organization model, is one of the prototypes for what later became known as community psychology. The Chicago Area Project is a 50-year case study, beginning in the 1930s, of delinquency prevention through environmental change. Located in a slum neighborhood in Chicago, the purpose of the project was to reduce the conditions leading to delinquency by improving the social environment. Powerless and distressed low-income residents were taught how to build an effective leadership structure, organize community support for law-abiding behavior, encourage active community participation in solving social problems, lobby for educational, recreational, employment, and other social services, reach out to gang members, and provide direct services to youths. A structure was created to integrate youth into meaningful community roles, bring adults into contact with youths in their own community, and open up new channels of communication between community residents and institutions of the larger world, such as the schools, civic organizations, police, juvenile courts, and city government, which were important in determining opportunities for local youth. Qualitative and quantitative research data suggest that the Chicago Area Project has achieved considerable success in building indigent leadership, mobilizing community residents, strengthening community networks, providing educational, recreational, and job services for youths, and reducing delinquency (Schlossman et al., 1984; Sedlak and Schlossman, 1983).

The schools have a vital role to play in delinquency prevention. Children who do well in school tend to receive positive reinforcement from teachers, parents, and nondelinquent peers. If young people from economically disadvantaged neighborhoods can graduate from high school with a mastery of basic educational skills, social competencies, and a belief that they can succeed in a competitive, technological job market, they will be more likely to select mainstream pathways. Conversely, if they drop out of school with an accumulative sense of failure and join other unskilled dropouts on the streets, chances are much greater they will become involved in a delinquent way of life. Currently, as many as half the students drop out in disadvantaged inner city school districts and another 20% to 30% are functionally illiterate. Sheppard Kellam, an educator from Johns Hopkins University, has designed a program for the Baltimore School System to increase success in school learning and promote prosocial behavior. The program, which started in September 1986, consists of two tracks, Mastery Learning and the Good Behavior Game. Mastery Learning is a foolproof, self-paced learning system. Students are given a chance to master each lesson before proceeding to the next sequence. The Good Behavior Game is based on social-learning principles. Students will earn reward points for prosocial behavior and lose points for destructive acts and antisocial behavior (Hurley, 1985).

At the preschool level, programs such as Head Start target young children before behavior, social, and academic problems develop. Evidence from the Perry Preschool Program in Ypsilanti, Michigan indicates that a solid preschool enrichment can significantly influence a child's behavior in life. A study released in 1984, which followed 123 economically disadvantaged children from preschool age to young adulthood, found that those who attended the preschool program were less likely to become pregnant as teenagers and more likely to be employed, to have graduated from high school, and to have attempted postsecondary education. The arrest rates for the preschool children were less than those for the children who did not attend preschool (Hurley, 1985).

Prosocial peer-group interaction has been investigated by Ronald Feldman and his associates (1983) in the St. Louis Project. Feldman and other delinquency experts have noted that in most group work with delinquents inside and outside of institutions, delinquents are mixed together with other delinquents. Placing young people together in predominately delinquent groups has the unintended effect of reinforcing antisocial behavior. Young people bond with other delinquents. In their 4-year study of group social behavior, Feldman and his colleagues were interested in finding out what would happen if one or two delinquent youngsters were mixed in with groups of prosocial young people in a suburban community center. Seven hundred boys were divided into small groups of predominately nondelinquent and delinquent youngsters. The delinquent and high-risk boys were referred by the juvenile courts, mental health clinics, special school programs, and group homes. One or two delinquent and high-risk youngsters were placed in prosocial groups, while others were placed in groups made up of delinquent youngsters. All together there were three groups, predominately delinquent, predominately prosocial, and a mixture of one or two antisocial youngsters with predominately prosocial kids. The youths took part in a daycamp of sorts where they participated in arts and crafts, athletics, trips, and group discussions. Trained and untrained leaders used behavior-modification techniques, traditional group therapy methods, or no formal style in working with the groups. The results showed the most important element in predicting future antisocial behavior was whether delinquent and high-risk boys were in groups with other delinquent boys, or in a predominately prosocial group. The delinquent boys in groups with other delinquent youths showed no decline in subsequent antisocial behavior, while 91% of the delinquent and high-risk youths in the prosocial groups showed a significant decrease in future antisocial behavior.

Several training programs are available to help parents with predelinquent and acting-out children. Gerald Patterson and his colleagues at the Oregon Social Learning Center in Eugene, Oregon have worked with over 250 families in the past decade whose children's behavior at home and at school has been characterized by fighting, lying, stealing, defiance of authority, running away, and vandalism. Patterson and his colleagues believe that most delinquent behavior develops because of ineffective parenting skills. Their training program used social learning techniques to teach parents more effective ways to monitor their children's behavior, at home and at school, by using a point system to reward prosocial behaviors and punish violations of the rules. Parents learn to maintain clear rules, monitor compliance, handle violations without resorting to physical punishment, and negotiate expectations and standards. Basic communication skills, crisis management, and family problem-solving strategies are also taught. The children participate individually and with their parents in family counseling. The end result is that parents are able to use more positive management techniques, improve the consistency of expectations and sanctions, praise their children more often and criticize less, and have more positive child-rearing attitudes (Patterson, 1981; Patterson and Stouthhamer-Loeber, 1984).

SUMMARY AND CONCLUSIONS

Juvenile delinquency is a complex term with many different meanings and nuances. Juvenile delinquency covers a wide range of behaviors from running away to murder. There are status versus nonstatus offenders, minor versus major offenders, occasional versus repeat offenders, hidden versus recorded delinquents, arrested delinquents versus those who are counseled and released, as well as diverted delinquents and those adjudicated by the courts and labeled delinquent. Most of the 4% to 5% of America's teenagers referred to juvenile courts each year are involved in minor, transitory, and episodic misconduct. Only 2% to 3% are repeat, serious offenders. Some degree of rebellion, testing the limits, and experimenting with behaviors violating adult rules is to be expected as part of the process of establishing autonomy and independence. Eighty to ninety percent of teenagers admit to taking part in mild misconduct that technically could be classified as delinquency, which never comes to the attention of juvenile authorities.

Most of the major factors correlating with serious, persistent delinquency can be incorporated into two theoretical models: a psychological model and a sociocultural model. According to psychological theory, delinquent behavior is symptomatic of an emotional disturbance resulting from unresolved conflicts in psychosocial development. Sociocultural or sociogenic theories of delinquency assume that delinquent behavior evolves from a normal, social learning process through reinforcement, emulation, and identification with antisocial role models and influences. Therapies derived from the psychological view are concerned with working through underlying feelings and conflicts, while therapies that emerged from the sociocultural model emphasized reinforcing prosocial behaviors and making social systems more responsive to the needs of the individual. Some delinquency experts focus their attention on prevention. A number of prevention programs across the country are demonstrating that it is possible to ward-off delinquency by spending money ahead of time, teaching prosocial behaviors, and working with such key social systems as the family, peer groups, educational systems, and community action groups.

The juvenile justice system is an umbrella term for the major organizational structure that society has put into place to work with juvenile offenders. The juvenile justice system consists of the police, juvenile courts, community-based programs, and custodial facilities. The first juvenile court was formed in Illinois in 1899. The original purpose of the juvenile court was to guide and rehabilitate, rather than to punish youthful lawbreakers. The juvenile justice system has a wide range of options in determining what happens to youths accused of lawbreaking. A storm of criticism of the juvenile justice system during the past 20 years has led to a combination of reforms and counter-reforms. On the liberal side, youths now enjoy a greater range of legal rights and emancipation. On the conservative side, there is greater concern with protecting the public and holding young people responsible and accountable for the consequences of their actions.

Since its inception at the dawn of the 20th century, the juvenile justice system has moved through successive stages characterized by rescuing children from the evils of adult jails, rehabilitating emotionally disturbed delinquent youth, and sociogenic causation with treatment by social learning and behavioral therapies. Society is now at a point where the focus is on accountability and holding young people responsible for the consequences of their actions. To the extent that society is going to hold young people responsible for the consequences of their behavior, four issues must be addressed to insure that justice is fairly administered and that young people have the opportunity to select nondelinquent life pathways. First, schools must be restructured to teach young people the psychosocial skills and academic competencies they need to handle responsibility and to adapt to a competitive job market. Young people cannot be expected to behave responsibly unless they have the tools to become economically self-supporting and capable decision-makers. Second, the movement toward equal rights under the law and emancipation of youth should continue. Society cannot, in all fairness, subject young people to the punitive consequences of the law without providing them with the guarantees and freedoms that come with equal protection under the law. Third, the structural socioeconomic conditions that breed juvenile crime in the inner cities of America must be changed. If low-income, minority young people do not perceive that they have a viable range of economic and social options, they will continue to make antisocial choices. Admittedly, there are no simple solutions to complex socioeconomic problems, but a lack of simple solutions is no excuse for the society to turn its back on these young people. Finally, there must be greater uniformity of law enforcement for juveniles across and within jurisdictions. Clear guidelines should be adopted for categories of offenses that will be ignored and those that will result in diversion, informal probation, formal probation, and placement in custodial facilities. Young people will not learn to respect the law, if they cannot reliably predict the consequences of misbehavior. Guidelines should take into consideration that 80% to 90% of juvenile lawbreaking is never reported.

SUGGESTIONS FOR PARENTS, TEACHERS, COUNSELORS, AND YOUTH WORKERS

1. Encourage your child to succeed in school and participate in extracurricular activities. Education is a key to success in a competitive, technological job market. Dropping out of school reduces the range of employment choices, leads to hanging around with other dropouts, and increases the chance of delinquent behaviors.

2. If your child does not seem interested in pursuing an academic education, check with the school counselors to see what options are available in the way of work-study or vocational education programs. Marketable skills and a career action plan are safeguards against drifting into delinquency.

3. Take an interest in your children's recreational and social activities. Peer influence is an important factor in determining delinquent and nondelinquent behavior; know who your children's friends are and what kinds of peer activities they participate in.

4. If you live or teach in an economically disadvantaged neighborhood, get in touch with local community action groups. Find out what kinds of social, recreational, and employment activities they sponsor for young people, and encourage your child or students to participate.

5. Try to establish clear, consistent rules, expectations, and consequences for violations. Negotiate these rules and expectations, try to achieve a consensus whenever possible. Reinforce positive behavior with approval and compliments. Make sure your child knows you are aware of efforts he or she is making toward personal growth and improvement.

6. If your child is taken into custody by the police, find out what alternatives are available before processing, through the juvenile justice system, begins. If diversion, restitution, or family counseling programs are available, request participation on a voluntary basis. Get to the source of the problem between you and your child as quickly as possible and talk through conflicts involving expectations, values, and standards for social conduct.

7. If you are an educator or school counselor, encourage juvenile officials and police officers to visit your school to explain the juvenile justice system to the staff and students. Students need to know ahead of time how the system will respond to misconduct and where the limits are. Staff members and teachers need to know what prevention programs are available so potentially delinquent students can be referred before serious misconduct becomes entrenched.

8. The years from 15 to 18 are the critical time frame for the development of serious, repetitive delinquent behavior. Educators, parents, and youth workers interested in delinquency prevention should begin working with

young people prior to their midteens by exposing them to prosocial peer groups, special education and preemployment programs, social skills, as well as psychosocial growth training and family education programs.

DISCUSSION QUESTIONS

1. What is hidden delinquency, how is it assessed, and how do hidden delinquency and social class bias affect the reliability of official delinquency statistics?
2. Some experts have concluded that the traditional juvenile justice system was partly responsible for juvenile delinquency. What is the basis for this conclusion?
3. Discuss the major components and sequence of decision-making outcomes in the juvenile justice system. How are the components connected, and what is the role of each component in processing youth through the system?
4. Discuss the major reforms and counter-reforms in the juvenile justice system during the past 20 years. How did these reforms come about, and what are the major assumptions underlying the reforms and counter-reforms?
5. Discuss the psychological and sociogenic theories of delinquency. Compare and contrast the major assumptions of each theory regarding psychological development, social reinforcement, treatment, and prevention.
6. Explain the term *diversion*. How did diversion come about, what is the rationale for diversion, and what are some of the major pros and cons associated with diversion?
7. Social learning and behavior approaches to delinquency treatment and prevention became very popular in recent years. Discuss the rationale on which these approaches are based. What are their advantages and disadvantages, and why are they considered superior to the psychodynamic approach? Give examples of family, peer, educational, and community interventions based on social learning and behavior models.
8. Why was the juvenile justice system created in the United States at the beginning of the 20th century, what were some of the legal, humanitarian, and psychological justifications for its existence, and on what bases were the original justifications seriously questioned in the 1960s?

10
Conclusions

The widespread presence of troubled and distressed youth in contemporary society is symptomatic of deeper unresolved social issues in American life. The psychosocial landscape confronting young people has changed radically since adolescence became a sociological reality at the beginning of the 20th century. Changes in cultural values and sex roles, the decline of the nuclear family and extended family support systems, and the accelerating pace of technological innovation, economic upheavals, population shifts, geographic dislocations, and transformations of the workplace from a manufacturing to a service economy have increased the complexity of the conflicts, challenges, and dilemmas confronting teenagers. In the last 30 years, society has changed more rapidly than during any comparable period. We now live in a postindustrial society in which teenagers are bombarded with conflicting information, value systems, and choices at earlier and earlier ages. Teenagers are confronted with mixed messages regarding sexual restraint versus sexual expressiveness, hard work and future preparation versus instant gratification, individuality and competition versus cooperation and harmonious living with others, and following the rules as opposed to doing one's own thing. Drugs and alcohol are glamorized and associated with being masculine, feminine, and sexually appealing. At the same time, society stresses the importance of saying no to drugs and exercising caution with sex. Teenagers are expected to make long-term commitments that involve years of preparation for jobs that may not exist when they finish their years of schooling and apprenticeship training. The conflicts, challenges, and demands of adolescents have extended downward to the preteens and early teens and extended upward to the post-teens. Young people are maturing earlier physically, dating earlier, experimenting with sex and drugs sooner, and worrying about what will happen to them in the future, long before they become middle-teenagers. Large numbers of youths well into their twenties, are still acquiring the tools for economic independence and occupational mastery.

Fundamental changes in family life have left many teenagers without clearly defined support systems, parental values, or expectations for social conduct. Many parents are psychologically unavailable because of family disruptions, work pressures, and the dilemmas of adult transitions. A 37-year-old, recently divorced mother who is unsure of her own standards for sexual conduct as she reenters the dating scene, may have difficulty counseling her 15-year-old daughter regarding the role of sexual behavior in male-female relationships. A 40-year-old father who uses cocaine and marijuana recreationally is likely to have trouble counseling his teenage son about drug use and abuse. Parents who are going through mid-life psychological and occupational crises may be too preoccupied with their own transitions to effectively counsel their teenage children regarding value conflicts and future choices. As the rate of future shock and social-change increases, parents suffer from a cultural lag wherein the standards of their own adolescence and young adulthood no longer fit the dilemmas confronting the now generation. Rapid social change creates role reversals where the teenagers, in many cases, become the trend setters (Elkind, 1984). Parents are either too confused or overwhelmed to take charge. The peer group replaces the parents as the source of support and guidance. Adolescents can no longer use the stable values of their elders as a foundation to develop personal standards and to arrive at decisions about goals, values, and who they would like to become. Some teenagers perceive their parents' reluctance to set clear limits as covert approval to do whatever they please.

Today's teenagers are growing up at a faster rate with fewer adult support systems and less clearly defined values and standards for social conduct. The modern mass media, by catering to teenage tastes, trends, and fads, has become a powerful socialization agent. Most young people spend more time watching TV than interacting in direct conversation with their parents.

The effect of accelerated teenage development without adequate adult support systems and clearly defined standards is increasing adolescent psychological stress and vulnerability. According to Elkind (1984), today's adolescents are not sufficiently protected or nurtured. Teenagers do not receive the time or guidance they need to integrate a personal identity, resolve value conflicts, and develop a sense of self based on a foundation of security and love. Teenagers are rushed from childhood to adulthood without being provided with the opportunities to gradually develop the skills they need to cope with the transformations in their bodies, feelings, and thoughts. Teenagers have more choices but are not well-prepared to deal with a greater range of choices.

The price of the increasing psychological stress and vulnerability on contemporary teenagers, caused by more choices with less preparation and support, is a greater number of troubled and distressed youths. It is not surprising that the number of runaways, suicides, depressions, eating disturbances, and adolescent drug abusers has increased to epidemic proportions in the last 20 years. The common psychological themes underlying the behaviors and symptoms of troubled and distressed youths are the absence of adult support systems, lack of preparation to cope with complex challenges and conflicting demands, and doubts about self-worth, which appear to be due to a loss of love and uncertainties about whether one is appreciated by significant others. Many troubled and distressed youths feel a lack of connectedness or bonding to the family, and alienation from the larger society. At a time when teenagers need to be developing a sense of power, influence, hope, meaning, and emotional bonding, many adolescents feel alone, powerless, inadequate, uncertain, and pessimistic about themselves and their future. They feel overwhelmed by demands they neither understand nor have the tools to handle. They perceive themselves to be growing up in a world that does not care and offers little in the way of support and genuine love.

As society grows more complex and the rapid pace of social and technological change continues, the uncertainties and stresses confronting adolescents will continue to multiply. No amount of wishful thinking can return society to the "good old days" when youths were expected to follow the authoritarian dictates of their elders in a monolithic value system. The days of rigidly defined roles, carefully controlled choices, and sacred rules are gone forever. The old social order, where youth was expected to blindly follow the values of conformity; denial of joy and sensuous pleasure, obedience, stoicism, and unquestioning commitment to traditional social norms in return for a promise of future happiness, security, love, and power, simply will not work in modern society. Contemporary teenagers need to be prepared to live in a world where they will have to cope with competing demands, conflicting values, changing social conditions, and moral dilemmas, without rigid guidelines or consensual agreement from their elders or solid adult support systems.

Adolescent conflict is both inevitable and an essential condition of psychological growth. The inevitability of conflict and competing demands stems from the complexity and rapid pace of social change. The necessity of conflict for healthy adolescent psychosocial growth is based on three conditions. First, adolescents must confront uncertainties, struggle, and challenge in order to achieve an integrated sense of their identity and values. Second, conflict can provide the motivation to move to higher levels of social maturity and personal integration. While conflict and stress are uncomfortable, discomfort with dissonant values can motivate youth to work through conflicting issues. Third, successful resolution of conflict builds self-confidence and trust in self. What youth need is not to avoid or be protected from conflict but help in developing the coping tools and psychosocial competencies that will allow them to utilize conflict in a growth-facilitating manner. It is the absence of adaptive coping skills that creates troubled and distressed adolescent behavior. When adolescents encounter stressful experiences that overtax their psychosocial competencies and coping abilities, we are likely to see running away, depression, drug abuse, suicidal behavior, and eating disturbances.

During the past 20 years, psychologists, mental health workers, and youth advocates have developed the psychosocial competency model to help adolescents acquire the new behavioral, cognitive, social, and emotional coping skills they will need to deal with the accelerated pace of personal and social demands, resolve identity issues, confront new assumptions about themselves and their sexuality, and to integrate a set of comprehensive values that can be used as guidelines in making critical decisions, exploring adventure, fulfilling needs for excitement and sensuousness, and establishing a sense of power, adequacy, and connectedness to others. Psychosocial competency is a term used to denote the adequacy of self-concept, social skills, interpersonal relationship skills, coping, decision-making and problem-solving strategies; conflict resolution skills; communication and negotiational skills; and one's ability to develop and utilize support systems, achieve non-chemical highs, and effectively manage stress. Psychosocial competency skills are taught through a combination of psychoeducational methods involving active participation, such as discussions, rehearsal, role-playing, modeling, feedback, and values clarification. The psychosocial competency approach is built on the assumption that if adolescents feel good about themselves and are equipped with the resources to develop positive support systems and employ competent courses of action when faced with stressful situations, they will be less vulnerable to maladaptive behavior.

The emergence of the social competency model is a step in the right direction toward enabling young people to effectively meet the challenges of growing up in a "hurry-up" society. The question now is how to make the psychosocial competency technology available to a larger number of youth in schools, work settings, families, youth groups, youth homes, adolescent psychiatric units, and community service agencies that work primarily with teenagers. Many school districts are integrating social competency techniques into drug and suicide prevention programs, self-esteem building workshops, personal effectiveness training and applied psychology classes, health and safety classes, and social studies. Peer counseling programs are being developed, which stress the basic helping skills of effective listening, empathy, positive regard, and knowledge about psychological services available to teenagers (Jensen, 1984; Ross, 1985). Young people who are troubled and distressed are more likely to express their thoughts, feelings, and intentions with peers, as opposed to adults who they feel will attempt to control the situation. Peers as confidants and resource persons can be helpful as support systems and in connecting troubled adolescents to appropriate mental health services.

Social competency and interpersonal effectiveness training within the family can strengthen relationships and improve understanding between parents and adolescents. Helping parents and teenagers learn to listen, empathize, share power, solve problems collaboratively, decrease intense negative emotions, and reestablish loving, supportive feelings will reduce the angry acting out, resentment, and fear, which exist in many families. Youths are less likely to feel alienated and alone if they are part of a family in which they are listened to and supported as they struggle with issues involving sexual behavior, drugs, peer relationships, future planning, self-conduct, and self-worth. Decreasing the intensity of family conflicts reduces the psychological burdens on parents and is likely to provide them with greater freedom to meaningfully explore the transitions their own lives are going through as they move from young adulthood to middle adulthood.

The psychosocial competency approach is part of a larger trend away from the use of pathology models in the explanation, treatment, and prevention of troubled and distressed adolescent behavior. The bad-sick approach is being replaced by an interactive view that holds maladaptive adolescent behavior is the result of faulty interaction between the teenager and the psychosocial environment that results in excessive stresses, conflicts, frustration, and disruptive behavior. To the extent that adolescent psychopathology exists as such, it is no longer perceived as a process that operates solely inside the internal psychological or psychobiological space of the adolescent. The current emphasis in the field of adolescent mental health is on wellness and prevention, rather than pathology./Adolescents are viewed as young people who have the power to initiate growth, master new challenges, recover from setbacks, and reach out to positive support systems. Changes in the treatment of runaway youths are an excellent example of how a behavior, once considered bad, deviant, or sick, has been brought into the normal range of adolescent behavior for treatment within a nonpathological framework. Runaway youths are now looked upon as potentially responsible, capable young people who need growth-facilitating experiences to develop the positive self-esteem, coping tools, and support systems necessary to resolve stressful intrapersonal and interpersonal conflicts. Reappraisal of the problems of runaway youth has led to major modifications in the juvenile justice system and in the adolescent's legal and human rights. The direction of the juvenile court has been away from confinement, coercive treatment, and involuntary mental health services for first-term offenders, status offenders, and minor juvenile lawbreakers. Runaways, minor juvenile offenders, and other troubled and distressed youths are not necessarily sick or bad but sometimes confused, angry, sad, and disappointed because they cannot change stressful psychosocial conditions and family turmoils blocking their growth. Because youth cannot change these dilemmas, they act out, take drugs, turn inward with signs of depression and suicide, or obsessively focus on the size of their bodies. Even in schizophrenia, where there is a definite trend toward biochemical explanations and treatment with antipsychotic drugs, experts acknowledge that community-based aftercare models cannot work unless recovering schizophrenics, and their families as care providers, are given psychosocial competency training and support services. Once disruptive schizophrenia behavior has been controlled by antipsychotic drugs and hospital treatment, the patient needs an array of psychosocial skills to reenter the mainstream of work, school, and interpersonal interaction.

The challenge ahead is twofold. First, adolescents themselves must be incorporated in significant roles in planning prevention and treatment programs. Second, a well-integrated infrastructure of treatment and prevention services needs to be created at the local community level. Well-meaning attempts on the part of adults, parents, educators, and mental health workers to reduce drug abuse, suicidal behavior, depression, eating disturbances, and runaways will not succeed unless young people participate in defining the causes of maladaptive behavior and strategies for prevention and treatment. Young people represent a vast source of creative energy and imagination unencumbered by the rigid views of the past. They have a wealth of ideas about why adolescent life is so stressful and what can be done about it. They do not want to be unhappy, miserable, self-deprecating, angry, or bummed out. To work effectively in the long run, treatment and prevention approaches must have a supportive consensus within the target group. Adults cannot mandate adaptive coping styles, values, or standards for drug use, sexual behavior, and body size. Incorporating youth in an ongoing dialogue about their mental health needs will increase their willingness to cooperate.

Efforts by Congress and youth advocates to address the runaway youth problem in the 1970s brought to the surface the absence of a well-coordinated network of prevention, counseling, employment, medical, and crisis services staffed by well-trained adolescent practitioners in many communities. Strategic planning at the federal, state, and local level is necessary to remedy this deficit. During the past 20 years, the public has responded to a series of adolescent mental health crises without fully recognizing that different symptom patterns of troubled and distressed behavior are due to a common set of stresses. At one time or another, suicide, drugs, running away, eating disturbances, and depression have captured the public's attention. Each of these syndromes is a signal that adolescents and their parents need stronger support services to cope with the dilemmas of growing up in a complex, fast-paced society.

Special programs are needed for low-income, minority urban youths and young women. The structural conditions breeding crime in the inner cities of America must be changed. If minority youths do not perceive they have a viable range of economic and social options, they will continue to make antisocial choices. Schools must be reorganized to teach low-income, minority young people the psychosocial skills and the academic and technical competencies they need to adapt to a competitive job market. Young people cannot be expected to behave responsibly, unless they have the tools to become economically self-supporting and responsible decision makers.

Young women are expected to be attractive, powerful, assertive, sensuous, and likeable. As adults, they will have to balance the roles of care givers, employees, homemakers, and companions. Many young women are having trouble integrating these conflicting challenges into a comprehensive identity and positive self-concept. Adolescent mental health workers and women's groups need to focus more attention on providing teenage females with positive role models and strategies they can utilize to enhance internal self-worth as opposed to excessive concentration on physical body image.

In closing this book on troubled and distressed youth, it is appropriate to briefly mention the adolescent passage of the generation of youths who are the parents of today's adolescents. David Wallechinsky's (1987) high school class of 1965 is now entering midlife. Youth of the mid-60s were at the cutting edge of revolutionary changes in American life. Young people of the 1960s protested U.S. involvement in Vietnam, experimented with drugs, sexual freedom, and alternative life-styles, and refused to blindly follow the racial and gender biases of their parents. Most observers agree that the overwhelming majority of these youths have become solid, productive citizens as adults. The hippies and war protesters of yesterday are the yuppies and trendy adults of today. If history has any value, it has taught us that most troubled and distressed youths ultimately make it through the adolescent passage to become productive adults.

References

Achenbach, T. M., & Edelbrock, C. S. (1981). Behavioral problems and competencies reported by parents of normal and disturbed children aged four through sixteen. *Monographs of the Society for Research in Child Development, 46*, 1–82.

Adams, G. R., & Gullotta, T. S. (1983). *Adolescent life experiences*. Monterey, CA: Brooks-Cole.

Adams, T., Resnik, H., Brann, J., & Wiltz, L. (1985). *Just say no. Stop drug abuse before it starts*. Oakland, CA: Pacific Institutes.

Adler, J. (1982, January 4). Looking back at 81. *Newsweek*, pp. 26–52.

Agras, W. E., & Kirkley, B. C. (1986). Bulimia: Theories of etiology. In K. D. Brownell & J. P. Foreyt (Eds.), *Handbook of eating disorders: Physiology, psychology, and treatment of eating disorders*. New York: Basic Books.

Albert, N., & Beck, A. T. (1975). Incidence of depression in early adolescence. *Journal of Youth and Adolescence, 4*, 301–307.

American Psychiatric Association. (1952). *Diagnostic and statistical manual of mental disorders* (1st ed.). Washington, DC: Author.

American Psychiatric Association. (1968). *Diagnostic and statistical manual of mental disorders* (2nd ed.). Washington, DC: Author.

American Psychiatric Association. (1980). *Diagnostic and statistical manual of mental disorders* (3rd ed.). Washington, DC: Author.

American Psychiatric Association. (1987). *Diagnostic and statistical manual of mental disorders* (3rd ed., rev. ed.). Washington, DC: Author.

Andersen, A. E. (1983). Anorexia nervosa and bulimia: A spectrum of eating disorders. *Journal of Adolescent Health Care, 4*, 15–21.

Andersen, A. E. (1986). Inpatient and outpatient treatment of anorexia nervosa. In K. D. Brownell & J. P. Forety (Eds.), *Handbook of eating disorders: Physiology, psychology, and treatment of eating disorders* (pp. 333–352). New York: Basic Books.

Angel, S. (1983, August 25). Incest novel breaks long silence. *Los Angeles Times*, pt. V, p. 1.

Armstrong, C. P. (1932). *660 runaway boys*. Boston: Badger.

Armstrong, C. P. (1937). A psychoneurotic reaction of delinquent boys and girls. *Journal of Abnormal and Social Psychology, 32*, 329–342.

Armstrong, T. L., & Altschuler, D. M. (1982). Conflicting trends in juvenile justice sanctioning: Divergent strategies in the handling of the serious juvenile offender. *Juvenile and Family Court Journal, 33*(4), 15–30.

Asarnow, J. R., & Goldstein, M. J. (1986). Schizophrenia during adolescence and a developmental perspective on risk research. *Clinical Psychology Review, 9*, 211–235.

Atkinson, R. L., Atkinson, R. C., & Hilgard, E. R. (1983). *Introduction to psychology* (8th ed.). New York: Harcourt, Brace and Jovanovich.

Bakan, D. (1971, Fall). Adolescence in America: From idea to social fact. *Daedalus, 100*, 979–995.

Bakwin, H. (1973). Suicide in children and adolescents. *Journal of the American Medical Women's Association, 28*(12), 603–650.

Bandura, A. (1977). *Social learning theory.* Englewood Cliffs, NJ: Prentice-Hall.

Banks, S. (1984, October 15). Runaways get a lift: Many arrive "Home free." *Los Angeles Times*, pp. 1, 3.

Bateson, G., Jackson, D. D., Haley, J., & Weakland, J. (1956). Toward a theory of schizophrenia. *Behavioral Sciences, 1*, 251–264.

Baum, L. F. (1982). *Wizard of Oz.* New York: Holt, Rinehart & Winston.

Bayer, A. E. (1984, December). Eating out of control. *Children Today*, pp. 7–11.

Beck, A. T. (1972). *Depression: Causes and treatment.* Philadelphia, PA: University of Pennsylvania.

Beck, A. T. (1974). The development of depression: A cognitive model. In R. Friedman & M. Katz (Eds.), *Psychology of depression: Contemporary theory and research.* Washington, DC: Winston-Wiley.

Beck, A. T. (1976). *Cognitive therapy and the emotional disorders.* New York: International Universities Press.

Beck, A. T. (1978). *Beck depression inventory.* Philadelphia, PA: Center for Cognitive Therapy.

Beck, A. T., Rush, A. G., Shaw, B. F., & Emery, G. (1979). *Cognitive therapy of depression.* New York: Guilford Press.

Beck, M. (1986, September 1). Drugs open a generation gap. *Newsweek*, p. 21.

Beckham, E. E., & Leber, W. R. (Eds.). (1985). *Handbook of depression: Treatment, assessment and research.* Homewood, IL: Dorsey Press.

Beggs, L. (1969). *Huckleberry's for runaways.* New York: Ballantine.

Bell, M., Mark, M. E., & McCall, C. (1985). *Streetwise* [Film]. Los Angeles: Angelika Films, a New World Co.

Bell, P. (1985, September). *Social policy prevention.* Paper delivered at the Conference on Alcohol and Drug Abuse Among Blacks, The Menninger Foundation, Topeka, KS.

Benalcazar, B. (1982). Study of fifteen runaway patients. *Adolescence, 17*(62), 553–566.

Berlin, J. (1981). Long-term care at Huckleberry. In J. S. Gordon & M. Beyer, *Reaching troubled youth: Runaways and community mental health.* Rockville, MD: U.S. Department of Health and Human Services.

Binder, A. (1983). The juvenile justice system and juvenile offenders: An overview. *The Counseling Psychologist, 11*(2), 65–68.

Binder, A., Bruce, D. D., Jr., & Geis, G. (1988). *Juvenile delinquency: Historical, cultural and legal perspectives.* New York: Macmillan.

Binder, A., & Geis, G. (1984, October). Ad populum argumentation in criminology: Juvenile diversion as rhetoric. *Crime and Delinquency, 30*(4), 624–647.

Binswanger, L. (1957). The case of Ellen West. In R. May (Ed.), *Existence* (pp. 236–262). New York: Basic Books.

Birlson, P. (1981). The validity of depressive disorder in childhood and the development of a self rating scale: A research project. *Journal of Child Psychiatry, 22*, 73–88.

Blaine, G. B. (1979). *Is adolescent suicide preventable?* Panel presented at the annual meeting of the American Association of Adolescent Psychiatry, Chicago, IL.

Blake, A. (1977, October 2). Outward bound: Is the experience lasting? *Boston Sunday Globe*, pp. 38–39.

Bleuler, E. (1950). *Dementia praecox or the group of schizophrenics*. New York: International Universities Press. (Original work published 1911)

Bleuler, M. (1978). There is hope: The long-term course of schizophrenic psychosis. In L. Wynne, R. Cromwell, & S. Mathysse, *The nature of schizophrenia: New approaches to research and treatment*. New York: Wiley & Sons.

Boffey, P. M. (1986, June 24). Technology helps research solve the schizophrenia puzzle. *Orange County Register* (Santa Ana, California), pt. A, pp. 1, 2.

Bollen, K. A., & Phillips, D. P. (1982). Imitation suicide: A national study of the effects of television news stories. *American Sociological Review, 47*, 802–809.

Bolton, R. H. (1979). *People skills: How to assert yourself, listen to others and resolve conflicts*. Englewood Cliffs, NJ: Prentice-Hall.

Bootzin, R. R., & Acocella, J. R. (1980). *Abnormal psychology: Current perspectives* (3rd ed.). New York: Random House.

Boskind-Lodhal, M. (1976). Cinderella's step sisters: A Feminist perspective on anorexia nervosa and bulimia. *Signs: The Journal of Women in Culture and Society, 2*, 342–356.

Boskind-White, M., & White, W. C. (1983). *Bulimarexia: The binge/purge cycle*. New York: W. W. Norton.

Boyer, J. L., & Guthrie, L. (1985). Assessment and treatment of the suicidal patient. In E. E. Beckham & W. R. Leber (Eds.), *Handbook of depression: Treatment, assessment, and research* (pp. 606–633). Homewood, IL: The Dorsey Press.

Brammer, L. M., & Abrego, P. J. (1981). Intervention strategies for coping with life transitions. *The Counseling Psychologist, 9*(2), 19–36.

Brennan, T. (1980). Mapping the diversity among runaways. *Journal of Family Issues, 1*(2), 189–209.

Brennan, T., Huizinga, D., & Elliott, D. (1978). *The social psychology of runaways*. Lexington, MA: D. C. Heath.

Brook, J. S., Gordon, A. S., Whiteman, M., & Cohen, D. (1986). Dynamics of childhood and adolescent personality traits and adolescent drug use. *Developmental Psychology, 22*(3), 403–414.

Brown, C. (1966). *Man-child in the promised land*. New York: Signet Books.

Brown, C. (1973). *The children of Ham*. Briar Cliff Manor, NY: Stein & Day.

Brown, D. (1987, January 29). Program aids self esteem of teen addicts. *Los Angeles Times*, pt. V, pp. 1–2.

Brownell, K. D., & Foreyt, J. P. (Eds.). (1986). *Handbook of eating disorders: Physiology, psychology, and treatment of eating disorders*. New York: Basic Books.

Bruch, H. (1973). *Eating disorders: Obesity, anorexia nervosa and the person within*. New York: Basic Books.

Bruch, H. (1978). *The golden cage: The enigma of anorexia nervosa*. Cambridge, MA: Harvard University Press.

Bruch, H. (1982). Anorexia nervosa: Therapy and theory. *American Journal of Psychiatry, 139*, 1531–1538.

Bruch, H. (1986). Anorexia nervosa: The therapeutic task. In K. D. Brownell & J. P.

Foreyt (Eds.), *Handbook of eating disorders: Physiology, psychology, and treatment of eating disorders* (pp. 328–332). New York: Basic Books.

Bryant, R., & Bates, B. (1985). Anorexia nervosa: Aeitiological theories and treatment methods. *Journal of Adolescence, 8*, 93–103.

Bucy, J. (1985, July). *To Whom do they belong? A profile of America's runaway and homeless youth and the programs that help them.* Testimony presented to the Sub-Committee on Children, Family, Drug and Alcoholism, United States Senate, October 1, 1985. Washington, DC: National Network of Runaway and Youth Services.

Burns, D. P. (1982, November). The perfectionist's script for self defeat. *Psychology Today*, pp. 34–52.

Burton, R. (Democritis Junior). (1621). *The anatomy of melancholy*. Oxford: Printed by John Lichfield and James Short for Henry Cripps.

Caine, E. (1978). Two contemporary tragedies: Adolescent suicide/adolescent alcoholism. *National Association of Private Psychiatric Hospitals Journal, 9*(3), 4–11.

Camus, A. (1955). *The myth of Sisyphus*. New York: Knopf.

Canton, P. (1985, February 18). These teenagers feel they have no options. *People Magazine*, pp. 84–87.

Cantwell, D. P., & Carlson, G. A. (Eds.). (1983). *Affective disorders in childhood and adolescence: An update*. New York: S. P. Medical and Scientific Books.

Caplan, G. (1964). *Principles of preventive psychiatry*. New York: Basic Books.

Caplan, G. (1974). *Support systems and community mental health*. New York: Behavioral Publications.

Care and treatment of schizophrenia—Part I. (1986, June). *The Harvard Medical School Mental Health Letter, 2*, pp. 1–4.

Care and treatment of schizophrenia—Part II. (1986, July). *The Harvard Medical School Mental Health Letter, 3*, pp. 1–4.

Carey, J. T., & McAnany, P. D. (1984). *Introduction to juvenile delinquency youth and the law*. Englewood Cliffs, NJ: Prentice-Hall.

Carlson, G. A. (1983). Depression and suicidal behavior in children and adolescents. In D. P. Cantwell & G. A. Carlson (Eds.), *Affective disorders in childhood and adolescence: An update* (pp. 335–353). New York: S. P. Medical and Scientific Books.

Carlson, G. A., & Garber, J. (1986). Developmental issues in the classification of depression in children. In M. Rutter, C. E. Izard, & P. B. Read (Eds.), *Depression in young people: Developmental and clinical perspectives*. New York: Guilford Press.

Carstensen, L. L., & Phillips, D. P. (1986, September 11). Clustering of teenage suicides after television news stories about suicide. *The New England Journal of Medicine, 315*(11), 685–689.

Cavan, R. S., & Ferdinand, T. N. (1981). *Juvenile delinquency* (4th ed.). New York: Harper & Row.

Chiles, J. A., Miller, M. L., & Cox, G. B. (1980). Depression in an adolescent delinquent population. *Archives of General Psychiatry, 87*, pp. 1179–1184.

Cimons, M. (1985, June 13). Panel cautiously backs shock therapy. *Los Angeles Times*, pt. I, p. 1.

Clark, M. (1979, November 12). Drugs and psychiatry: A new era. *Newsweek*, pp. 98–104.

Cloward, R. A., & Ohlin, L. E. (1960). *Delinquency and opportunity: A theory of delinquent gangs*. New York: Free Press.

Cohen, H. L., & Filipczak, J. (1971). *A new learning environment*. San Francisco: Jossey-Bass.

Coleman, J. C., Butcher, J. N., & Carson, R. C. (1984). *Abnormal psychology and modern life* (7th ed.). Glenview, IL: Scott, Foresman.

Coles, R. (1972). *Farewell to the south*. Boston: Little, Brown.

Conger, J. J., & Petersen, A. C. (1984). *Adolescence and youth: Psychological development in a changing world* (3rd ed.). New York: Harper & Row.

Covington, J. (1983). Adolescent deviation and age. *Journal of Youth and Adolescence, 11*(4).

Coyne, J. C. (1976). Depression and the responses of others. *Journal of Abnormal Psychology, 85*, 186–193.

Craig, M., & Glueck, S. J. (1963). Ten years experience with the Glueck social prediction scale. *Crime and Delinquency, 24*, pp. 231–232.

Cramer, P., & Carter, T. (1978). The relationship between sexual identification and the use of defense mechanisms. *Journal of Personality Assessment, 42*, 63–73.

Crisp, A. H. (1980). *Anorexia nervosa: Let me be*. New York: Grune & Stratton.

Cross, H. J., & Kleinhesselink, R. R. (1980). Psychological perspectives on drugs and youth. In J. F. Adams (Ed.), *Understanding adolescence: Current developments in adolescent psychology* (4th ed.). Boston: Allyn & Bacon.

Dacey, J. S. (1986). *Adolescents today* (3rd ed.). Glenview, IL: Scott, Foresman.

Davis, P. A. (1983). *Suicidal adolescents*. Springfield, IL: Charles C Thomas.

Davison, G. C., & Neale, J. M. (1982). *Abnormal psychology* (3rd ed.). New York: Wiley & Sons.

Delay, J., & Deniker, P. (1952). Le traitement des psychoses par une methods neurolytique derivee de l'hibernotherapie. In *Congres de Medicins Alienistes et Neurologistes de France et des pays de langues francaise*. Luxembourg.

Doan, M., & Peterson, S. (1984, November 12). As cluster suicide takes toll of teenagers. *U.S. News & World Report*, pp. 49–50.

Dolan, M. (1986, September 15). Crusade on drugs urged by Reagans. *Los Angeles Times*, pp. 1, 14.

Dublin, L. L. (1963). *Suicide: A sociological and statistical study*. New York: Ronald Press.

Duffy, B. (1986, September 29). War on drugs: More than a short term high. *U.S. News & World Report*, pp. 28–29.

Dupont, R. L. (1984). Bulimia: A modern epidemic among adolescents. *Pediatric Annals, 13*, 908–914.

Durkheim, E. (1951). *Suicide: A sociological study*. New York: Free Press.

Dusek, J. B. (1987). *Adolescent development and behavior*. Englewood Cliffs, NJ: Prentice-Hall.

Elkind, D. (1967). Ego centrism in adolescence. *Child Development, 38*, 1025–1034.

Elkind, D. (1981). *The hurried child: Growing up too fast too soon*. Reading, MA: Addison-Wesley.

Elkind, D. (1984). *All grown up and no place to go, teenagers in crisis*. Reading, MA: Addison-Wesley.

Ellis, A. (1970). Rational emotive therapy. In L. Hershen (Ed.), *Four psychotherapies* (pp. 47–72). New York: Appleton-Century-Crofts.

Emery, G., Bedrosian, R., & Garber, J. (1983). Cognitive therapy with depressed children and adolescents. In D. P. Cantwell & G. A. Carlson (Eds.), *Affective disorders in childhood and adolescence: An update*. New York: S. P. Medical and Scientific Books pp. 445–471.

Emery, P. E. (1983, Summer). Adolescent depression and suicide. *Adolescence, 18*(70), 245–258.

Erikson, E. H. (1956). The problem of ego identity. *The Journal of American Psychoanalytic Association, 11*, 56–121.

Erikson, E. H. (1963). *Childhood and society* (2nd ed.). New York: Norton.

Erikson, E. H. (1968). *Identity: youth and crisis.* New York: Norton.

Fairburn, C. (1981). A cognitive behavioural approach to the treatment of bulimia. *Psychological Medicine, 11*, 707–711.

Fairburn, C. G. (1985). Cognitive-behavioral treatment for bulimia. In D. M. Garner & P. E. Garfinkel (Eds.), *Handbook of psychotherapy for anorexia nervosa and bulimia* (pp. 161–192). New York: Guilford Press.

Fairburn, C. G., & Cooper, P. J. (1982). Self induced vomiting and bulimia nervosa: An undetected problem. *British Medical Journal, 284*, 1153–1155.

Fairburn, C. G., Cooper, Z., & Cooper, P. J. (1986). The clinical features and maintenance of bulimia nervosa. In K. D. Brownell & J. P. Foreyt (Eds.), *Handbook of eating disorders: Physiology, psychology, and treatment of eating disorders* (pp. 389–404). New York: Basic Books.

Fairburn, C. G., & Garner, D. M. (1986, March). The diagnosis of bulimia nervosa. *International Journal of Eating Disorders, 5*, 403–419.

Falloon, I. R., Boyd, J., & McGill, C. W. (1984). Family care of schizophrenia: A problem solving approach in the treatment of mental illness. New York: Guilford Press.

Farberow, N. L. (1977). Adolescent suicide. In V. Aalberg (Ed.), *Proceedings of the 9th International Congress for Suicide Prevention.* Helsinki: Finnish Association for Mental Health.

Farberow, N. L. (1985). Youth suicide: A summary. In M. L. Peck, N. L. Farberow, & R. E. Litman (Eds.), *Youth suicide* (pp. 191–203). New York: Springer.

Farberow, N. L., & Shneidman, E. S. (Eds.). (1961). *The cry for help.* New York: McGraw-Hill.

Feldman, R. A., Caplinger, T. E., & Wodarski, J. S. (1983). *The St. Louis conundrum: The effective treatment of anti-social youths.* Englewood Cliffs, NJ: Prentice-Hall.

Finckenauer, J. O. (1982). *Scared straight and the panacea phenomenon.* Englewood Cliffs, NJ: Prentice-Hall.

Fischer, D. G. (1983). Parental supervision and delinquency. *Perceptual and Motor Skills, 56*, 635–640.

Fixen, D. L., Phillips, E. L., Phillips, E. A., & Wolf, M. M. (1976). The teaching family model group home treatment. In W. E. Craighead, A. E. Kazdin, & M. J. Mahoney (Eds.), *Behavior Modification.* Boston: Houghton Mifflin.

Flanagan, T. J., & McCloud, M. (1983). *Source book of criminal justice statistics.* Washington, DC: U.S. Department of Justice.

Flanagan, T. J., Van Alstyne, D. J., & Gottfredson, M. R. (Eds.). (1982). *Source book of criminal justice statistics — 1981.* Washington, DC: U.S. Department of Justice.

Forisha-Kovach, B. (1983). *The experience of adolescence: Development in context.* Glenview, IL: Scott, Foresman.

Frederick, C. J. (1985). An introduction and overview of youth suicide. In M. L. Peck, N. L. Farberow, & R. E. Litman (Eds.), *Youth suicide.* New York: Springer.

Freud, A. (1937). *The ego and the mechanisms of defense.* New York: International Universities Press.

Freud, S. (1949). *An outline of psychoanalysis.* New York: Norton. (Original work published 1933).

Freud, S. (1950). *Mourning and melancholia* (Collected Papers, Vol. 4). London: Hogarth Press and Institute of Psychoanalysis. (Original work published 1917).

Freud, S. (1966). *New introductory lectures on psychoanalysis* (J. Strachey, Ed., & Trans.). New York: Norton. (Original work published 1933).

Freud, S. (1974). *The ego and the id*. London: Hogarth. (Original work published 1923).

Freud, S. (1977). *A general introduction to psychoanalysis* (J. Strachey, Ed., & Trans.). New York: Liveright. (Original work published 1920).

Friedman, P. (Ed.). (1967). *Symposium on suicide with particular reference to suicide among young students*. New York: International Universities Press.

Fromm, E. (1941). *Escape from freedom*. New York: Norton.

Fromm, E. (1955). *The sane society*. New York: Norton.

Fromm-Reichmann, F. (1948). Notes on the development of treatment of schizophrenia by psychoanalytic psychotherapy. *Psychiatry, 11*, 263–273.

Fuhrmann-Schneider, B. S. (1986). *Adolescence, adolescents*. Boston: Little, Brown.

Gallup, G., Jr. (1985). *The Gallup poll-public opinion, 1985*. Wilmington, DE: Scholarly Resources.

Galvin, J., & Polk, K. (1983). Juvenile justice: Time for a new direction. *Crime and Delinquency, 29*, 325–331.

Gandour, M. J. (1984, Spring). Bulimia: Clinical description, assessment, etiology and treatment. *International Journal of Eating Disorders, 3*(3), 3–37.

Garfinkel, B. D., Froese, M. D., & Hood, J. (1982, October). Suicide attempts in adolescence. *American Journal of Psychiatry, 139*(10), 1257–1261.

Garfinkel, P. E., & Garner, D. M. (1982). *Anorexia nervosa: A multidimensional perspective*. New York: Brunner/Mazel.

Garfinkel, P. E., & Kaplan, A. S. (1986). Anorexia nervosa: Diagnostic conceptualizations. In K. D. Brownell & J. P. Forety (Eds.), *Handbook of eating disorders: Physiology, psychology, and treatment of eating disorders* (pp. 266–282). New York: Basic Books.

Garmezy, N. (1978). Observations on high risk research and premorbid development in schizophrenia. In L. C. Wynne, R. L. Cromwell, & S. Mathysse (Eds.), *The nature of schizophrenia*. New York: Wiley & Sons.

Garner, D. M. (1986). Cognitive therapy for anorexia. In K. D. Brownell & J. P. Foreyt (Eds.), *Handbook of eating disorders: Physiology, psychology, and treatment of eating disorders* (pp. 301–327). New York: Basic Books.

Garner, D. M., & Bemis, K. M. (1985). Cognitive therapy for anorexia nervosa. In D. M. Gardner & P. E. Garfinkel (Eds.), *Handbook of psychotherapy for anorexia nervosa and bulimia* (pp. 107–147). New York: Guilford Press.

Garner, D. M., & Garfinkel, P. E. (Eds.). (1979). The eating attitude test: An index of the symptoms of anorexia nervosa. *Psychological Medicine, 9*, 273–279.

Garner, D. M., & Garfinkel, P. E. (Eds.). (1985). *Handbook of psychotherapy for anorexia nervosa and bulimia*. New York: Guilford Press.

Garner, D. M., Garfinkel, P. E., Swartz, D., & Thompson, M. (1980). Cultural expectations of thinness in women. *Psychological Reports, 47*, 483–491.

Garner, D. M., Olmstead, M. P., & Polivy, J. (1983). Development and validation of a multidimensional eating disorder inventory for anorexia and bulimia. *International Journal of Eating Disorders, 2*, 15–34.

Garner, D. M., Rockert, W., Olmstead, M. P., Johnson, C., & Coseina, P. V. (1985). Psychoeducational principles in the treatment of bulimia and anorexia nervosa. In D. M. Gardner & P. E. Garfinkel (Eds.), *Handbook of psychotherapy for anorexia nervosa and bulimia* (pp. 513–572). New York: Guilford Press.

Gelman, V. (1986, January 20). Treating teens in trouble. *Newsweek*, pp. 52–54.

Gentry, B. (Singer). (1967). *Ode to Billy Joe* (Phonograph Record), Los Angeles: Capitol Records.

Gibbons, P. C., & Krohn, M. D. (1986). *Delinquent behavior* (4th ed.). Englewood Cliffs, NJ: Prentice-Hall.

Gilbert, E. H., & DeBlassie, R. R. (1984). Anorexia nervosa: Adolescent starvation by choice. *Adolescence, 19*, 839–846.

Gilead, M. P., & Mulaik, J. S. (1983). Adolescent suicide: A response to developmental crisis. *Perspectives in Psychiatric Care, 21*(3), 94–101.

Gilligan, C. (1982). *In a different voice: Psychological theory and women's development.* Cambridge, MA: Harvard University Press.

Glueck, S., & Glueck, E. (1950). *Unraveling juvenile delinquency.* Cambridge, MA: Harvard University Press.

Gold, M., & Petronio, R. (1980). Delinquent behavior in adolescence. In J. Adelson (Ed.), *Handbook of adolescent psychology.* New York: John Wiley & Sons.

Goldberg, S. C., Halmi, K. A., Eckert, E. D., Casper, R. C., Davis, J. A., & Roper, M. (1980). Attitudinal dimensions in anorexia nervosa. *Journal of Psychiatric Research, 15*, 239–251.

Goldenberg, H. (1977). *Abnormal psychology: A social community approach.* Monterey, CA: Brooks-Cole.

Goldenson, R. M. (Ed.). (1984). *Longman dictionary of psychology and psychiatry.* New York: Longman.

Goldstein, A. P., Sprafkin, R. P., Gershaw, N. J., & Klein, P. (1980). *Skill streaming the adolescent.* Champaign, IL: Research Press.

Goldstein, M. J. (1985). Family factors that antedate the onset of schizophrenia and related disorders: The results of a fifteen year prospective longitudinal study. *Acta Psychiatrica Scandinavica Supplementum, 71*(319), 7–18.

Goldstein, M. J., Baker, B. L., & Jamison, K. R. (1980). *Abnormal psychology: Experiences, origins and interventions.* Boston: Little, Brown.

Goldstein, M. J., & Doane, J. A. (1982). Family factors in the onset, course and treatment of schizophrenic spectrum disorders. *The Journal of Nervous and Mental Disease, 170*(11), 692–700.

Goldstein, M. J., & Doane, J. A. (1985). Interventions with families and the course of schizophrenia. In M. Alpert (Ed.), *Controversies in schizophrenia* (pp. 381–397). New York: Guilford Press.

Goodwin, D. W. (1976). *Is alcoholism hereditary?* New York: Oxford.

Gordon, J. S. (1981). Running away: Reaction or revolution. In J. S. Gordon & M. Beyer (Eds.), *Reaching troubled youth: Runaways and community mental health.* Rockville, MD: U.S. Department of Health and Human Services.

Gordon, J. S., & Beyer, M. (Eds.). (1981). *Reaching troubled youth: Runaways and community mental health* (DHHS Publication #ADM 81-955). Rockville, MD: U.S. Department of Health and Human Services.

Gould, M. S., & Shaffer, D. (1986, September 11). The impact of suicide in television movies: Evidence of imitation. *The New England Journal of Medicine, 315*(11), 690–693.

Gould, R. E. (1965). Suicide problems in children and adolescents. *American Journal of Psychiatry, 19*, 228–246.

Greeley, H. (1850). *Hints toward reform.* New York: Harper & Row.

Green, H. (1964). *I never promised you a rose garden.* New York: New American Library.

Greenblatt, M., Levinson, D. J., & Williams, R. H. (1957). *The patient and the mental hospital*. New York: Free Press.

Greene, N. B., & Esselstyn, T. C. (1972). The beyond control girl. *Juvenile Justice, 23*, 13–19.

Greuling, J. W., & DeBlassie, R. R. (1980, Fall). Adolescent suicide. *Adolescence, 15*(59), 589–601.

Gross, B., & Gross, R. (1977). *The children's rights movement*. Garden City, NY: Anchor Books.

Guilford, J. P. (1954). *Psychometric methods*. New York: McGraw-Hill.

Gull, W. W. (1964). Anorexic nervosa. In R. M. Kaufman & M. Helman (Eds.), *Evolution of psychosomatic concepts. Anorexia nervosa: A paradigm*. New York: International Universities Press. (Original work published 1874, *Trans. Clin. Soc.* Vol. 7, pp. 22–28).

Gullotta, T. P. (1978). Runaways, reality or myth. *Adolescence, 13*(52), 543–550.

Gullotta, T. P., & Adams, G. R. (1982). Substance abuse minimization: Conceptualizing prevention in adolescent and youth programs. *Journal of Youth and Adolescence, 11*(5), 409–424.

Haan, N. (1977). *Coping and defending*. New York: Academic Press.

Hall, G. S. (1904). *Adolescence*. New York: Appleton.

Halmi, K. A. (1985a). Anorexia nervosa. In H. I. Kaplan & B. J. Sadock (Eds.), *Comprehensive textbook of psychiatry* (4th ed., Vol. 2, pp. 1143–1148). Baltimore, MD: Williams & Wilkins.

Halmi, K. A. (1985b). Eating disorders. In H. I. Kaplan & B. J. Sadock (Eds.), *Comprehensive textbook of psychiatry* (4th ed., Vol. 2, pp. 1731–1736). Baltimore, MD: Williams & Wilkins.

Halmi, K. A., Falk, J. R., & Schwartz, E. (1981). Binge-eating and vomiting: A survey of a college population. *Psychological Medicine, 11*, 697–706.

Hammond, W. A. (1879). *Fasting girls: Their physiology and pathology*. New York: Putnam.

Hanson, D. J. (1980). Drug education—Does it work? In F. R. Scarpihi & S. K. Datesman (Eds.), *Drugs and the youth culture* (pp. 251–282). Beverly Hills, CA: Sage Publications.

Hatton, C. L., Valente, S. M.,& Rink, A. (1977). *Suicide: Assessment and intervention*. New York: Appleton-Century-Crofts.

Hawkins, S. (1985, March 11). Ratpack youth: Teenage rebels in suburbia. *U.S. News & World Report*, pp. 51–54.

Healey, W. (1915). *The individual delinquent*. Boston: Little, Brown.

Hendin, H. (1975). Growing up dead. Student suicide. *American Journal of Psychotherapy, 29*(3), 327–338.

Hendin, H. (1985). Suicide among the young: Psychodynamics and demography. In M. L. Peck, N. L. Farberow, & R. E. Litman (Eds.), *Youth suicide* (pp. 19–38). New York: Springer.

Herbert, W. (1982, March 13). Schizophrenia: From adolescent insanity to dopamine disease. *Science News, 121*, pp. 173–175.

Herman, J. (1981). *Father-daughter incest*. Cambridge, MA: Harvard University Press.

Herzog, A., & Resnik, H. L. (1968). A clinical study of parental response to adolescent death by suicide and recommendations for approaching the survivors. In N. L. Farberow (Ed.), *Proceedings of the Fourth International Conference for Suicide Prevention* (pp. 381–390). Los Angeles: Suicide Prevention Center, Inc./Delmar.

Herzog, D. B. (1984, December). Are anorexic and bulimic patients depressed? *American Journal of Psychiatry, 141*(12), 1594–1597.

Hildebrand, J. A. (1968). Reasons for runaways. *Crime and Delinquency, 14*(1), 42–48.

Hill, W. H. (1984). Intervention and postvention in schools. In H. S. Sudak, H. B. Ford, & N. S. Rusforth (Eds.), *Suicide in the young.* Littleson, MA: Wright PSG.

Hinsie, L. E., & Campbell, R. J. (1970). *Psychiatric dictionary* (4th ed.). New York: Oxford University Press.

Hirschi, T. (1969). *Causes of delinquency.* Berkeley, CA: University of California Press.

Hodges, K., Kline, J., Stern, L., Cytryn, L., & McKnew, D. (1982a). The development of a child assessment interview for research and clinical use. *Journal of Abnormal Child Psychology, 10,* 173–189.

Hodges, K., McKnew, D., Cytryn, L., Stern, L., & Kline, J. (1982b). Child Assessment Schedule (CAS) diagnostic interview: A report on reliability and validity. *Journal of the American Academy of Child Psychiatry, 21,* 468–473.

Hodges, K. K., & Seigel, L. J. (1985). Depression in children and adolescents. In E. E. Beckham & W. R. Leber (Eds.), *Handbook of depression: Treatment, assessment and research.* Homewood, IL: The Dorsey Press.

Holden, C. (1985, January). Genes, personality and alcoholism. *Psychology Today,* pp. 38–44.

Holzman, P. S., & Grinker, R. R. (1974). Schizophrenia in adolescence. *Journal of Youth and Adolescence, 3*(4), 276–290.

Homer, L. E. (1973). Community-based resources for R. *Social Case Work, 54*(8), 473–479.

Hopkins, J. R. (1983). *Adolescence: The transitional years.* New York: Academic Press.

Horney, K. (1937). *The neurotic personality of our time.* New York: Norton.

Horney, K. (1945). *Our inner conflicts: A constructive theory of neurosis.* New York: Norton.

Howlett, H. S. (1986, February 23–25). Teen overcomes drug addiction. *Newport Daily Pilot* (Newport Beach, California), Section A2.

Hsu, L. K. G. (1980). Outcome of anorexic nervosa: A review of the literature (1954–1978). *The Archives of General Psychiatry, 37,* 1041–1046.

Huba, G. J., Wingard, J. A., & Benher, P. M. (1979). Beginning adolescent drug use and peer and adult interaction systems. *Journal of Consulting and Clinical Psychology, 49*(2), 265–276.

Hunt, I. (1970). *No promises in the wind.* Chicago: Follett.

Hurley, P. (1985, March). Arresting delinquency. *Psychology Today,* pp. 63–68.

Husain, S. A., & Vandiver, T. (1984). *Suicide in children and adolescents.* New York: Spectrum Books.

Hussein, Waris (Director). (1985). *Surviving* [Film]. Los Angeles: American Broadcasting Company TV Studios.

Institute of Judicial Administration and American Bar Association Juvenile Justice Standards Project. (1977). *Standards relating to administration.* Cambridge, MA: Ballinger.

Jacobs, J. (1971). *Adolescent suicide.* New York: Wiley.

Janis, I. L. (Ed.). (1969). *Personality: Dynamics, development and assessment.* New York: Harcourt, Brace and World.

Jenkins, R. L. (1969). Classification of behavior problems of children. *American Journal of Psychiatry, 125*(8), 1032–1039.

Jenkins, R. L. (1971). The runaway reaction. *American Journal of Psychiatry, 128*(2), 168–173.

Jenkins, R. L., & Boyer, A. (1968). Types of delinquent behaviors and background factors. *International Journal of Social Psychiatry, 14*, 65–76.

Jensen, L. C. (1985). *Adolescence: Theories, research, applications.* New York: West.

Joel, B. (Singer). (1973–75). *You're only human* (From the album *Greatest Hits*, Vol. 1 & 2; Phonograph Record). New York: Columbia Records.

John E., & Taupin, B. (Singers). (1972). *I think I'm going to kill myself* (Phonograph Record). New York: Dick James Music Ltd.

Johnson, C., & Larson, R. (1982). Bulimia: An analysis of moods and behavior. *Psychosomatic Medicine, 44*, 341–351.

Johnson, C., Lewis, C., Love, S., Lewis, L., & Stuckey, M. (1984). Incidence and correlates of bulimic behavior in a female H. S. population. *Journal of Youth and Adolescence, 13*(1), 15–25.

Johnson, C., & Pure, D. L. (1986). Assessment of bulimia: A multidimensional model. In K. D. Brownell & J. P. Foreyt (Eds.), *Handbook of eating disorders: Physiology, psychology, and treatment of eating disorders* (pp. 405–449). New York: Basic Books.

Johnson, D. W. (1981). *Reaching out: Interpersonal effectiveness and self-actualization* (2nd ed.). Englewood Cliffs, NJ: Prentice-Hall.

Johnson, G. M., & Shontz, F. C. (1974, Summer). Relationship between adolescent drug use and parental drug behaviors. *Adolescence, 19*, 295–299.

Johnston, L. D. (1985). The etiology and prevention of substance use: What can we learn from recent historical changes. In C. L. Jones & R. J. Battjes, *Etiology of drug abuse: Implementation for prevention—NIDA Research Monograph 56.* Washington, DC: Department of Health and Human Services.

Johnston, L. D., O'Malley, P. M., & Bachman, J. G. (1986). *The use of licit and illicit drugs by America's high school students, 1975–1984.* Ann Arbor, MI: University of Michigan Survey Research Institute.

Jones, C. L., & Bell-Bolek, C. S. (1986, May–June). Kids and drugs. *Children Today, 15*(3), pp. 5–10.

Jones, M. (1953). *The therapeutic community.* New York: Basic Books.

Jones, V. (1980). *Adolescents with behavior problems.* Boston: Allyn & Bacon.

Jorgensen, S. R., Thornberg, H. D., & Williams, J. K. (1980). The experience of running away: Perceptions of adolescents seeking help in a shelter care facility. *High School Journal, 64*(3), 87–96.

Jourard, S. (1967). *Personal adjustment* (2nd ed.). New York: Macmillan.

Justice, B., & Duncan, D. F. (1976). Running away: An epidemic problem of adolescence. *Adolescence, 11*(43), 365–371.

Kagan, D. M., & Squires, R. L. (1984, Spring). Eating disorders among adolescents: Patterns and prevalence. *Adolescence, 19*(73), 14–28.

Kalish, R. A. (1981). *Death, grief and caring relationships.* Monterey, CA: Brooks-Cole.

Kandel, D. B. (1985, Summer). On processes of peer influence and adolescent drug use: A developmental perspective. *Advances in Alcohol and Substance Abuse, 4*(3/4), 139–164.

Kandel, D., Kessler, R., & Margulies, R. (1978). Antecedents of adolescent initiation into stages of drug use: A developmental analysis. *Journal of Youth and Adolescence, 7*, 13–40.

Kaslow, N. J., & Rehm, L. P. (1983). Child depression. In R. J. Morris & T. R. Kratochwill (Eds.), *The practice of child therapy.* New York: Pergamon Press.

Kelly, F., & Baer, D. (1971, October). Physical challenges as a treatment for delinquency. *Crime and Delinquency*, pp. 437–445.

Kesey, K. (1962). *One flew over the cuckoo's nest*. New York: Viking Press.

Kety, S. S., Rosenthal, D., Wender, P. H., Schulsinger, F., & Jacobson, B. (1975). Mental illness in the biological and adoptive families of adopted individuals who have become schizophrenic: A preliminary report based on psychiatric interviews. In R. Fieve, D. Rosenthal, & H. Brill (Eds.), *Genetic research in psychiatry*. Baltimore, MD: Johns Hopkins University Press.

Keys, A., Brozek, J., Henschel, A., Mickelsen, O., & Taylor, H. L. (1950). *The biology of human starvation*. Minneapolis, MN: University of Minnesota Press.

Kilpatrick, J. J. (1987, June 17). Inouye Bill could save much agony and anguish. *The Kansas City Times*, p. A-15.

Kimmel, D. C., & Weiner, I. B. (1985). *Adolescence: A developmental transition*. Hillsdale, NJ: Lawrence Erlbaum Associates.

Kirk, W. J. (1980). Juvenile justice and delinquency. In R. E. Muuss (Ed.), *Adolescent behavior and society* (3rd ed.). New York: Random House.

Kirkley, B. G., Schneider, J. A., Agras, W. S., & Bachman, J. A. (1985). Comparisons of two group treatments for bulimia. *Journal of Counseling and Clinical Psychology, 53*(1), 43–48.

Kohlberg, L. (1975). The cognitive development to moral education. *Phi Delta Kappan, 56*, 670–677.

Kohlberg, L. (1976). Moral stages and moralization: The cognitive-developmental approach. In T. Likona (Ed.), *Moral development and behavior, theory research and social issues*. New York: Holt, Rinehart & Winston.

Konopka, G. (1966). *The adolescent girl in conflict*. Englewood Cliffs, NJ: Prentice-Hall.

Korchin, S. J. (1976). *Modern clinical psychology: Principles of intervention in the clinic and community*. New York: Basic Books.

Kovacs, M., & Beck, A. T. (1977). An empirical-clinical approach toward a definition of childhood depression. In J. G. Schulterbrandt & A. Raskin (Eds.), *Depression in childhood: Diagnosis, treatment and conceptual models*. New York: Raven Press.

Kovacs, M., Beck, A. T., & Weissman, A. (1975). Hopelessness: An indicator of suicide. *Suicide, 5*, 98–103.

Kraepelin, E. (1971). *Dementia praecox and paraphrenia* (R. M. Barclay, Trans.: G. M. Robertson, Ed.). New York: Krieger. (Original work published 1919, 8th ed.).

Kraft, S. (1983, April 4). Youth suicide: Eighth grader declares "I never was OK." *The Daily Pilot* (Newport Beach, California).

Krisberg, B., & Schwartz, I. (1983). Rethinking juvenile justice. *Crime and Delinquency, 29*, 333–364.

Kroeber, G. (1963). The coping functions of ego defense mechanisms. In R. W. White (Ed.), *The study of lives* (chap 8). New York: Atherton Press.

Kübler-Ross, E. (1969). *On death and dying*. New York: Macmillan.

Laing, R. D. (1965). Mystification, confusion and conflict. In I. Boszormenyi-Nagy & J. Framo (Eds.), *Intensive family therapy*. New York: Harper & Row.

Langway, L. (1982, October 18). A nation of runaway kids. *Newsweek*, pp. 97–98.

Lasch, C. (1977). *The culture of narcissism*. New York: Warner Books.

Lasch, C. (1979). *The culture of narcissism: American life in an age of diminishing expectations*. New York: W. W. Norton.

Lasegue, C. (1964). De l'anorexie hysterique. In R. M. Kaufman & M. Heiman (Eds.), *Evolution of psychosomatic concepts. Anorexia nervosa: A paradigm*.

New York: International Universities Press. (Original work published 1873, *Arch. Gen. de Med.*, Vol. 385)

Lazarus, R. S., & Folkman, S. (1984). *Stress, appraisal and coping.* New York: Springer.

LeCoq, L. L., & Capuzzi, P. (1984, June). Preventing adolescent drug abuse. *Humanistic Education and Development*, 155–167.

Lester, D., Beck, A. T., & Mitchell, B. (1979). Extrapolation from attempted suicides to completed suicides: A test. *Journal of Abnormal and Social Psychology, 88*(1), 78–80.

Lettieri, D. J. (1985, Summer). Drug abuse: A review of explanations and models of explanation. *Advances in Alcohol and Substance Abuse, 4*(3/4), 9–40.

Levenkron, S. (1978). *The best little girl in the world.* New York: Warner Books.

Levin, E., Adelson, S., Buchalter, G., & Bilcher, J. (1983, February 21). Karen Carpenter. *People Magazine*, pp. 52–59.

Levin, Peter (Director). (1985). *Reason to live* [Film]. Burbank, CA: National Broadcasting Company TV Studios.

Levinson, D. J., Darrow, C. N., Klein, E. B., Levinson, M. H., & McKee, B. (1978). *The seasons of a man's life.* New York: Knopf.

Levy, R. (1982). *The new language of psychiatry-learning and using DSM-III.* Boston: Little, Brown.

Lewinsohn, P. M. (1974). A behavioral approach to depression. In R. J. Friedman, & M. M. Katz (Eds.), *The psychology of depression.* Washington, DC: Winston.

Lewinsohn, P. M., & Arconad, M. (1981). Behavioral treatment in depression: A social learning approach. In J. Clarkin & H. Glazer (Eds.), *Behavioral and directive treatment strategies.* New York: Garland Press.

Lewinsohn, P. M., & Talkington, J. (1979). Studies on the measurement on unpleasant events and relations with depression. *Applied Psychological Measurement, 3*, 83–101.

Lewis, J. M., Rodnick, E. H., & Goldstein, M. (1981). Intra-familial interactive behavior, parental communication deviance, and risk for schizophrenia. *Journal of Abnormal Psychology, 90*, 448–457.

Lidz, T. (1975). *The origin and treatment of schizophrenic disorders.* New York: Basic Books.

Liebertoff, K. (1980). The runaway child in America: A social history. *Journal of Family Issues, 1*(2), 151–164.

Liebman, R., Sargent, J., & Silver, M. (1983). A family systems orientation to the treatment of anorexia nervosa. *Journal of the American Academy of Child Psychiatry, 22*(2), 128–133.

Lindner, R. (1955). *The fifty minute hour.* New York: Holt, Rinehart.

Lipton, D., Martinson, R., & Wilks, J. (1975). *The effectiveness of correctional treatment: A survey of treatment evaluation studies.* Springfield, MA: Praeger.

Litman, R. E., & Diller, J. (1985). Case studies in youth suicide. In M. L. Peck, N. L. Farberow, & R. E. Litman (Eds.), *Youth suicide.* New York: Springer.

Lourie, I. S., Campiglia, P. J., Rick, L., & Dewitt, J. (1979, November). Adolescent abuse and neglect: The role of runaway youth programs. *Children Today*, pp. 27–29, 40.

Loveless, J. (a). (1981, November 26). 2 million children run away annually. *Los Angeles Times*, pt. 1A, pp. 2–4.

Loveless, J. (b). (1981, November 26). Life on the outside is seldom an improvement. *Los Angeles Times*, pt. 1A, pp. 2–4.

Luft, J. (1970). *Group processes, an introduction to group dynamics* (2nd ed.). Palo Alto, CA: Mayfield.

Lundman, R. (1984). *Prevention and control of juvenile delinquency*. New York: Oxford Press.

Maloney, M. J., & Klykylo, W. M. (1983). An overview of anorexia nervosa, bulimia and obesity in children and adolescence. *Journal of the American Academy of Child Psychiatry, 22*(2), 99–107.

Mann, J. (1983, January 17). An endless parade of runaway kids. *U.S. News & World Report*, p. 64.

Mann, P. (1985, September 24). Drugs? Not my child! *Family Circle*, pp. 18–20, 78–80.

Marshall, K. (1981, December). Transcending trendiness: Treatment of runaways in adolescent fiction. *English Journal*, pp. 58–63.

Martin, B. (1977). *Abnormal psychology*. New York: Holt, Rinehart & Winston.

Martz, L. (1986, August 11). Trying to say no: The drug crisis. *Newsweek*, pp. 14–20.

Mashek, J. (1986, September 29). As politicians jockey for advantage in wars battles. *U.S. News & World Report*, p. 29.

Maslow, A. H. (1968). *Toward a psychology of being* (2nd ed.). Princeton, NJ: Van Nostrand.

Mazel, J. (1981). *The Beverly Hills diet*. New York: Macmillan.

McCoy, K. (1982). *Coping with teenage depression: A parent's guide*. New York: New American Library.

McDermott, D. (1984, Spring). The relationship of parental drug use and parent's attitude concerning adolescent drug use to adolescent drug use. *Adolescence, 19*, 89–97.

McGill, C. W., & Lee, E. (1986). Family psychoeducational intervention in the treatment of schizophrenia. *Bulletin of the Menninger Clinic, 50*, pp. 269–286.

McIntire, M. S., & Angle, C. R. (1973). Psychological biopsy in self poisoning of children. *American Journal of Diseases of Children, 126*, 42–46.

McIntire, M. S., & Angle, C. R. (1980). *Suicide attempts in children and youth*. Hagerstown, MD: Harper & Row.

McNab, W. L. (1983, September). Anorexia and the adolescent. *JOSH, 53*(7), 427–430.

Mednick, S. (1985, March). Crime in the family tree. *Psychology Today*, pp. 58–61.

Mednick, S. A., & Schulsinger, I. (1965). A longitudinal study of children with a high risk of schizophrenia. A preliminary report. In S. Vandenberg (Ed.), *Methods and goals in behavior genetics*. New York: Academic Press.

Meichenbaum, D. H. (1985). *Stress inoculation training*. New York: Pergamon.

Merton, R. K. (1957). *Social theory and social structure*. New York: Free Press.

Meyer, A. (1906). Fundamental conceptions of dementia praecox. *British Medical Journal, 2*, 757–760.

Mezzich, J. E. (1979). Patterns and issues in multiaxial psychiatric diagnosis, *Psychological Medicine, 9*, 125–137.

Michaels, R. (Director). (1984). *Silence of the heart* [Film]. Los Angeles: Columbia Broadcasting System TV Studios.

Miller, D. (1981). Adolescent suicide: Etiology and treatment. In S. C. Feinstein & P. L. Giovacchini (Eds.), *Adolescent psychiatry*, (Vol. 9, pp. 327–342). Chicago: University of Chicago Press.

Miller, D., Miller, D., Hoffman, F., & Duggan, R. (1980). *Runaways: Illegal aliens in their own land*. New York: Praeger.

Miller, R. S. (1981, November). Health is a share creation, the evolution of a physician. *Science of Mind*, pp. 9–19, 107–108.

Mintz, L. B., & Betz, N. E. (1986). Sex differences in the nature, realism and correlates of body image. *Sex Roles, 15*(3/4), 185–195.

Mintz, L. B., & Betz, N. E. (1988). Prevalence and correlates of eating disordered behavior among university women. *Journal of Counseling Psychology, 35*(4), 463–471.

Mitchell, J. E. (1986). Bulimia: Medical and physiological aspects. In K. D. Brownell & J. P. Foreyt (Eds.), *Handbook of eating disorders: Physiology, psychology, and treatment of eating disorders* (pp. 379–388). New York: Basic Books.

Mitchell, J. E., & Pyle, R. L. (1982). The bulimic syndrome in normal weight individuals: A review. *International Journal of Eating Disorders, 2*, 61–73.

Mitchell, J. T., & Resnik, H. L. (1981). *Emergency responses to crisis*. Bowie, MD: Brady.

Morgan, L. (1980, February 28). Path of suicide taken by rising number of youths. *Los Angeles Times*, pt. I, pp. 1, 20, 21.

Morganthau, T. (1986, January 6). Abandoned. *Newsweek*, pp. 14–19.

Morganthau, T. (1986a, March 17). Kids and cocaine. *Newsweek*, pp. 58–65.

Morganthau, T. (1986b, June 16). Crack and crime. *Newsweek*, pp. 16–22.

Moriarty, A. E., & Toussieng, P. W. (1976). *Adolescent coping*. New York: Grune and Stratton.

Morton, R. (1694). *Phthisiologica: On a treatise of consumptions*. London: S. Smith & B. Walford.

Moses, A. B. (1978). The runaway youth act: Paradoxes of reform. *The Social Science Review, 52*(2), 227–243.

Mosher, L., Kresky-Wolff, M., Mathews, S., & Menn, A. (1986). Milieu therapy in the 1980s: A comparison of two residential alternatives to hospitalization. *Bulletin of the Menninger Clinic, 50*, pp. 257–268.

Moss, R. A., Jennings, G., McFarland, J. H., & Center, P. (1984). Binge eating, vomiting and weight fear in a female high school population. *The Journal of Family Practice, 18*(2), 313–320.

Motto, J. A. (1967). Suicide and suggestibility—The role of the press. *American Journal of Psychiatry, 124*(2), 252–256.

Motto, J. A. (1985). Treatment concerns in preventing youth suicide. In M. L. Peck, N. L. Farberow, & R. E. Litman (Eds.), *Youth suicide*. New York: Springer.

Musto, D. (1986, September 16). Drug use and abstinence: Two routes to the most you can be. *Los Angeles Times*, pt. II, p. 9.

National Center for Health Care Statistics. (1985). *Vital statistics of the United States*. Washington, DC: U.S. Government Printing Office.

National Youth Workers Alliance (Eds.). (1979). *Runaway Youth Program Directory*. Washington, DC: The Office of Juvenile Justice and Delinquency Prevention, U.S. Department of Justice.

Nelson, D. D., & Noland, J. T. (1983). *Young winners' way: A twelve step guide for teenagers*. Minneapolis, MN: Comp Care.

Newman, B. M., & Newman, P. R. (1986). *Adolescent development*. Columbus, OH: Merrill.

Newman, B. M., & Newman, P. R. (1984). *Development through life, a psychosocial approach* (3rd ed.). Homewood, IL: Dorsey Press.

Nye, F. (1980). A theoretical perspective on running away. *Journal of Family Issues, 1*(2), 274–299.

Nye, F. I., & Edelbrock, C. (1980). Introduction: Some social characteristics of runaways. *Journal of Family Issues, 1*(2), 147–151.

O'Neal, P., & Lee, R. (1959). Childhood patterns predictive of adult schizophrenia: 30 year follow up. *American Journal of Psychiatry, 115*, 391–395.

O'Neill, C. B. (1982). *Starving for attention*. New York: Continuum.

Opinion Research Corporation. (1976). *National statistical summary on runaway youth*. Princeton, NJ: Author.

Orten, J. S., & Soll, S. K. (1980). Runaway children and their families: A treatment typology. *Journal of Family Issues, 1*(2), 249–261.

Otto, V. (1972). Suicidal acts by children and adolescents: A follow-up study. *Acta Psychiatrica Scandinavica, 233*, 5–123 (Supplement).

Palmer, W., & Patterson, B. (1981). If you loved my son you would take out the trash. In J. S. Gordon & M. Beyer (Eds.), *Reaching troubled youth: Runaways and community mental health*. Rockville, MD: U.S. Department of Health and Human Services.

Patterson, G. R. (1981). *Coercive family processes*. Eugene, OR: Castala.

Patterson, G. R., & Stouthhamer-Loeber, M. (1984). The correlation of family management practice and delinquency. *Child Development, 55*, 1299–1307.

Peck, M. L. (1985). Crisis intervention treatment with chronically and acutely suicidal adolescents. In M. L. Peck, N. L. Farberow, & R. E. Litman (Eds.), *Youth suicide* (pp. 112–122). New York: Springer.

Peck, M. L., Farberow, N. L., & Litman, R. E. (Eds.). (1985). *Youth suicide*. New York: Springer.

Petzel, S., & Riddle, M. (1981). Adolescent suicide: Psychosocial and cognitive aspects. In S. C. Feinstein & P. L. Giovacchini (Eds.), *Adolescent psychiatry*, (Vol. 9, pp. 343–397). Chicago: University of Chicago Press.

Phillips, E. L. (1968). Achievement place: Token reinforcement in a home style rehabilitation setting for predelinquent boys. *Journal of Applied Behavioral Analysis, 1*, 213–223.

Polk, K. (1984, October). Juvenile diversion: A look at the record. *Crime and Delinquency, 30*(4), 648–659.

Prescott, P. S. (1981). *The child savers*. New York: Knopf.

President's Commission on Law Enforcement and the Administration of Justice. (1967). *Task force report: Juvenile delinquency*. Washington, DC: U.S. Government Printing Office.

Puig-Antich, J. (1986). Psychobiological markers: Effects of age and puberty. In M. Rutter, C. E. Izard, & P. B. Read (Eds.), *Depression in young people: Developmental and clinical perspectives*. New York: Guilford Press.

Rader, D. (1982, February 7). Runaways. *Parade*, pp. 6–8.

Ray, L., & Johnson, N. (1983, November). Adolescent suicide. *Personnel and Guidance Journal*, 131–135.

Reckless, W. C. (1961, December). A new theory of delinquency and crime. *Federal Probation, 25*, 42–46.

Reckless, W. C. (1967). *The crime problem*. New York: Appleton-Century-Crofts.

Redner, R., Snellman, L., & Davidson, W. (1983). Juvenile delinquency. In R. J. Morris & T. R. Kratochill (Eds.), *The practice of child therapy* (pp. 193–220). New York: Pergamon Press.

Rice, F. P. (1978). *The adolescent: Development, relationships, and culture* (2nd ed.). Boston: Allyn & Bacon.

Rice, F. P. (1984). *The Adolescent: Development, relationships, and culture* (4th ed.). Boston: Allyn & Bacon.

Riemer, J. W. (1981). Deviance as fun. *Adolescence, 16*(61), 39–43.

Ritter, O. F. (1979, March). The runaway adolescent: A national problem. *USA Today*, pp. 24–28.

Roark, A. C. (1985, May 30). Mystery of the brain-technology opens wonders. *Los Angeles Times*, pt. I, p. 3.

Roberts, A. R. (1982). Adolescent runaways in suburbia: A new typology. *Adolescence, 17*(66), 387–396.

Robinson, S. M. (1979). *Identification of suicidal persons at a suicide prevention center based on their initial contact data.* Unpublished master's thesis, California School of Professional Psychology, Los Angeles, CA.

Rodin, J., Silberstein, L. R., & Striegel-Moore, R. H. (1985). Women and weight: A normative discontent. In Theo B. Sonderegger (Ed.), *Nebraska Symposium on Motivation, 1984: Psychology and Gender* (Vol. 32, pp. 267–307). Nebraska: University of Nebraska Press, 267–307.

Rogers, C. R. (1959). A theory of therapy, personality and interpersonal relationships, as developed in the client centered framework. In Koch (Ed.), *Psychology: A study of a science* (Vol. 3, pp. 184–256). New York: McGraw-Hill.

Rogers, C. R. (1980). *A way of being.* Boston: Houghton Mifflin.

Romero, F. F. (1984, Fall). Adolescence, sexual conflict and anorexia nervosa. *Adolescence, 19*(75), 551–555.

Romig, D. A. (1978). *Justice for our children.* Lexington, MA: D. C. Heath.

Rosenfeld, A. H. (1985, June). Depression. Dispelling despair. *Psychology Today*, pp. 29–34.

Rosenhan, D. L. (1973). On being sane in insane places. *Science, 179*, 250–258.

Rosenhan, D. L., & Seligman, M. E. (1984). *Abnormal psychology.* New York: W. W. Norton.

Rosenthal, R., & Jacobson, L. (1968). *Pygmalion in the classroom.* New York: Holt, Rinehart & Winston.

Rosenthal, T. L., & Zimmerman, B. J. (1978). *Social learning and cognition.* New York: Academic Press.

Ross, C. P. (1985). Teaching children the facts of life and death. In M. L. Peck, N. L. Farberow, & R. E. Litman (Eds.), *Youth suicide* (pp. 147–169). New York: Springer.

Rossman, P. (1981, April). Appropriate punishment: The key to rehabilitating criminals. *The Futurist*, pp. 41–47.

Rubel, J. A. (1984, June). The functioning of self help groups in recovery from anorexia nervosa and bulimia. *Psychiatric Clinic of North America, 7*(2), 381–393.

Runaway Youth Act. (1974). *Laws of the 93 Congress* (Title III, P.L. 93-415). Washington, DC: Government Printing Office.

Russell, G. F. (1979). Bulimia nervosa: An ominous variant of anorexia nervosa. *Psychological Medicine, 9*, 429–448.

Ruterman, N. A., & Hughes, T. R. (1984). Developments in the juvenile justice system during the decade of the 1970s: Juvenile detention facilities. *Criminal Justice, 12*, 325–333.

Rutter, M., Izard, C. E., & Read, P. B. (Eds.). (1986). *Depression in young people: Developmental and clinical perspectives.* New York: Guilford Press.

Sacco, W. P., & Beck, A. T. (1985). Cognitive therapy of depression. In E. E. Beckham & W. R. Leber (Eds.), *Handbook of depression: Treatment assessment and research.* Homewood, IL: Dorsey Press.

Sackheim, H. A. (1985, June). The case for ECT. *Psychology Today*, pp. 37–40.

Sansome, W. (1962, May). The smile on the face of tagus. *Harper's Magazine*, pp. 23–25.

Sarason, I. G., & Sarason, B. G. (1984). *Abnormal psychology, the problem of maladaptive behavior* (4th ed.). Englewood Cliffs, NJ: Prentice-Hall.

Sarri, R. C. (1983). Gender issues in juvenile justice. *Crime and Delinquency, 29*, 381–397.

Satchell, M. (1986, July 20). Kids for sale: The exploitation of runaway and throw away children continues to be a national tragedy. *Parade Magazine*, pp. 4–7.

Satir, V. (1983). *Conjoint family therapy*. Palo Alto, CA: Science and Behavior Books.

Schacter, J. (1986, September 11). Studies rise in teen suicides linked to TV programs. *Los Angeles Times*, pt. I, pp. 3, 33.

Scharf, M. (1980). *Unfinished business: Pressure points in the lives of women*. New York: Ballantine.

Schizophrenic: I feel like I'm trapped inside my head. (1986, June 24). *Orange County Register* (Santa Ana, California), Section A, p. 2.

Schlossberg, N. (1981). A model for analyzing human adaptation to transition. *The Counseling Psychologist, 9*, 2–18.

Schlossman, S., & Wallach, S. (1978). The crime of precocious sexuality: Female delinquency in the progressive era. *Harvard Educational Review, 48*(1), 65–94.

Schlossman, S., Zellman, G., & Shavelson, R. (with M. Sedlak & J. Cobb). (1984, May). *Delinquency prevention in south Chicago: A fifty-year assessment of the Chicago area project*. Santa Monica, CA: Rand Corporation.

Schmeck, H. M. (1986, June 24). Dramatic differences found in brain structure. *Orange County Register* (Santa Ana, California), Section A, p. 1.

Schulsinger, H. A. (1976). A 10 year follow up of children of schizophrenic mothers: Clinical assessment. *Acta Psychiatrica Scandinavica, 53*, 371–386.

Schumer, F. (1983). *Abnormal psychology*. Lexington, MA: D. C. Heath.

Scientific Analysis Corporation. (1974). *The sick, the bad and the free: A review of runaway literature*. San Francisco, CA: Unpublished.

Scott, R. N. (1980). Coordinating services for runaway youth: The case of New York City. *Journal of Family Issues, 1*(2), 308–310.

Sechehaye, M. (1968). *Autobiography of a schizophrenic girl*. New York: New American Library.

Sedlak, M., & Schlossman, S. (1983, July). The Chicago area project revisited. *Crime and Delinquency, 29*(3), 398–462.

Seligman, M. E. (1975). *Helplessness: On depression, development and death*. San Francisco, CA: Freeman.

Seligman, M. E., & Peterson, C. (1986). A learned helplessness perspective on childhood depression: Theory and research. In M. Rutter, C. E. Izard, & P. B. Read (Eds.), *Depression in young people: Developmental and clinical perspectives*. New York: Guilford Press.

Seligman, J., & Zabarsky, M. A. (1983, March 7). A deadly feast and famine. *Newsweek*, pp. 59–60.

Selye, H. (1976). *The stress of life* (rev. ed.). New York: McGraw-Hill.

Services to runaways. . . . " (1984, January–February). *Children Today*, pp. 23–24.

Shaffer, D. (1986). Development of factors in adolescent suicide. In M. Rutter, C. E. Izard, & P. B. Read (Eds.), *Depression in young people: Developmental and clinical perspectives* (pp. 383–398). New York: Guilford Press.

Shaffer, D., & Fisher, P. (1981). The epidemiology of suicide in children and young adolescents. *Journal of the American Academy of Child Psychiatry, 20*, 545–565.

Shakespeare, W. (1982). *The complete works of William Shakespeare*. London, England: Octopus Books Unlimited.

Shamsk, S. J. (1981). Antisocial adolescents: Our treatments do not work — Where do we go from here? *Canadian Journal of Psychiatry, 26*(5), 357–364.

Shapiro, S. A. (1981). *Contemporary theories of schizophrenia: Review and synthesis*. New York: McGraw-Hill.

Sherrill, M. (1979, June 23). The search for juvenile justice. *Saturday Review*, pp. 20–24.

Shneidman, E. S. (1976a). Suicide among the gifted. In E. S. Shneidman (Ed.), *Suicidology: Contemporary developments*. New York: Grune & Stratton.

Shneidman, E. S. (1976b). *Suicidology: Contemporary developments*. New York: Grune & Stratton.

Shneidman, E. S. (1977). The psychological autopsy guide. In *Guide to the investigation and reporting of drug abuse deaths* (Vol. 6). Washington, DC: U.S. Department of Health, Education and Welfare.

Shneidman, E. S. (1984, July). Aphorisms of suicide and some implications for psychotherapy. *American Journal of Psychiatry, 38*(3), 319–328.

Short, J. F., & Nye, I. F. (1958). Extent of unrecorded juvenile delinquency: Tentative conclusions. *Journal of Law, Criminology and Police Science, 49*, pp. 296–302.

Siegel, B. S. (1986). *Love, medicine and miracles*. New York: Harper & Row.

Silverman, J. (1974). Anorexia nervosa: Clinical observations in a successful treatment plan. *Journal of Pediatrics, 84*(1), 68–73.

Sinatra, F. (Singer). (1969). *My way* (Phonograph Record). Los Angeles: Warner Bros. Records.

Skinner, B. F. (1953). *Science and human behavior*. New York: Macmillan.

Smith, D. M. (1980). Adolescent suicide. In R. E. Muuss (Ed.), *Adolescent behavior and society* (pp. 402–409). New York: Random House.

Smith, M. C. (1984). Anorexia nervosa and bulimia. *The Journal of Family Practice, 18*(5), 757–766.

Sours, J. (1980). *Starving to death in a sea of objects: The anorexia nervosa syndrome*. New York: Jason Aronson.

Squire, S. (1983). *The slender balance*. New York: Pinnacle.

Steel, C. I. (1980, Winter). Weight loss among teenage girls: An adolescent crisis. *Adolescence, 15*(60), 823–829.

Steinberg, L. (1985). *Adolescence*. New York: Knopf.

Stephens, J. H. (1978). Long-term prognosis and follow-up in schizophrenia. *Schizophrenia Bulletin, 4*, 25–47.

Stierlin, H. (1973). Family perspective on adolescent runaways. *Archives of General Psychiatry, 29*, 56–62.

Striegel-Moore, R. H., Silberstein, L. R., & Rodin, J. (1986). Toward an understanding of risk factors for bulimia. *American Psychologist, 41*(3), 246–263.

Strober, M. (1986). Anorexia nervosa: History and psychological concepts. In K. D. Brownell & J. P. Foreyt (Eds.), *Handbook of eating disorders: Physiology, psychology, and treatment of eating disorders* (pp. 232–246). New York: Basic Books.

Strober, M., & Yager, J. (1985). A developmental perspective on the treatment of anorexia nervosa. In D. M. Gardner & P. E. Garfinkel (Eds.), *Handbook of psychotherapy for anorexia nervosa and bulimia* (pp. 363–390). New York: Guilford Press.

Stunkard, A. (1959). Eating patterns and obesity. *Psychiatric Quarterly, 33*, 284–295.

Sudak, H. S., Ford, A. B., & Rushford, N. B. (1984, July). *American Journal of Psychotherapy, 38*(3), 350–363.

Suicide belt rates up for affluent teenagers. (1980, September 1). *Time*, p. 56.

Sullivan, H. S. (1953). *The interpersonal theory of psychiatry*. New York: Norton.

Sullivan, H. S. (1962). *Schizophrenia as a human process*. New York: Norton.

Sullivan, I., & Maiken, P. (1984). *Killer clown: The John Wayne Gacy murders*. New York: Pinnacle Books.

Sutherland, E. H., & Cressy, D. R. (1978). *Criminology* (10th ed.). Philadelphia, PA: Lippincott.

Szasz, T. S. (1961). *The myth of mental illness's foundation of a theory of personal conduct*. New York: Harper and Hoeber.

Szasz, T. S. (1963). *Law, liberty and psychiatry: An inquiry into the social uses of mental health practices*. New York: Macmillan.

Szasz, T. S. (1973). *The age of madness: The history of involuntary mental hospitalization presented in selected texts*. Garden City, NY: Anchor Press/Doubleday.

Tabachnick, N. (1981). The interlocking psychologies of suicide and adolescence. In S. C. Feinstein & P. L. Giovacchini (Eds.), *Adolescent psychiatry*, (Vol. 9, pp. 399–410). Chicago: University of Chicago Press.

The golden girl's disease. (1975, June). *Playgirl*.

The Holy Bible: King James Version. (1976). Nashville, TN: The Gideons International.

Thompson, W. E., & Dodder, R. A. (1983). Juvenile delinquency explained: A test of containment theory. *Youth and Society, 15*(2), 171–194.

Thornberg, H. D. (1982). *Development in adolescence* (2nd ed.). Monterey, CA: Brooks-Cole.

Thornton, J. (1983, June 20). Behind a surge in suicides of young people. *U.S. News & World Report*.

Tishler, C. L., & McHenry, P. C. (1982). Parental negative self and adolescent suicidal attempts. *Journal of the American Academy of Child Psychiatry, 21*.

Toffler, A. (1971). *Future shock*. New York: Bantam Books.

Toolan, J. M. (1962). Suicide and suicide attempts in children and adolescents. *American Journal of Psychiatry, 118*, 719–724.

Toolan, J. M. (1974). Masked depression in children and adolescents. In S. Lesse (Ed.), *Masked depression*. New York: Aronson.

Topol, P., & Reznikoff, M. (1982). Perceived peer and family relationships, hopelessness and locus of control as factors in adolescent suicide attempts. *Suicide and Life Threatening Behavior, 12*(3), 381–392.

Torrey, E. F. (1983). *Surviving schizophrenia: A family manual*. New York: Harper & Row.

Turkington, C. (1985, August). Support helps schizophrenics meet needs. *APA Monitor*.

Twain, Mark. (1981). *Tom Sawyer*. New York: Bantam Books.

Twain, Mark. (1981). *Huckleberry Finn*. New York: Bantam Books.

Tyerman, A., & Humphrey, M. (1983). Life stresses, family support and adolescent disturbance. *Journal of Adolescence, 6*, 1–12.

United States Bureau of the Census. (1980). *Statistical Abstract of the United States—1980*. Washington, DC: U.S. Government Printing Office.

United States Bureau of the Census. (1987). *Statistical Abstract of the United States—1987*. Washington, DC: U.S. Government Printing Office.

United States Congress. (1986). *Hearings on Youth Suicide Prevention Act of 1985*

(Serial No. 99-56). Committee on Education and Labor, September 10, 1985 and October 21, 1985. Washington, DC: U.S. Government Printing Office.

United States Supreme Court. (1967). *In Re: Gault* (387 U.S. 1).

Valliant, G. (1977). *Adaptation to life*. Boston: Little, Brown.

Walker, D. (1975). *Runaway youth: Annotated bibliography and literature overview*. Washington, DC: Department of Health, Education and Welfare.

Wallachinsky, D. (1987). *Class reunion '65, tales of an American generation*. New York: Penguin Books.

Walrond-Skinner, S. (1986). *Dictionary of psychotherapy*. New York: Routledge and Kegan Paul.

Walsh, M. E. (1985). *Schizophrenia: Straight talk for family and friends*. New York: Warner Books.

Washton, K. (1974). Running away from home. *Journal of Social Issues, 30*(1), pp. 181–188.

Wasserman, I. M. (1984, June). Imitation and suicide: A reexamination of the Werther effect. *American Sociological Review, 49*, 427–436.

Webb, L. J., Clemente, C. C., Johnstone, E. E., Sanders, J. L., & Perky, R. A. (Eds.). (1981). *DSM-III training guide*. New York: Brunner/Mazel.

Wechler, J. A. (1972). *In a darkness*. New York: W. W. Norton.

Weiner, I. B. (1970). *Psychological disturbances in adolescence*. New York: John Wiley & Sons.

Weiner, I. B. (1974). Depression in adolescence. In F. Fisch & S. Draghi (Eds.), *The nature and treatment of depression*. New York: John Wiley & Sons.

Weiner, I. B. (1980). Psychopathology in adolescence. In J. Adelson (Ed.), *Handbook of the psychology of adolescence*. New York: John Wiley & Sons.

Weiner, I. B. (1982). *Child and adolescent psychopathology*. New York: John Wiley & Sons.

Weisheit, R. A. (1984, Summer). Alcohol and drug abuse prevention: Implications for delinquency prevention. *Journal of Drug Issues*, 469–476.

Wenar, C. (1982). *Psychopathology from infancy through adolescence*. New York: Random House.

Wenz, F. V. (1979a). Sociological correlates of alienation among adolescent suicidal attempts. *Adolescence, 14*, 19–30.

Wenz, F. V. (1979b). Self injury behavior, economic status and the family anomie syndrome among adolescents. *Adolescence, 14*, 387–397.

Wetzel, J. W. (1984). *Clinical handbook of depression*. New York: Gardner Press.

White, J. L. (1984). *The psychology of Blacks: An Afro-American perspective*. Englewood Cliffs, NJ: Prentice-Hall.

White, R. W., & Watt, N. F. (1981). *The abnormal personality* (5th ed.). New York: Wiley & Sons.

Wilford, B. B. (1981). *Drug abuse: A guide for the primary care physician*. Chicago, IL: American Medical Association.

Williams, J. R., & Gold, M. (1972). From juvenile delinquency to official delinquency. *Social Problems, 20*, 209–229.

Wilson, T. G. (1986). Cognitive-behavioral and pharmacological therapies for bulimia. In K. D. Brownell & J. P. Foreyt (Eds.), *Handbook of eating disorders: Physiology, psychology, and treatment of eating disorders* (pp. 450–474). New York: Basic Books.

Wolk, S., & Brandon, J. (1977). Runaway adolescent's perceptions of parents and self. *Adolescence, 12*, 175–188.

Wooley, S. C., & Kearney-Cooke, A. (1986). Intensive treatment of bulimia and body image disturbances. In K. D. Brownell & J. P. Foreyt (Eds.), *Handbook of eating disorders: Physiology, psychology, and treatment of eating disorders* (pp. 476–502). New York: Basic Books.

Wooley, S. C., & Wooley, O. W. (1982). The Beverly Hills eating disorder: The mass marketing of anorexia nervosa. *International Journal of Psychiatry, 1*(3), 57–69.

Wooley, S. C., & Wooley, O. W. (1984, February). Feeling fat in a thin society. *Glamour*, pp. 198–201, 251–252.

Wynne, L. C., & Singer, M. T. (1963a). Thought disorder and family relations of schizophrenics, I. A research study. *Archives of General Psychiatry, 19*, 191–198.

Wynne, L. C., & Singer, M. T. (1963b). Thought disorder and family relations of schizophrenics, II. A classification of forms of thinking. *Archives of General Psychiatry, 19*, 199–206.

York, P., York, D., & Wachtel. (1983). *Toughlove*. New York: Bantam.

Young, B., Godfrey, W., Mathews, B., & Adams, G. (1983, April). Runaways: A review of negative consequences. *Family Relations*, pp. 151–281.

Zober, E. (1981). The socialization of adolescents into juvenile delinquency. *Adolescence, 16*(62).

Index

About the Author

Dr. Joseph L. White has been a professor of psychology and a practicing clinical-consulting psychologist for the past twenty-seven years. He received his Ph.D. in clinical psychology from Michigan State University in 1961 after completing his Bachelor's and Master's Degrees in psychology at San Francisco State University. He is currently a professor of Psychology, Psychiatry, and Comparative Culture at the University of California, Irvine, where he also serves as a supervising psychologist in the counseling psychology internship program. Past university affiliations include teaching and administrative posts at Washington University; California State University, Long Beach; San Francisco State University; and Portland State University. Dr. White has held administrative posts as a Dean of Undergraduate Studies, Assistant Vice Chancellor, and Director of Special Projects. He has served as a consultant with a wide variety of governmental, educational, and health agencies and is an affiliate staff psychologist at five hospitals in Southern California. His clinical practice is with the firm of Cal-Psych Associates in Santa Ana, California. Dr. White's primary interests are in life span development, wellness, and cross-cultural psychology. His first book, *The Psychology of Blacks: An Afro-American Perspective*, was published by Prentice-Hall in 1984.

Dr. White was appointed to the Board of Trustees of The Menninger Foundation in May of 1983 and served as the chairman of the State Licensing Board of Psychology of California from 1981 to 1984.

Pergamon General Psychology Series

Editors: **Arnold P. Goldstein,** Syracuse University
Leonard Krasner, Stanford University &
SUNY at Stony Brook

*Out of print in original format. Available in custom reprint edition.